AF593970

Our Texas

A Celebration of The University of Texas in Pictures

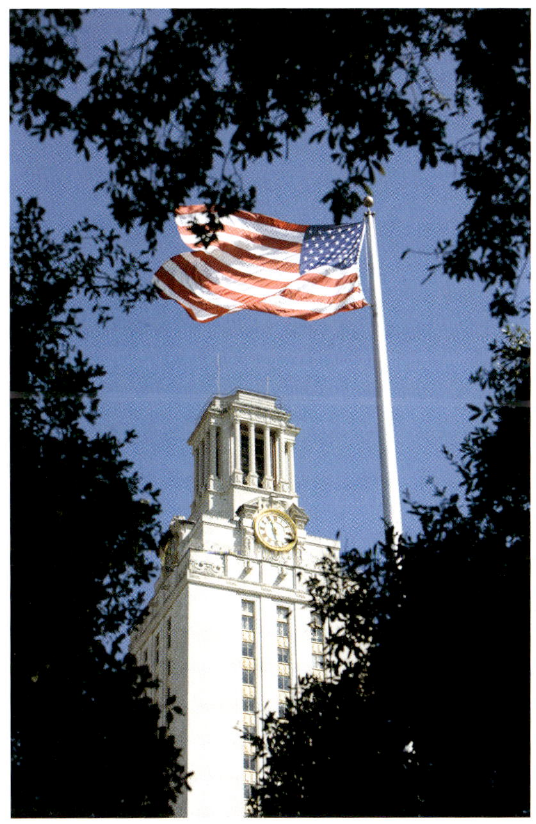

Photography by Susan and Jim Sigmon
Foreword by Avrel Seale ⋆ Historical Essay by Jim Nicar

Published by

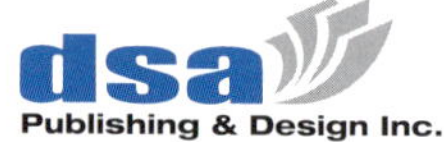

203 W. Belmont Drive
Allen, Texas 75013
972-747-7866
FAX 972-747-0226
www.dsapubs.com

Publisher: Duff Tussing

Associate Publisher: Steve Boston

Photography: Susan and Jim Sigmon

Design: Donnie Jones, The Press Group

Printed in the US

PUBLISHER'S DATA

Our Texas

Library of Congress Control Number: 2008908023

ISBN Number: 978-0-9818229-2-1

First Printing 2008

10 9 8 7 6 5 4 3 2 1

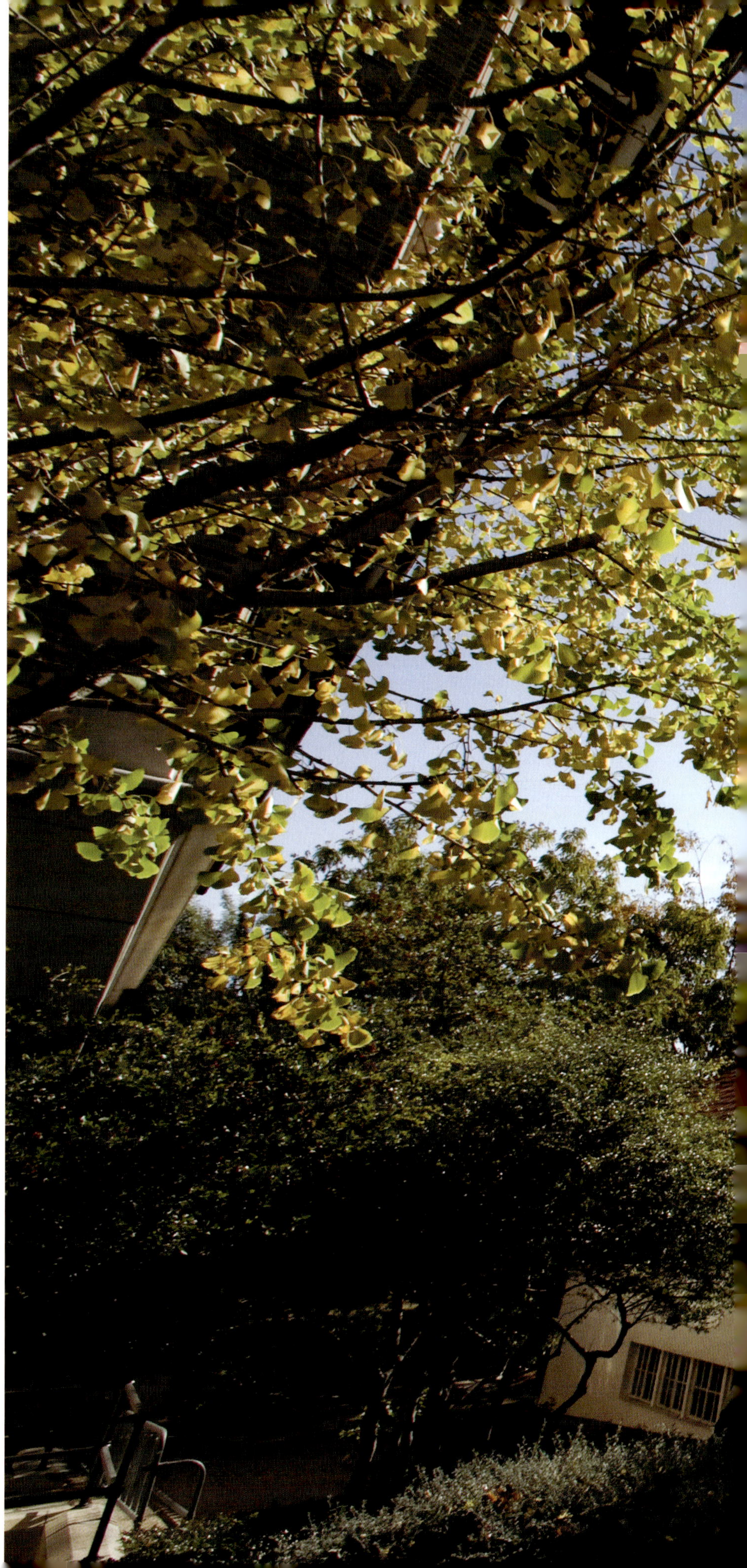

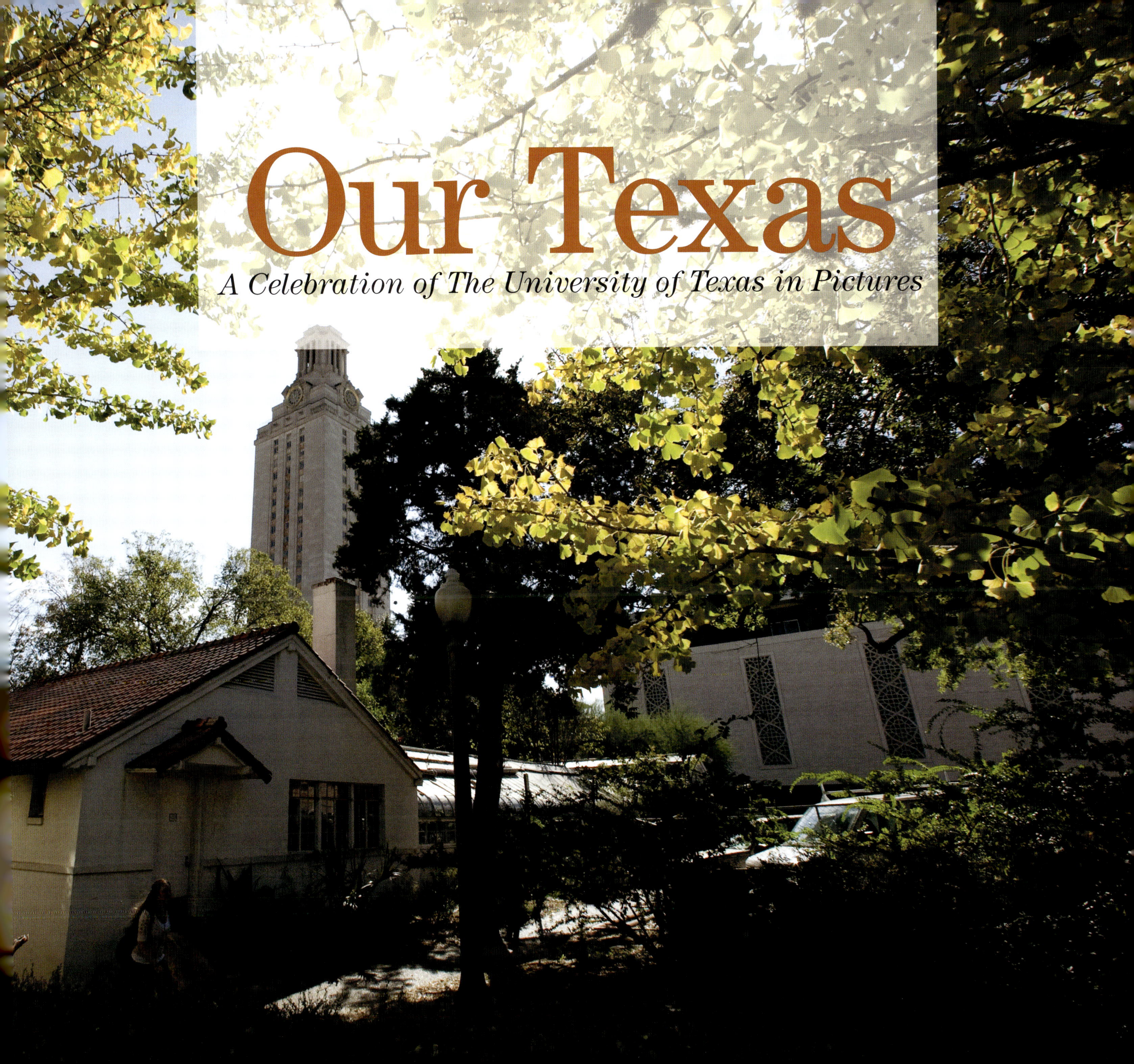

Our Texas

A Celebration of The University of Texas in Pictures

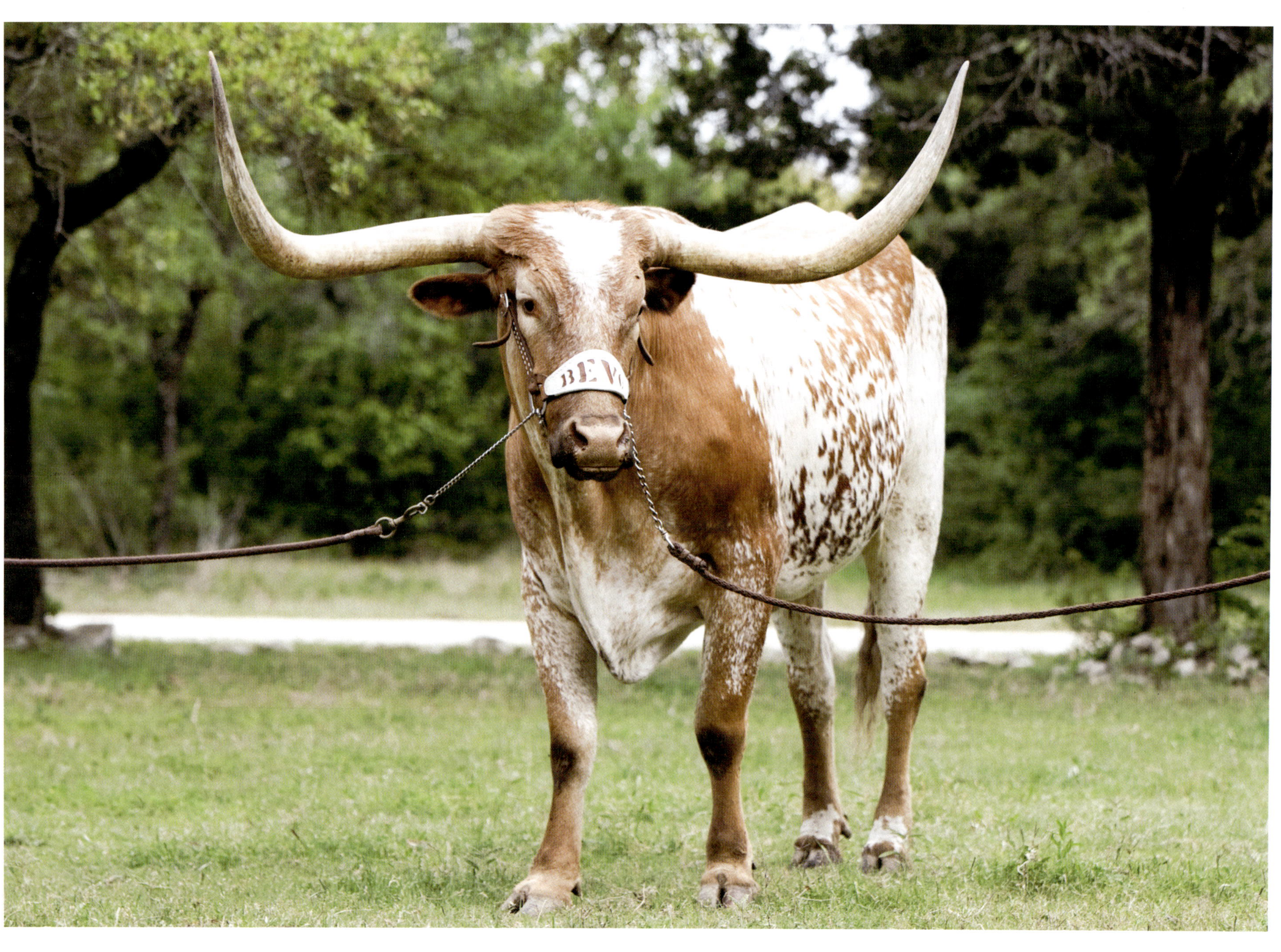
BEV

CONTENTS

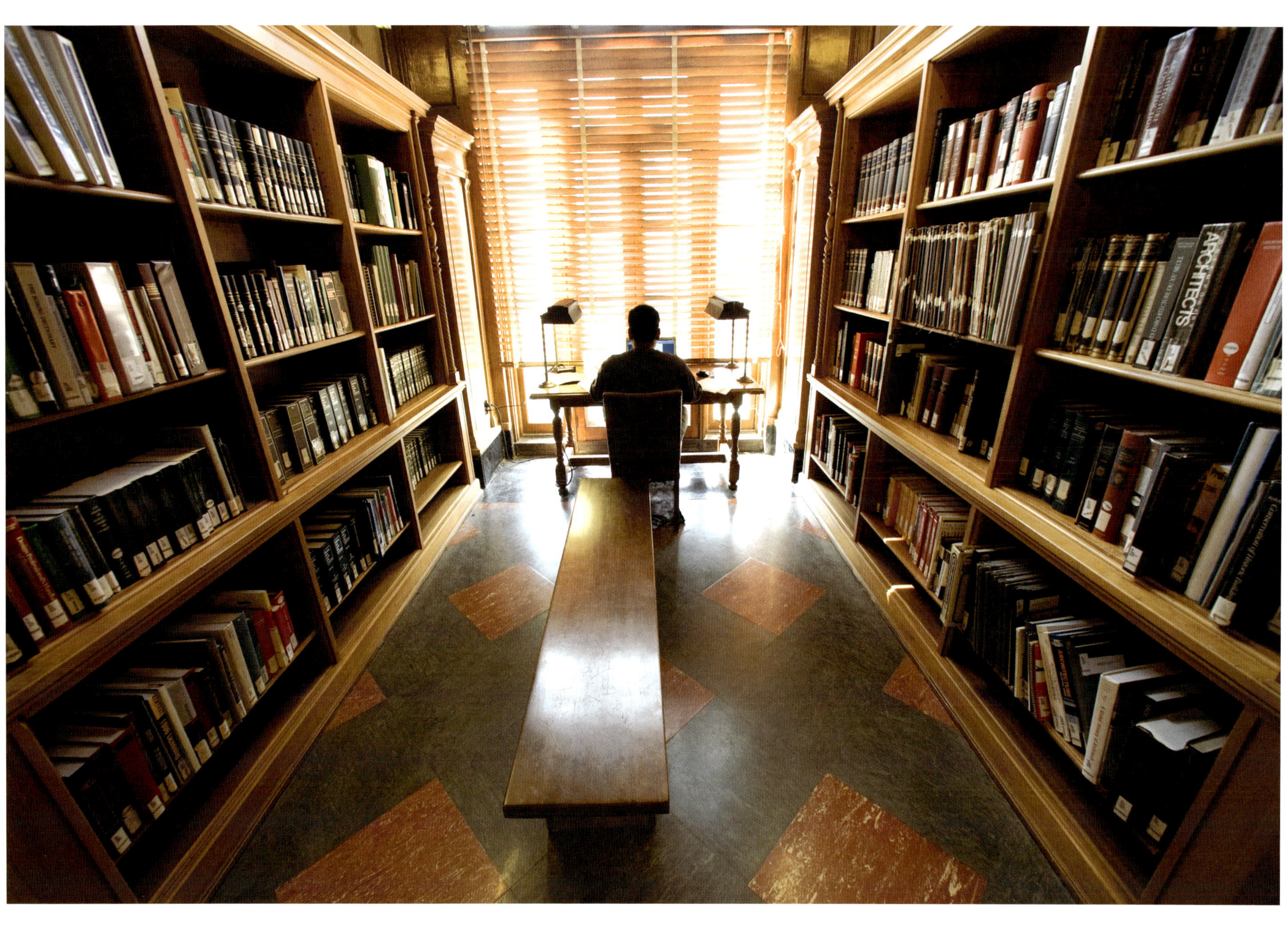
ARCHITECTS

FOREWORD

What began as 221 students, eight professors, and a few head of cattle is now a university that, if it were its own city, would be bigger than Galveston, Huntsville, Harlingen, Eagle Pass, and dozens of other Texas towns that send their young women and men here every fall.

For all intents and purposes, The University of Texas is not only its own city, but its own nation, complete with a capitol building, symbols and flags, a national anthem. It is a society whose members have spread around the world. It has transcended geography into the realm of lofty ideals, complex international consortia, business connections, government leaders, lifelong friendships. But all of it does start in a place—a place bounded by a few streets in Austin, Texas.

A place covered in live oaks, grackles, and squirrels. A place built up in a hodgepodge of architectural styles that tell the tale of rapid, at times crazy, growth. A place where buttoned-down pre-professionals and generously pierced neo-primitives queue up together at coffee carts, where old traditions like fraternities and sororities rub up against rag-tag radicalism like tectonic plates, where ironies and creative tensions linger around every limestone corner.

What is it about this place that gets into people's hearts? We'll spare you the clichés about Texas' can-do attitude and swagger, all true though they may be. For many who grew up in-state, The University of Texas represents the continuation of an affinity that began in the mists of childhood, an attraction to things that appeal to the kid in us all—a lovable mascot, a catchy song, the pageantry and drama of autumn Saturdays. For others, the University represents not the nostalgia of a Texas childhood but a bold, sometimes frightening, new frontier, hours from home, across state lines, across oceans and continents, a new language, a new bustling culture, a new life altogether. But whichever way it gets to us, get to us it does.

So how best to communicate these varied feelings to the family? How best to hold up a mirror to the Longhorn Nation itself? If the axiom holds true that a picture is worth a thousand words, then it is a simple calculus that we can say more with 130 pages of photos than with the same volume of squiggly black lines. And beyond that equation, there is something ineffable about a photograph, something that cannot be communicated even in a thousand words, nor in a million. Like music and other art forms, photography, whether high-end coffee table fare or a faded family snapshot, enjoys direct access to the heart.

And so what follows are photos—some old, some new—that celebrate a place moving through time, alive with all the dynamics and tensions that are at play in society at large: the inclusion of people previously excluded, a huge engine of economic mobility, a crucible of change for thousands of people—young and not so young—who enter it every year.

The contemporary photos were taken mostly in 2007 and 2008 by a photographic power couple, Susan and Jim Sigmon, who have honed their considerable skills during their long tenure as the University's primary sports photographers. They were commissioned by this book's publisher, the same organization responsible for many of the subjects you'll see in these pages: the Texas Union, Hogg Auditorium, and Gregory Gym, the Torchlight Parade and the Hex Rally, the same group responsible for millions of dollars in scholarships to worthy students and thousands in awards to worthy professors. We are the organized manifestation of those whose lives were changed in this crucible, the alumni association of The University, The Texas Exes.

Thanks for enjoying this pictorial love letter to a unique place, and Hook 'em Horns. ✯

Avrel Seale, Editor
The Alcalde

Our Mission
an idea is born

by Jim Nicar

Bolstered by crisp autumn breezes and sapphire-blue skies, The University of Texas celebrated its 25th anniversary in grand style. The last full week of November 1908 was a blur of parades, concerts, rallies, speeches, and receptions, highlighted by the inauguration of Dr. Sidney Mezes as the University's fifth president, the dedication of a new law school building, and the annual Thanksgiving Day football bout against the A&M College of Texas. Gridiron fans weren't disappointed, as the Longhorns overcame a 12-point deficit at halftime to win 29-12. The week ended with a post-game formal dance at the Driskill Hotel in downtown Austin. Under a canopy of electric lights and green garlands, and with music provided by Besserer's Orchestra, almost five hundred revelers packed the hotel's second-floor ballroom until 4 a.m. the following morning.

One of the week's most anticipated events was the Alumni Barbecue, slated for Wednesday, November 25th, the day before Thanksgiving. Eager to make the pilgrimage to Austin, University alumni arrived from all parts of the state. Some came on horseback, a few in the newfangled "Model T" automobiles introduced earlier in the year by the Ford Motor Company, but most made the journey by train. Alumni in Dallas chartered three Pullman cars for the trip, those living in Houston and San Antonio each filled two more, and a group in Fort Worth claimed another. Tickets to the barbecue were $1 apiece, and organizers predicted it to be the largest gathering of UT alumni ever seen.

At half past noon on Wednesday, more than 700 alumni assembled on the sun-drenched lawn that fronted the yellow-brick old Main Building. The men sported dark suits, starched collars and bowlers, while the women wore their best Victorian dresses and wide, fashionable hats. It wasn't an easy task to get everyone organized, but the group eventually managed to arrange itself by graduation year, and with members of the first graduating class of 1884 leading the way, a noisy and colorful procession marched down the hill to the east of campus and across Waller Creek, to a wooded area known as Wheeler's Grove. Waiting for them, sprawled under the dappled branches of live oak trees, was an immense barbecue feast of beef, mutton, and pork served with bread, pickles, and coffee. With enough chairs and long tables for everyone, the alumni dined, talked, and reminisced through the afternoon. "The time was so pleasantly spent by all," reported *The Texan* student newspaper, "that it was with much regret that the crowd was persuaded to leave such a scene of good fellowship, happiness and shade."

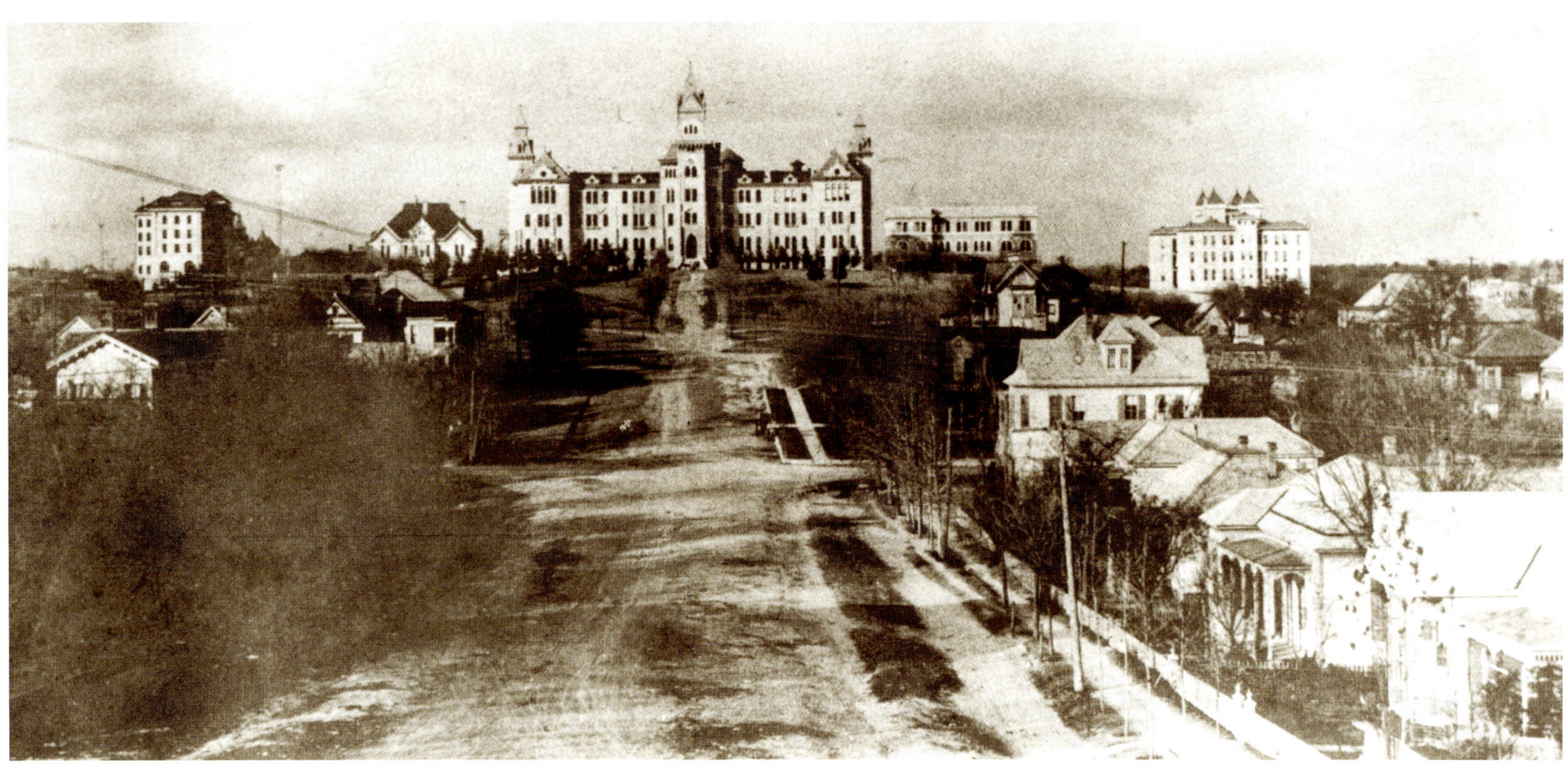

When most of the "eatables" had been finished, the group gathered under two of the largest trees, where Dr. Harry Benedict called the proceedings to order. Benedict was the immediate past president of the Texas Exes, and a professor of astronomy and applied mathematics. To be seen and heard above the crowd, he climbed atop the only platform available: a rather shaky wheelbarrow.

"Fellow old students and old fellow students," Benedict began, "rejoice, make merry and be of good cheer; more than half of our speakers for this event have been unavoidably detained, and it's necessary for us to pretend that we're sorry." Always witty and genial, with broad shoulders, a quick smile and a mop of dirty-blond hair that looked as if he'd combed it with his fingers, Benedict was a popular figure on the campus. He often was invited to speak at University events, but swore that a good long speech was a "psychological impossibility," and was always careful not to overstay his welcome.

"The University welcomes you," announced Benedict from his precarious perch. "She rejoices in your triumphs, sorrows over your misfortunes, and is ashamed at your misdeeds." After a few quips about the smiles on the faces of local innkeepers at the sight of the alumni, Benedict finished his opening remarks by revealing what he claimed was already an open secret: "This celebration is largely a fraud, and its basis a deception." The events surrounding the University's 25th anniversary were all well and good, he argued, but the real reason so many alumni had gathered under the oaks at Wheeler's Grove was to meet each other and renew old friendships. A University milestone, a presidential inauguration, and the new law building were all merely "decoys to bring us back, wooden ducks to lure out of the distant skies the real ducks, namely us. Verily, rejoice, for when before has there been such a quacking in these parts?"

First on the program was Thomas Watt Gregory, known as "Watt" to his friends, who finished at the head of UT's second graduating law class in 1885. He was an intense, passionate, and persuasive speaker, and the affairs of the University were among his favorite topics. "As soon as the ink dried on his diploma he took up alumnising," wrote his classmate Venable Proctor. "Whenever the University needed anything, and of course, it has needed everything, Gregory proceeded to go after whatever gender the thing was." Considered by some as the most vocal advocate for the University, Gregory also was touted as one of the

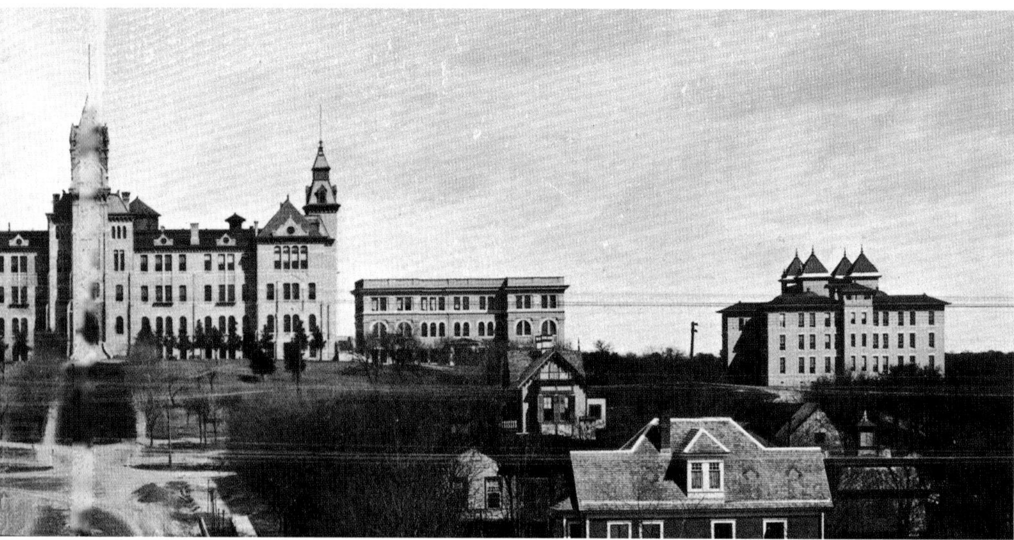

best lawyers in the state and later would serve as U.S. attorney general under Woodrow Wilson. In the spring of 1899, Gregory became the first UT graduate appointed to the Board of Regents. He had just completed an active eight-year term on the board when he was asked to speak at the barbecue. "Watt Gregory is a man who could not be uninteresting if he tried," Proctor declared.

Gregory's talk was not so much a remembrance of bygone college days as a State of the University Address, and it lasted well over eight minutes. Taking Benedict's place on the wheelbarrow, he reminded everyone of the Texas constitutional mandate for the state to provide a "University of the first class" and then asked, "Now what has the state done for this institution?" Gregory asserted that while the University had prospered in its first quarter-century, it had done so in spite of the fact "that we have been starvelings at the hands of the state."

Warming to his subject, the former regent pointed out the two million acres of West Texas land given to the University to establish a permanent fund, "thrown to us, out upon the far distant border, where they were supposed to have, and did then have little value." He compared the legislative appropriations given to other state universities and found that those in Illinois, Wisconsin, and California, among others, had been awarded more in a single session than The University of Texas had received over its entire history. The Austin campus was beset with overcrowded classrooms, a library of 50,000 volumes housed in tight quarters that wasn't fireproof and was bulging at the seams, and no University gymnasium "except an unsanitary old den under the auditorium, where the health of several students has been injured." Even the heating plant was inadequate. "I call your attention to a fact that may astonish some, but that is literally true: two years ago when we had a cold spell of weather, all the work of the University was stopped and the doors closed, and the institution waited until milder weather would permit a continuation of the work."

For over half an hour, an animated Watt Gregory lectured his fellow alumni, and somehow kept his balance atop the wheelbarrow. "Before leaving this meeting," he urged, "before leaving the pleasant associations which are revived here, swear an oath more solemn than that of Hannibal, not to destroy Rome, but to save Carthage." Gregory demanded "to see that the guarantee and the promise of the Constitution of Texas is not a matter of sounding brass and tinkling cymbals, but that this institution shall be in fact and in deed a university of the first class!"

The alumni roared with applause, and many who listened were inspired by Gregory's call to "wage a crusade" and convey UT's cause to their state representatives. But to others, the campus shortcomings were nothing new. The older graduates recalled their days as students, enrolled in a fledgling university with a smattering of books in the library, coal stoves for heat, and a campus plagued by stray cattle.

The arrival of The University of Texas was anything but auspicious. Its modest opening ceremonies on September 15, 1883, were held in the still unfinished west wing of a Gothic-styled Main Building, which rose on the crest of a hill of an unremarkable 40-acre campus. Because of the University's meager finances, the Main Building wasn't completed all at once, but had to be constructed in three segments. The west wing was to have been ready by June 1883, three months before classes began in September, but a bricklayers strike and the sudden death of a contractor postponed its completion until the following January. Instead, the University spent its inaugural fall term in the cramped quarters of the temporary Capitol building in downtown Austin.

The campus itself was almost devoid of flora, save for a thicket of mesquite trees and a handful of live oaks, some festooned with Spanish moss. A great gulley extended from the top of the hill to the southeast, dry most of the time but a quagmire in wet weather. According to Halbert Randolph, who earned his law degree in 1885, the ornamental shrubbery consisted of "cactus sporting its full-grown fruit, looking like the ripe nose of a drunkard." But for a few weeks in the spring, when the campus was aglow with a blanket of Texas bluebonnets, the forlorn state of the Forty Acres was temporarily forgotten.

To the east, just beyond the University grounds, lay vast tracts of pasture and open prairie, while to the west, along a dusty and unpaved Guadalupe Street, stood two grocery stores, a dry goods shop, and a saloon.

The sprawling town of Austin filled the landscape to the south, its 15,000 inhabitants still abuzz over the local telephone service that was installed two years previously. Austin won the privilege to host the main campus of the University after a hotly contested statewide election, and as it was already the seat of Texas government, civic leaders predicted Austin would soon be the "Athens of the Southwest." Fortunately, there were no proposals to change the city's name accordingly. (Through much of the 19th century, as the United States expanded westward,

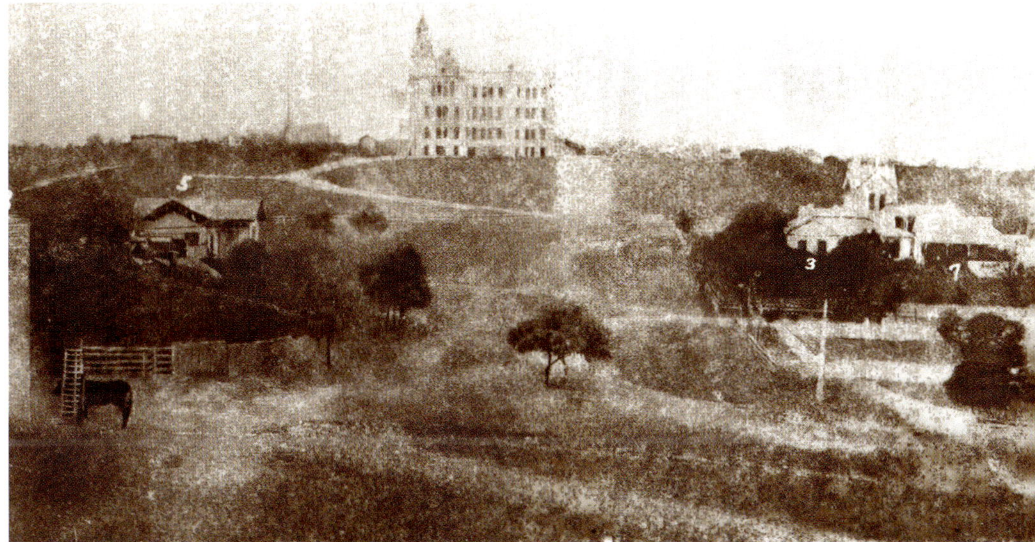

colleges and universities were desired assets of newly founded, up-and-coming towns with lofty ambitions, and communities sometimes renamed themselves to reflect their goals. It's no accident that two of Ohio's state universities reside in towns named Oxford and Athens, that students enrolled at The University of Mississippi travel to Oxford, or that The University of Georgia is found in Athens.)

Ashbel Smith, a 76-year-old physician from Galveston, was selected to chair the first Board of Regents, and was entrusted with the Herculean task of creating the new university. A graduate of Yale, Smith had served as secretary of state for the Republic of Texas and had been elected to multiple terms in the state legislature. The University of Texas was Smith's passion in the conclusive years of his life, and his top priority was to recruit the best faculty possible. He traveled extensively, visited colleges throughout the country, and spent many late nights devoted to University-related correspondence, scribbling letters by candlelight.

After nearly two years of effort, Smith and the Board of Regents selected eight professors. Six of them formed the Academic Department, and most were assigned to teach multiple disciplines: English, literature, and history; chemistry and physics; mathematics; metaphysics, logic, and ethics; ancient Greek and Latin; and Spanish, French and German. The remaining two professors comprised the Law Department. Salaries averaged $2,500 per year, a generous sum in the 1880s.

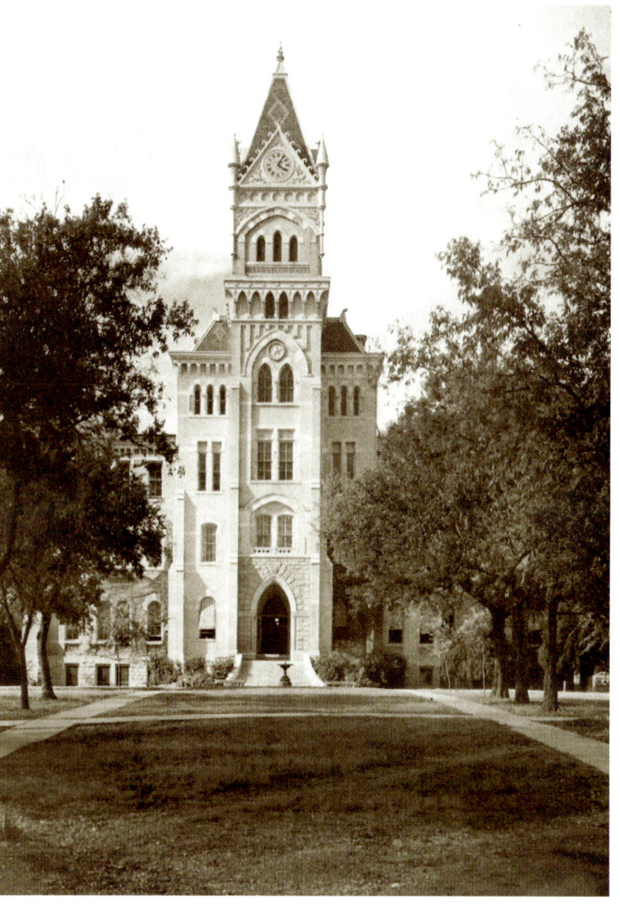

The initial entrance requirements were determined by the faculty. Candidates for the Academic Department were expected to know elementary Greek and Latin, though French and German could be substituted for those planning to pursue science or literature. Competency in algebra and plane geometry, English composition, history, and political geography were also required. Prospective law students needed to have a strong background in reading and writing English, and a "familiarity of the history of the United States and England."

In the weeks before the University was scheduled to open, college-aged youth made their way to Austin to present their credentials and be interviewed by the faculty for admission. In a state where 90 percent of the population was classified as rural, many of the candidates were from farms and ranches, the children of pioneers, raised in log cabins with few luxuries. They were practical and self-motivated, but their preparatory education was incomplete, they often did not possess high school diplomas, and the standards for admission were too high. One prospective student who hoped to study mathematics, when asked how much math he had taken, proudly answered that he'd completed a class in "discount and bankruptcy." Though hindered by a lack of formal education, the young Texans managed to impress the faculty. According to chemistry professor John Mallet, "Boys whose spelling and arithmetic were much behind their years, talked and thought like grown men of house building on the prairie, of cattle driving, even of social and political movements." At the end of the first day of entrance examinations, the faculty met, discussed the situation, and with a collective shrug decided not to rigidly enforce the "grade of scholarship" established for admission, due to the "limited advantages for education in this state."

From the beginning, the University was open to men and women, a progressive statement at a time when opportunities for women in higher education were rare. That UT would be coeducational was the result of a compromise in the state legislature as it debated the bill to create the University. Some members of the House who were opposed to female students were also political opponents of then-Governor Oran Roberts, and they feared that Roberts would be named UT's first president. In order to support the inclusion of women, the legislators demanded that the University be modeled after the University of Virginia, which was then led by a faculty chairman instead of a president. An agreement was reached, and for its first decade, University affairs were the responsibility of the elected head of the faculty. Roberts was denied the possibility of serving as UT's president, but he was appointed one of the two initial law professors.

With an incomplete building sitting on a mostly barren campus, boasting an inaugural faculty of eight professors, and joined by 221 students, most of whom hailed from Austin or the surrounding countryside of Central Texas, the University took its first, tentative steps upon the stage of Academe.

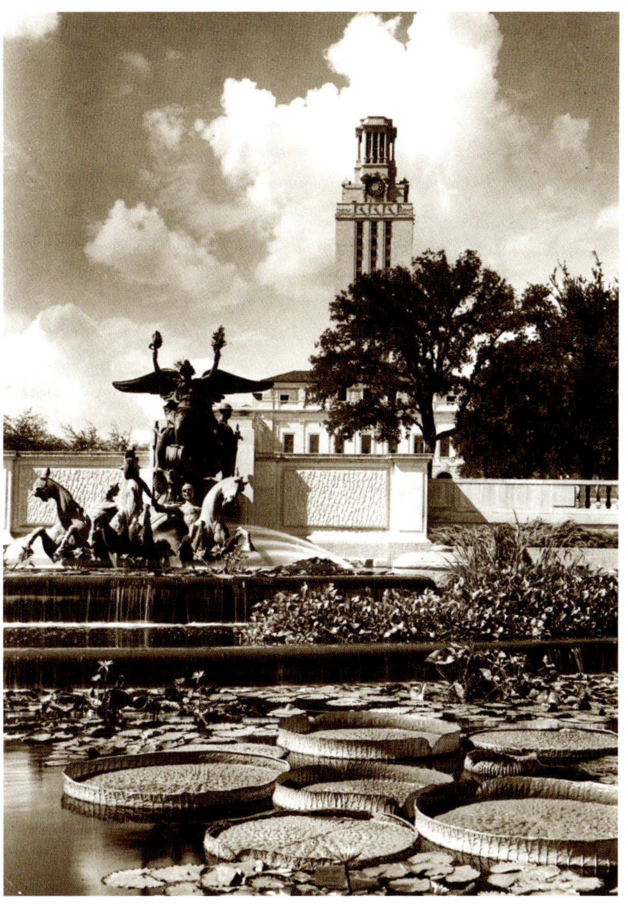

In 2008, a century after Gregory's wheelbarrow speech, The University of Texas opened its 125th academic year. Through the intervening decades, it has overcome adversities, celebrated hard-won successes, and built a strong and vibrant community. It claims internationally recognized academic programs and research facilities, as well as incredible libraries and museums filled with priceless treasures, and it boasts top-notch athletic squads. The acres of West Texas lands that Gregory had so lamented as worthless in 1908 turned out to have riches underneath. Less than a decade after the Santa Rita oil rig made its discovery in 1923, UT had embarked on a massive construction program that included a new Main Building and Tower. The University of Texas has participated in two world wars, persevered through the Great Depression, suffered through tense debates on academic freedom, and challenged itself to open its doors to everyone. It has grown and matured and has earned a prominent position on that academic platform.

And the alumni have heeded Gregory's challenge. In 1917, Governor James Ferguson threatened to veto appropriations and close the University unless President Robert Vinson and several professors resigned their posts. The Texas Exes rallied to defend their alma mater, and Ferguson was impeached and removed from office. The Union Project, an ambitious fundraising effort to build the Texas Union, two gymnasiums and an auditorium, encountered the economic depression of the 1930s. But the Texas Exes were adamant, alumni sometimes scrimping on necessities to send in meager $5 pledges with heartfelt notes so that the $600,000 goal could be met. In the 1960s, the alumni association created "Operation Brainpower" to recruit the brightest high school students to UT, and in more recent years it has developed a world-class scholarship program and a strong legislative advocacy group, always striving to live up to its mission to "praise, promote, and protect The University of Texas."

Gregory would most certainly have been proud. ★

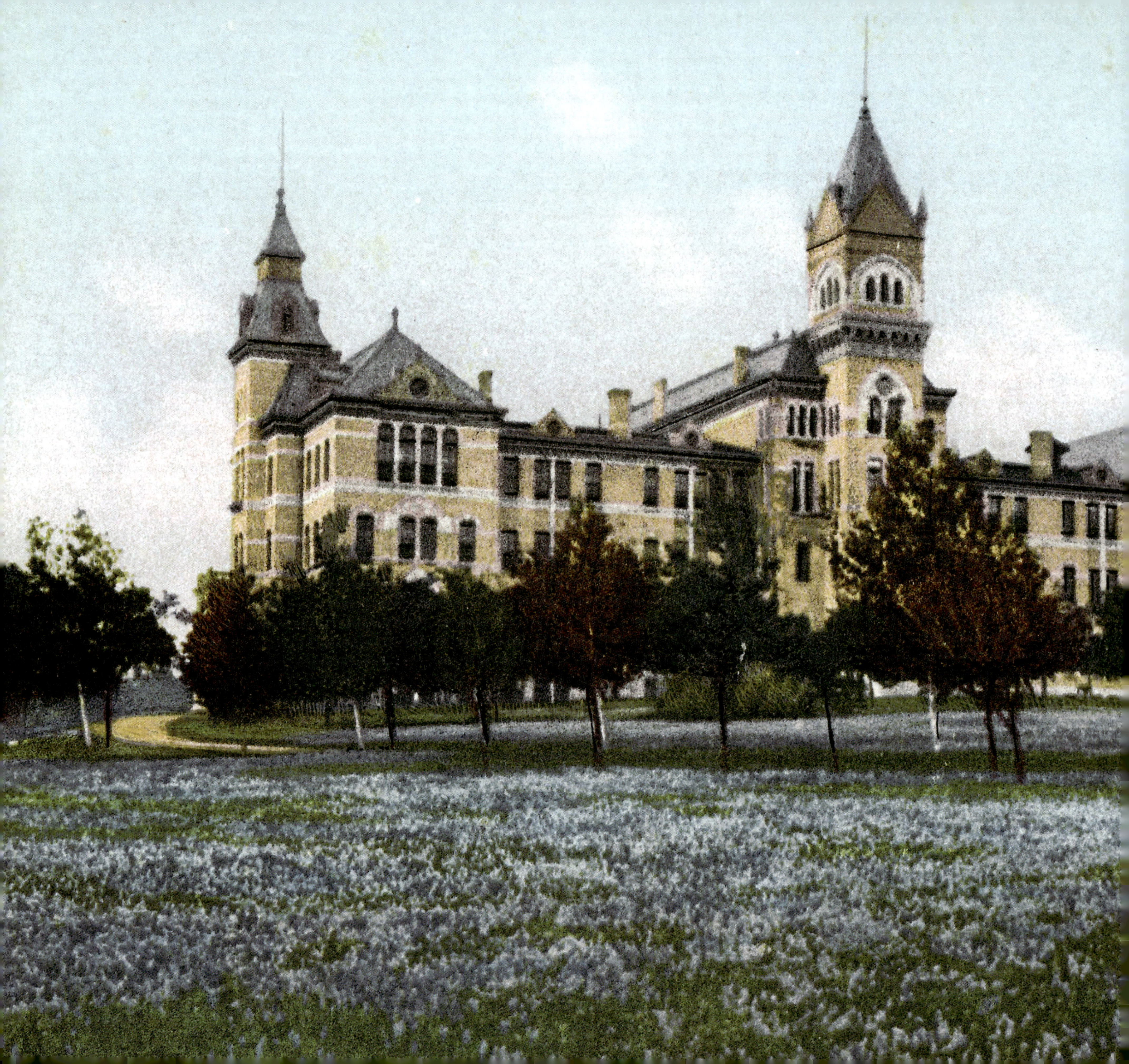

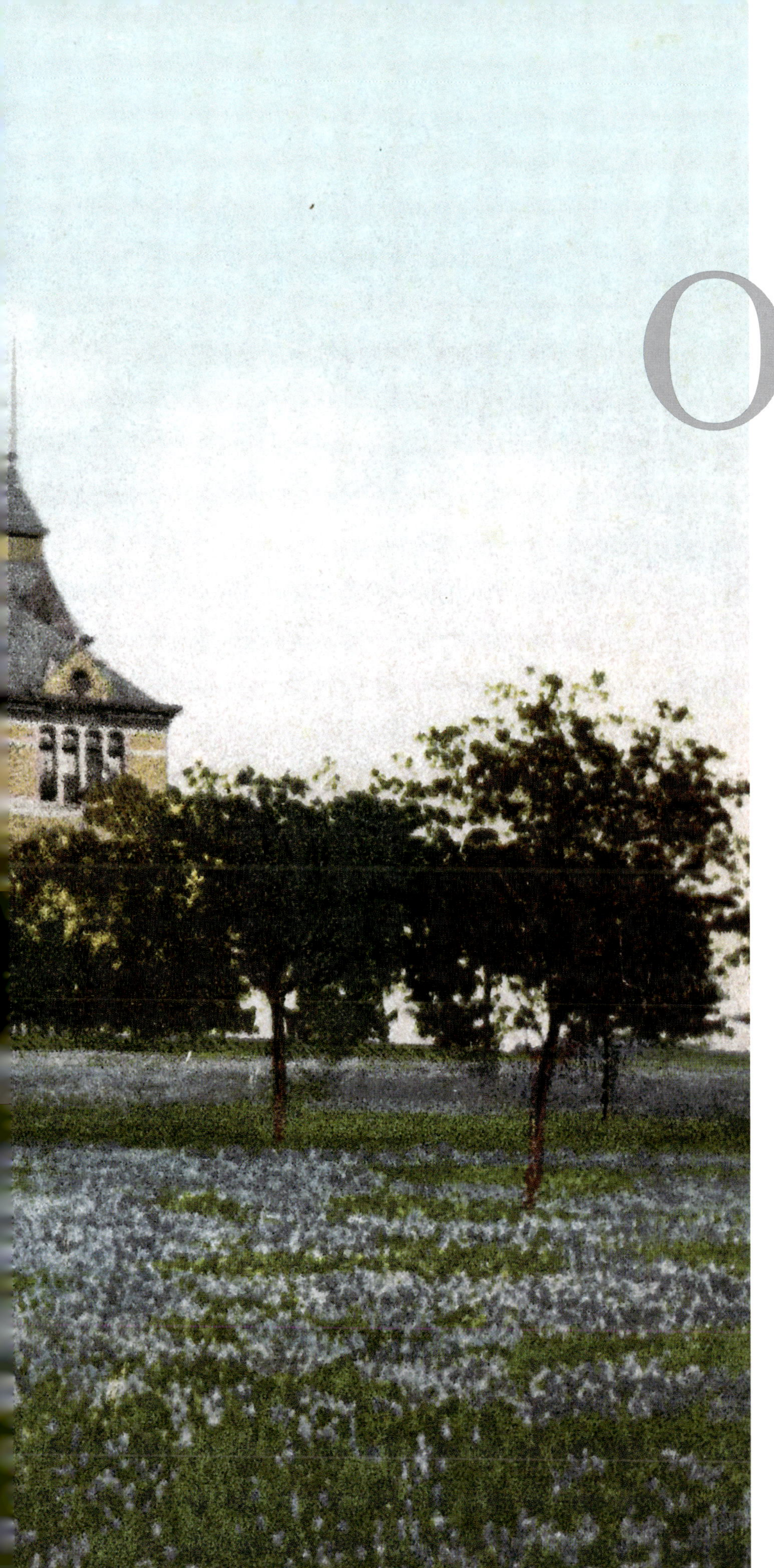

Our Story
rites of passage

The old Main Building, the University's first building, sits majestically on the crest of College Hill, in the middle of a 40-acre campus awash in bluebonnets.

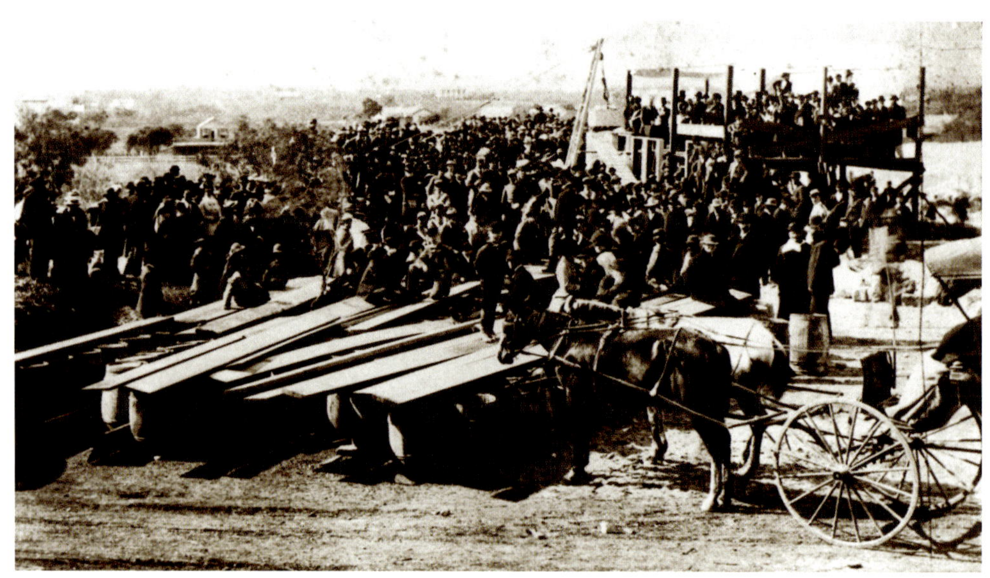

Left On Friday, November 17, 1882, several thousand braved chilly and damp conditions to attend the cornerstone ceremony for the old Main Building. The University opened the following autumn.

Below The University's original 40-acre campus was a haven for hackberry, mesquite, and cedar trees, and at its center stood the Victorian-Gothic old Main Building. Made from yellow buff brick and cream limestone trim, its pointed central tower was flanked by two shorter towers that marked the east and west entrances of the building. The decorative cornices were made from galvanized iron, and a pink granite arch guarded the main southern doorway. *John M. Kuehne Photograph Collection, Center for American History, UT-Austin*

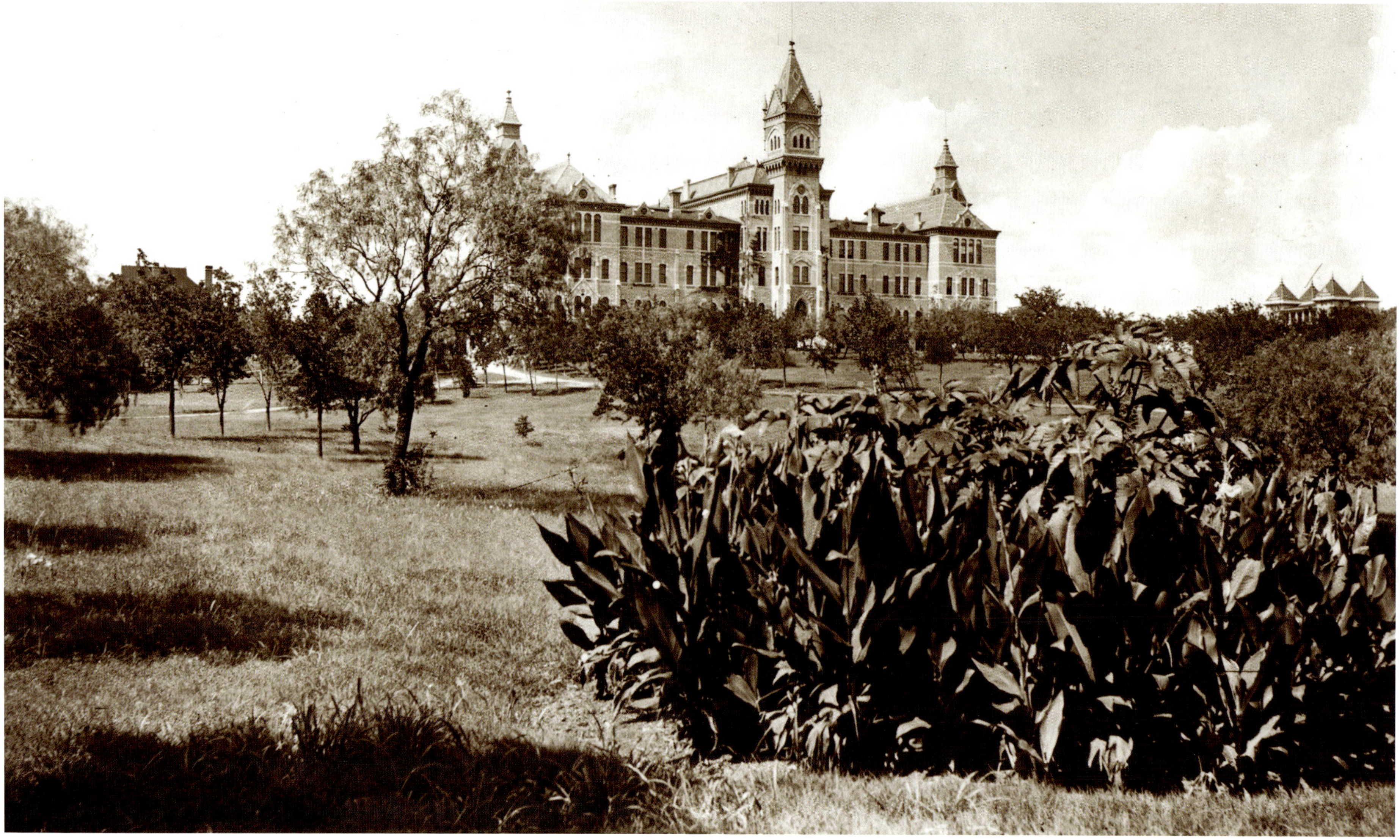

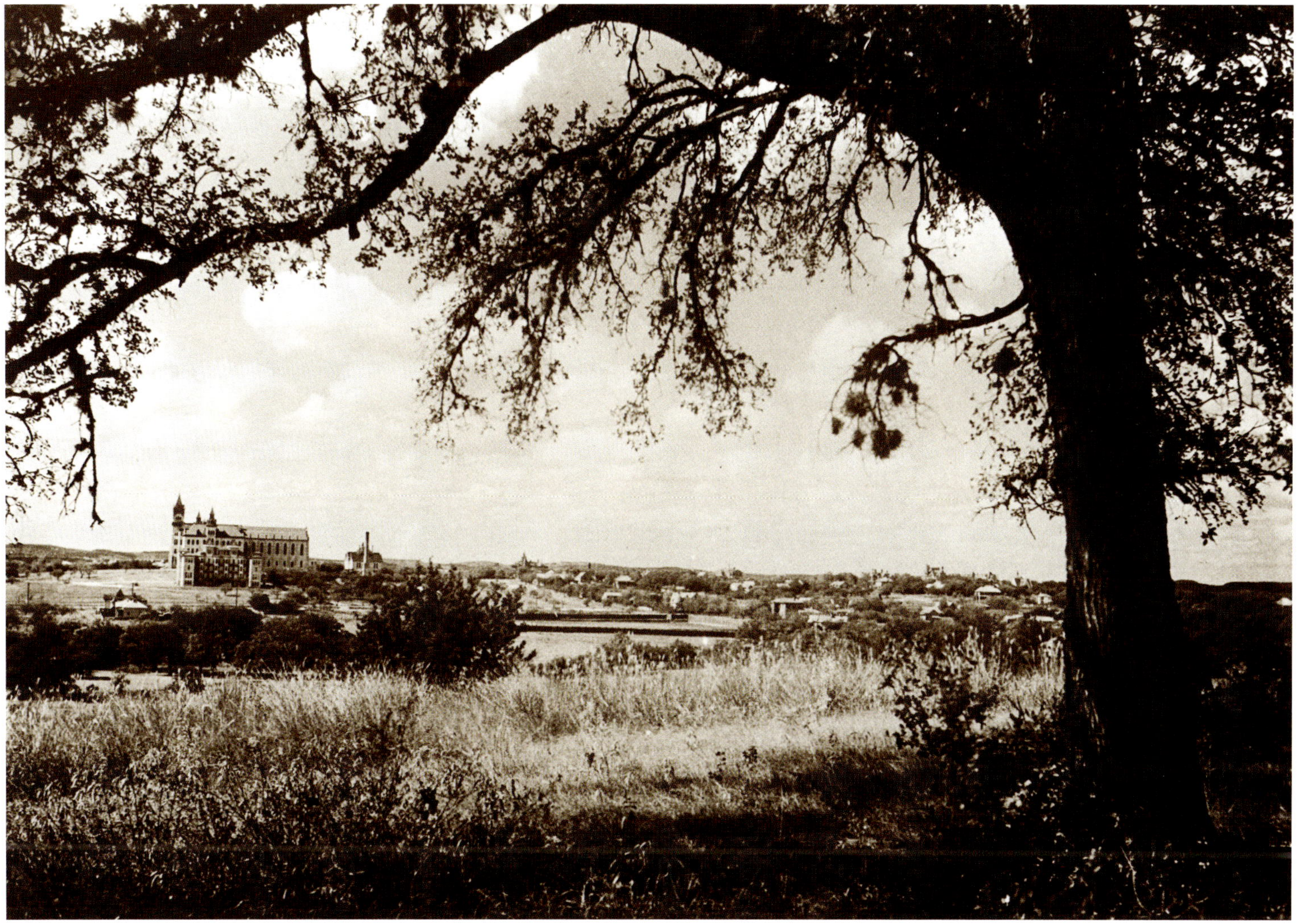

Above A view of the early UT campus from the east, near where the LBJ Library now stands. Old Main sits at the top of the hill and faces south toward downtown Austin. Down the slope and just to the right is Clark Field, the University's first athletic field.

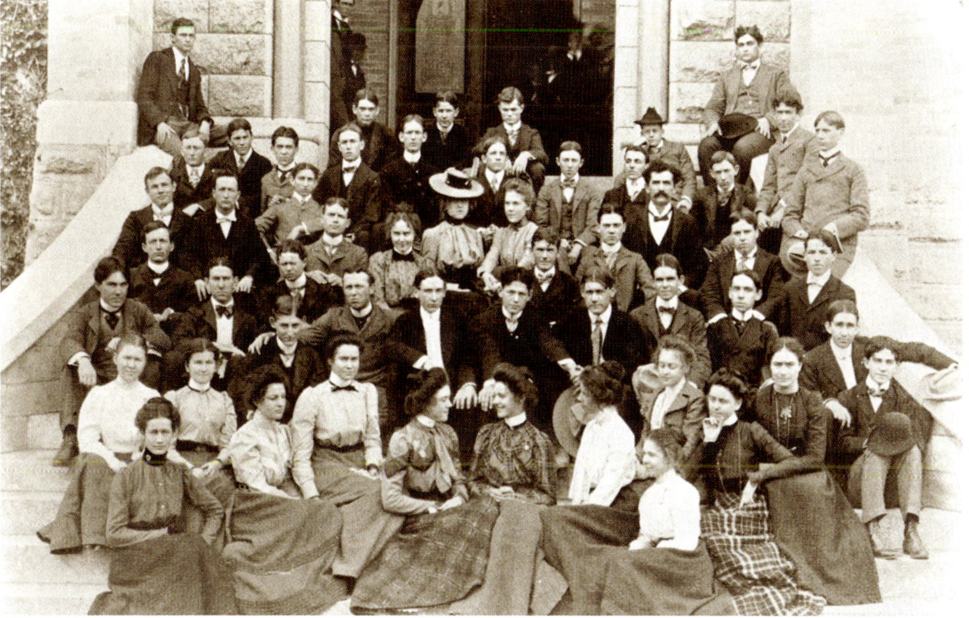

Right Freshman students of 1901 sit on the front stairs of Old Main for a class portrait. From its opening session in 1883, The University of Texas admitted both men and women, progressive for its time.

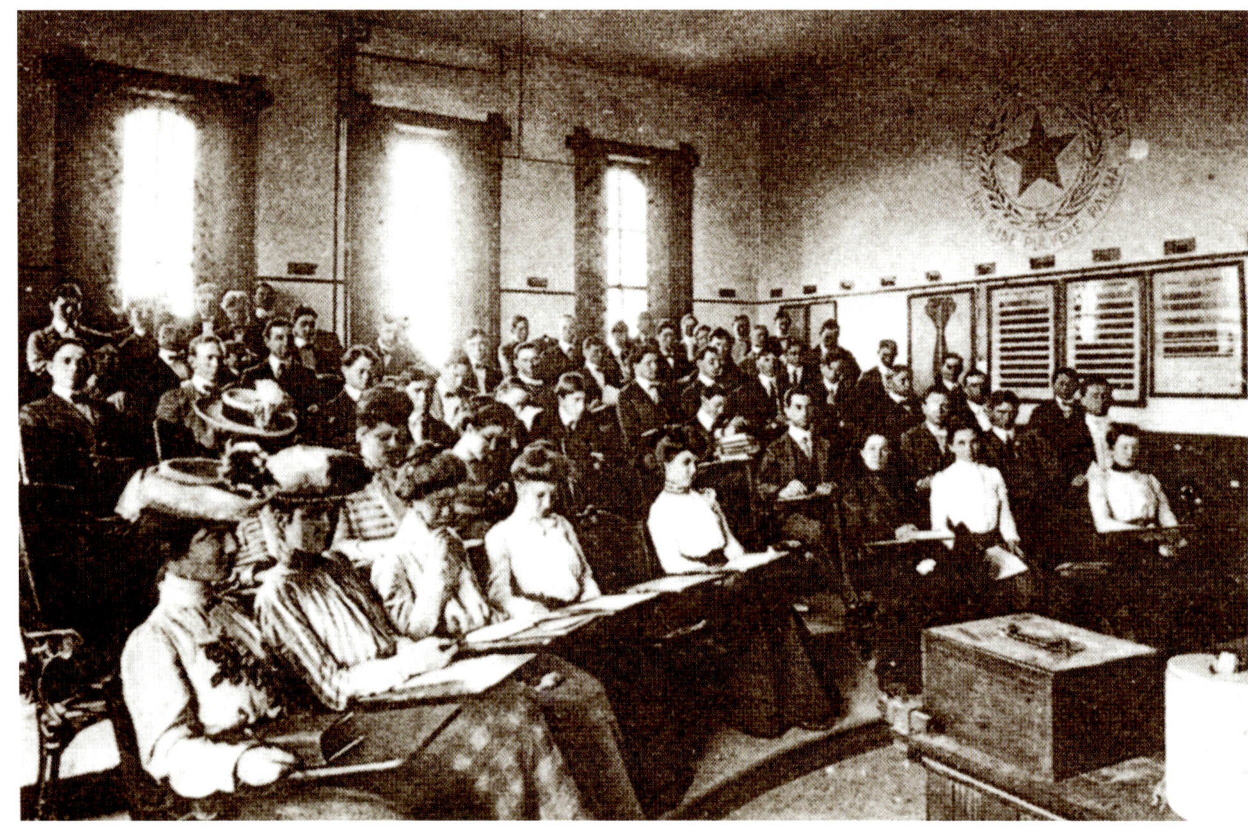

The History Room was one of the few auditorium-style classrooms in Old Main. Classes were held from Monday through Saturday, and professors sent monthly attendance reports to parents. Here, the coeds sit in the front, while the gentlemen fill the seats behind.

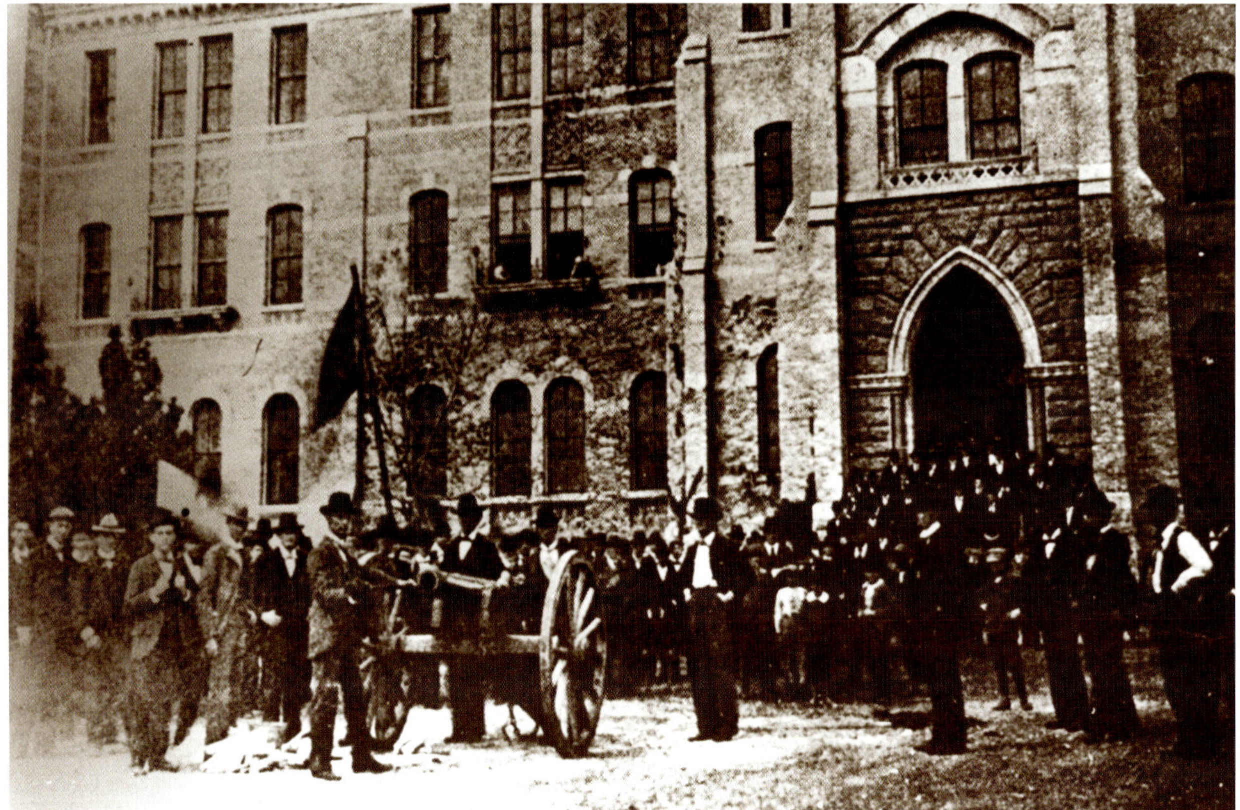

On March 2, 1897, the senior law class borrowed a cannon from the state capitol grounds and fired it all afternoon in front of the old Main Building to celebrate Texas Independence Day. For decades afterward, March 2nd was one of the few official University holidays.

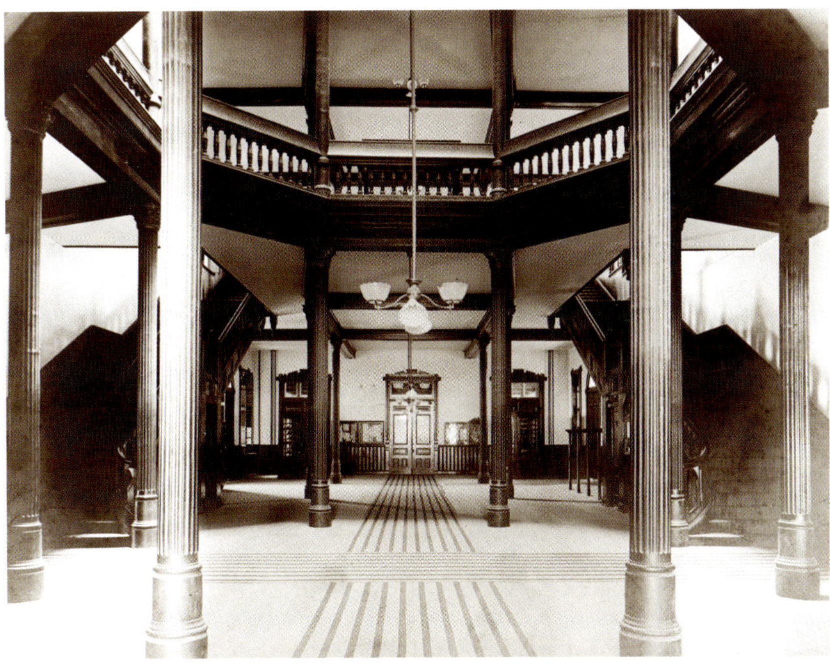

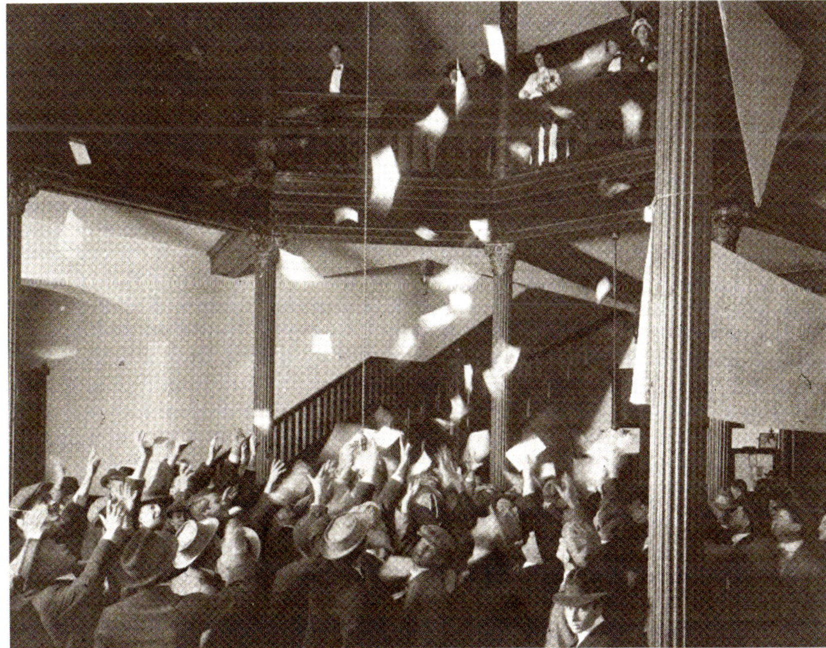

Top Visitors who passed through the south entrance to Old Main were greeted to a four-story rotunda capped by an octagonal skylight. In the days before a student union, the rotunda was a popular gathering place for students and provided an important means of communication.

Above Announcements of upcoming campus events were printed on handbills, called "dodgers," taken to the fourth floor and tossed en masse out into the rotunda, where they dropped into the hands of students waiting below.

1902

FRESHMEN

HEARKEN!

We, the mighty Junior Laws, realizing that the male contingent of the Freshman Class is an abomination to the State and a pest to the University, do propose to

Wipe Up the Earth

with the individuals of the above mentioned aggregation possessing sufficient indescretion to remain on the Athletic Field after the Foot-Ball Game to-day.

All those desirous of seeing this performance are requested to remain.

We are the noble Junior Laws,
We feed on Freshmen squeals,
At the very sight of us
The freshman's blood congeals.

Oh we're the lusty Junior Laws!
Come Freshies if ye dare,
By the gods we'll eat you
Flesh and bone and hair.

MORGAN-PRESCOTT PRINTING CO., AUSTIN

Above Not all of the dodgers were friendly. This challenge to the freshman class was written by first-year law students. *Prints and Photographs Collection, Center for American History, UT-Austin*

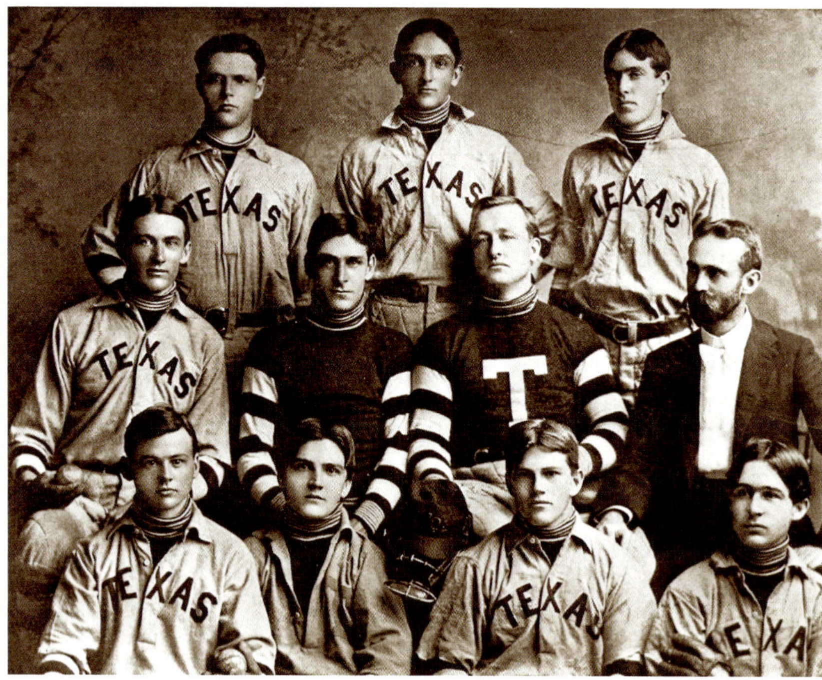

Baseball, not football, was the favorite diversion among students in the University's infant years, and afternoon inter-class games were played on the relatively flat northwest corner of the campus, where the Texas Union now stands. The team waiting to bat often took shade under one of the old trees that are today known as the Battle Oaks. This is the 1902 UT Baseball Team.

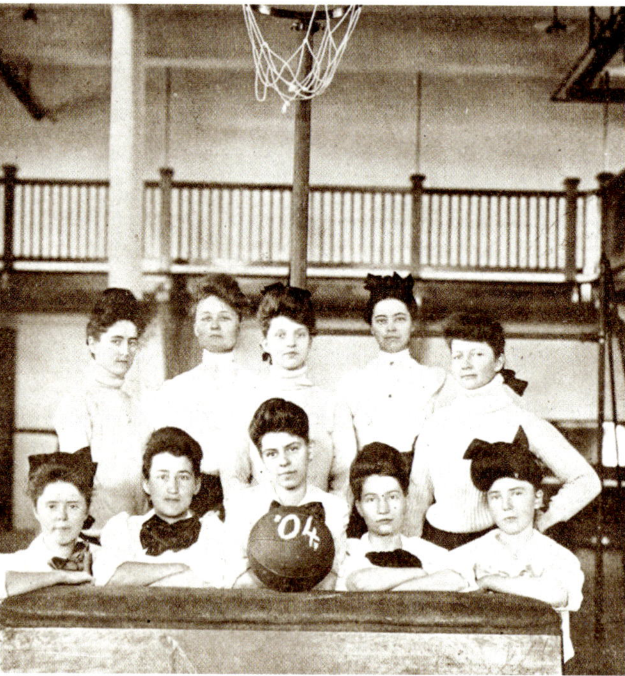

Basketball debuted in the 1890s as a woman's game, first played in makeshift quarters in Old Main, and later in the basement gymnasium of the Woman's Building, the first residence hall for UT coeds. Ladies were still required to wear dresses, and Mrs. Carothers, the head matron of the hall, sometimes covered the windows so that nothing "inappropriate" would be seen.

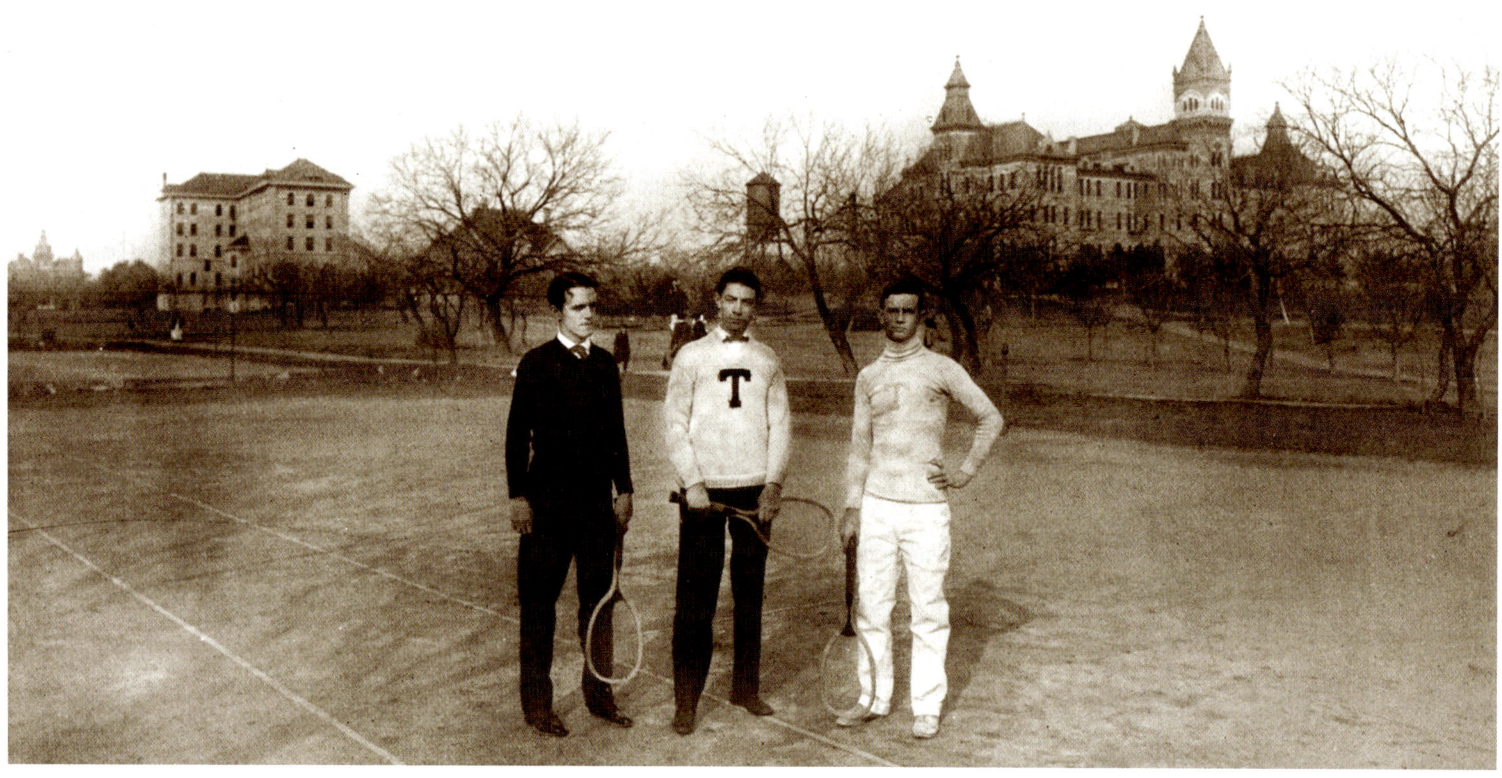

With Old Main in the background, members of the UT Tennis Association pose on a clay court in the southwest corner of the Forty Acres, where the Ransom Center stands today. The University Athletic Association, along with a faculty-chaired Athletic Council, was formed in 1892 to oversee sports events and facilities. At the time, baseball and tennis were popular. Football was added in 1893.

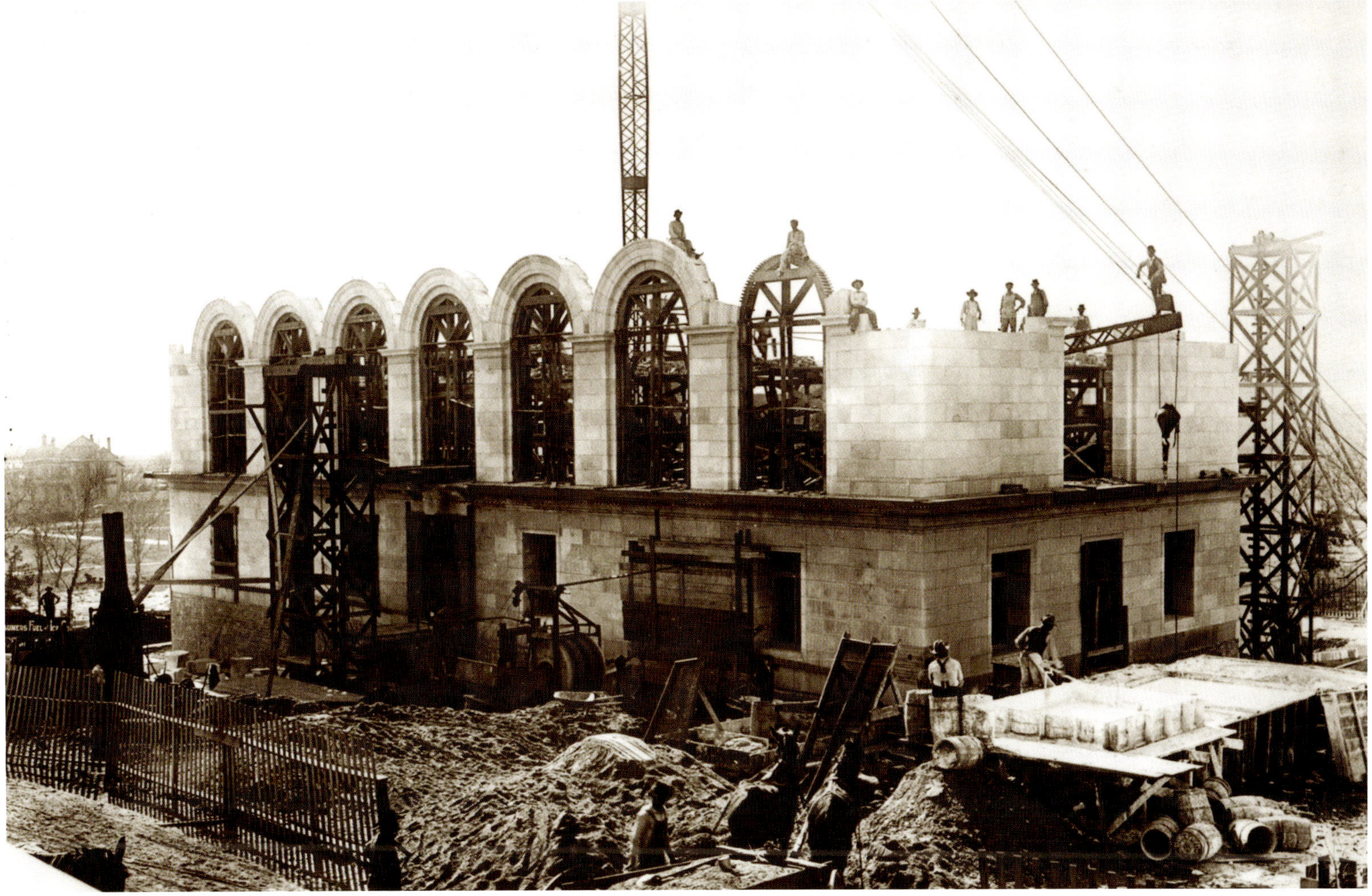

In 1910, with the library in Old Main hopelessly overcrowded, the Board of Regents hired Cass Gilbert of New York as the first University Architect, and assigned him the task of designing a new, separate library building (now known as Battle Hall). Among the most renowned architects of his time, Gilbert also created the Minnesota State Capitol, the Woolworth Tower in New York, and the U.S. Supreme Court Building. The library's Mediterranean-Renaissance style was to set the tone for future campus buildings. *Prints and Photographs Collection, Center for American History, UT-Austin*

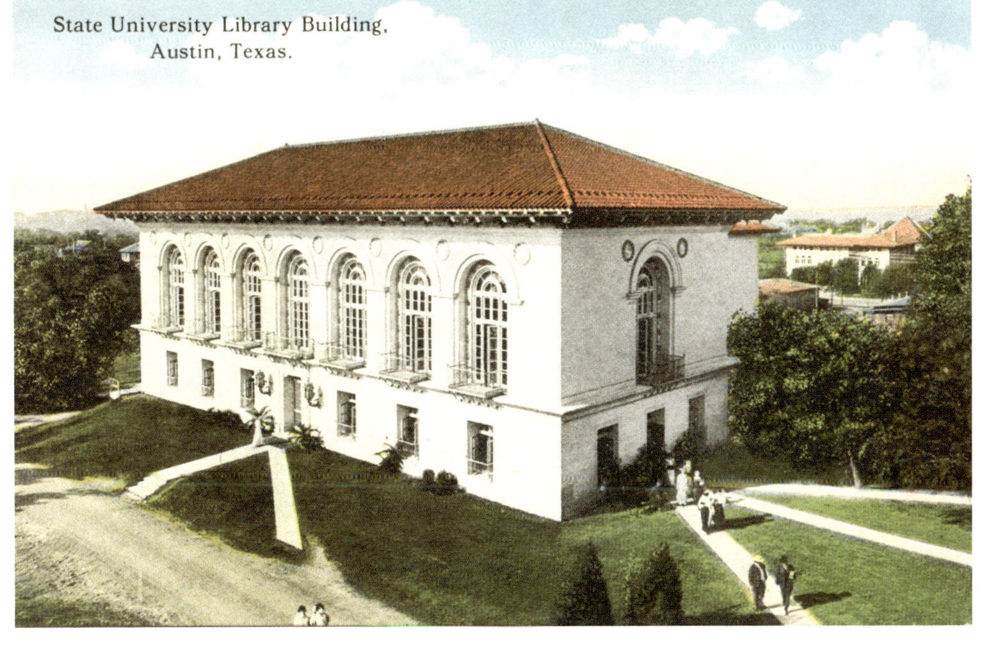

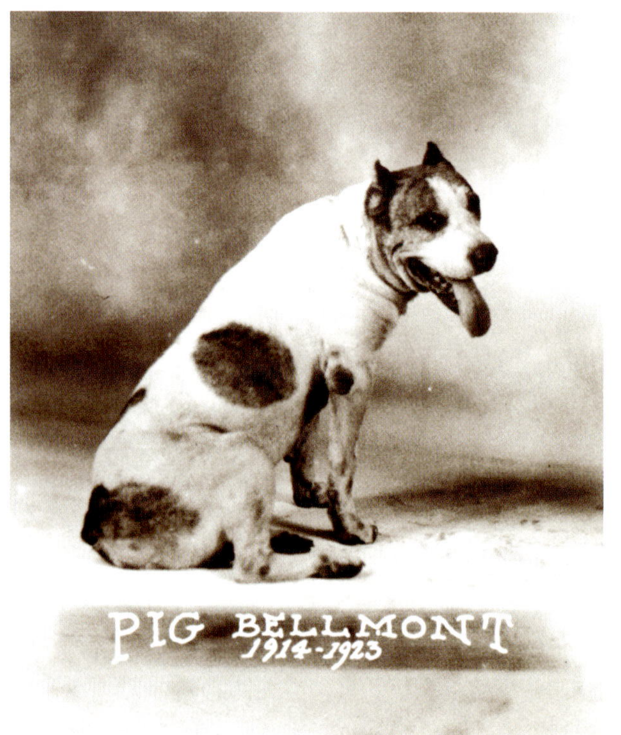

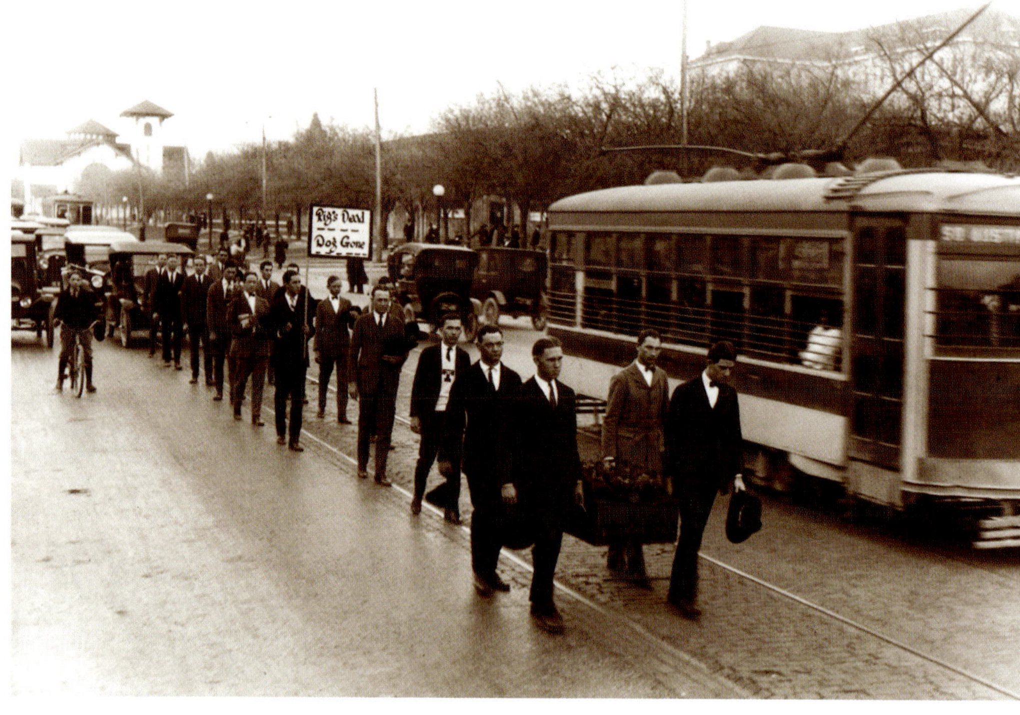

Above Left and Above Brought to Austin in 1914 by Theo Bellmont, UT's first athletics director, Pig Bellmont inhabited the campus, attended home and away athletic games, and was beloved among students as the University's first live mascot. He was named after Gus "Pig" Dittmar, a center for the football team, when students discovered that both dog and athlete were bowlegged. Pig Bellmont was tragically killed by a Model T Ford on New Year's Day, 1923, and students held an appropriate funeral march down Guadalupe Street. He was buried on campus; a marker was left with the epitaph, "Pig's Dead . . . Dog Gone."

Left Purchased for $125 by a group of UT alumni, Bevo I was introduced at halftime of the 1916 Thanksgiving football bout between the University and the A&M College of Texas. The following month, *The Alcalde* magazine, in its report of the game, announced: "His name is Bevo. Long may he reign!" Bevo was later branded by a group of prankster Aggies, but contrary to some popular accounts, the steer was named well before being branded, and the brand was never altered to read "Bevo."

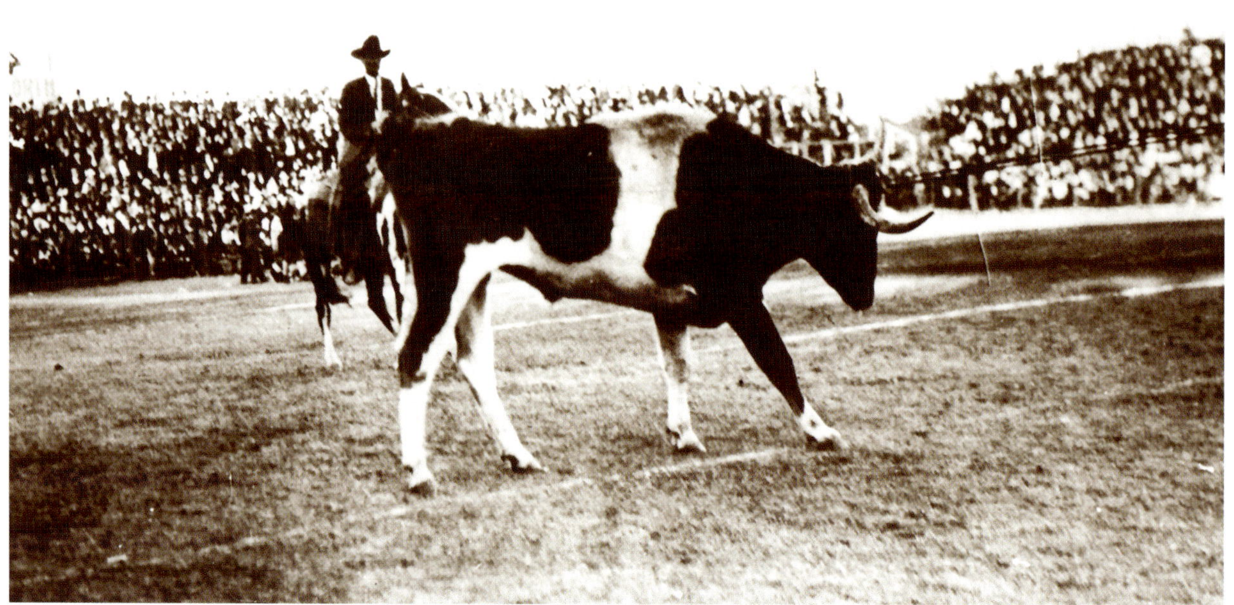

Right For almost half a century, springtime on the campus was heralded by a sea of bluebonnets that would blanket the Forty Acres. In the 1910s, the wildflowers helped to create an annual tradition among University coeds. Graduating seniors passed an immense, handmade chain of real bluebonnets, representing tradition and responsibility, onto the shoulders of the junior girls. The ceremony continued into the early 1960s.

Below and Right Opened in 1890, Brackenridge Hall, or "B. Hall," was a gift from UT regent George Brackenridge of San Antonio. Intended to make college affordable for the "poor boys" of Texas, rent in the hall was $2.50 per month. Making the best use of their education, the hall's residents went on to become well-known professors, doctors, lawyers, and state and national lawmakers. B. Hall was also the source of many University traditions and organizations, including "The Eyes of Texas," the Longhorn Band, student government, *The Daily Texan* newspaper, the Texas Cowboys, and the Tejas Club.

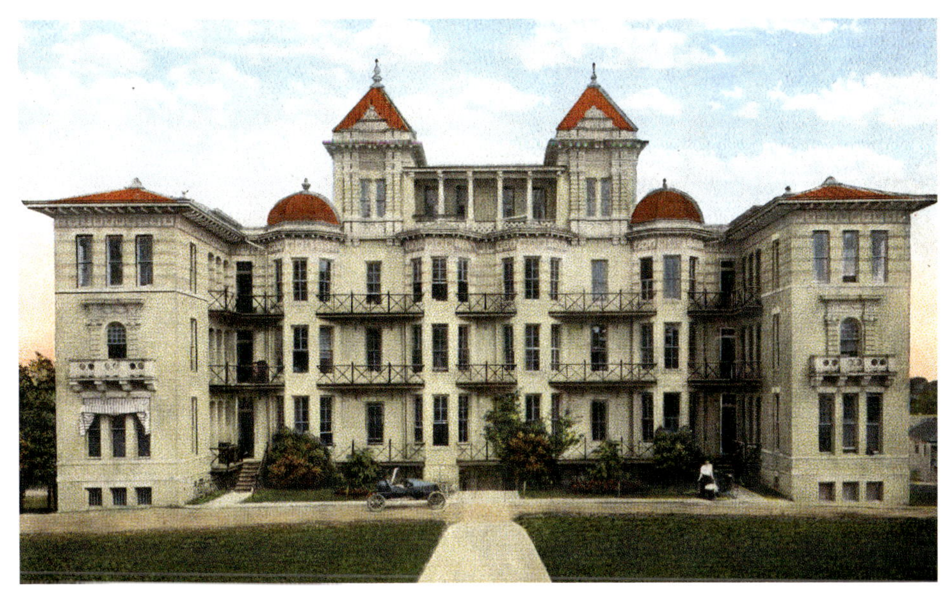

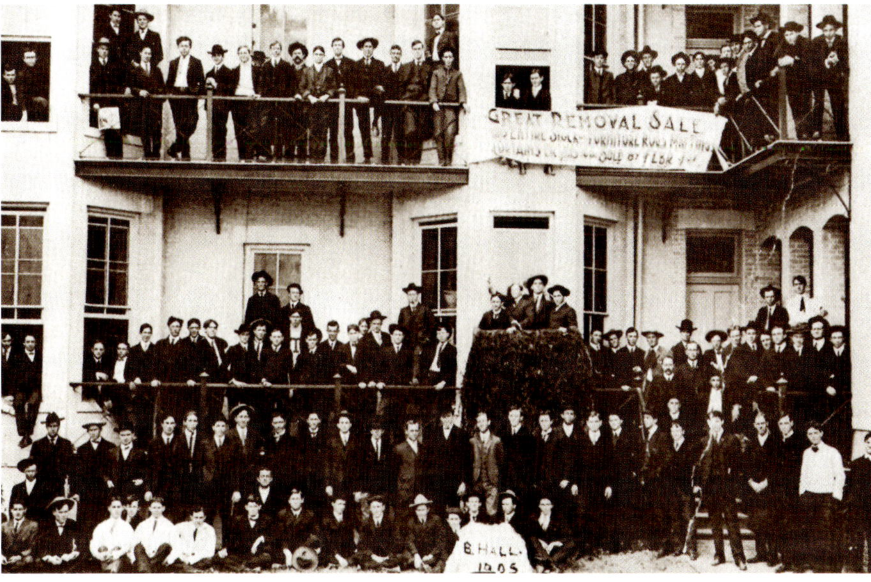

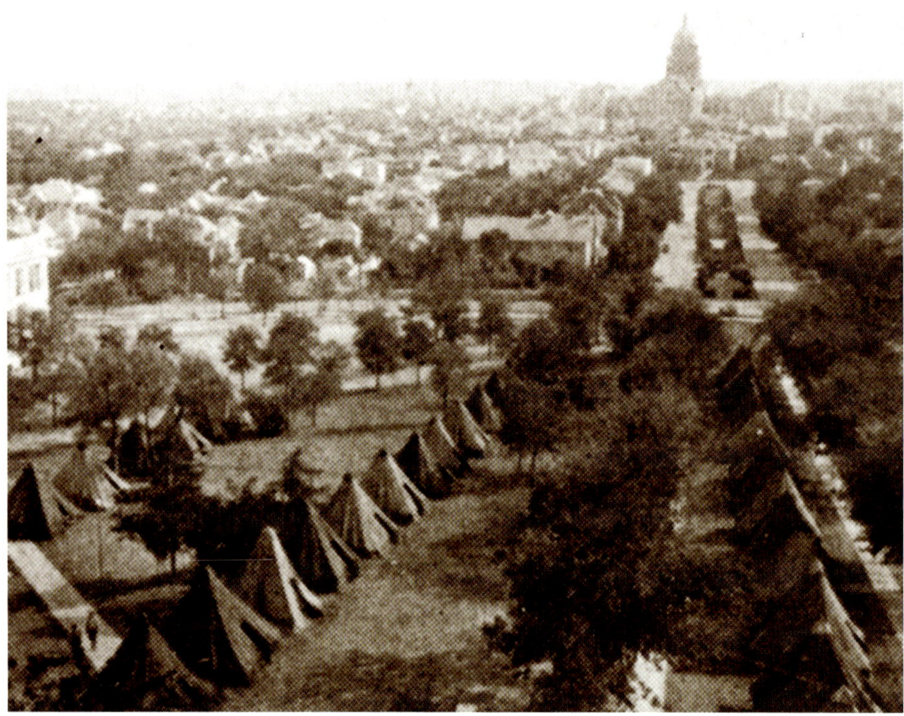

During World War I, the campus better resembled a military encampment, with canvas army tents lining what would later become the South Mall. The University hosted military schools for radio operators and automobile mechanics, along with the nation's largest School of Military Aeronautics, dubbed the "West Point of the Air."

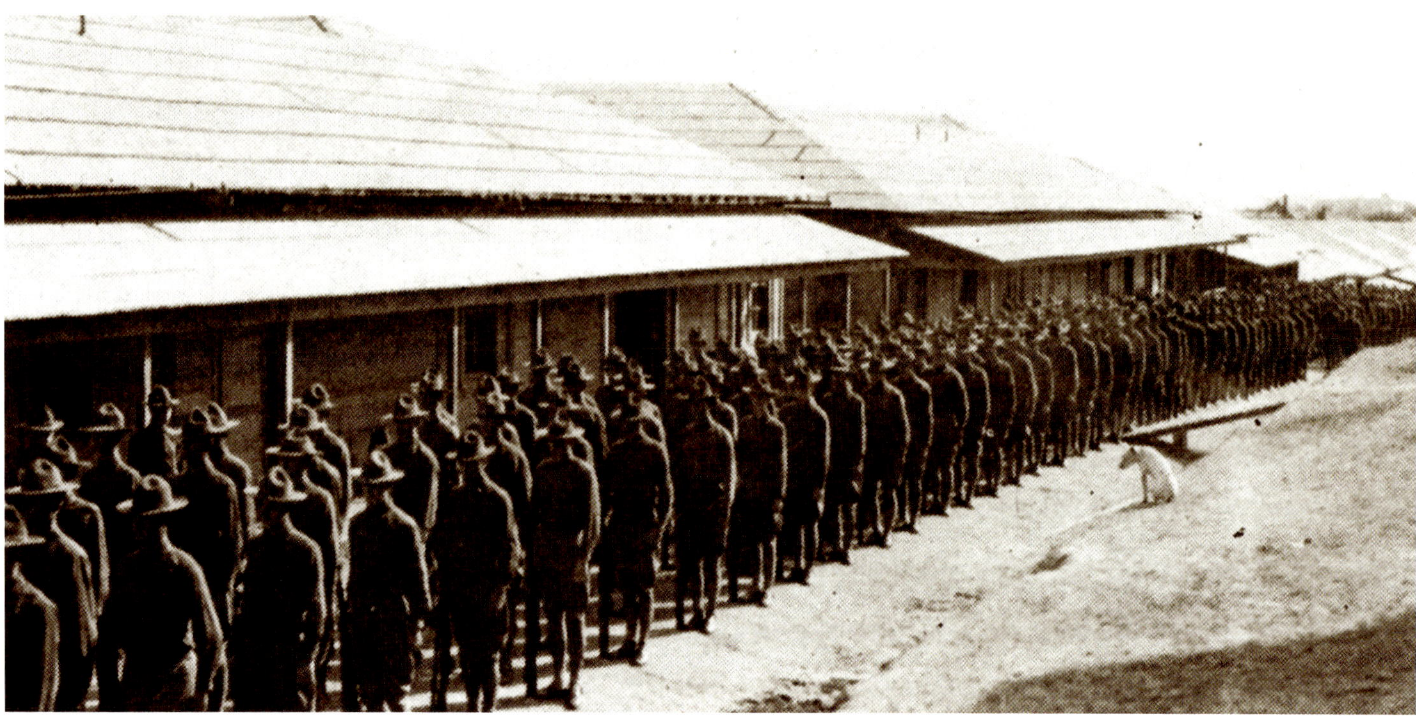

Atten-shun! In 1918, as part of the war effort, most male students participated in the Student Army Training Corps, resided in wooden barracks along the east side of campus (where Waggener Hall and the McCombs School are today), and marched to class and meals. Here, students fall out in formation while Pig Bellmont inspects the troops.

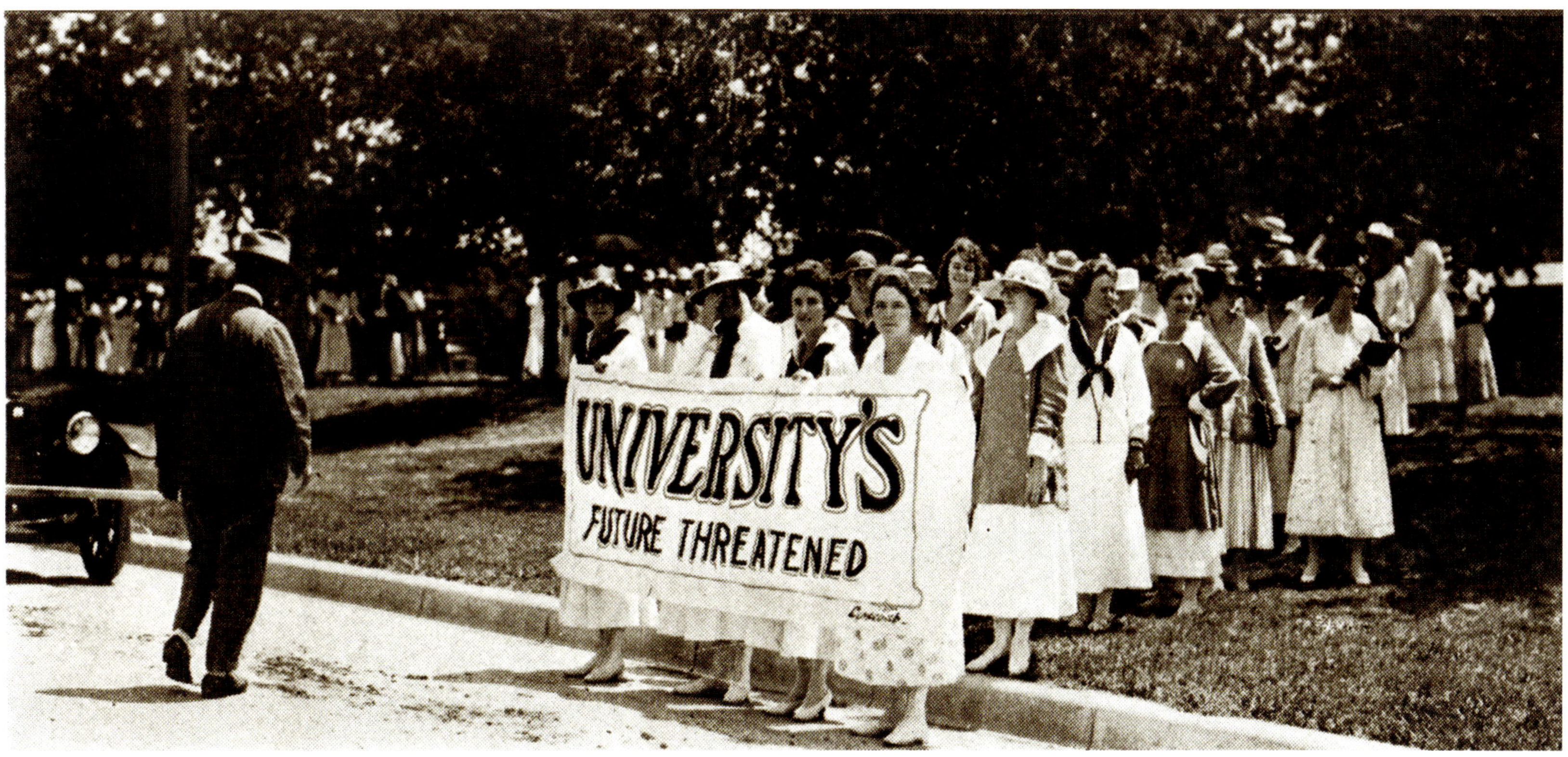

In 1917, while supporting the nation's war efforts, the University also was embroiled in a controversy with Governor James Ferguson, who threatened to veto appropriations and close the University unless President Robert Vinson and several professors resigned their posts. In May, students responded with a protest march to the Capitol grounds.

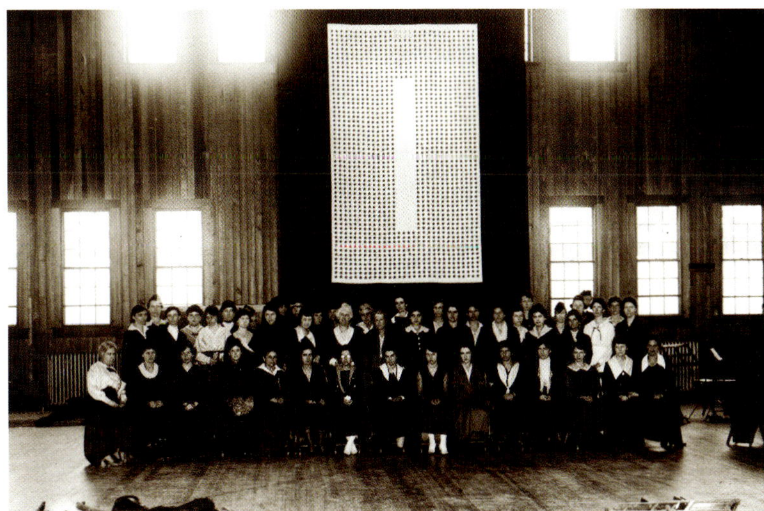

On March 2, 1918, the University Ladies Club presented a hand-made service flag, 10 1/2 feet wide and 16 feet long. It contained 1,570 blue stars on a white flannel background, with a red border. The stars represented the number of UT alumni then in military service. Eight of the stars had white centers, noting those who had died in service to their country.
Prints and Photographs Collection, Center for American History, UT-Austin

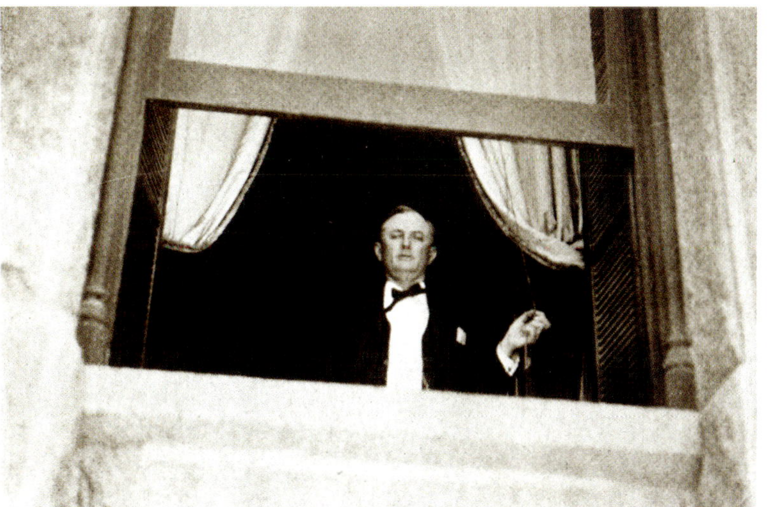

An unhappy Governor Ferguson glares at a student demonstration from his office window. The controversy galvanized the Ex-Students' Association to defend the University, and Governor Ferguson was impeached and removed from office in August 1917. Two years later, the Association elected to separate itself from UT and become a self-governing organization in order to "praise, promote and protect The University of Texas."

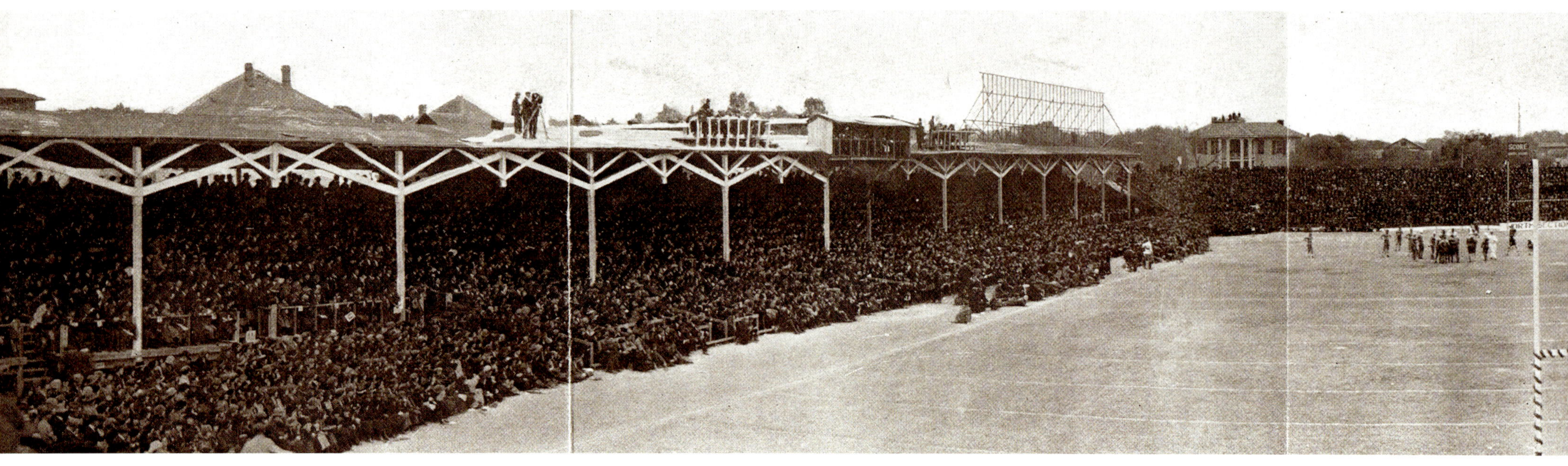

Clark Field, the University's first athletic field, was east of the Forty Acres, where Taylor Hall and the ACES Building now stand. Named for James Clark, a beloved University proctor, the land for the field was purchased in 1899 with contributions from students, faculty, and alumni.

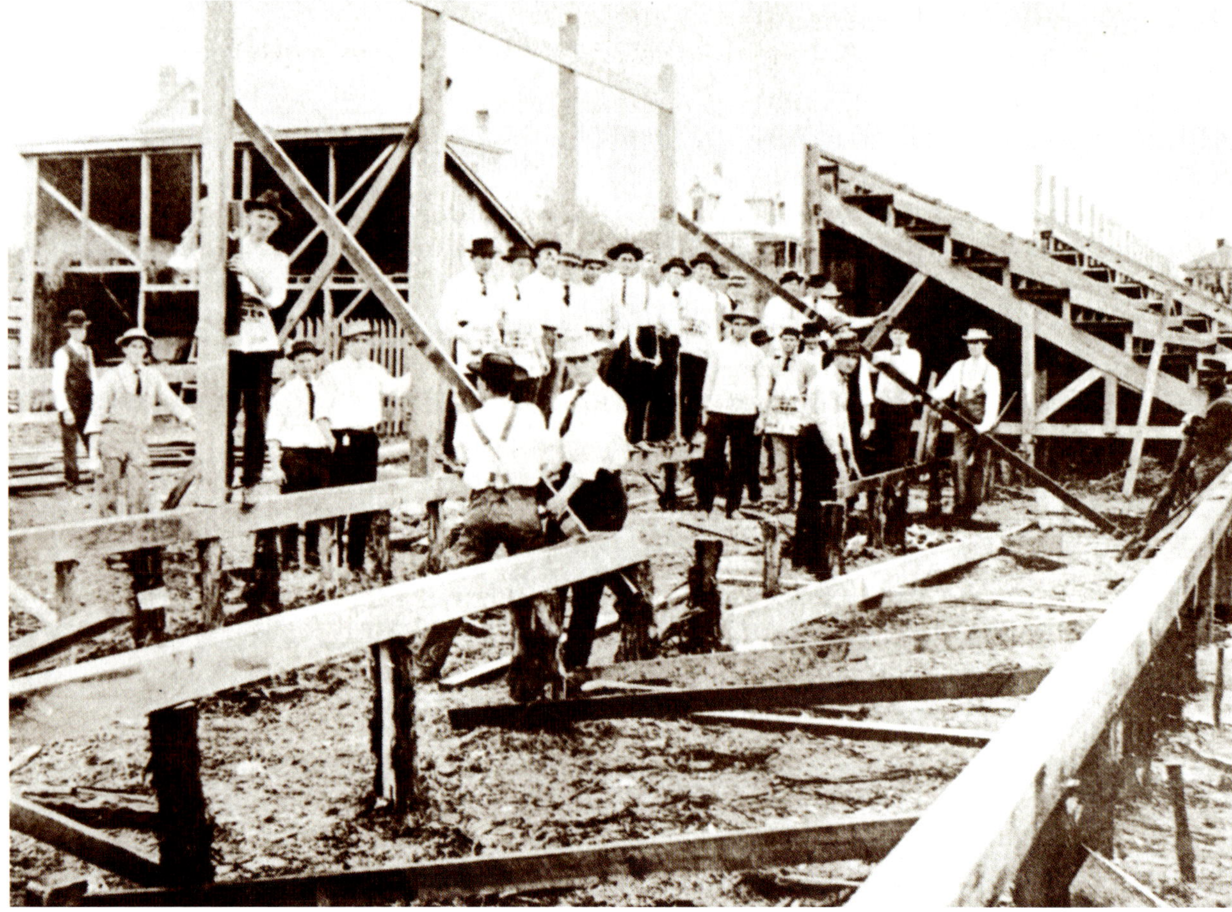

Hardworking students rush to finish wooden bleachers for Clark Field before the 1907 football game against Texas A&M. The initial bleachers were planned, financed, and constructed by UT students in about two weeks, with a capacity of 3,000 persons. Over the years, the students continued to add seating until it reached almost 20,000 in the early 1920s.

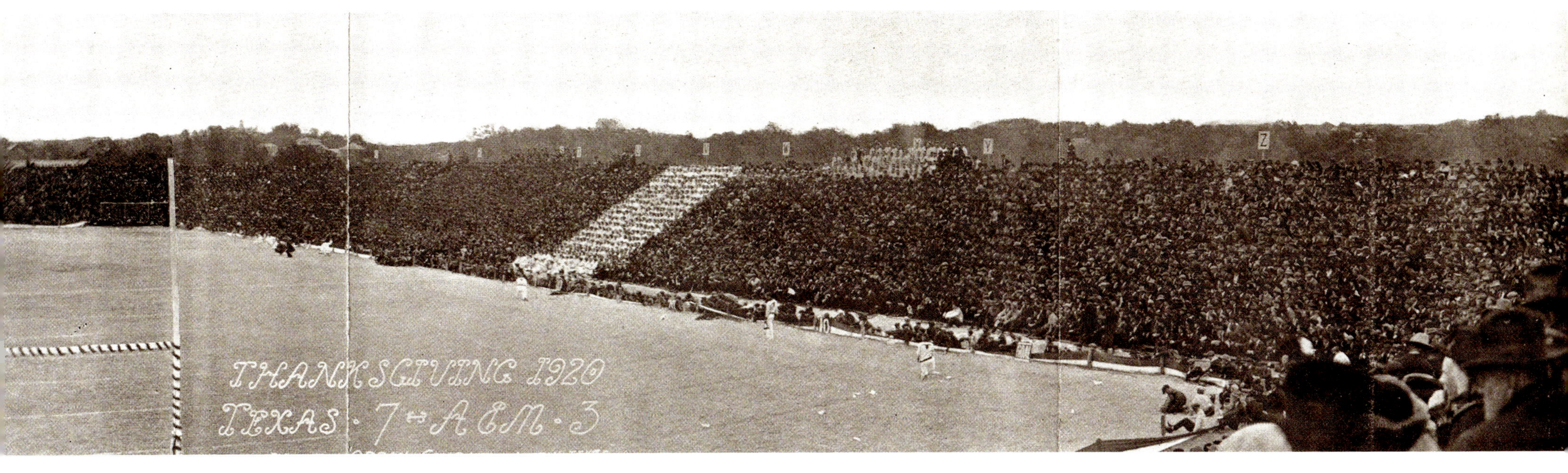

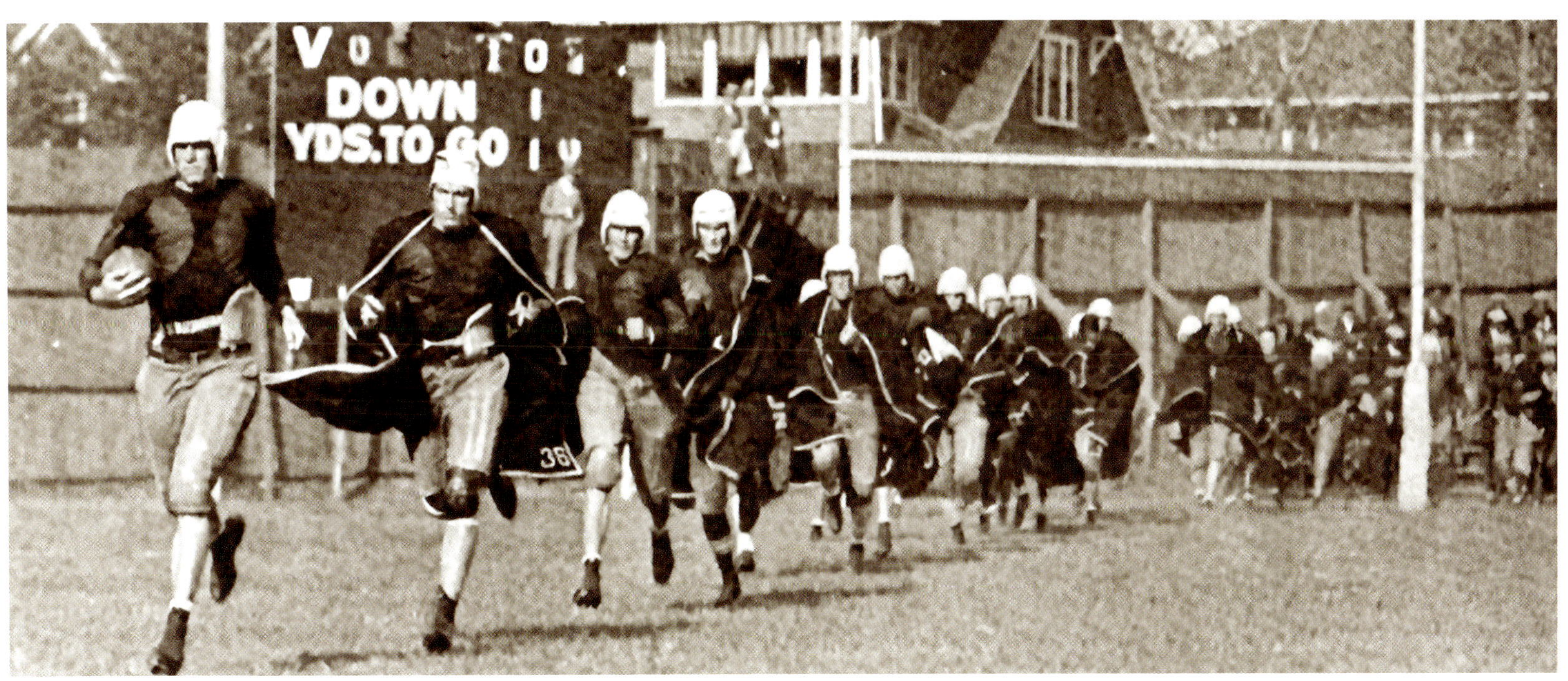

All hail the Longhorns! With bright orange jerseys and white leather helmets, the University of Texas football team charges into Clark Field in the 1920s.

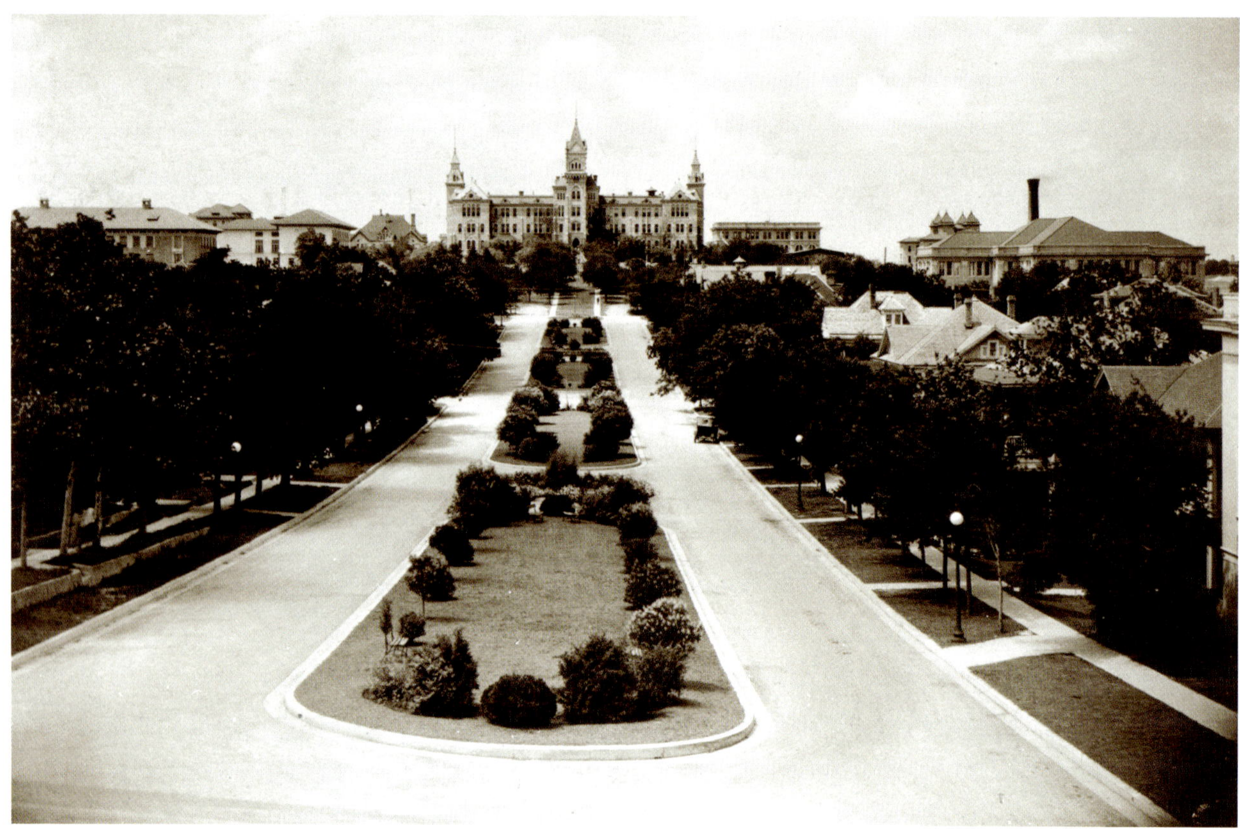

A panorama from University Avenue, about 1925. While the stately Old Main still dominated College Hill, it shared the campus with an increasing number of other buildings.
Prints and Photographs Collection, Center for American History, UT-Austin

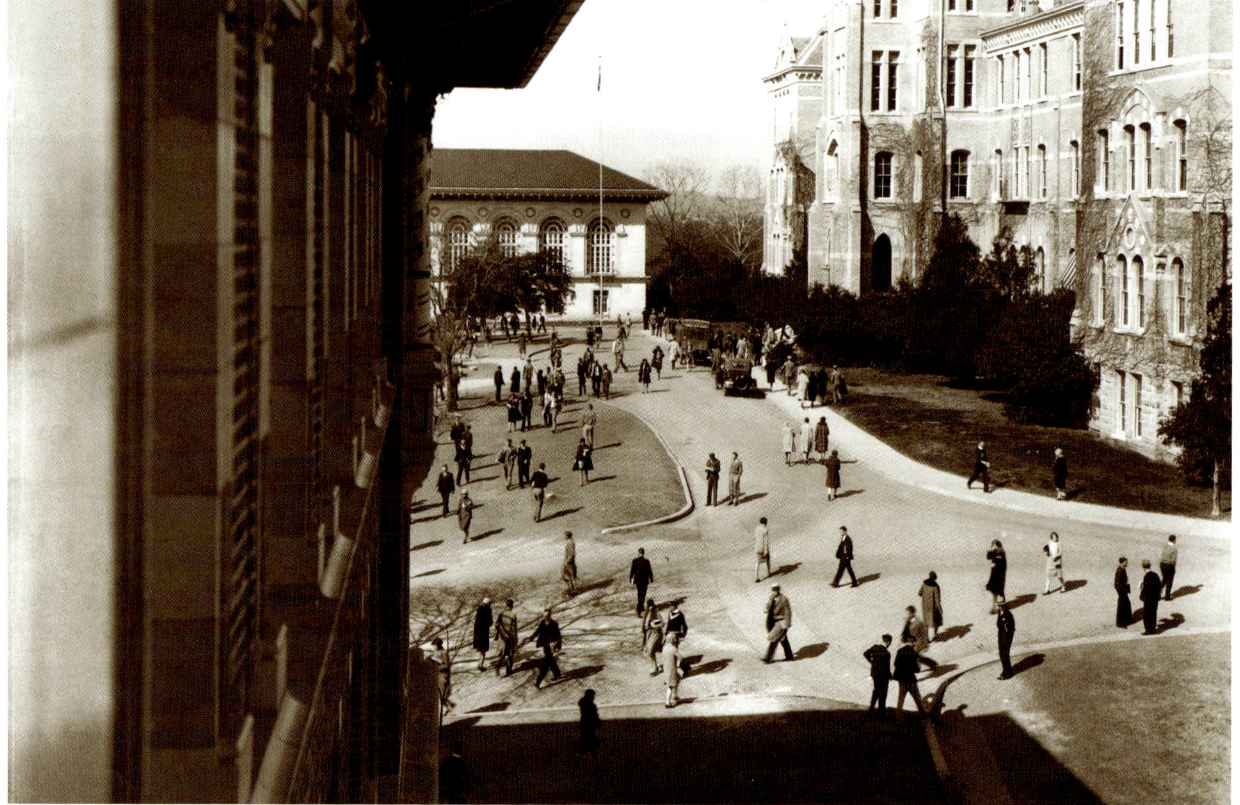

A view of class change from the top floor of the newly finished Garrison Hall. Old Main is to the right, and the library (later Battle Hall) can be seen across what would become the Main Mall.
Prints and Photographs Collection, Center for American History, UT-Austin

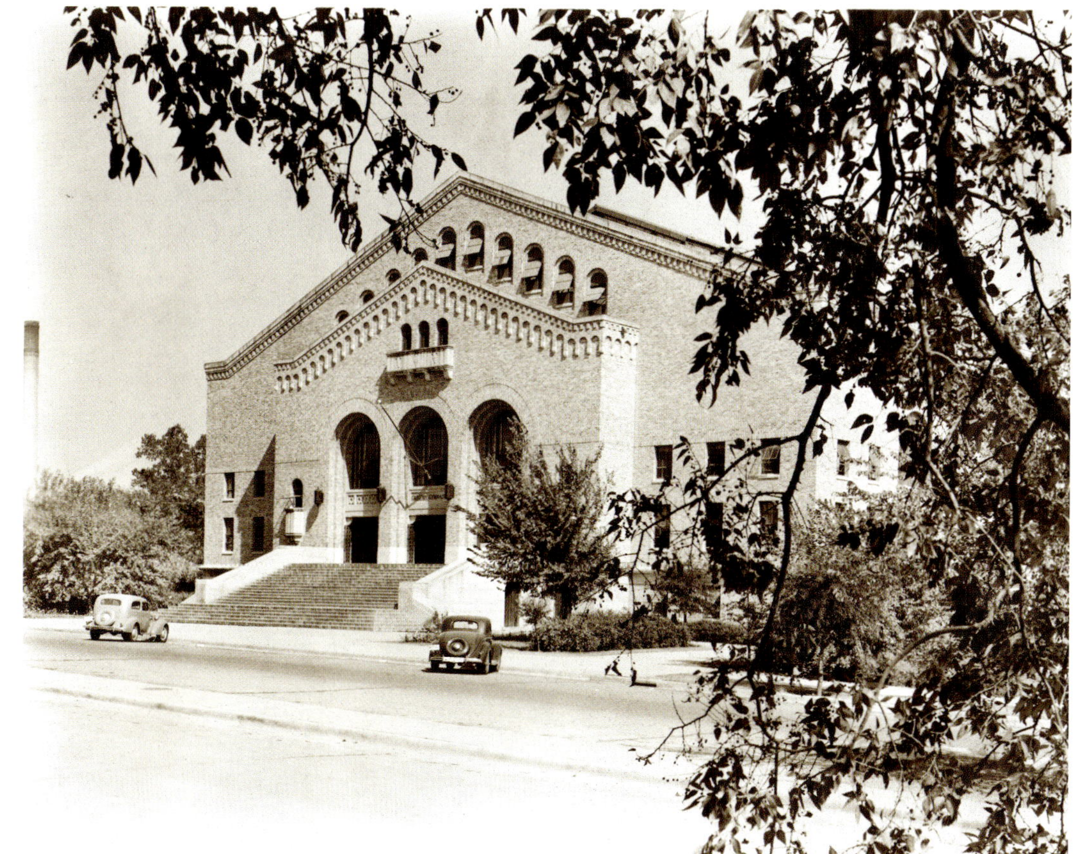

Right As early as 1907, the Ex-Students' Association appointed Thomas Watt Gregory (LL.B. 1885) to chair a committee that would raise funds for a new men's gymnasium. Almost $65,000 was raised and invested, and when Gregory became president of the Association in 1927, he asked the Board of Regents to expand the project to include a women's gym and student union building. Under Gregory's spirited leadership, "The Union Project" was off and running. The Texas Exes contributed more than $600,000 to build the Texas Union, Gregory Gym, Anna Hiss Gym, and Hogg Auditorium, all completed during the Great Depression of the 1930s.

Below University coeds participate in the dedication ceremonies for the Texas Memorial Stadium on Thanksgiving Day, 1924. The stadium was financed by an intense fundraising effort by both students and alumni, under the slogan "For Texas, I Will." Old Main and the Forty Acres are on the hill behind the stadium.

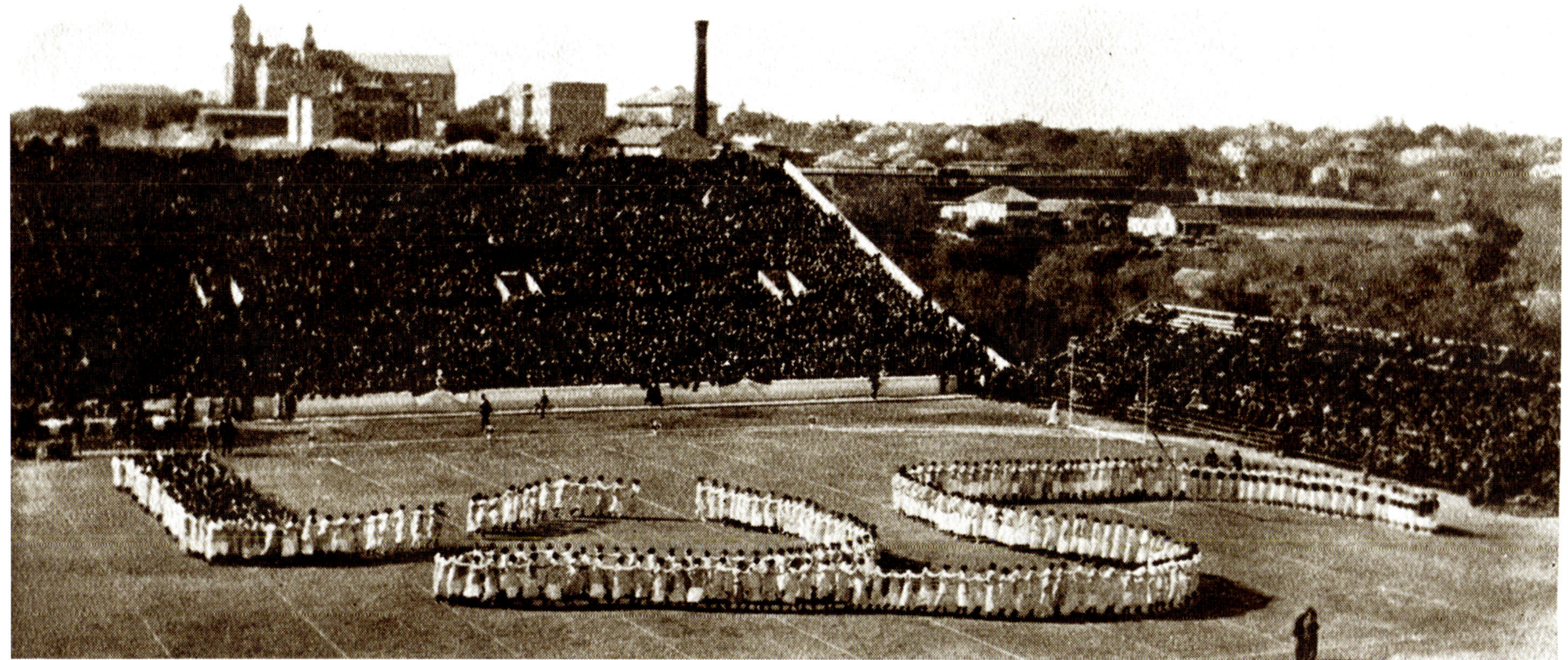

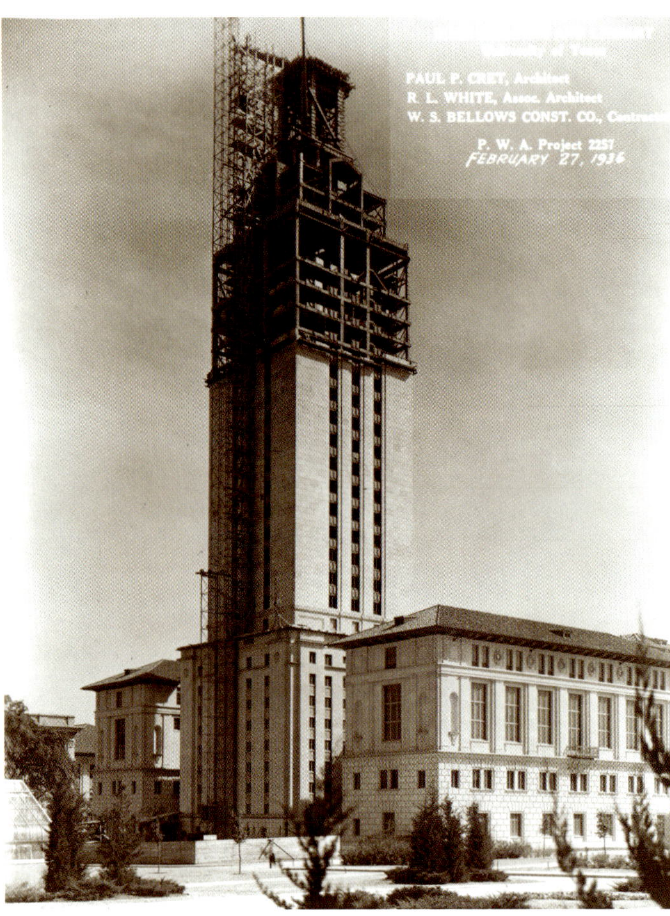

Rising 27 floors above the reading rooms, the Tower contained the library's book stacks. Constructed of Indiana limestone, it was financed by the Works Progress Administration, a New Deal program created during the Great Depression. Because it was a closed-stack library, patrons searched an immense card catalog, and then requested books at the front desk. Orders were forwarded to a Tower librarian, who often wore roller skates to navigate the bookshelves. Once collected, the books were sent downstairs in an elevator to be checked out. *Alexander Architecture Archives, UT-Austin*

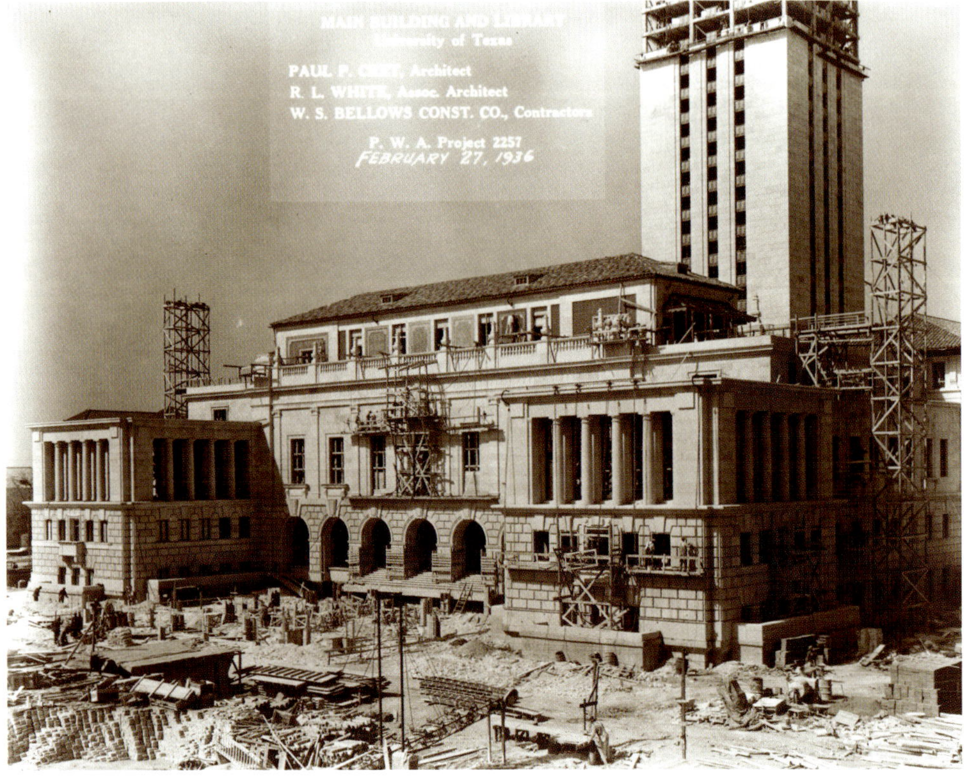

Designed by Paul Cret and completed in 1937, the Main Building, with its 307-foot Tower, replaced the Gothic old Main Building. Created to house the University's central library, it featured a pair of spacious reading rooms: the "Hall of Texas" and the "Hall of Noble Words," connected to a great central reference room. *Alexander Architecture Archives, UT-Austin*

Facing Page In 1930, Paul Cret, a French immigrant who chaired the architecture program at the University of Pennsylvania, was hired as consulting architect to produce a campus master plan for The University of Texas. Within a decade, as this photograph shows, many of Cret's key buildings were already in place: the Main Building and Tower, the Littlefield Gateway and South Mall, and Goldsmith Hall and the Texas Union, which would mark the western entrance to the campus. *Prints and Photographs Collection, Center for American History, UT-Austin*

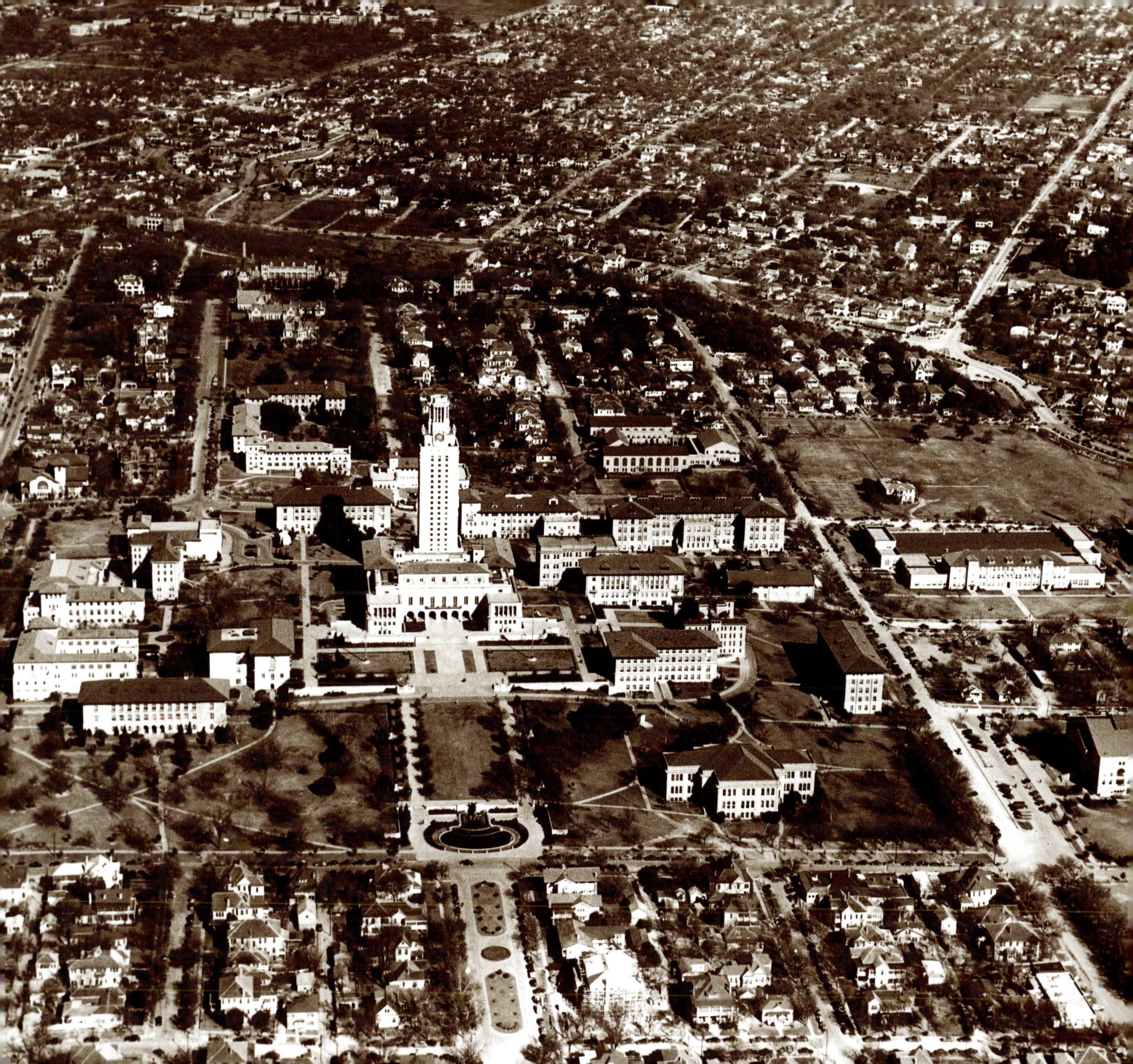

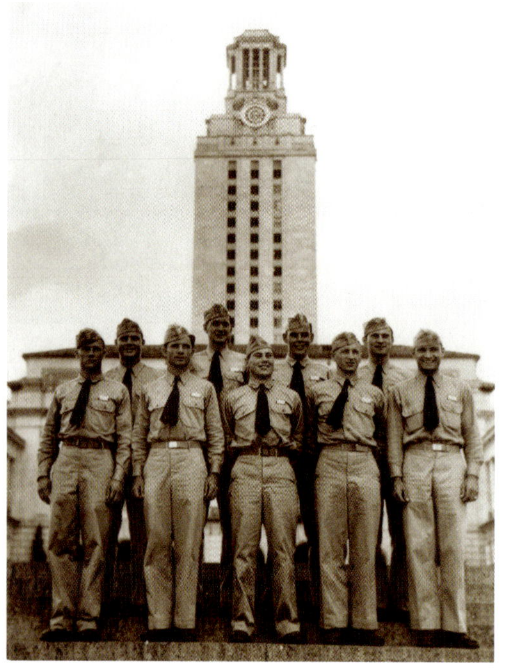

When World War II preoccupied the nation, the University contributed to the war effort by offering more classes during breaks; hosting naval units in the women's residence halls and Gregory Gym; and sponsoring a dating service in the Union. There, coeds declared it their "patriotic duty" to go out with local GIs. *Prints and Photographs Collection, Center for American History, UT-Austin*

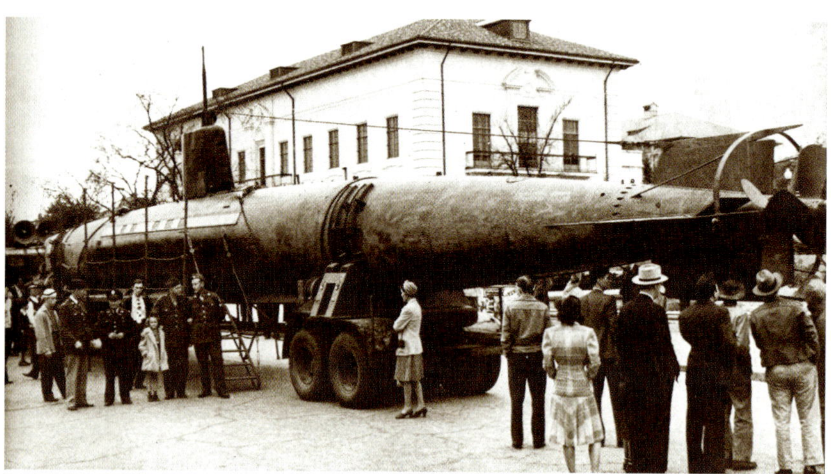

A captured Japanese submarine on a national tour stops in front of Littlefield Fountain. Rainey Hall is in the background.

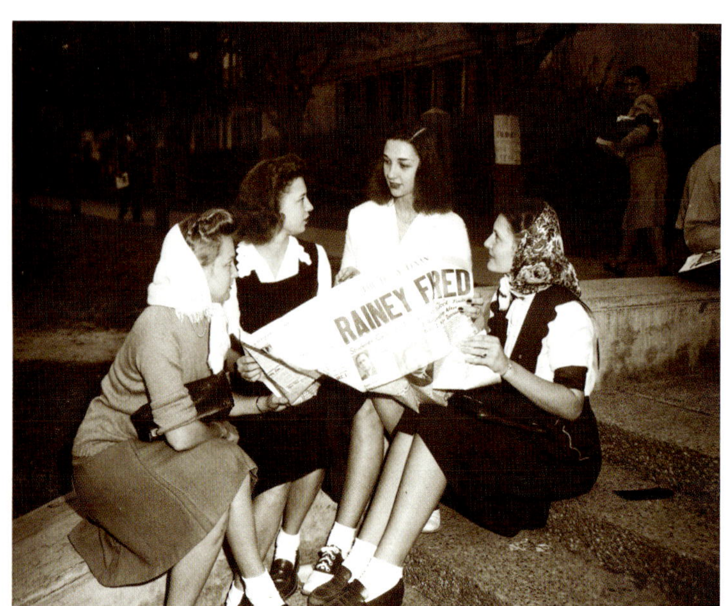

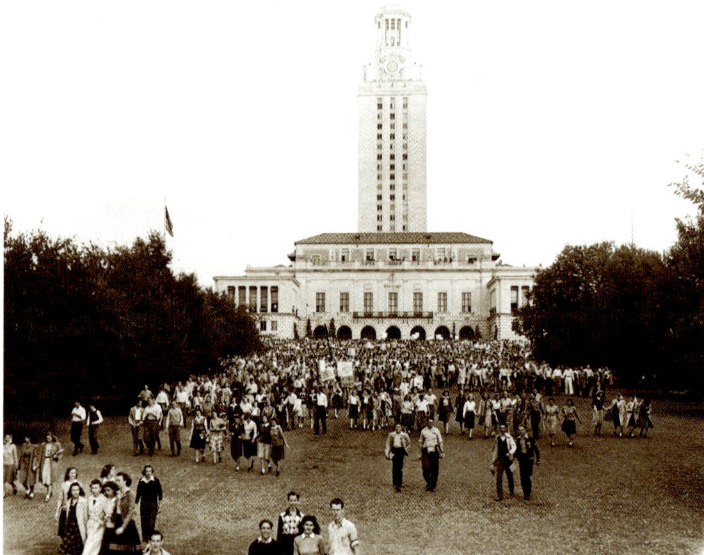

Left and Above On November 1, 1944, after several years of disagreements between the Board of Regents and UT president Homer Rainey, the board voted to fire Rainey, and several of the regents resigned. Most of the University community supported Rainey; the students boycotted class for a week and held two protest marches, one through downtown Austin as a funeral procession for "academic freedom." *Prints and Photographs Collection, Center for American History, UT-Austin*

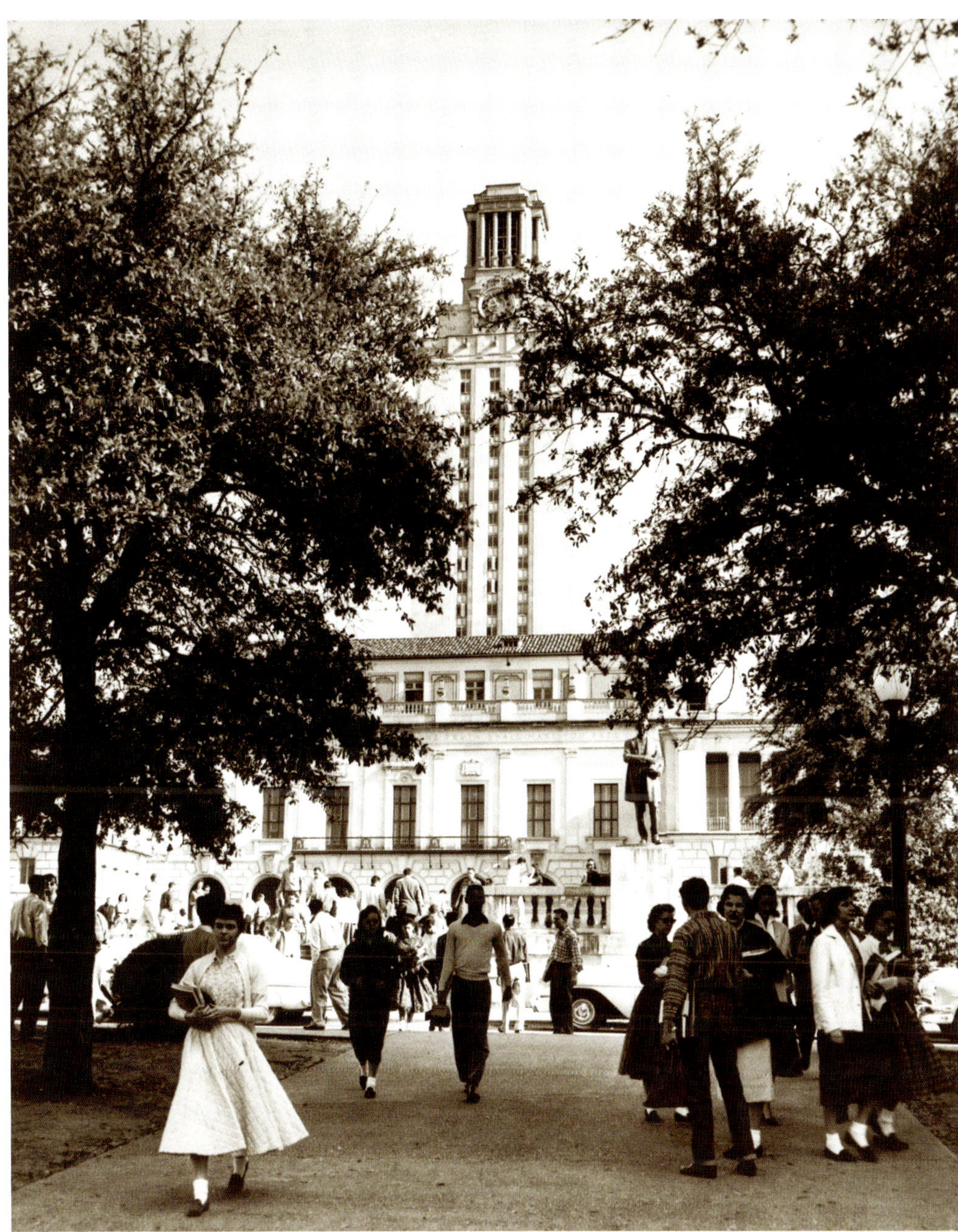

With the passage of the GI Bill in 1944, post World War II enrollment surged at campuses nationwide. By the mid-1950s, UT enrollment swelled to more than 17,000, and penny loafers, bobby socks, poodle skirts, and button-down shirts filled the South Mall. *Prints and Photographs Collection, Center for American History, UT-Austin*

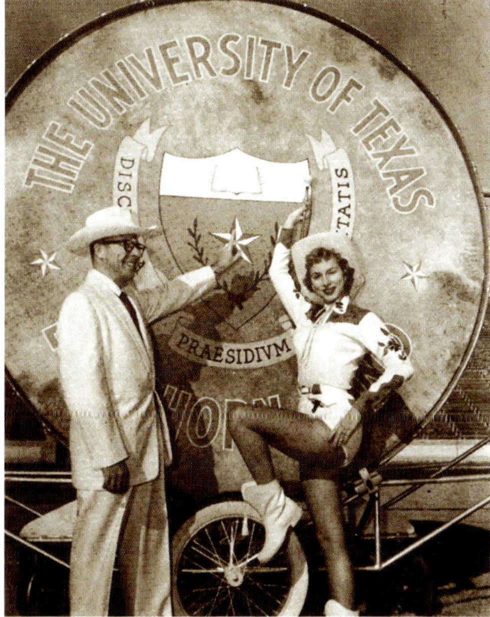

Originally built for the University of Chicago in 1922, Big Bertha, "the world's largest bass drum," was presented to the Longhorn Band in 1955 by Harold Byrd of Dallas.

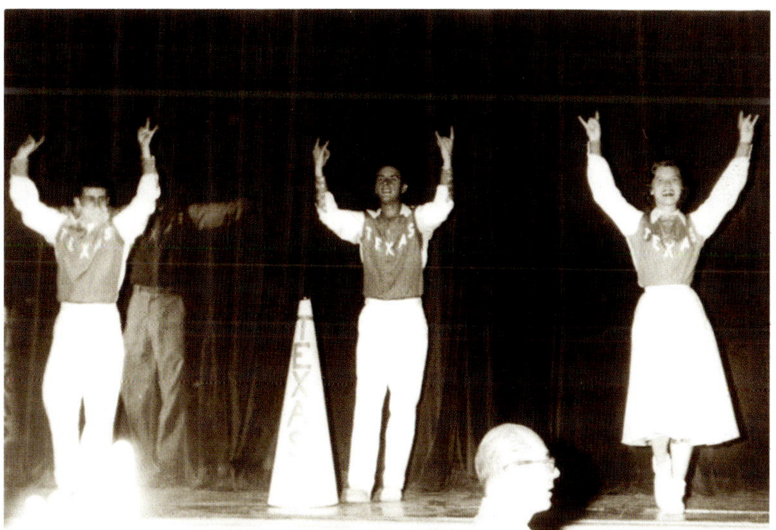

Hook 'em Horns! A UT tradition debuted on November 11, 1955, at a Friday night football rally in Gregory Gym. Pictured here is the moment UT cheerleaders first introduced the signal to students. At the Texas vs. TCU football game the next day, the hand sign was an instant hit. *Photo courtesy Jane Rhodes*

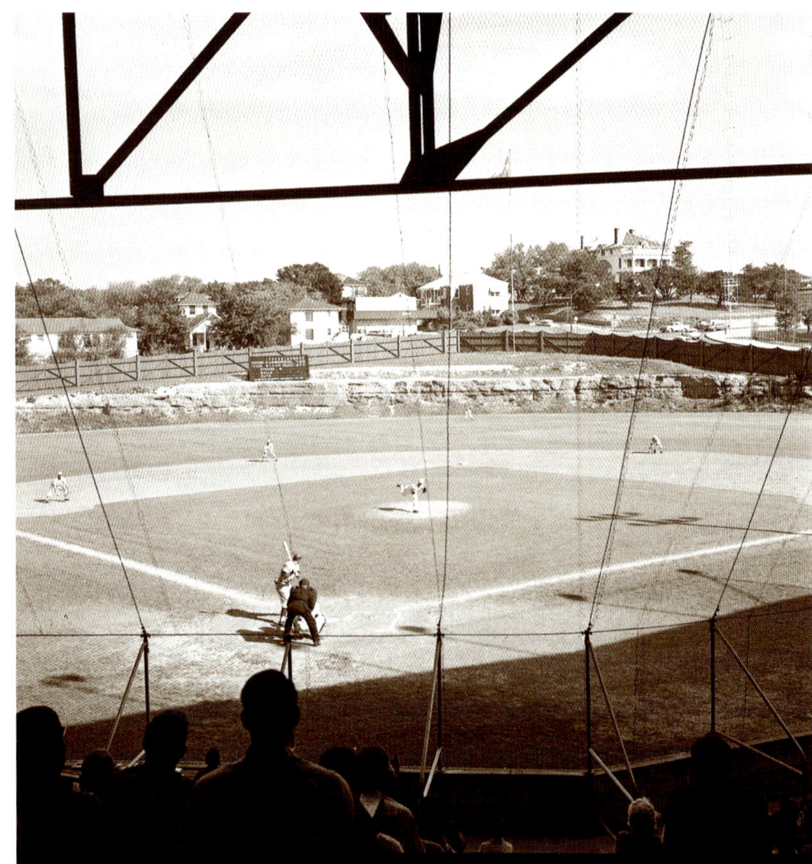

While the original Clark Field was closed after the construction of Memorial Stadium, a second, baseball-only version was built just north of the stadium, where the Bass Concert Hall now stands. The land just past the outfield fence is now used for the LBJ Library and School of Public Affairs.

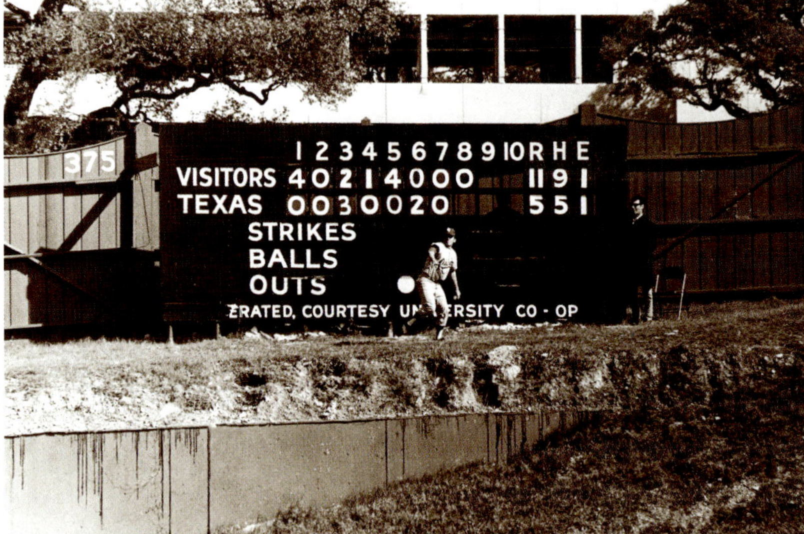

Split-level baseball. The limestone outcropping at the back of center field was named "Billy Goat Hill." Balls batted to the top of the hill remained in play, and only UT players knew the quickest trails to the summit.

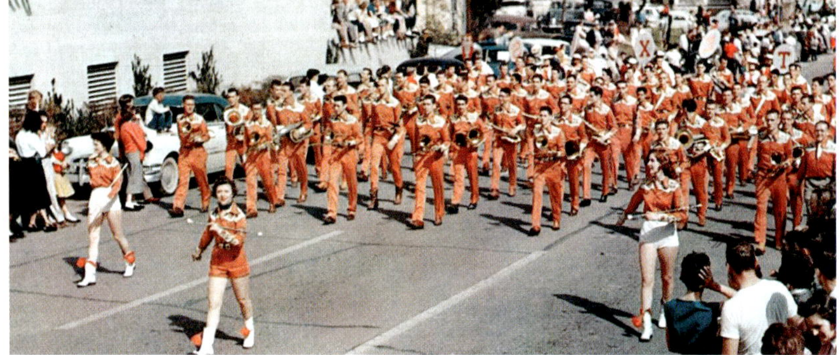

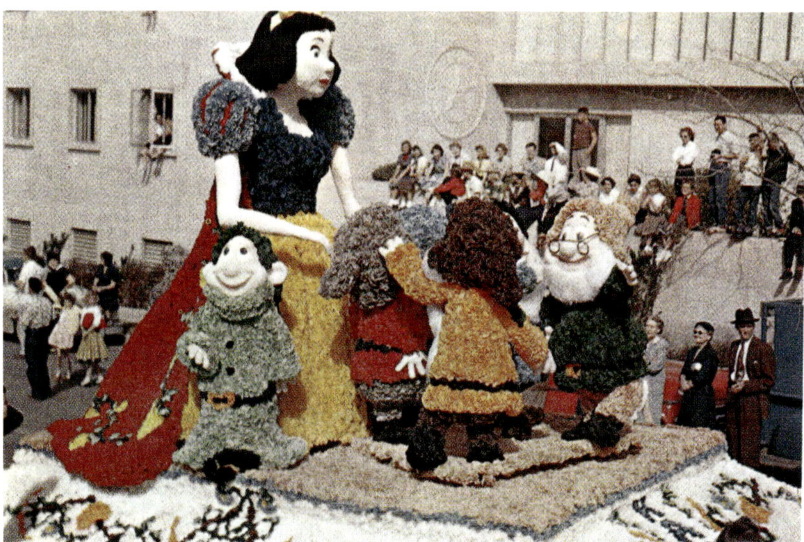

Above and Right In the 1950s and 1960s, the popular Round-up Parades featured the Longhorn Band as well as intricate floats built by UT students. Inaugurated by the Texas Exes in 1930 as a spring homecoming festival, the annual Round-up continued until 1990.

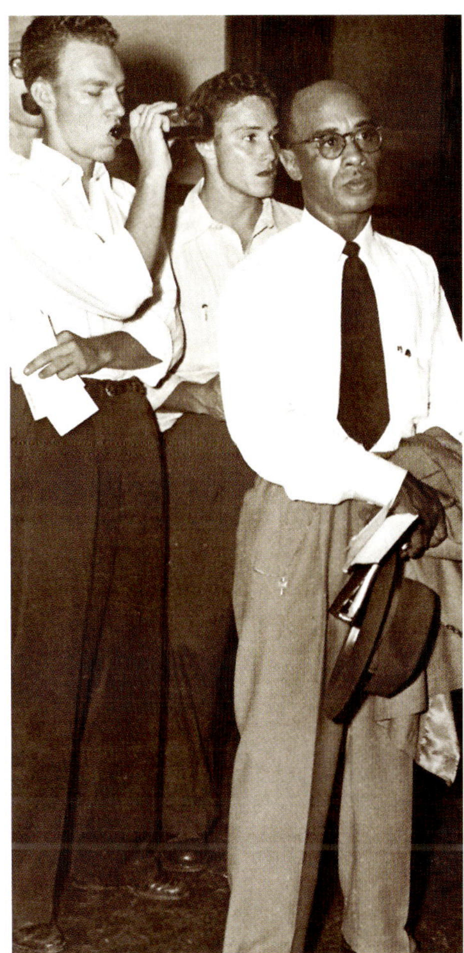

In September 1950, after a four-year court battle and final decision from the U.S. Supreme Court, the University opened its law school to all persons, regardless of race, and Heman Sweatt became the first African American to enroll. Integrating campus was a gradual process that lasted well over a decade; not until 1956 were African-American undergraduates admitted to the University.

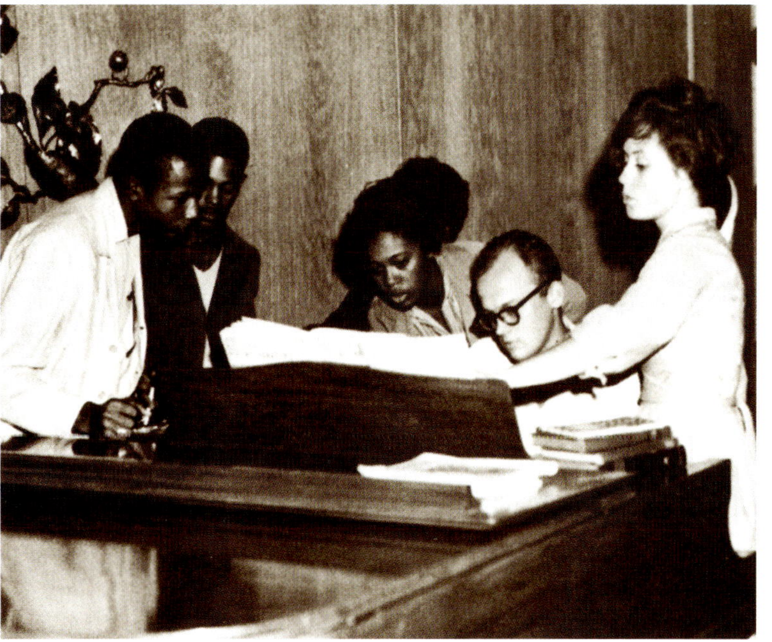

By 1960, while the University no longer denied admission based on race, campus residence halls were still limited to whites only. In October 1961, a group of African-American undergraduates, along with other supportive UT students, held a one-hour "sing along" in the parlor of Kinsolving. With mounting public pressure, the residence halls were open to everyone in the summer of 1964.

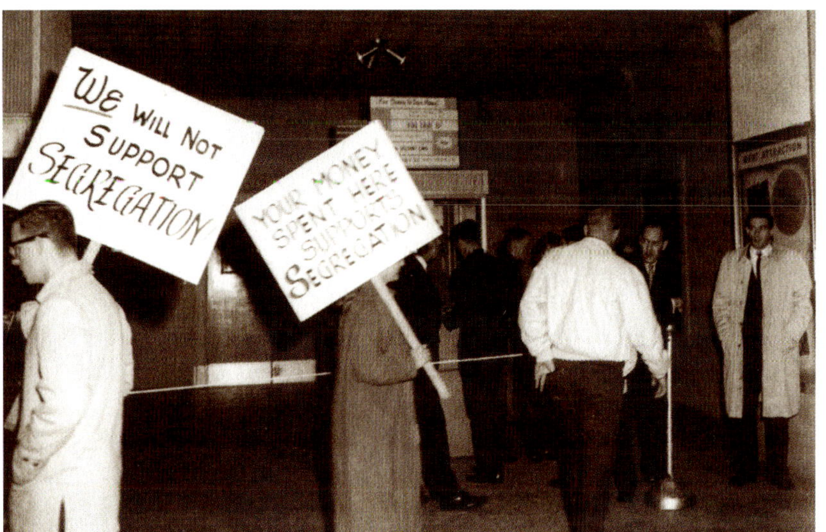

University students also protested the segregation of shops, cafes, and movie theaters along Guadalupe Street. By 1962, most of the stores on the Drag had removed their "Whites Only" window signs.

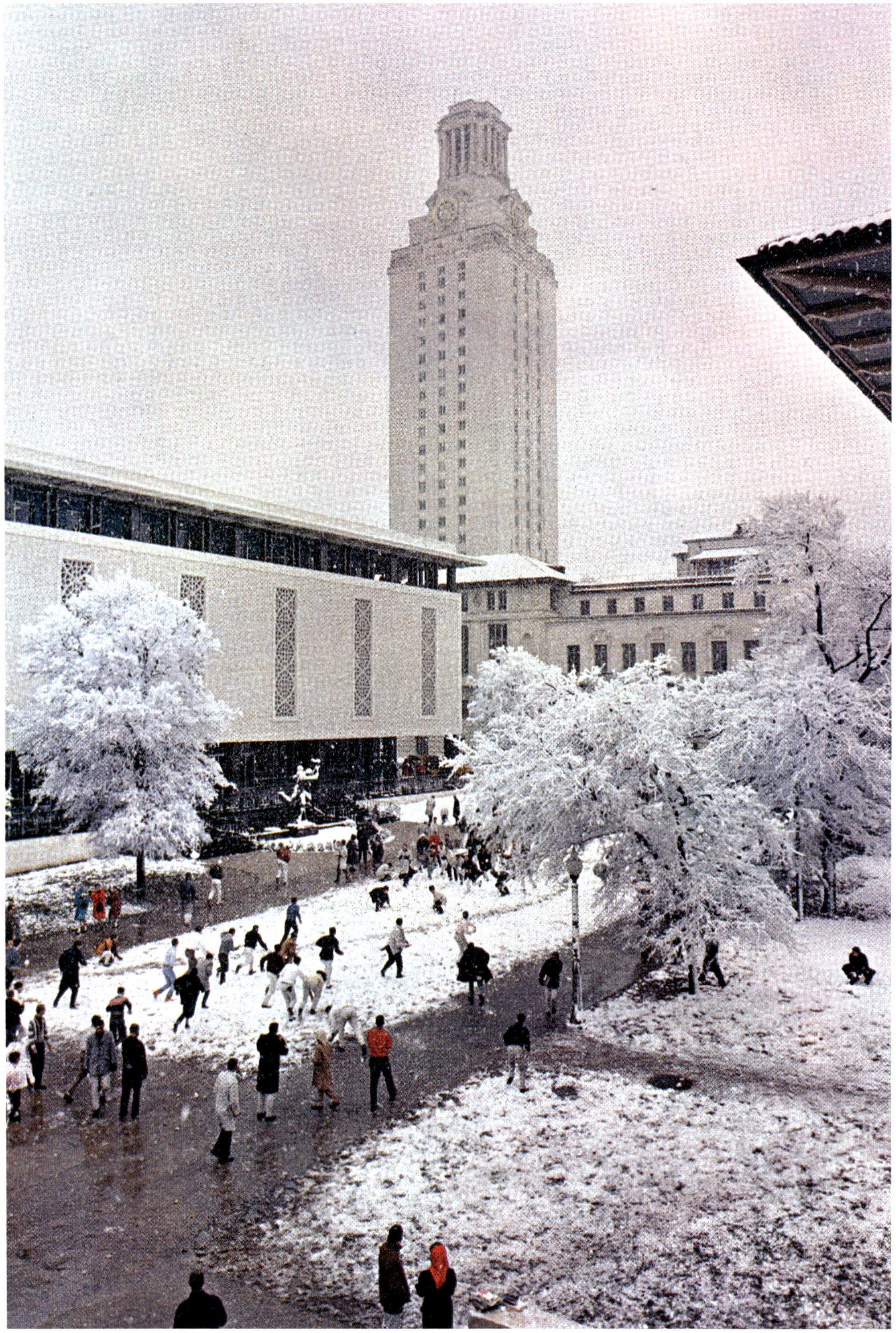

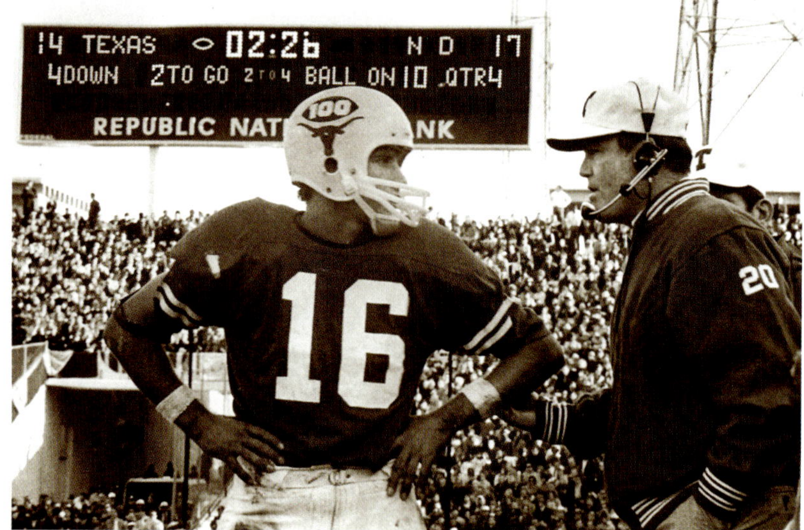

Above On fourth down, two yards to go, and with just over two minutes left, Coach Darrell Royal confers with quarterback James Street at the 1970 Cotton Bowl. The play called would gain eight yards and a first down and would lead to a last-minute score to lift Texas over Notre Dame 21-17. The Texas Longhorns completed an 11-0 season and were crowned the 1969 National Football Champions.

Left Snowball fight! Students on the West Mall engage in some extracurricular activity after a rare Austin snowstorm in January 1963. When this photograph was taken, the Undergraduate Library, now known as the Flawn Academic Center, was the newest addition to campus.

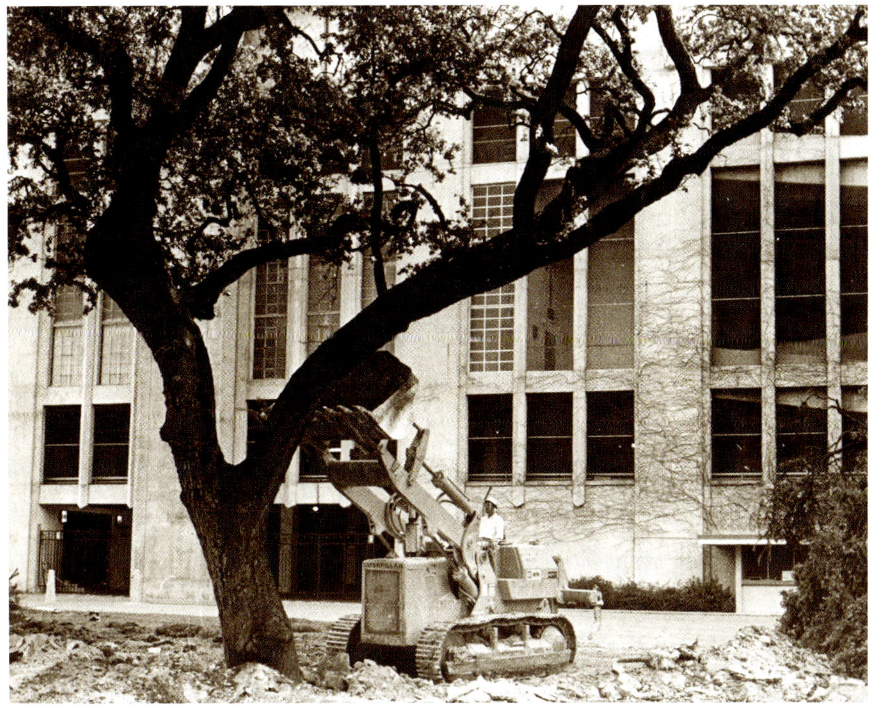

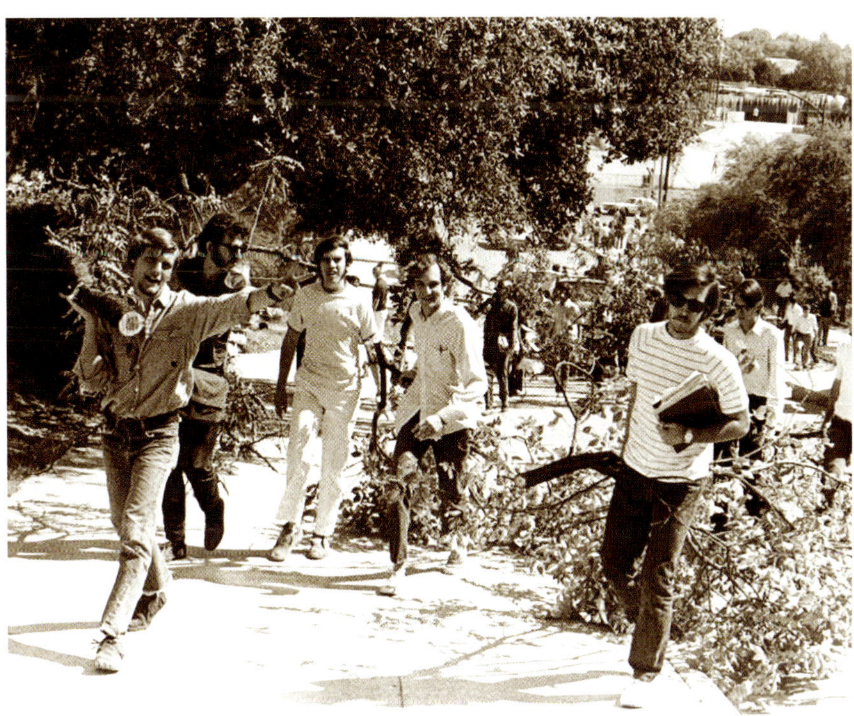

Left and Below Left In order to make room for the Bellmont Hall addition to the stadium, the route of San Jacinto Boulevard had to be altered, and several trees along Waller Creek were tagged for removal. On October 5, 1969, construction workers arrived to find protesters firmly lodged in the trees. With UT regent Frank Erwin present, city, state, and campus police were summoned to remove the protesters, and the trees were bulldozed. Students gathered up branches and stuffed them into the entrances of the Main Building.

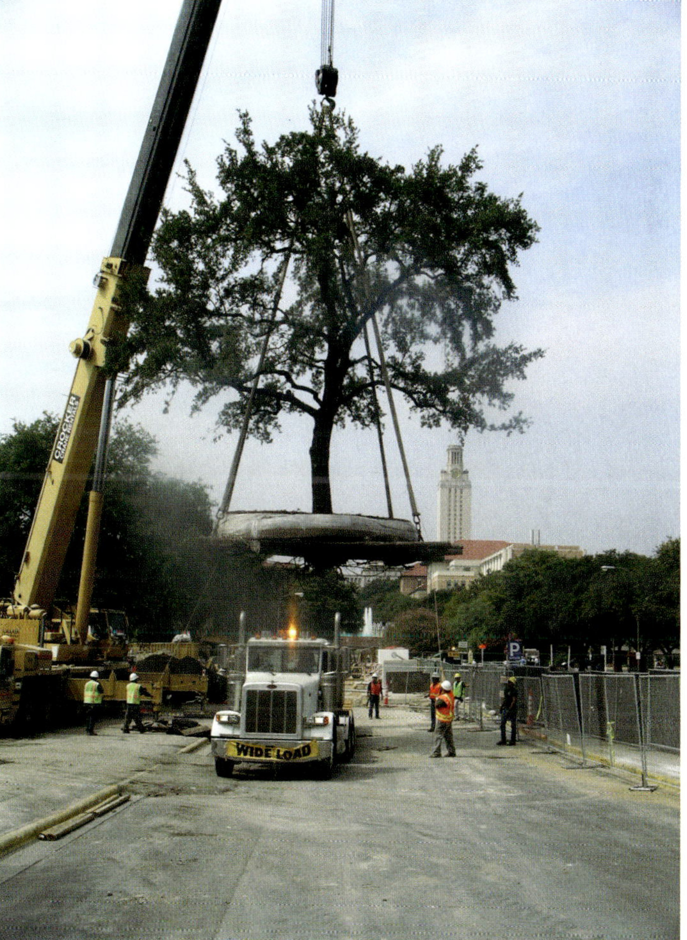

In recent years, the University has recognized its campus trees as a valuable asset. In 2007, as part of another renovation to the stadium, the trees were moved and replanted on other parts of the campus. *Photo courtesy Larry Maginnis*

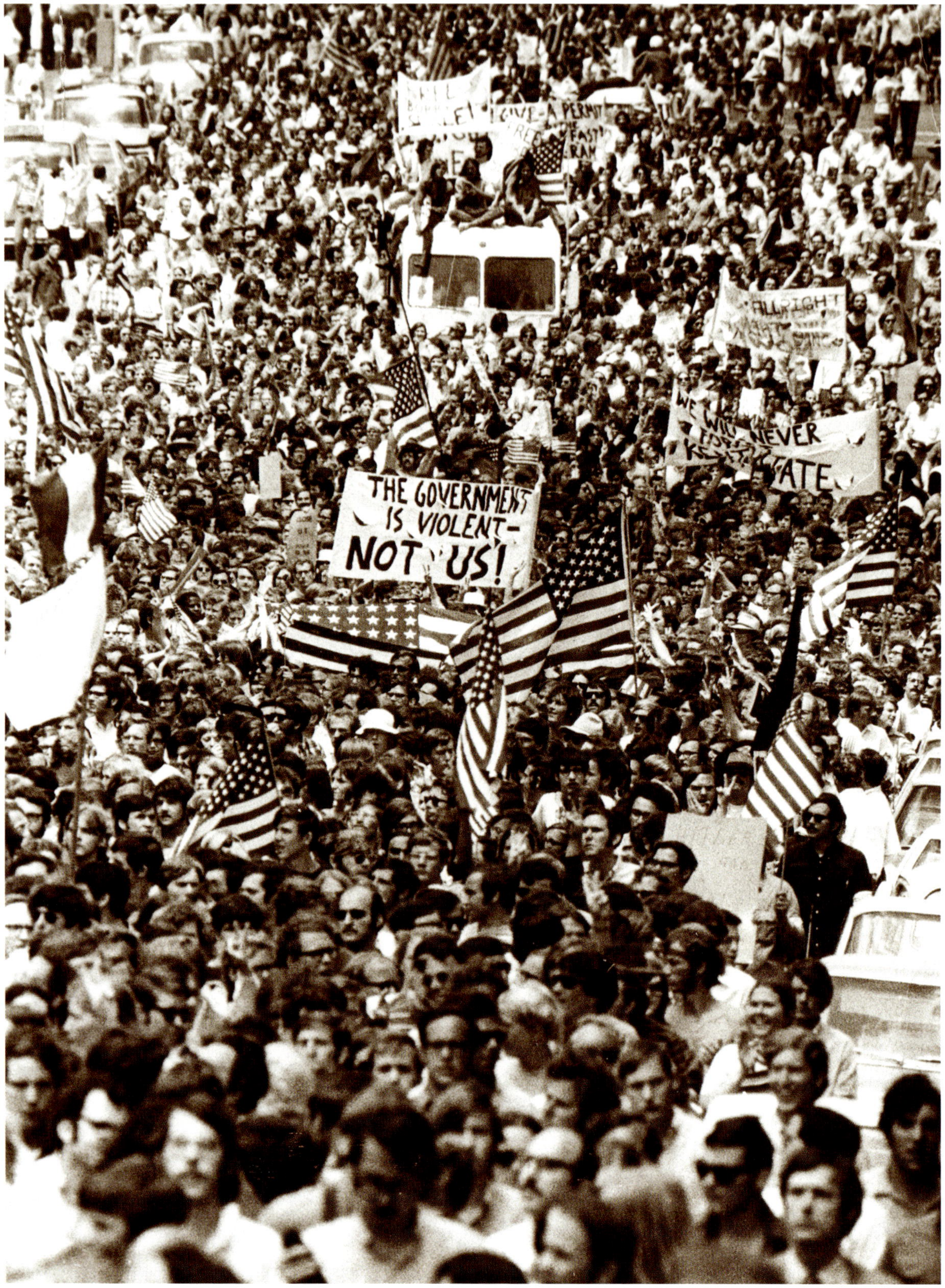

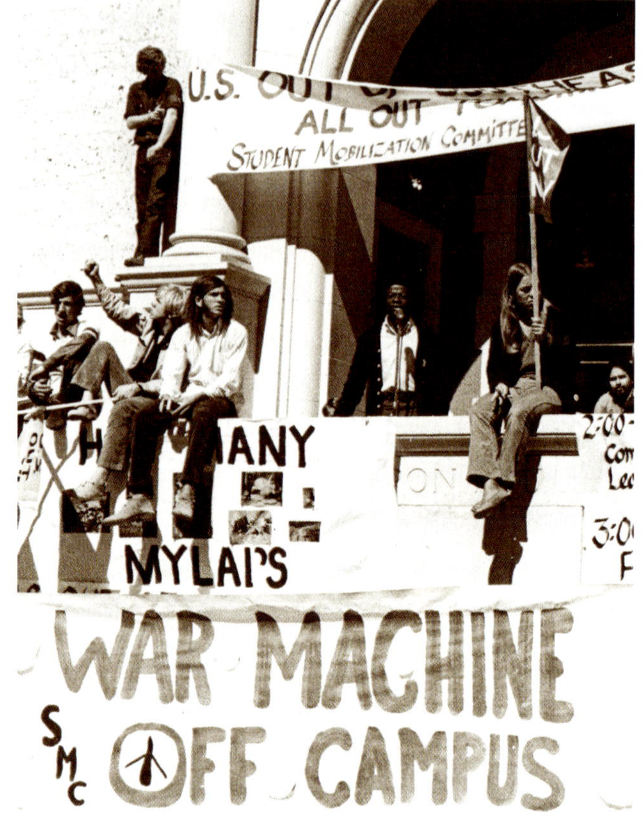

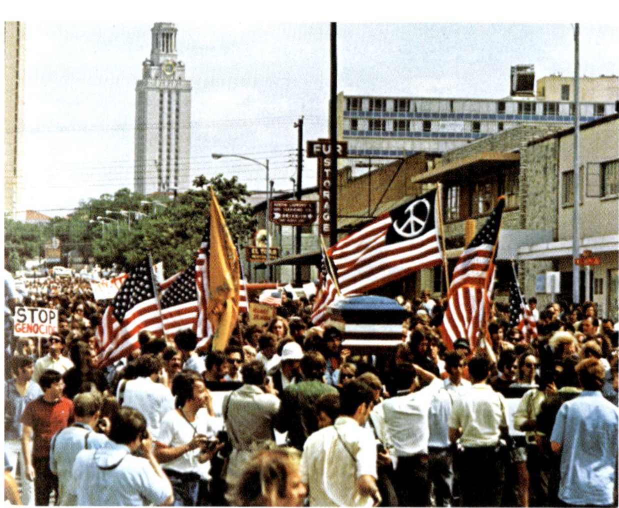

On May 8, 1970, more than 20,000 marched in peaceful protest against the Vietnam War and the recent deaths of four students at Kent State. The procession began on Guadalupe Street, moved south and east through downtown Austin, and then returned along San Jacinto Boulevard to the East Mall Fountain. It was the largest protest in the University's history.
Prints and Photographs Collection, Center for American History, UT-Austin

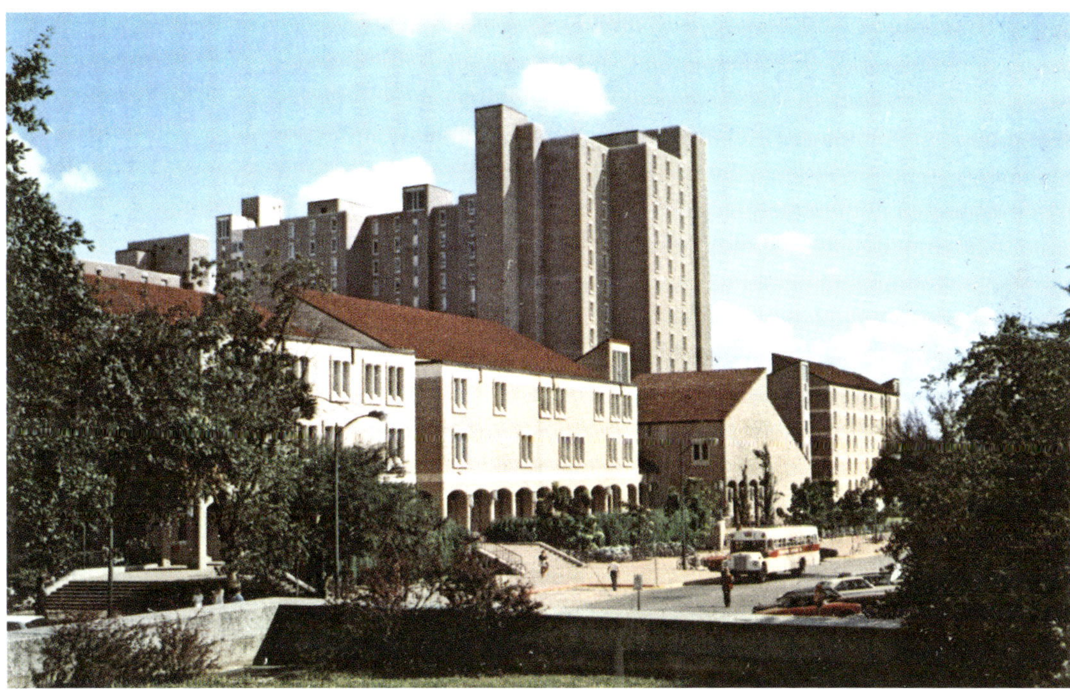

Jester Center opened in 1969 as a "residential college," where students could live and attend classes in the same facility. Parked in front of the building is a UT shuttle bus, which initiated service the same year.

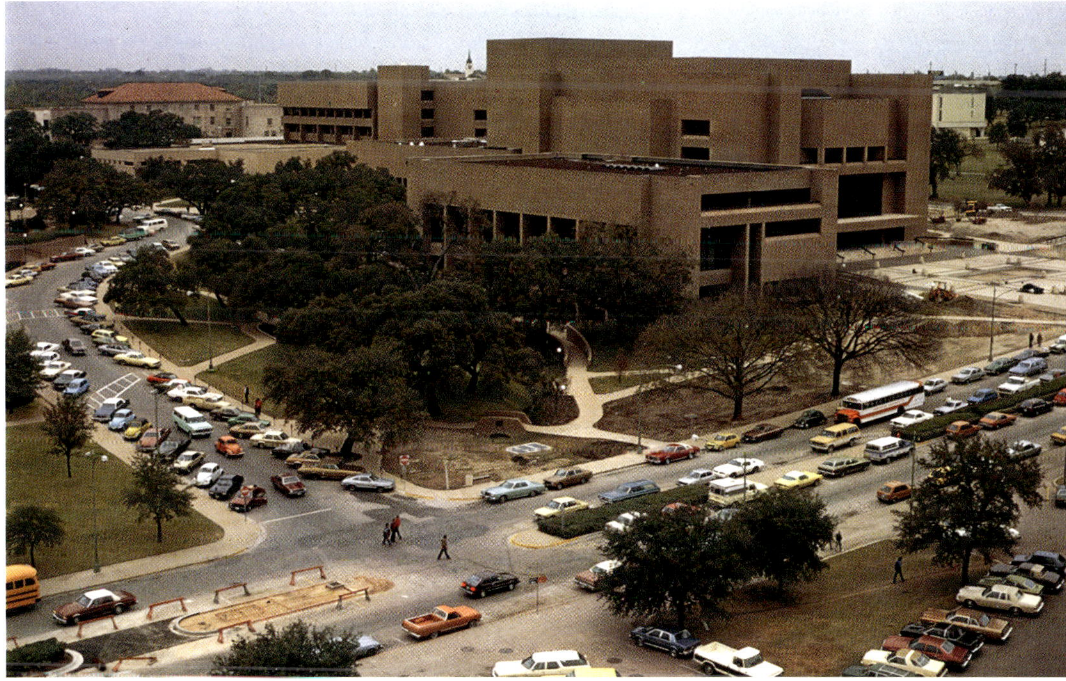

The University's Fine Arts Complex, which includes the Winship Drama Building, the Art Building and Museum, and the Music Building, was completed in 1981 with the addition of the Bass Concert Hall, McCullough Theater, and Doty Fine Arts Library.

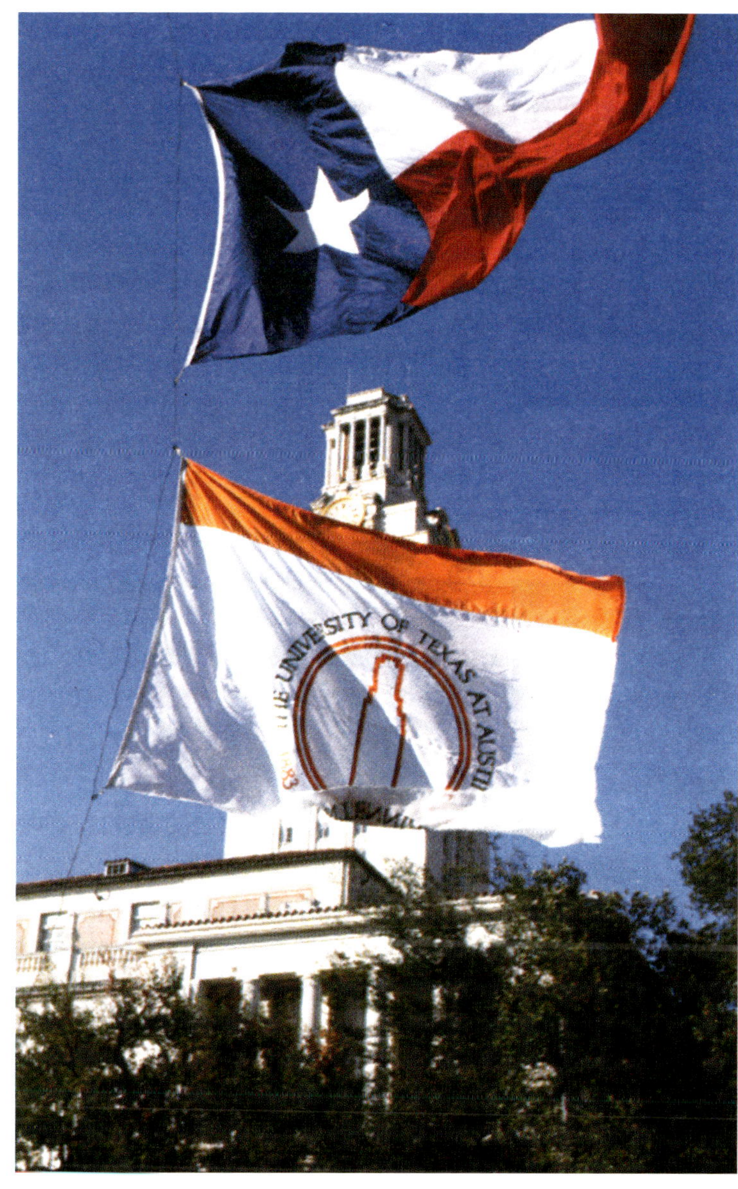

In 1983, UT observed its 100th anniversary with parties, lectures, exhibits, and a campus-wide University Showcase. Throughout the year, a special Centennial Flag flew from the flag pole on the Main Mall.

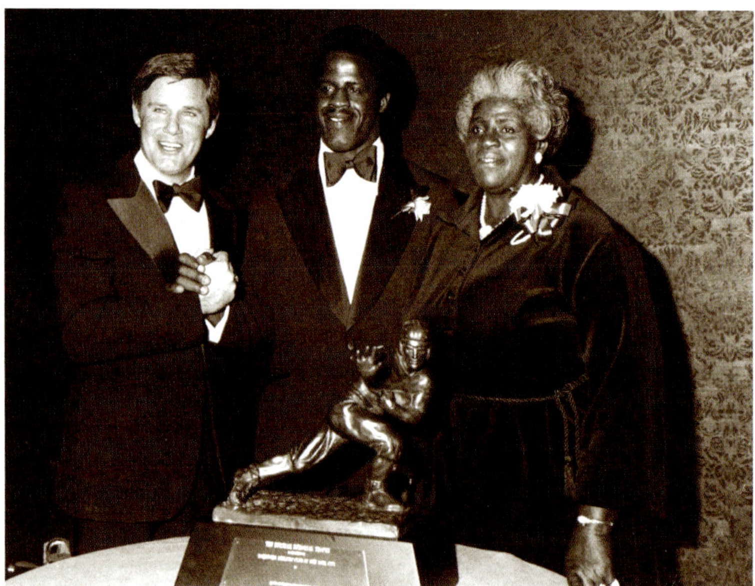

Left Football coach Fred Akers joins Earl Campbell and his mother, Ann Campbell, in celebrating the University's first Heisman Trophy winner in 1977. Ricky Williams was awarded the Heisman in 1998 after setting an NCAA rushing record of 6,279 yards.

Below As UT women's basketball coach from 1976–2007, Jody Conradt guided her 1986 squad to an undefeated 34-win season and national championship. Her outstanding career included 900 wins, six times named as National Coach of the Year, and induction into the Naismith Memorial Basketball Hall of Fame.

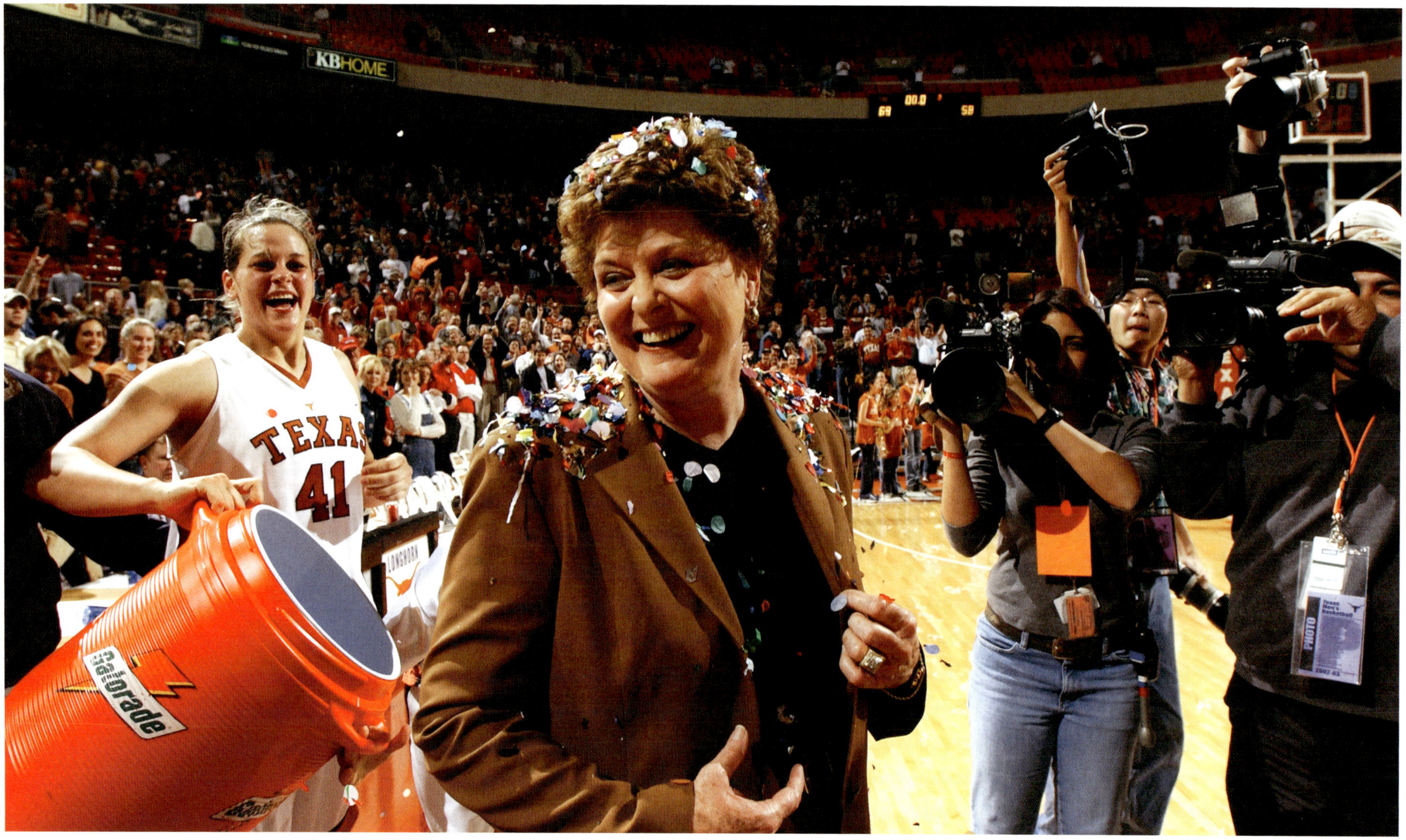

Along with the main campus, the University boasts the McDonald Observatory on Mount Locke in West Texas (pictured); the J.J. "Jake" Pickle Research Campus in north Austin; the Lady Bird Johnson Wildflower Center; the Brackenridge Field Laboratory for biology; the Marine Sciences Institute in Port Aransas; J. Frank Dobie's Paisano Ranch, used by Texas authors; and the Winedale Historical Center in Round Top, best known for its Shakespeare at Winedale program.

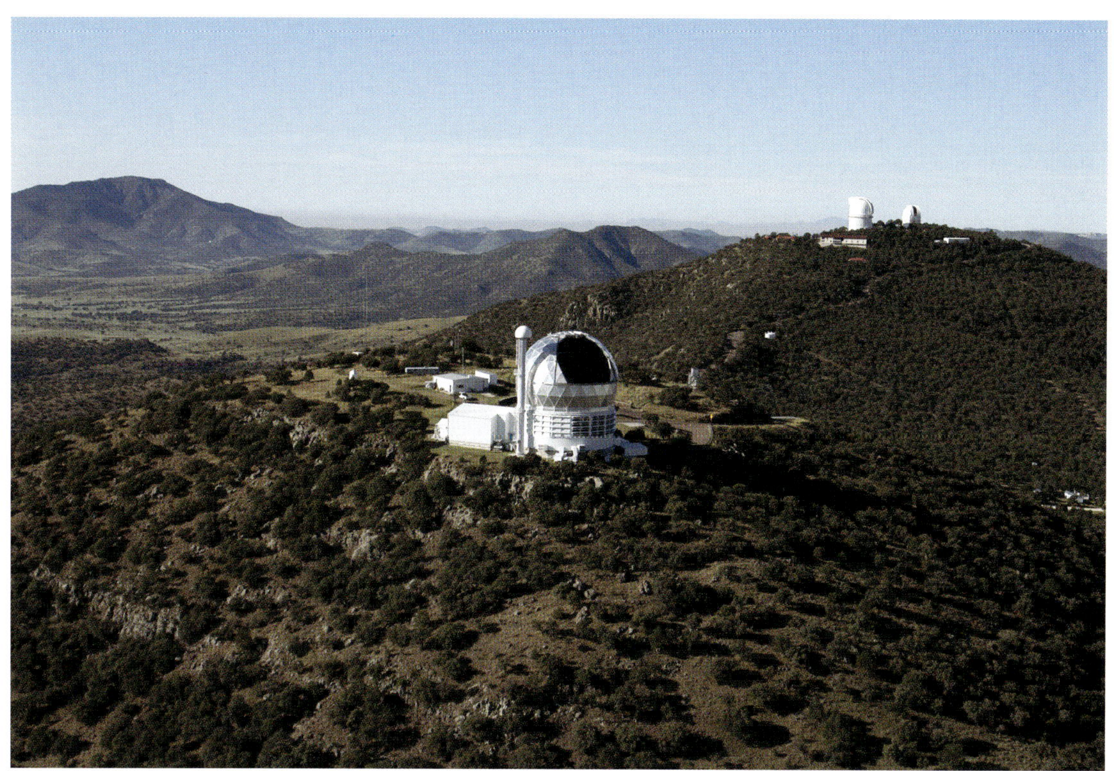

The Applied Computational Engineering and Sciences (ACES) Building, completed in 2000, is a state-of-the-art facility for research and graduate study in computer sciences, electrical and computer engineering, mathematical modeling, and software engineering. Among its many features is the Visualization Laboratory, with a 10-foot tall, 180 degree stereo-capable display used for large-scale data analysis.

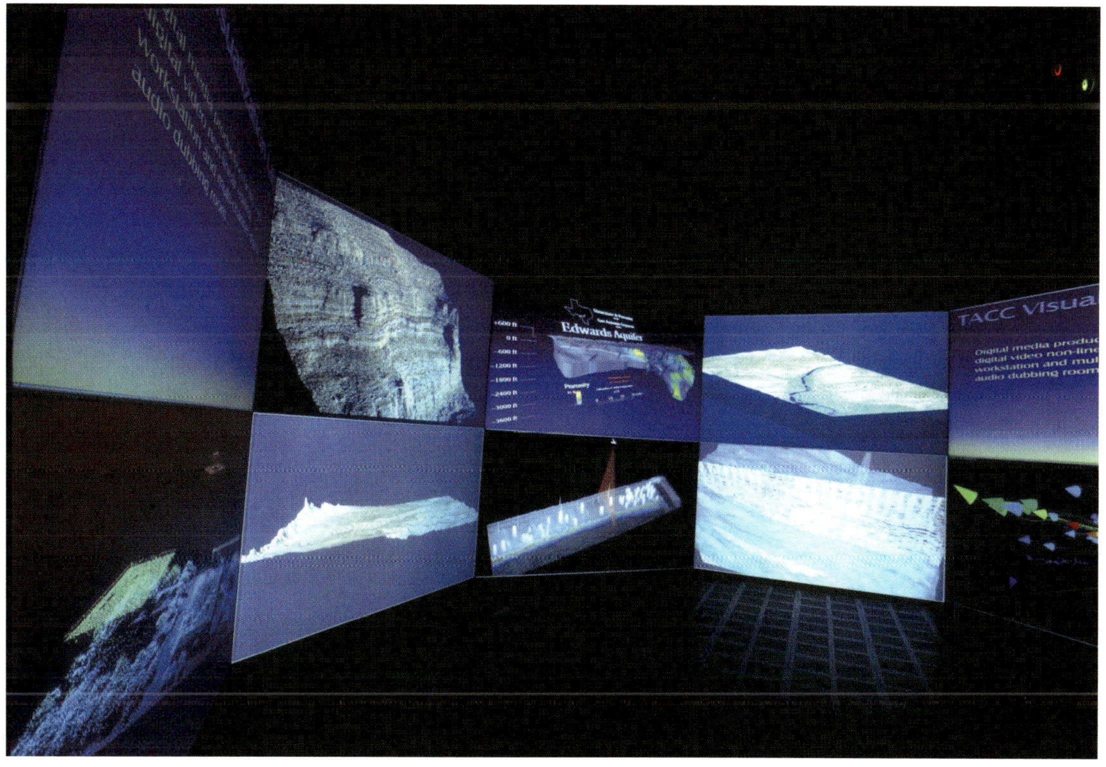

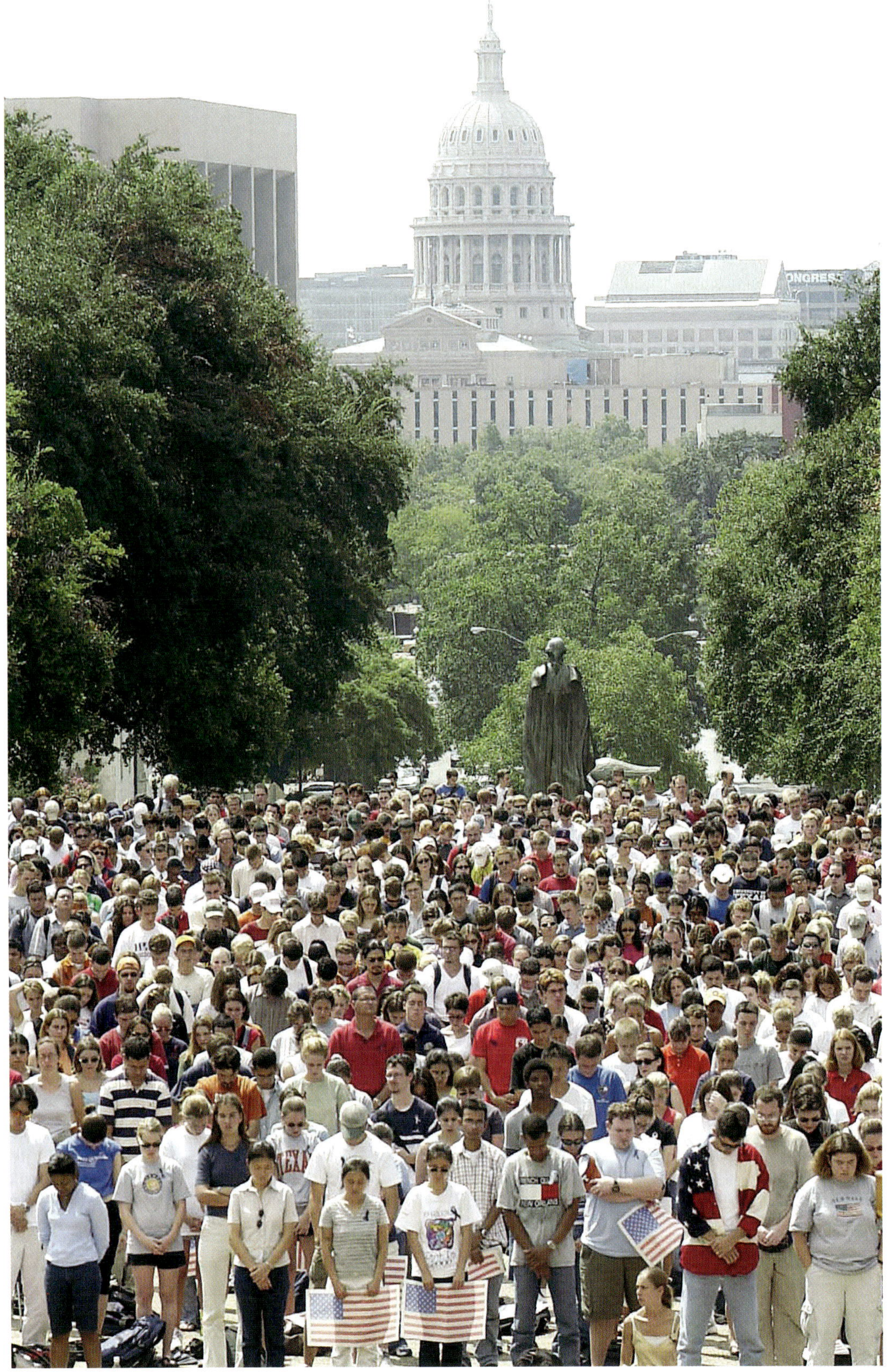

The events of September 11, 2001, were felt across the country, including at UT. An American flag was solemnly displayed on the front of the Main Building. Friday, September 14, was declared a National Day of Remembrance, and more than 5,000 attended a noon memorial service on the Main Mall.

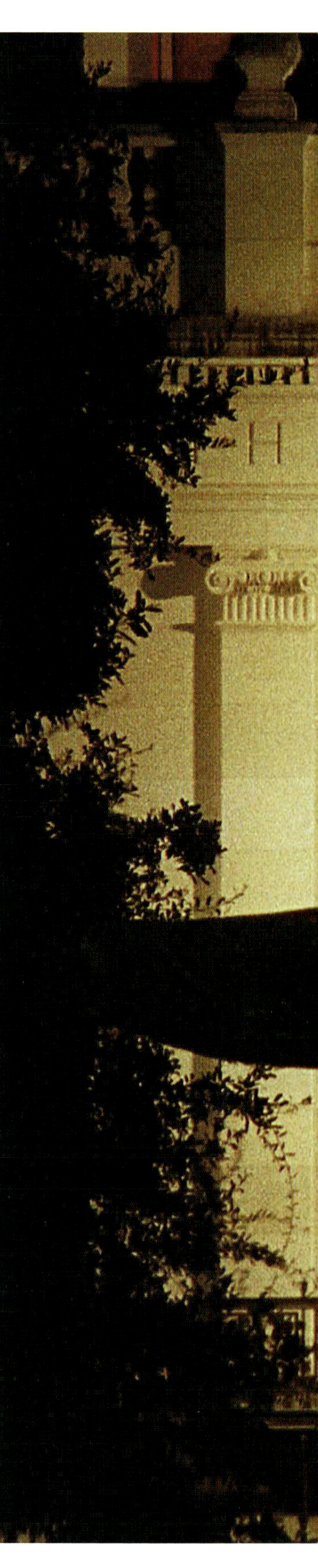

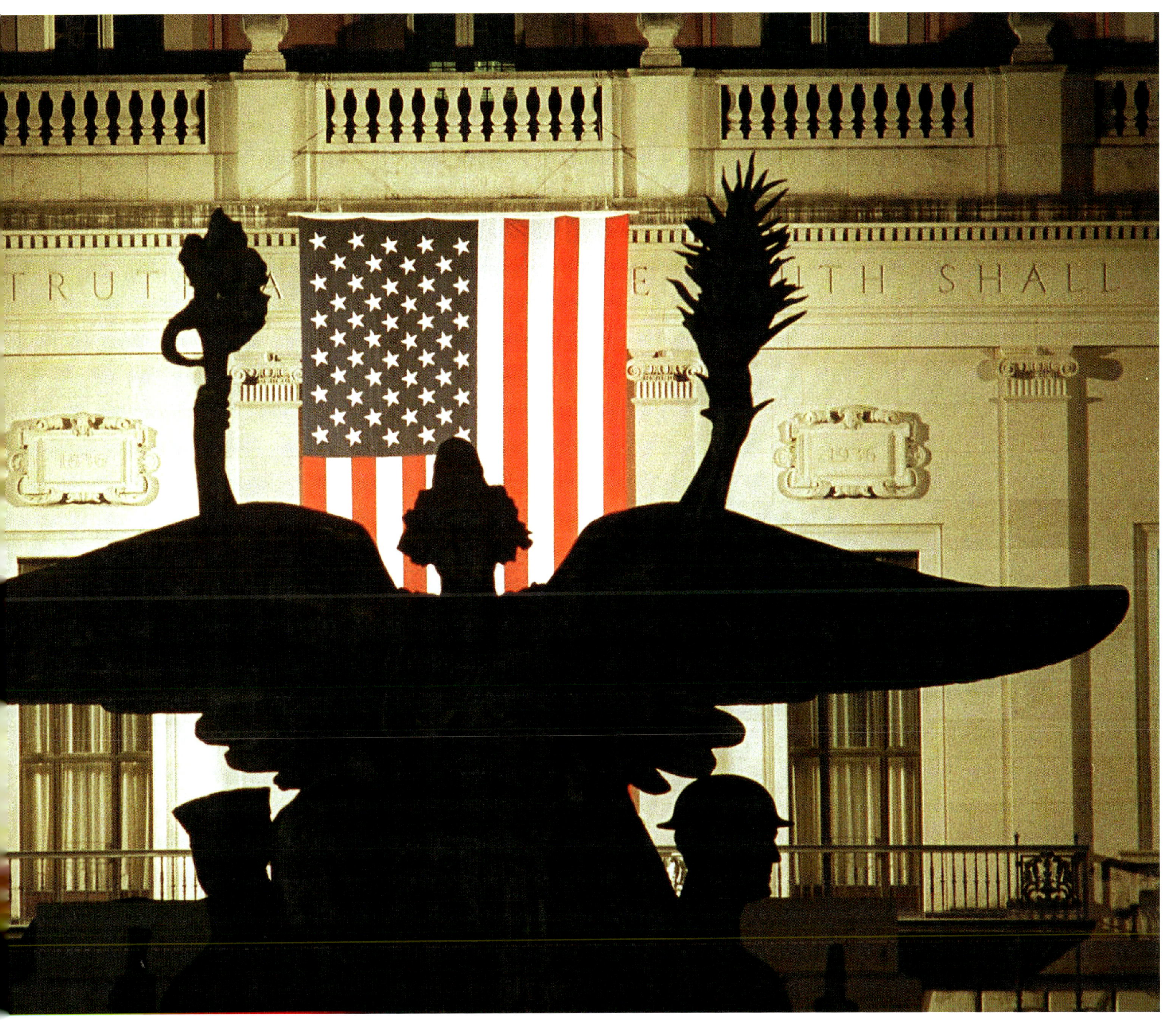

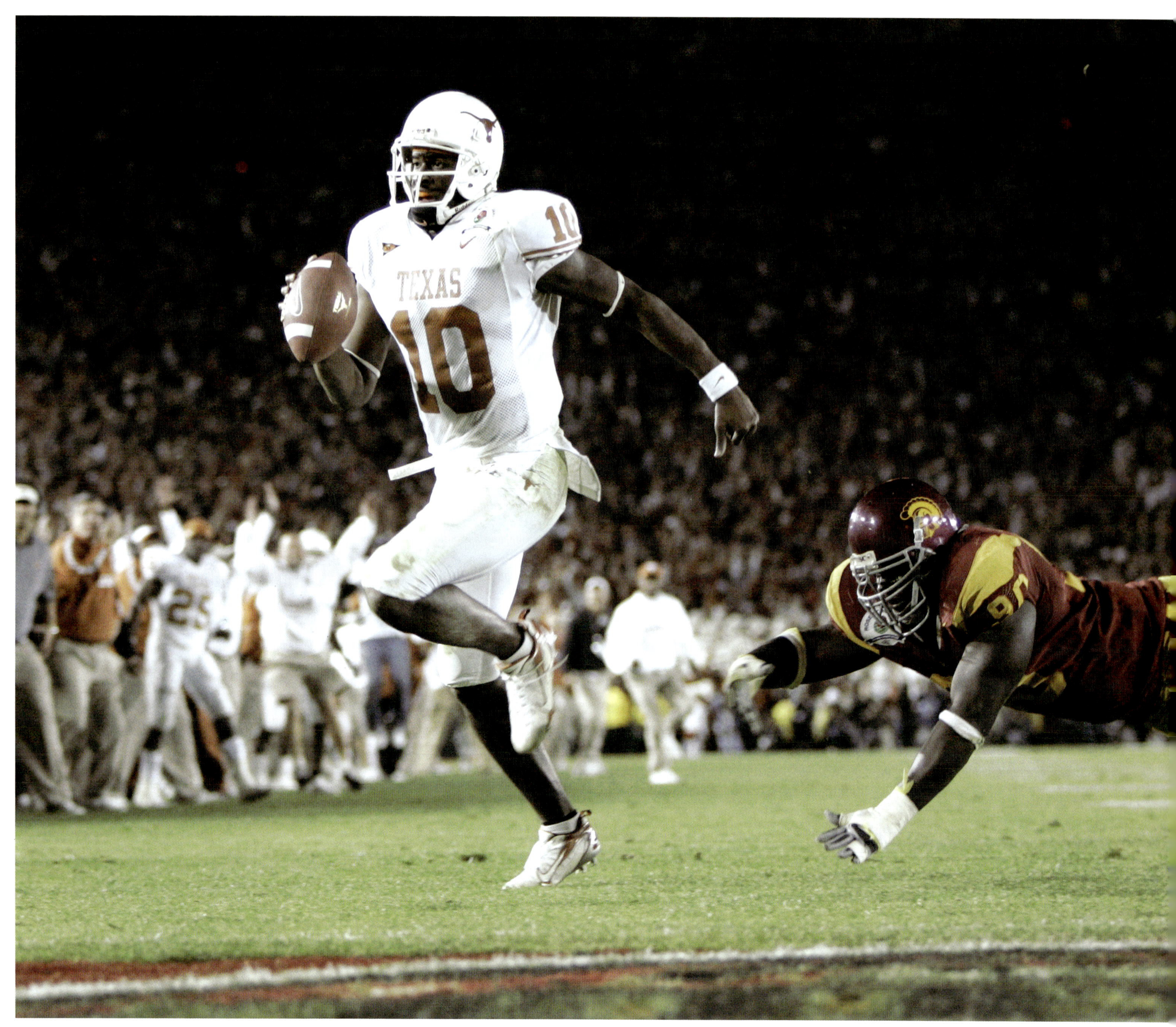
TEXAS
10

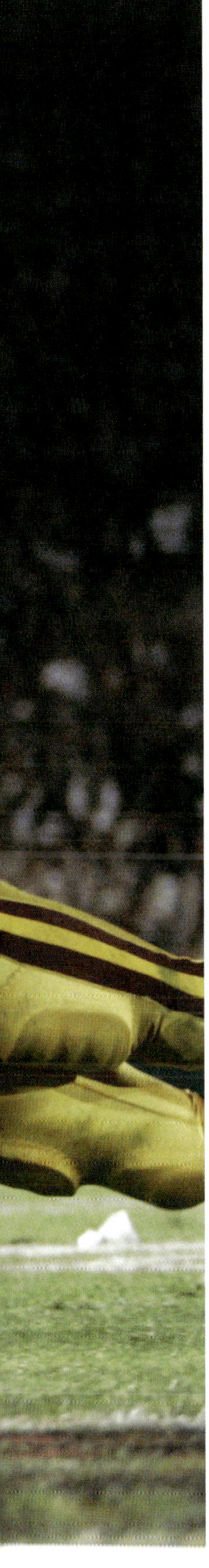

Left Quarterback Vince Young eludes the USC Trojans and scores a touchdown to give UT a 2006 Rose Bowl victory and its fourth national football championship.

Right Entering the 21st century, the University has matured into a world-class center of higher education, with internationally recognized academic programs, research facilities, libraries and museums, and a strong and vibrant campus community.

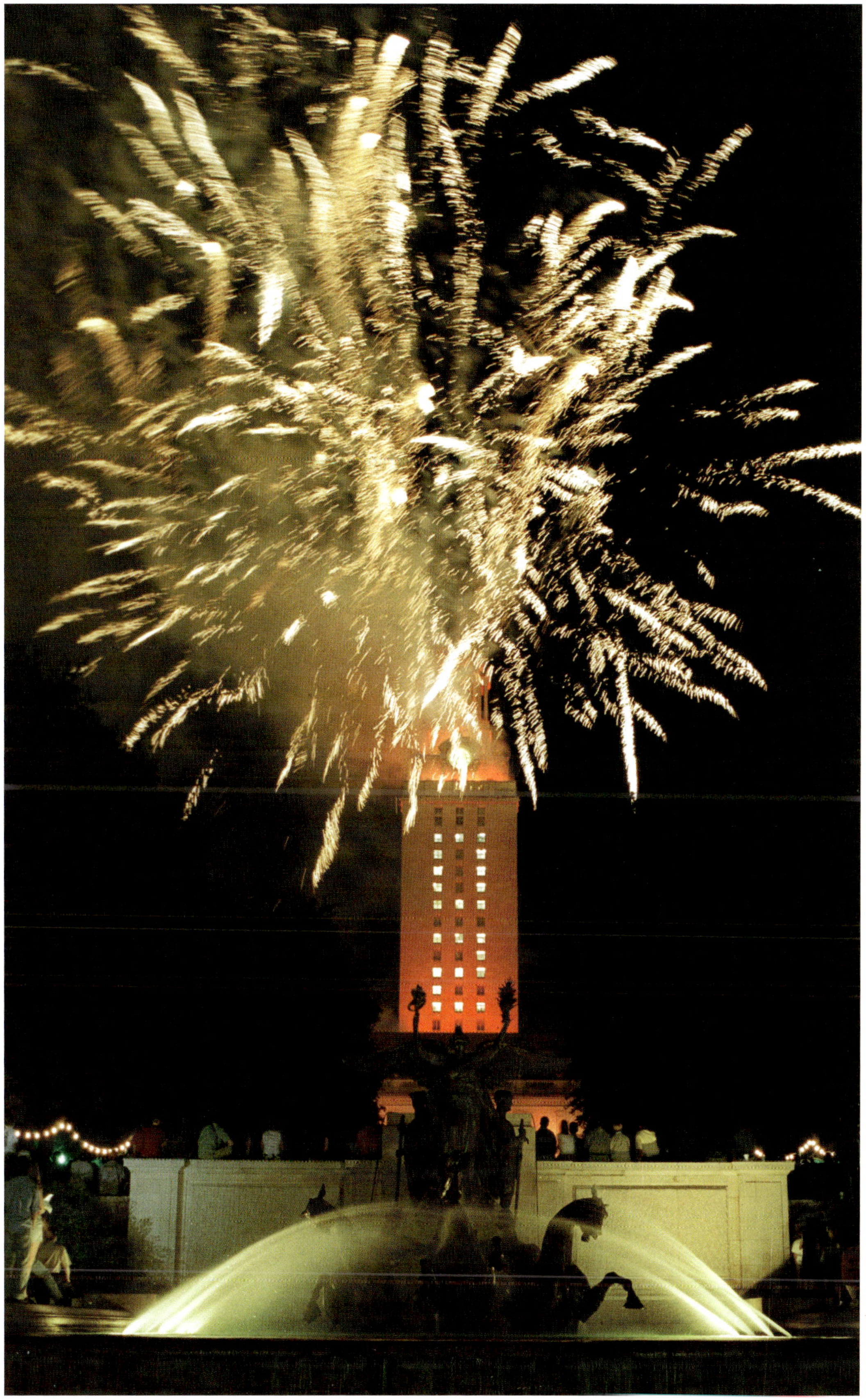

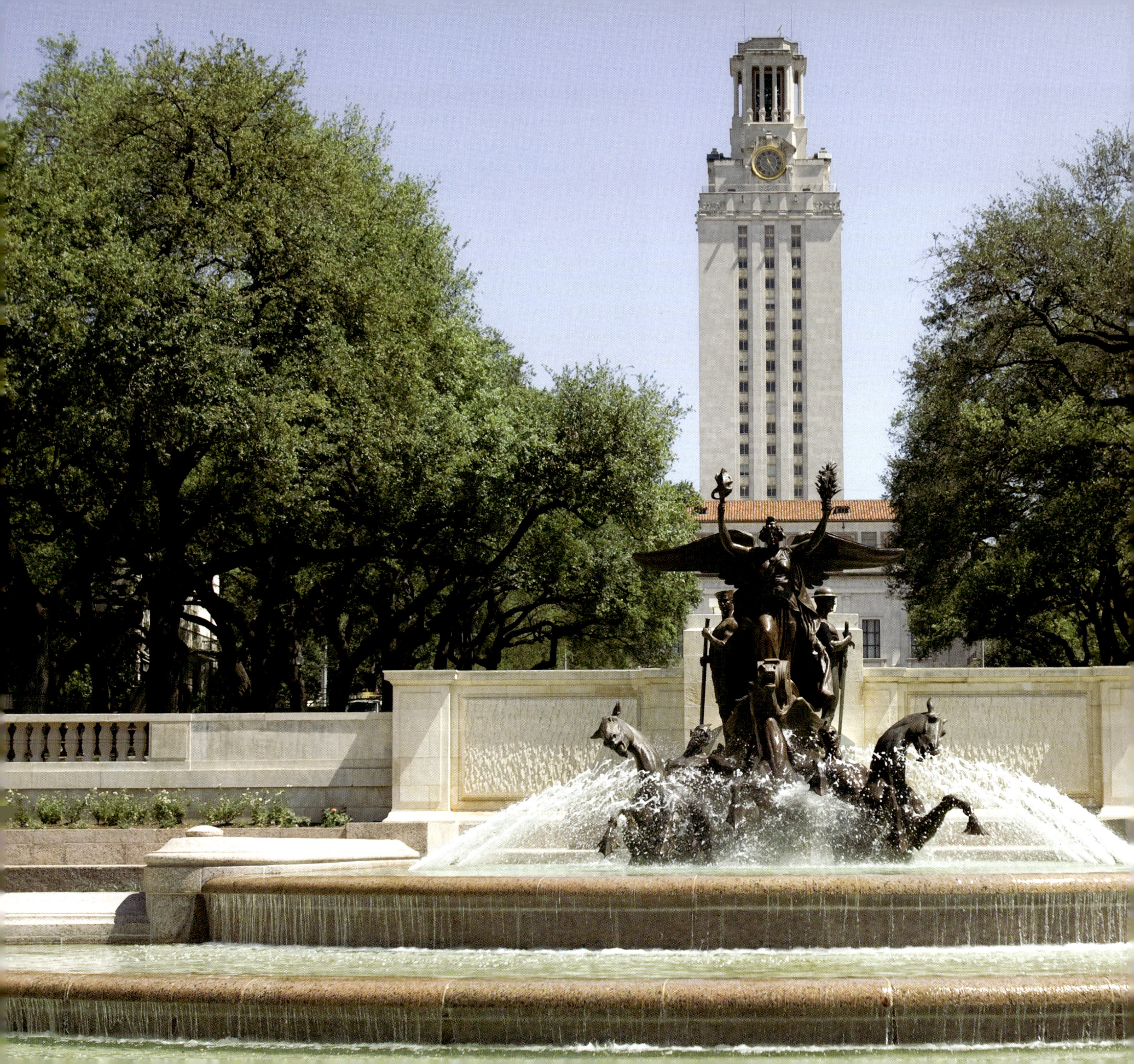

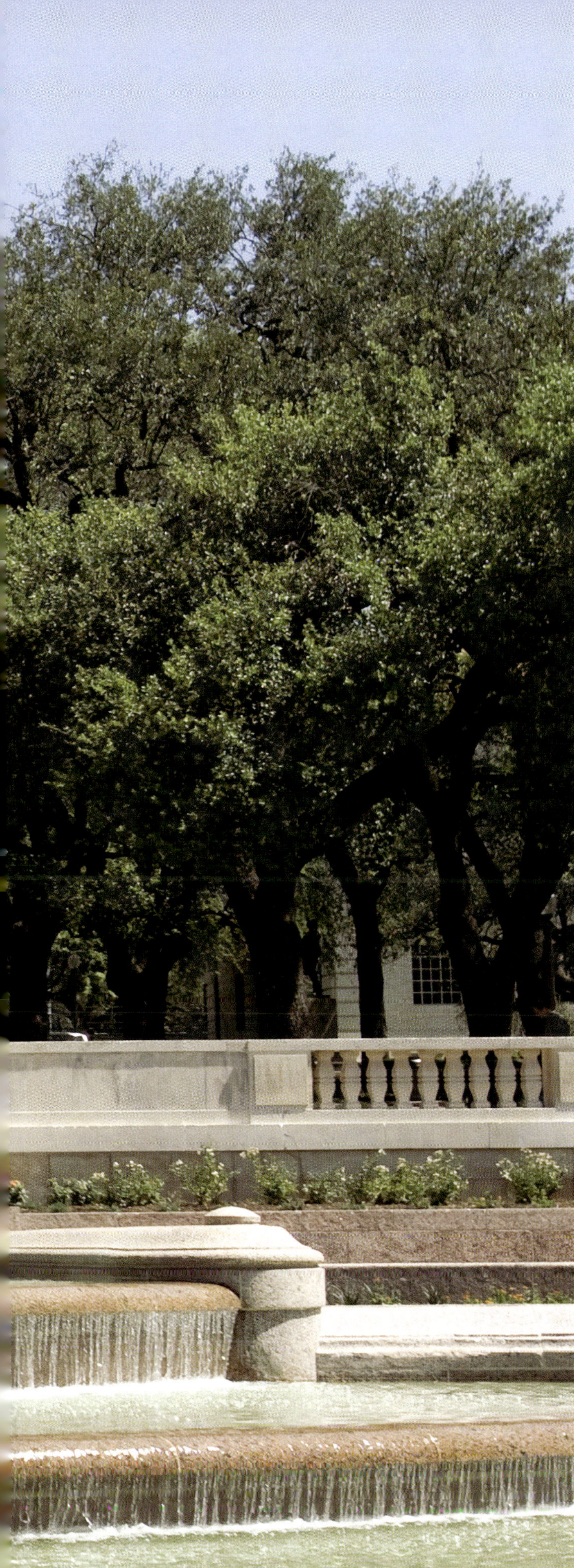

Our Time

what starts here changes the world

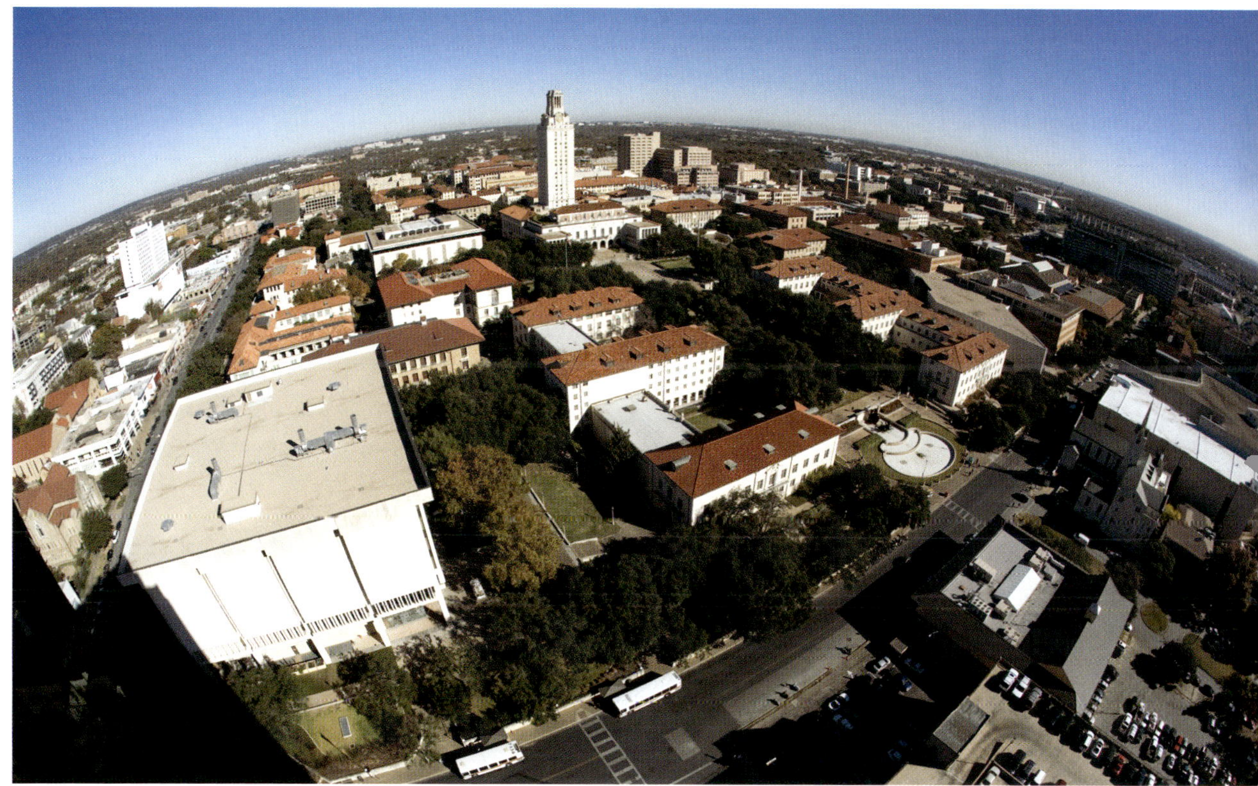

The Littlefield Fountain, with the Tower soaring behind it, is a favorite vista on the campus. Completed in 1932, the Littlefield Memorial Gateway was a gift of former regent George Littlefield, and was conceived by Italian-born sculptor Pompeo Coppini. Since the project was proposed just a year after World War I, Coppini intended to show the final reunification of America after its division in the Civil War. Behind the fountain, a brass door leading to the underground pump room bears the names of members of the UT community who lost their lives in World War I. On each side of the door is a quote from Cicero on patriotism. One reads *Brevis a natura nobis vita data est, at memoria bene redditae vitae Sempiturna*, which translates as, "Short is the life given to us by nature, but the memory of a life nobly surrendered is everlasting."

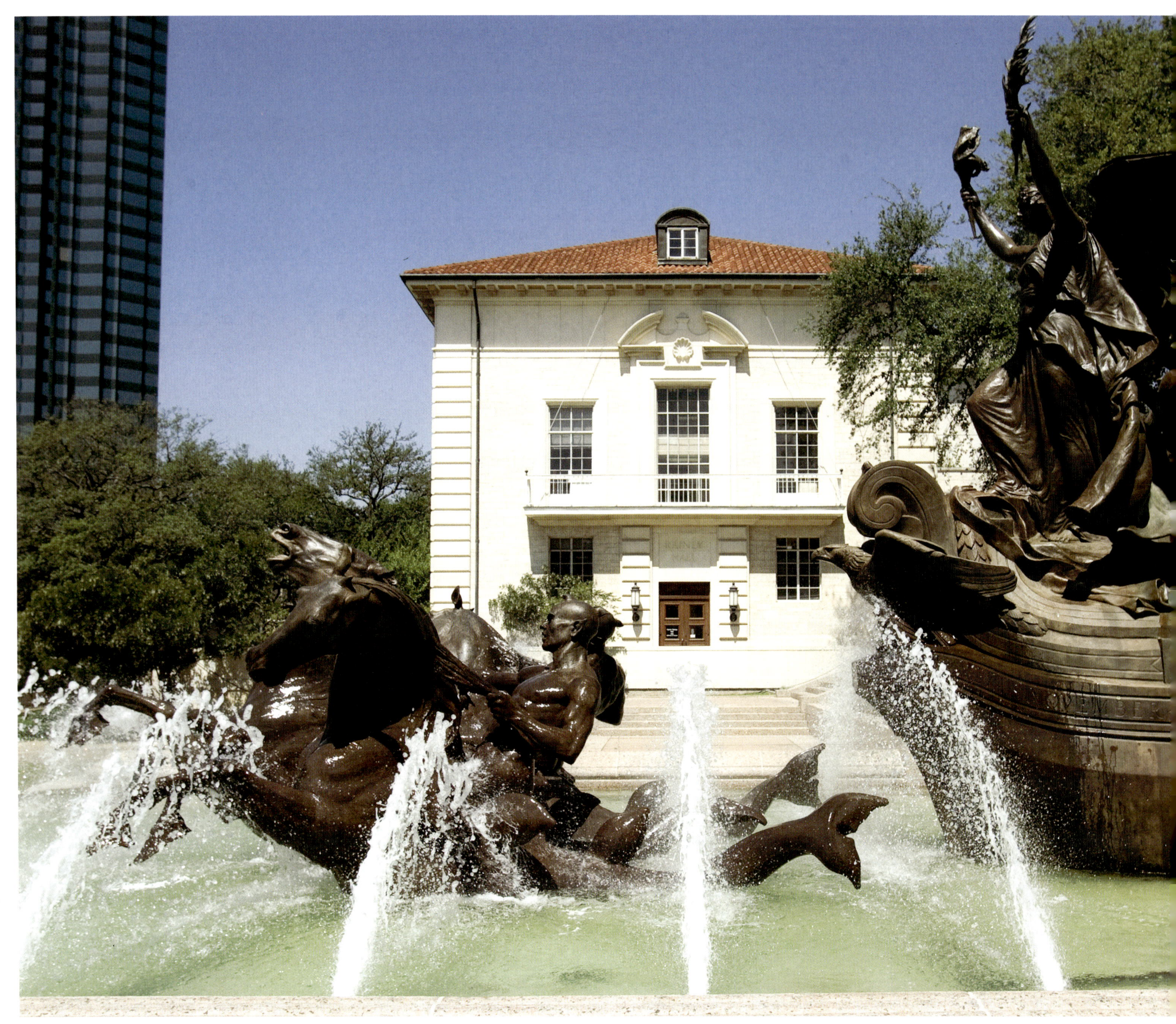

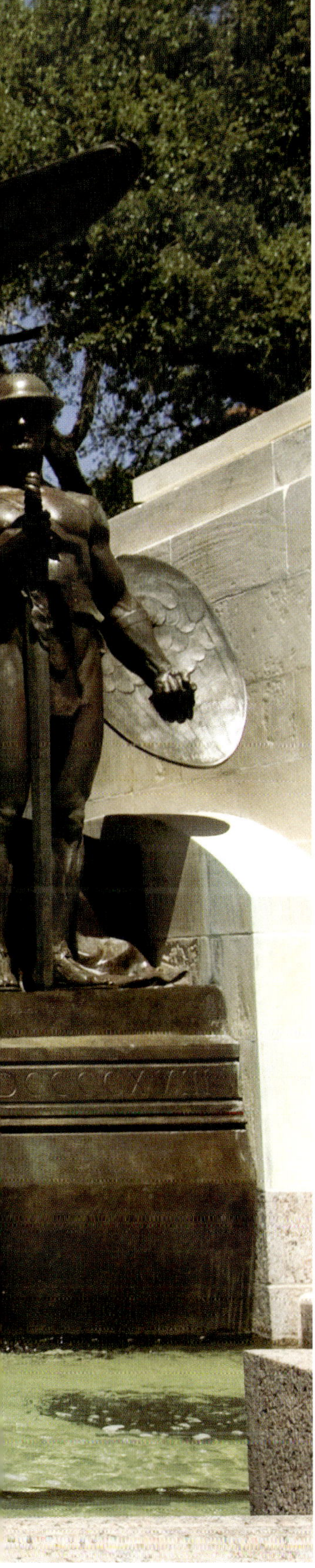

Left On the bow of a ship stands Columbia, the symbol of the American spirit, bearing the torch of freedom in her right hand and the palm leaves of peace in her left. Behind her are representatives of the country's armed forces, while the ship is being pulled by three sea tritons. This was Coppini's vision of a strong, reunified nation sailing across the ocean to protect democracy abroad.

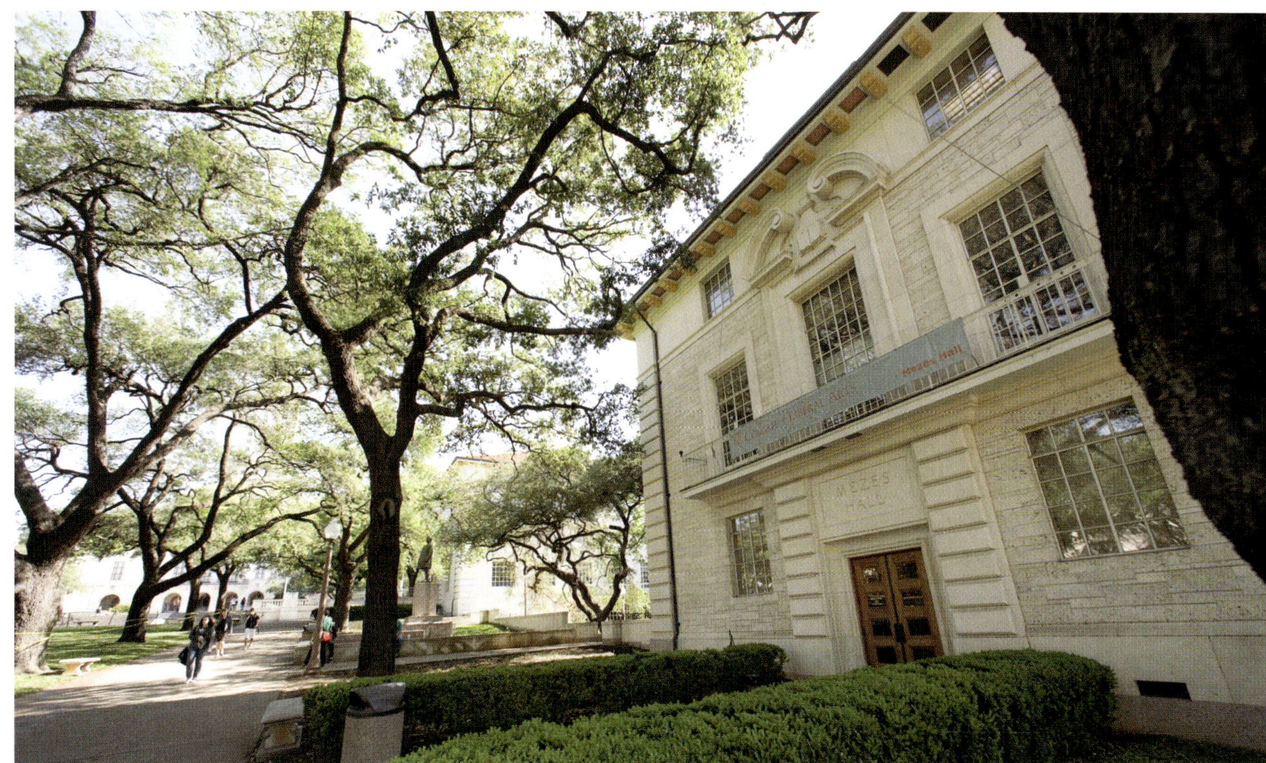

Above Beyond the Littlefield Fountain, the walks of the South Mall are shaded by a canopy of live oak trees, acquired in Orange, Texas, and planted in 1933. The six buildings along the mall, known by students as the "six pack," house language departments.

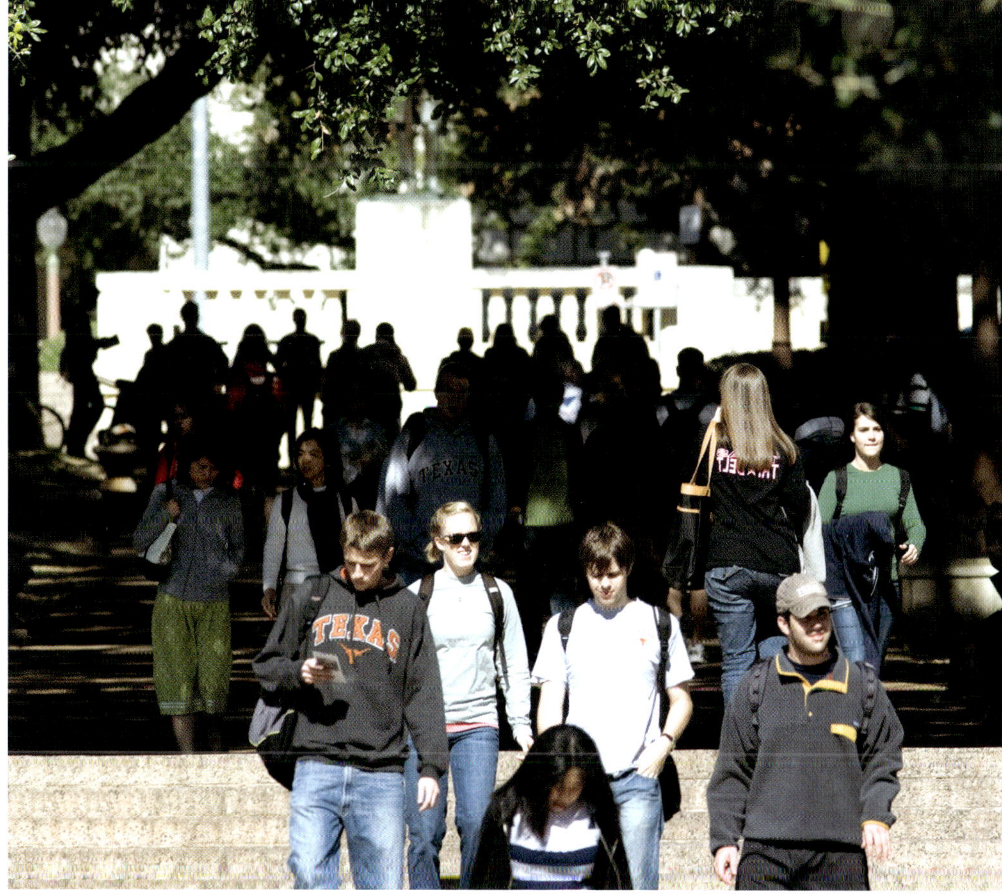

Right In between classes on the South Mall

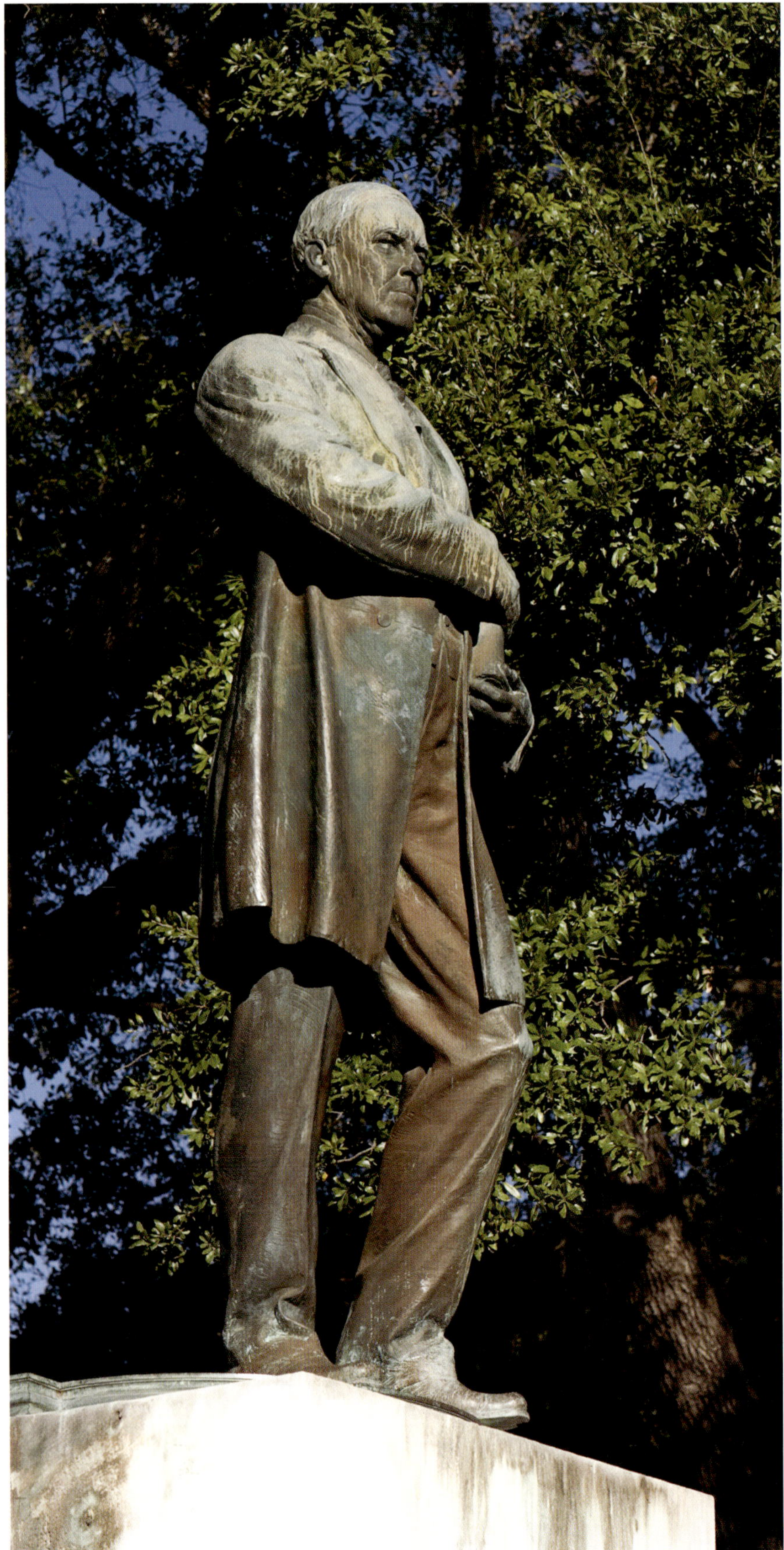

Left A part of the Littlefield Gateway, Pompeo Coppini's likeness of Woodrow Wilson was planned to sit directly behind the fountain, along with a statue of Jefferson Davis. Its intent was to portray leaders when the country was divided (Davis) and later reunited (Wilson). The statues were deemed too crowded, however, and spread about the South Mall.

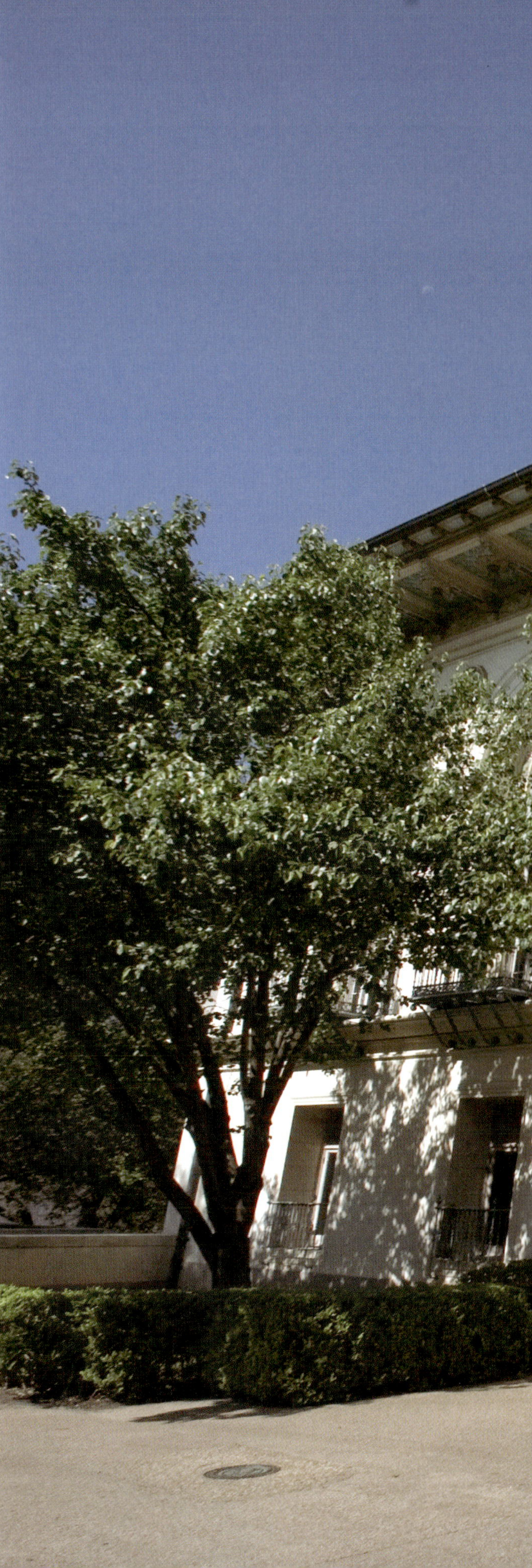

Right Opened in 1911 as the University's first library building, Battle Hall now houses the Architecture and Planning Libraries. Its walls are made of Cordoba Cream limestone, quarried just north of Austin in Cedar Park.

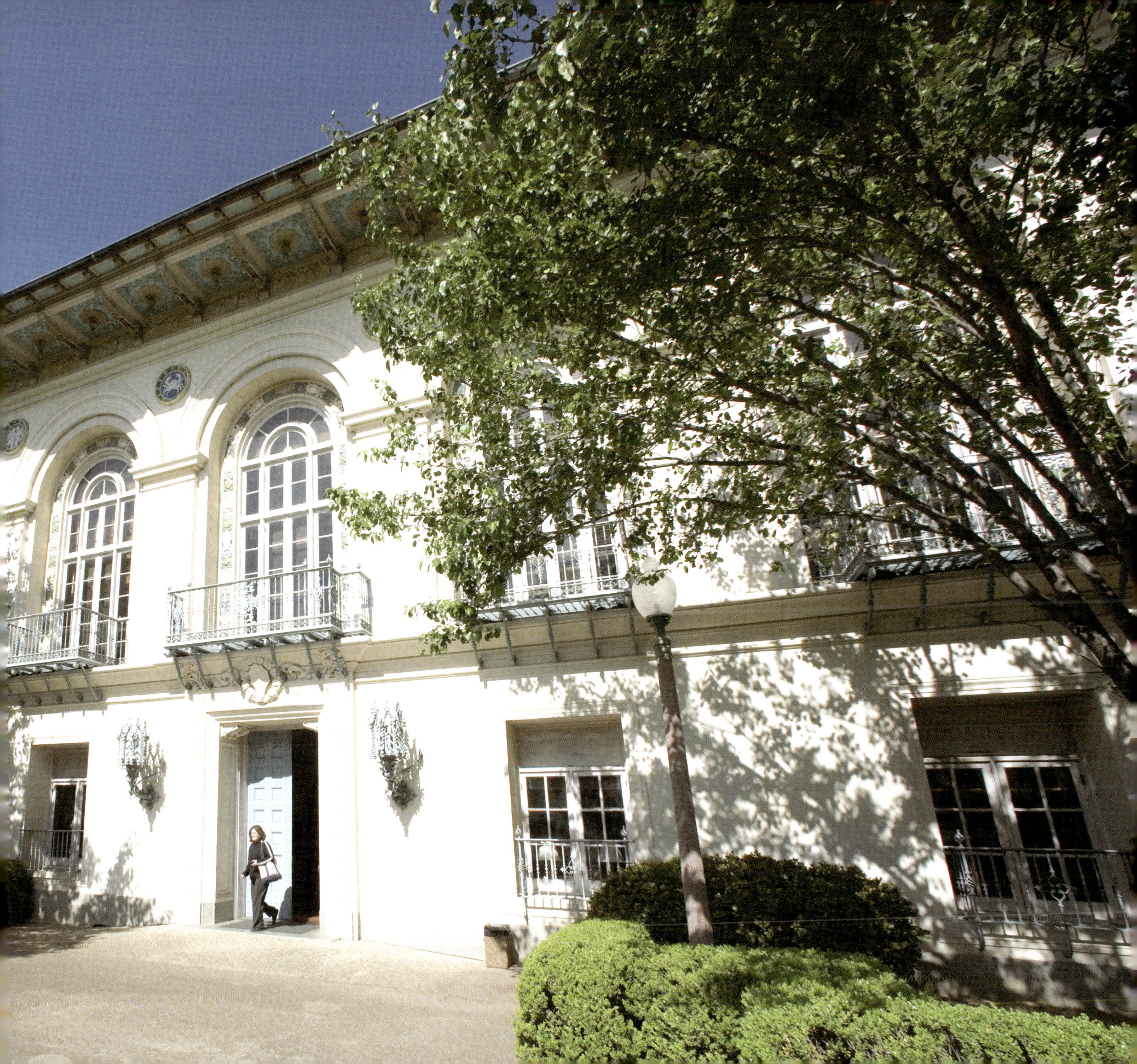

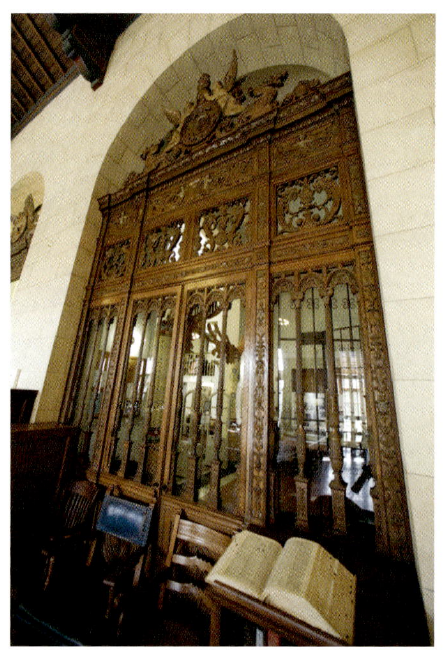

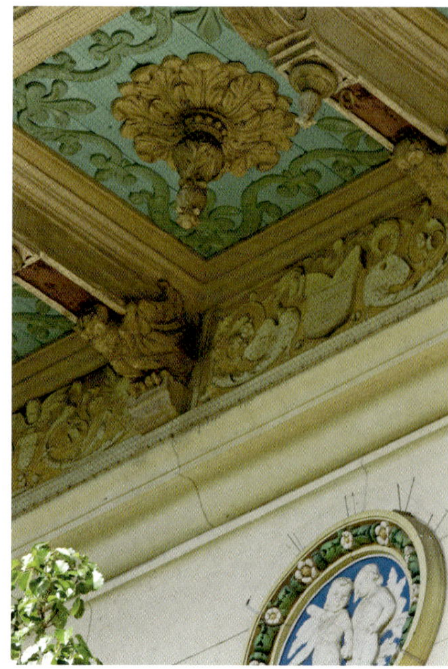

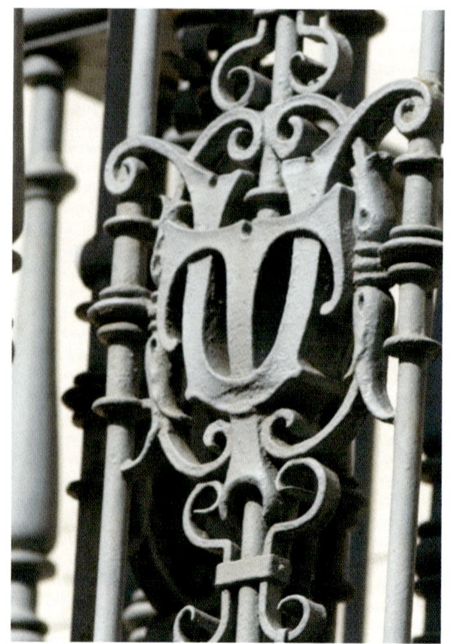

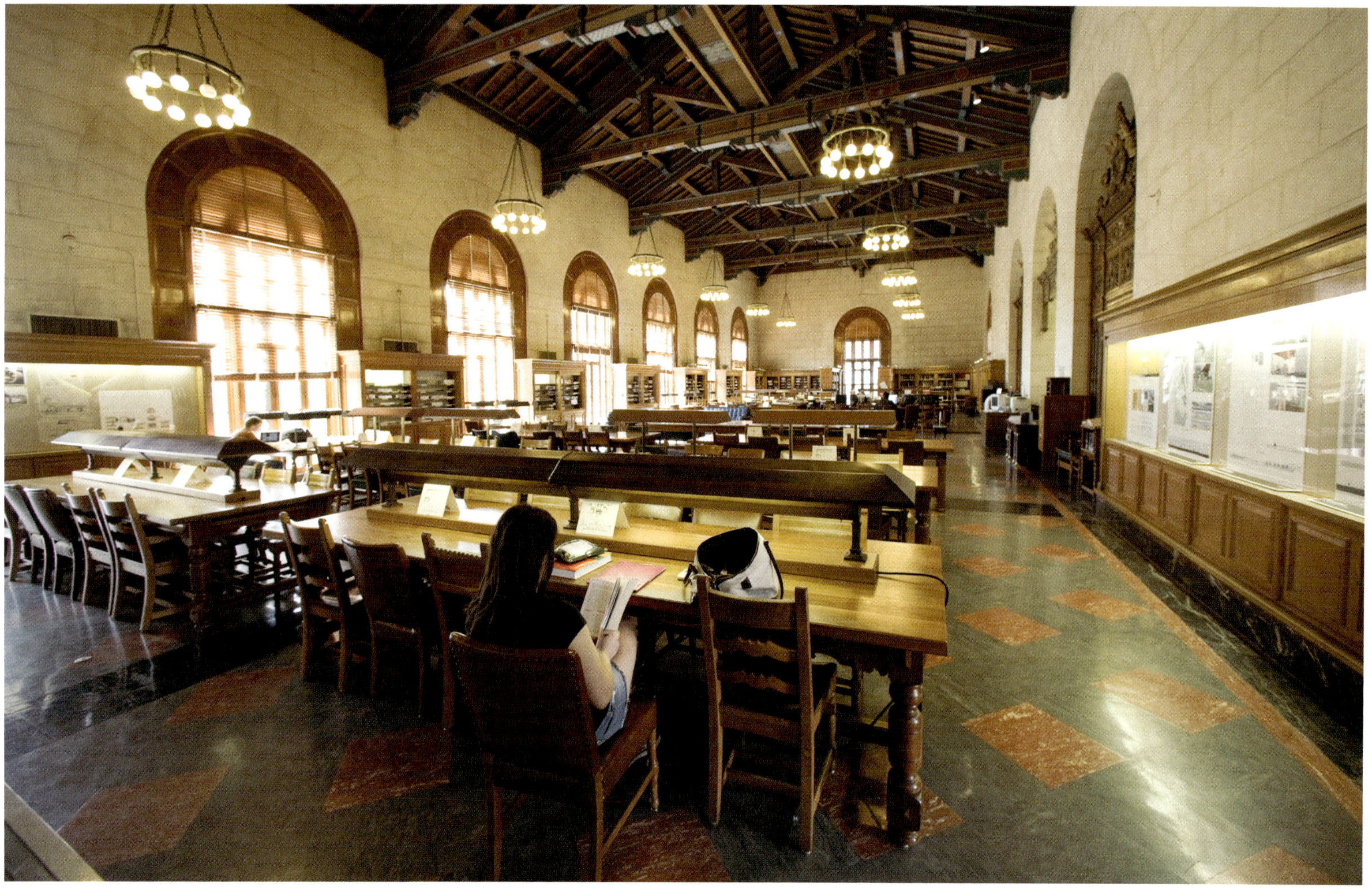

Facing Page, Top Images
Architect Cass Gilbert believed a library should appear "literate," and as such, Battle Hall is richly decorated in classical themes. Medallions depict the signs of the zodiac to communicate a sense of time or "permanence" of the building and its important contents. Beams under the eaves are supported by sculpted owls, an ancient symbol of Athena, the goddess of wisdom. The intricate wrought-iron work is the finest on the campus. Interlocking UTs can be seen on the front balcony.

Facing Page, Bottom
The second-floor reading room. Constructed well before the advent of air conditioning, Battle Hall was positioned so that its wide, arched windows could admit the southeastern breezes from the Gulf of Mexico.

Right In 2007, a bronze statue of civil rights leader Cesar Chavez was unveiled on the north side of Battle Hall, along the West Mall. Approved by a student referendum in 2003, the statue honors Chavez' legacy as an advocate of social justice.

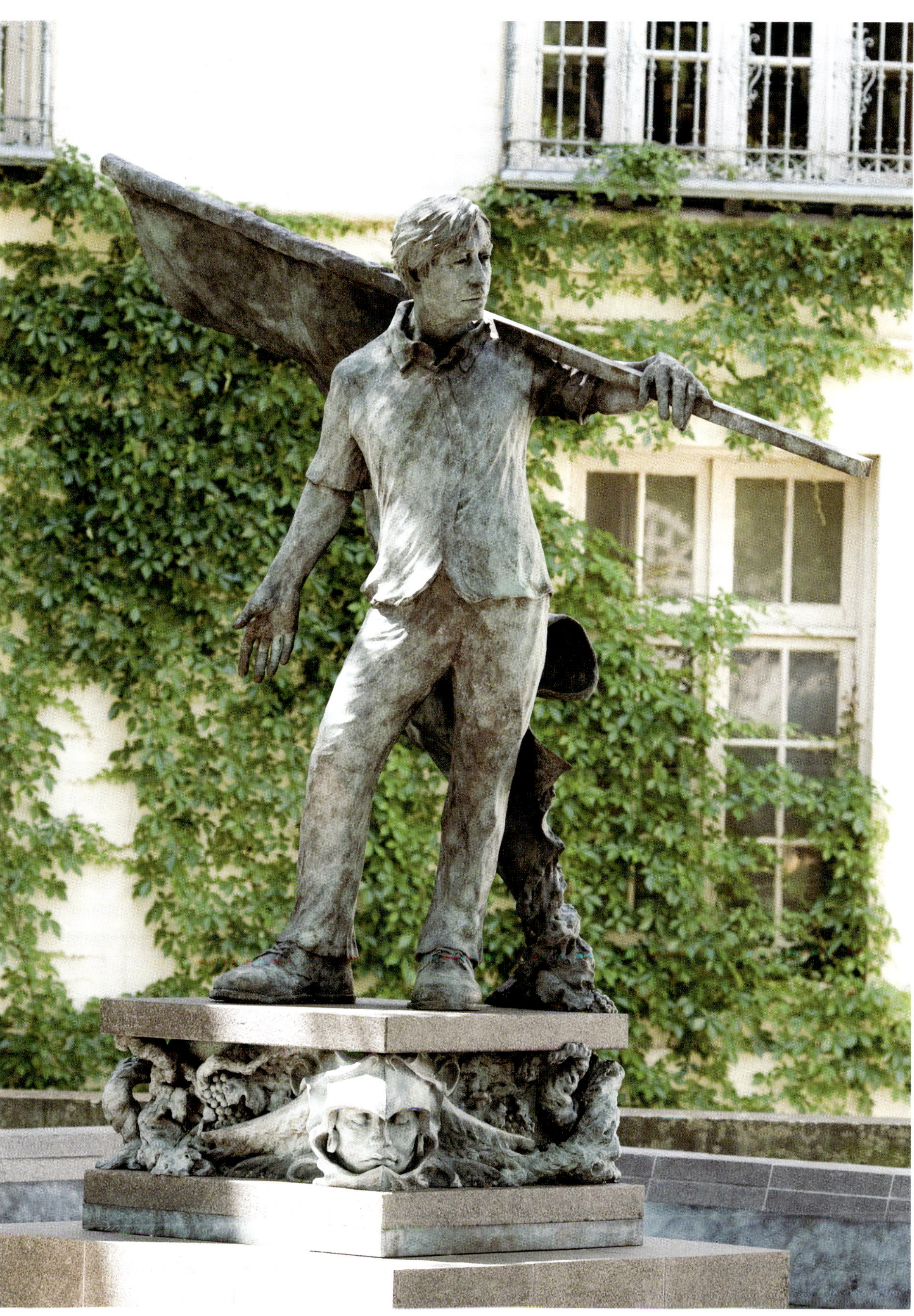

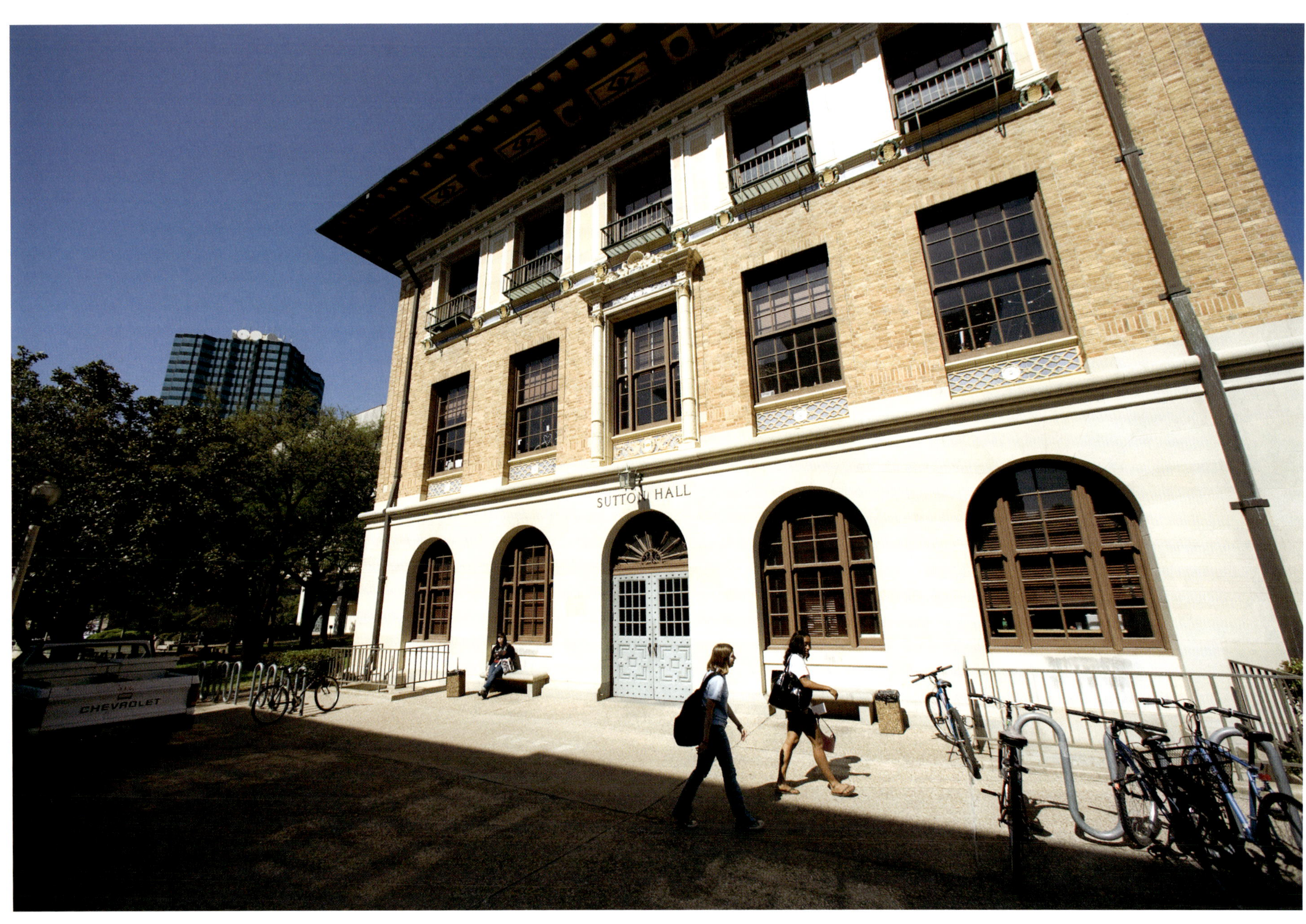

Sutton Hall was constructed in 1917 for the Education Department but is now used by the School of Architecture. Designed by Cass Gilbert in a Mediterranean-Renaissance style, Battle and Sutton Halls set the tone for campus architecture.

Right Look closely. The rope decoration near the top left, created from a series of five terra cotta tiles, is even and unbroken, but two of the tiles on the right panel were mistakenly placed upside down, making the rope pattern disjointed. Of the 32 panels around the building, only one was installed correctly!

Below Like Battle Hall, Sutton Hall boasts elaborate decoration. A pair of cherubs gazes down from the east entrance of the building, along with Griffins, legendary creatures with the body of a lion and the head of an eagle, which were mythological protectors of precious things. The scallop shell is emblematic of Venus, the Goddess of Truth and Beauty.

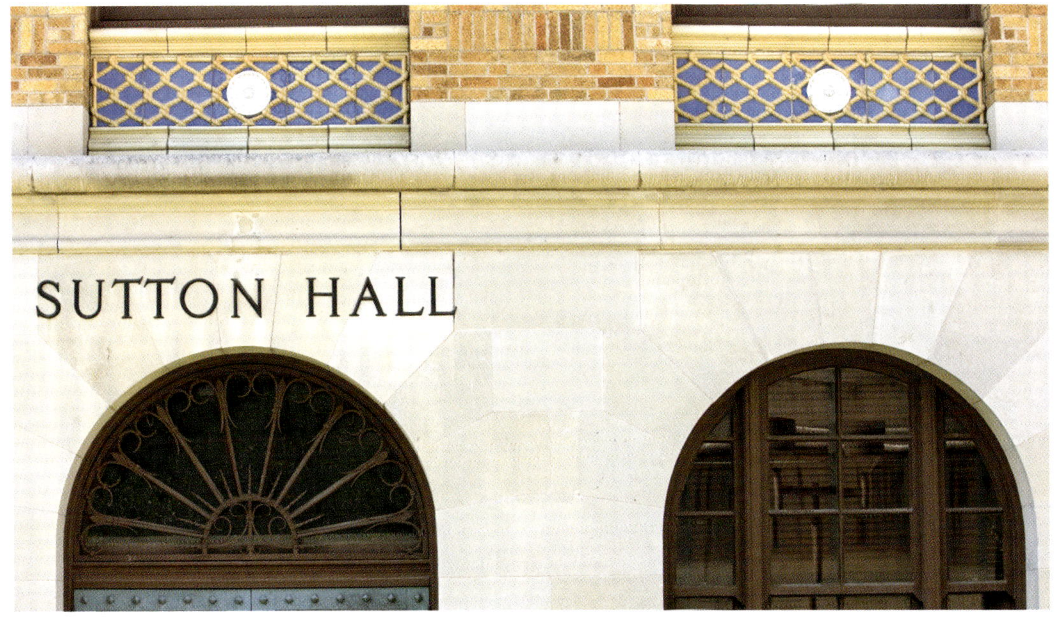

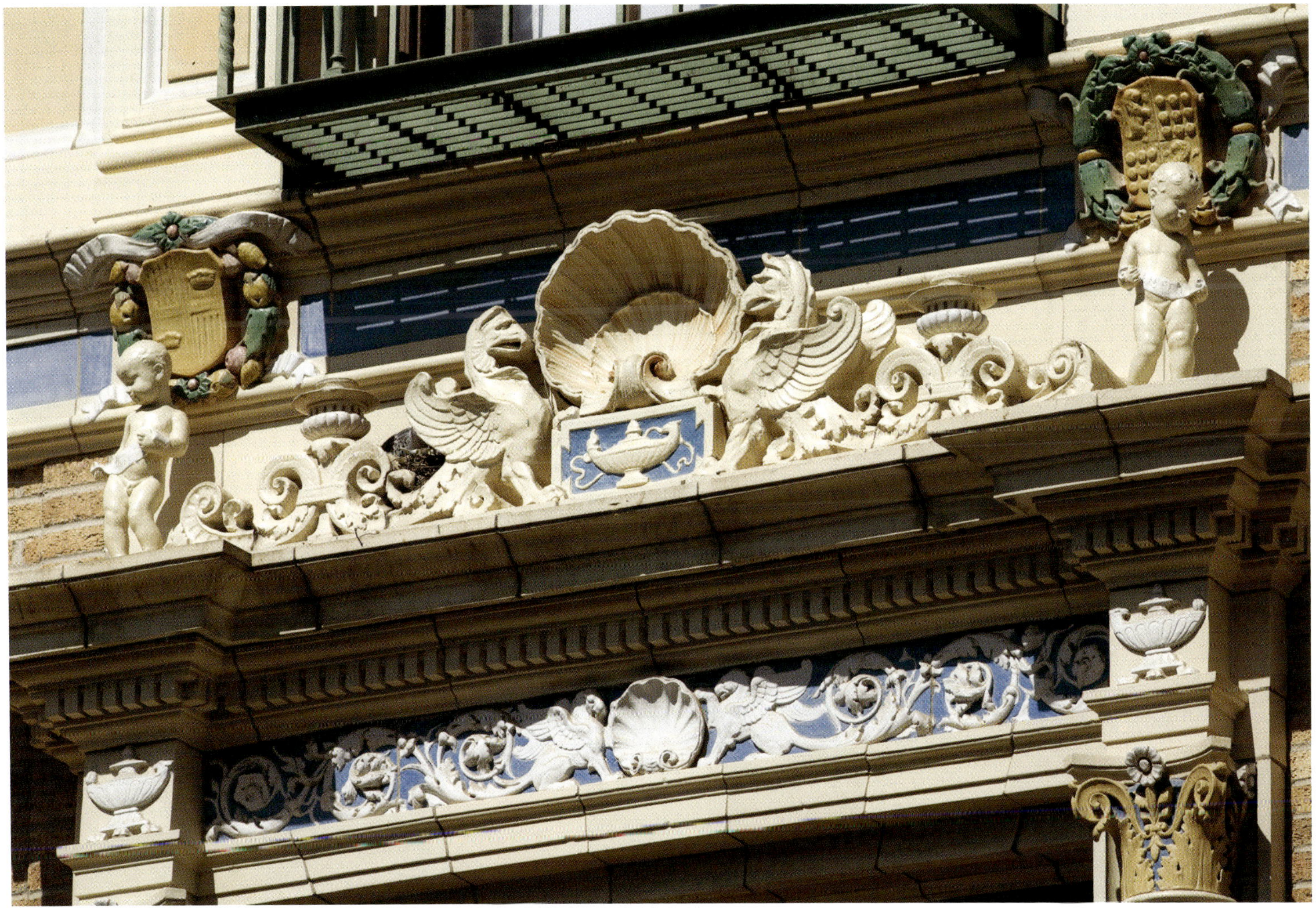

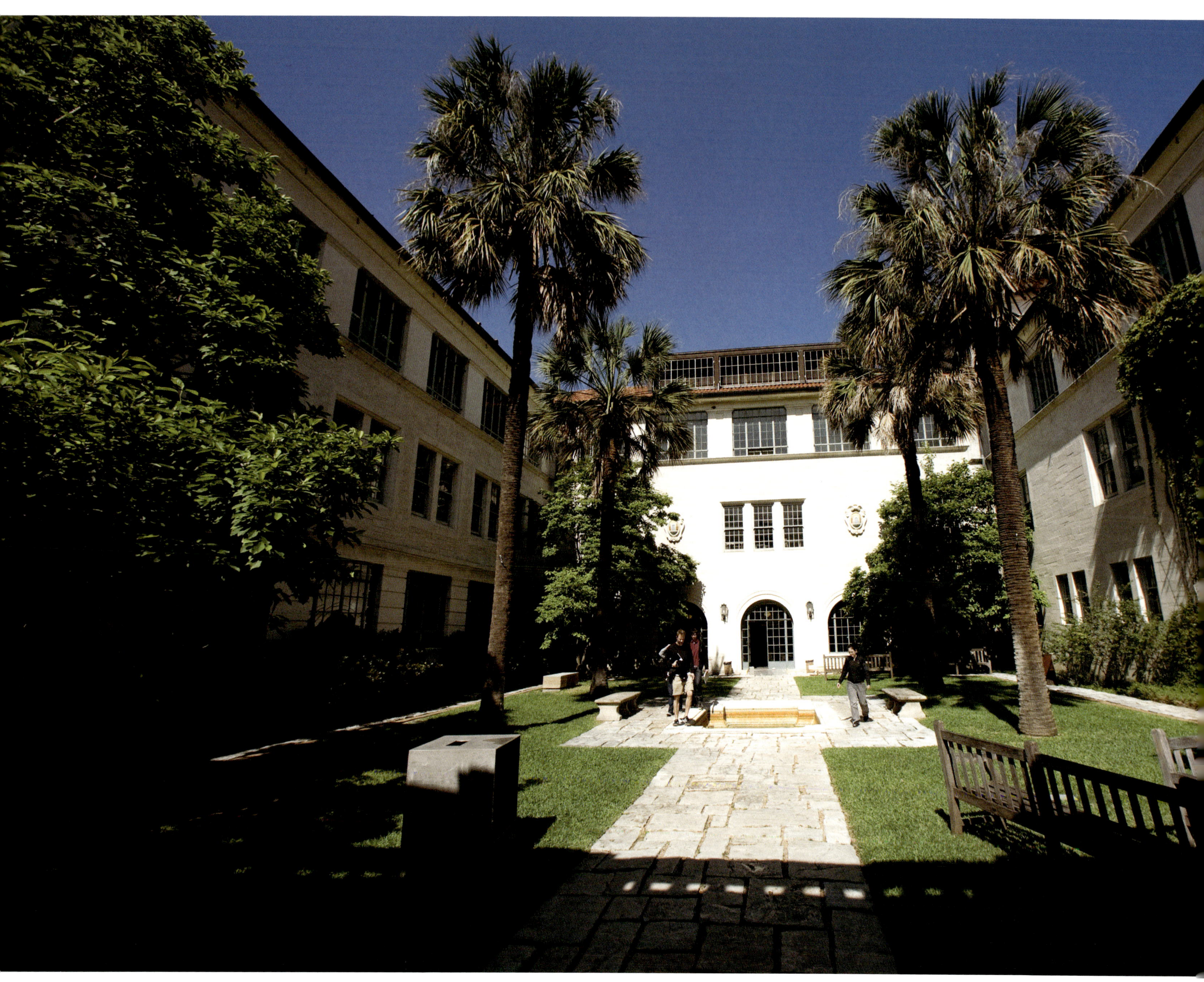

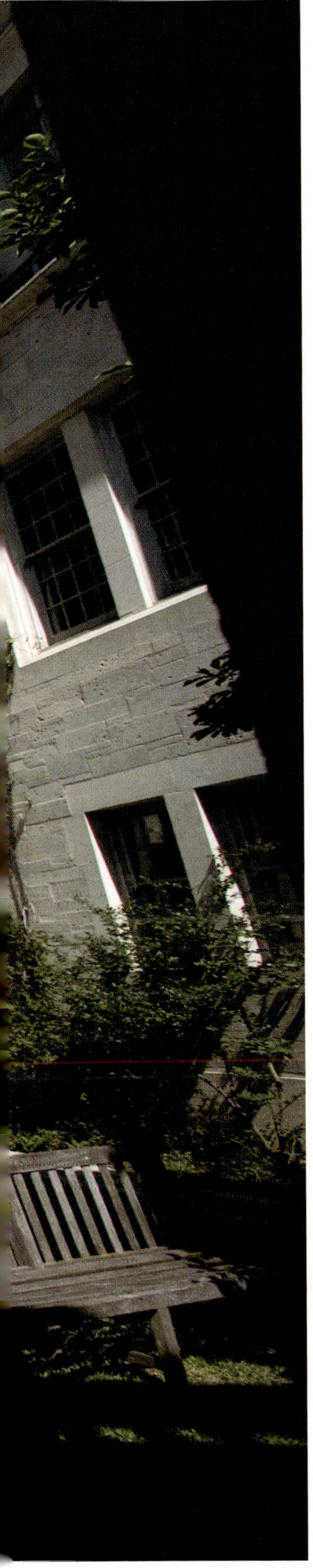

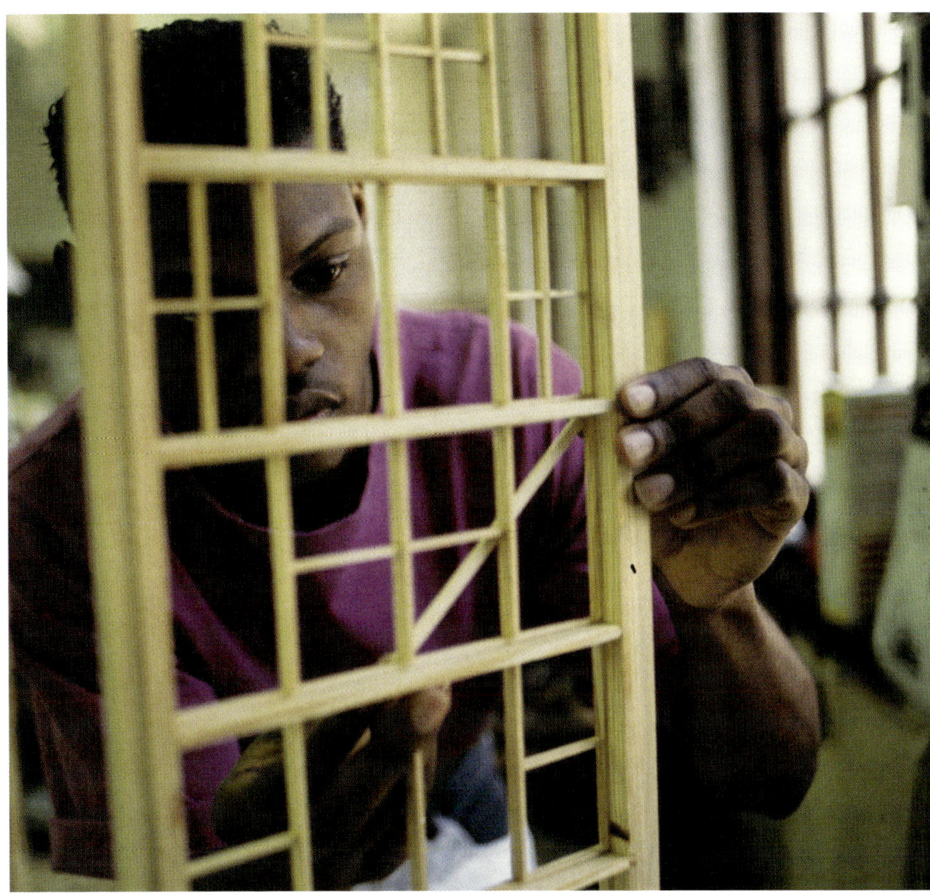

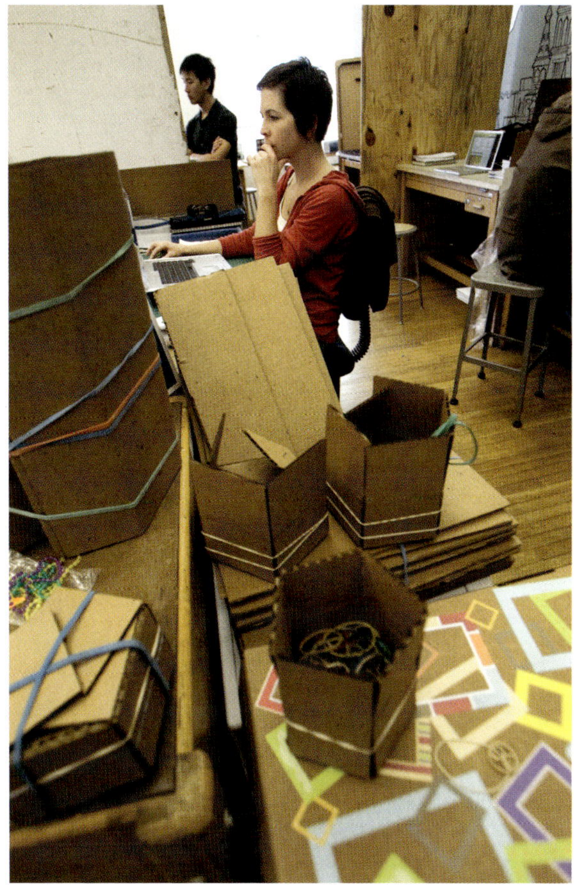

Left The tranquil courtyard of Goldsmith Hall, headquarters for the School of Architecture. The open space allows abundant sunlight to flood the upper-floor studios.

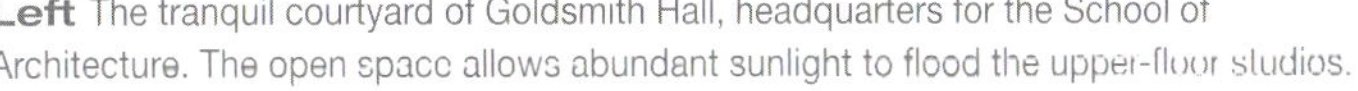

Above and Right Students in the School of Architecture work long hours with little sleep to finish their projects.

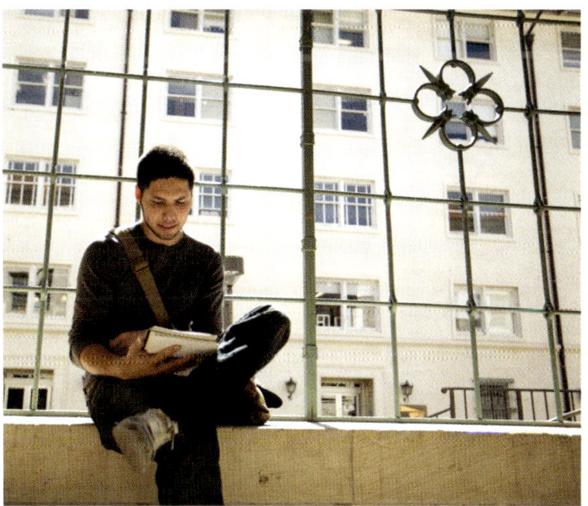

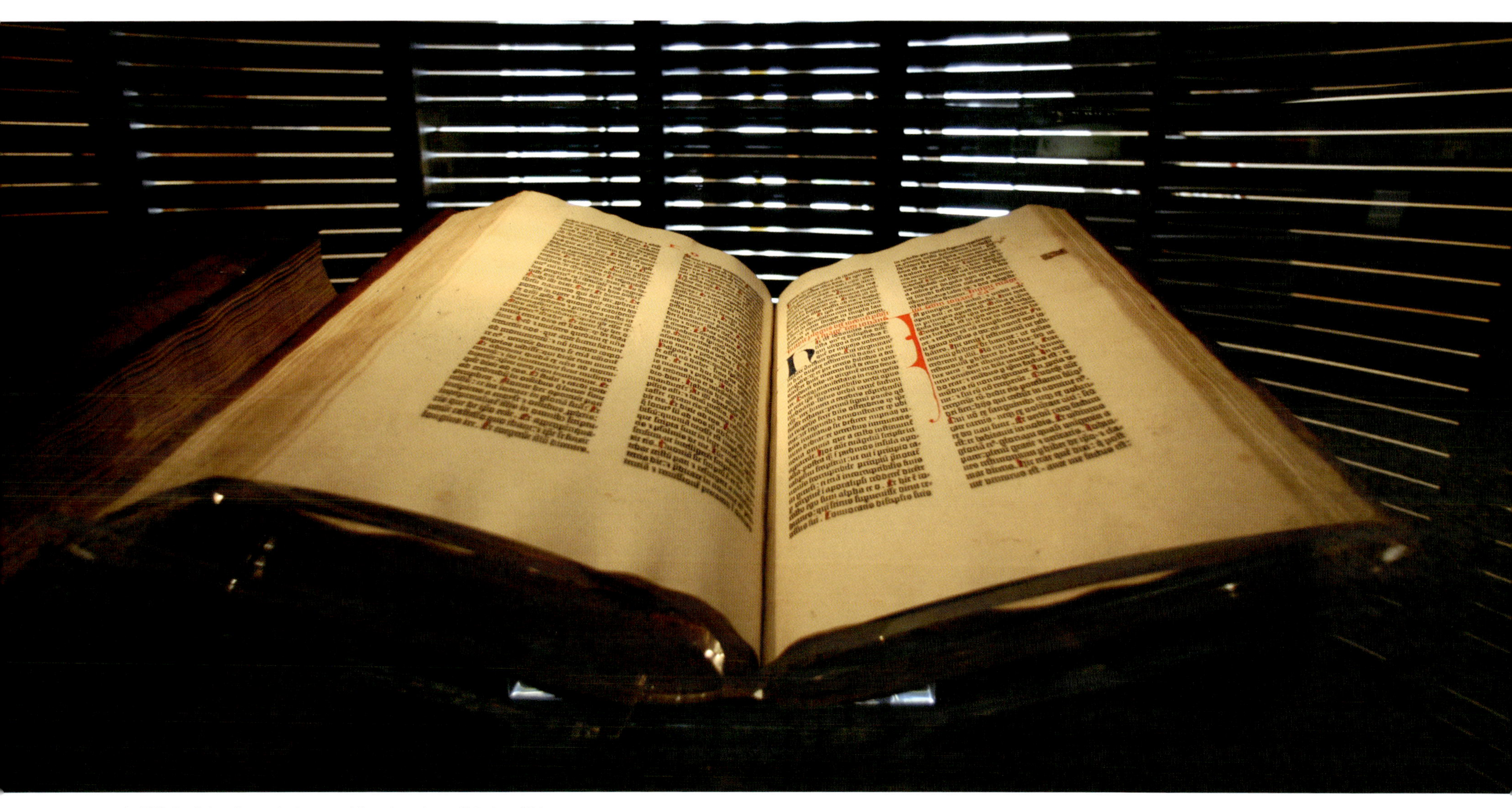

In 1978, the University acquired a copy of the extremely rare Gutenberg Bible. Published in the mid-15th century, it was the first substantial book printed with movable type and is on permanent display in the Harry Ransom Center.

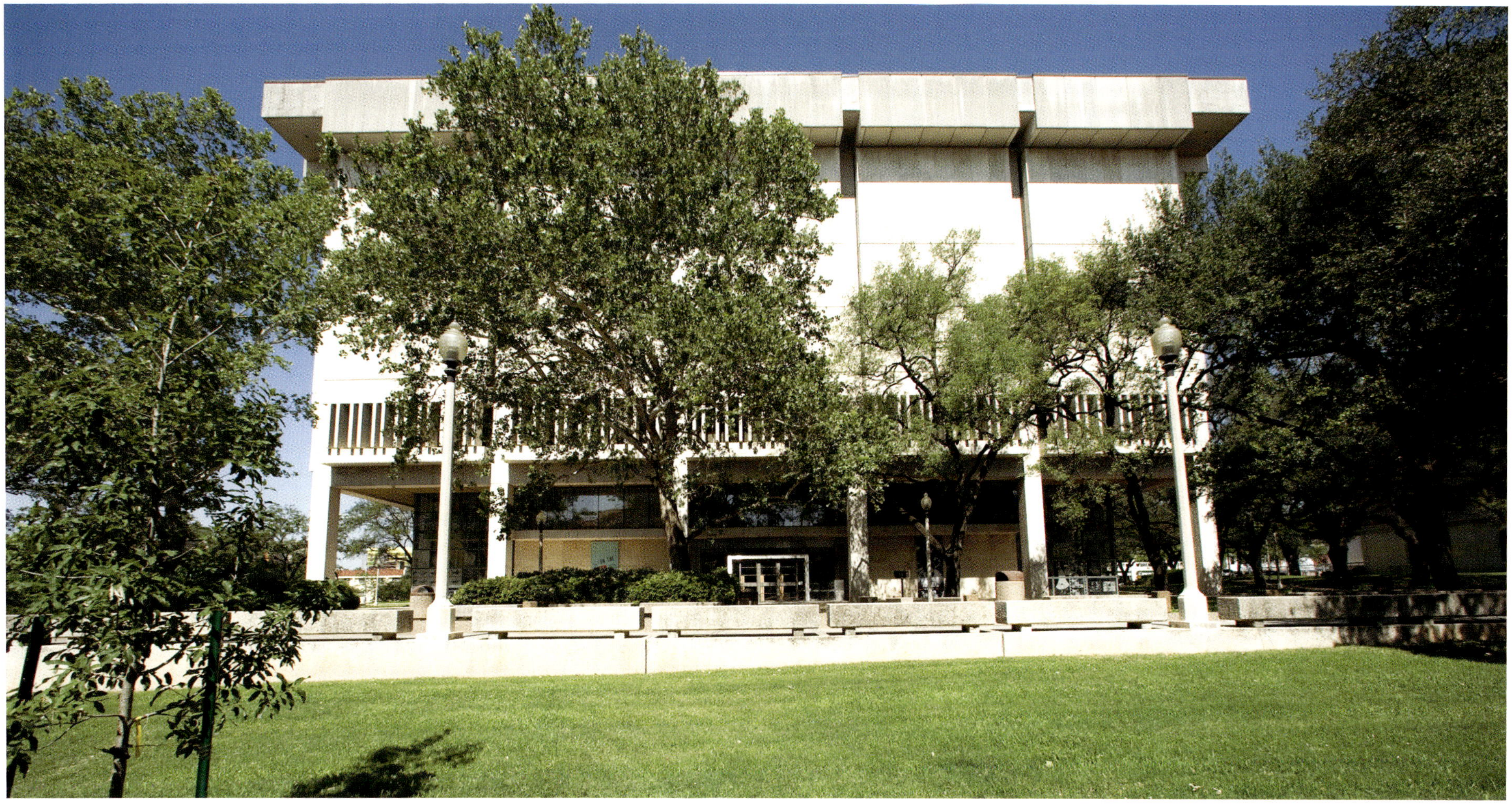

Founded in 1957 by then-Provost Harry Ransom, the Humanities Research Center houses an incredible collection of rare books, manuscripts, photographs, art, film, and other items. Dedicated to "advance the study of the arts and humanities," its diverse holdings include the first known photograph; manuscript collections of James Joyce, Lewis Carroll, and Norman Mailer; papers of Gloria Swanson and George Bernard Shaw; costumes used in the film *Gone with the Wind*; and the Woodward and Bernstein Watergate Papers. The Center moved into its current quarters, named for Harry Ransom, in 1972.

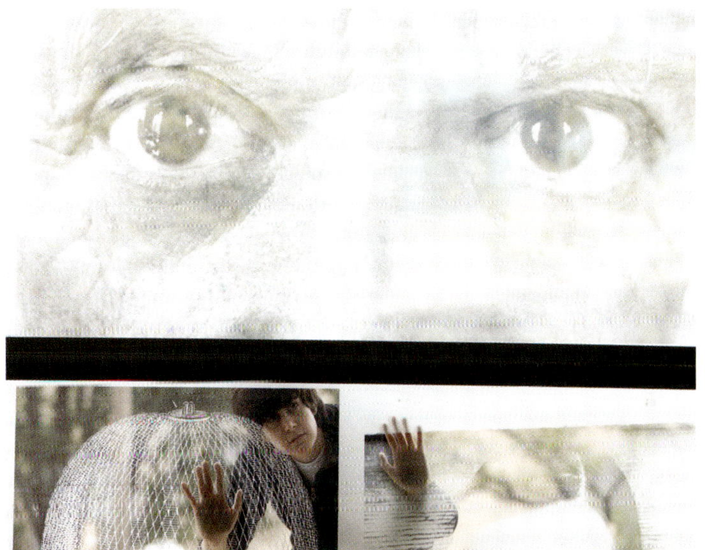

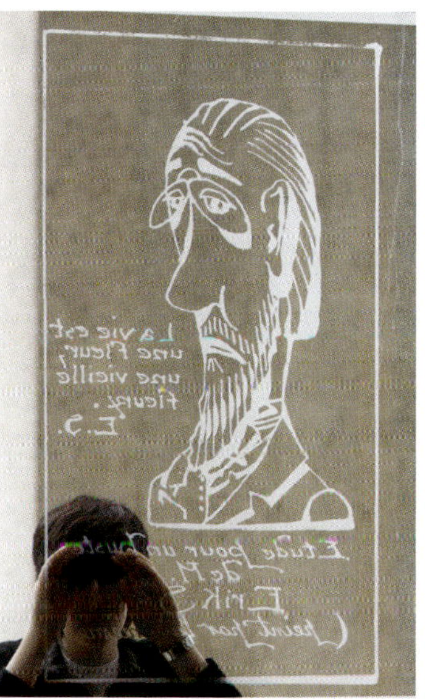

The etched glass, added to the front of the building as part of a renovation in 2003, hints at the literary and photographic treasures stored within.

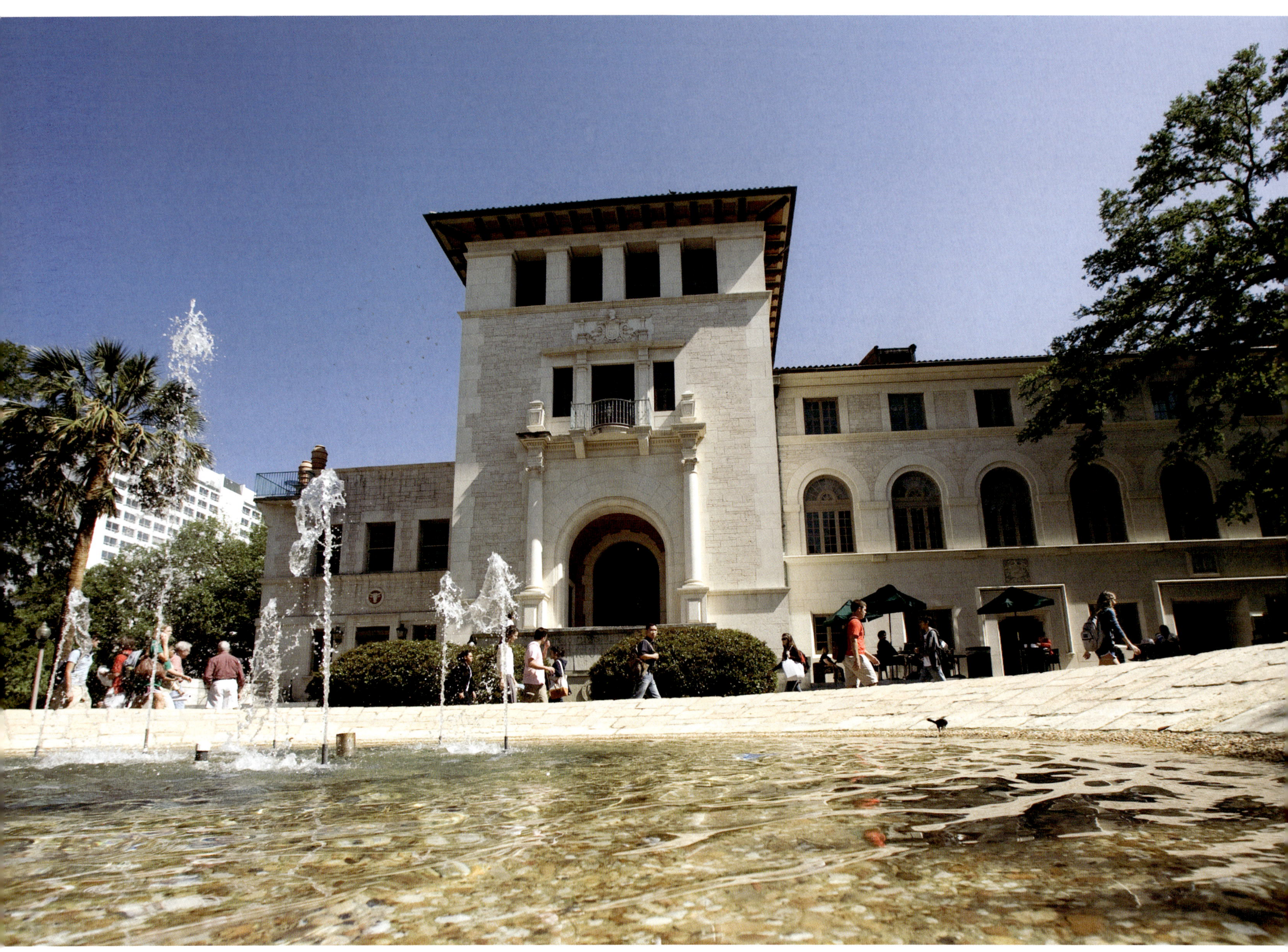

The Texas Union was opened in 1933 as part of the Union Project, a massive fundraising effort undertaken by the Texas Exes in the midst of the Great Depression. Guarding the west entrance of the campus, the Union has long been a bustling hub of student life.

Below Inside the Union's main entrance and up a flight of stairs, a visitor will encounter the Presidential Lobby. Following the University's Mediterranean architecture, the lobby was designed to resemble the open courtyard of a Spanish palace. The Bodhi tree was installed to coincide with a visit to the University by the Dalai Lama in 2005.

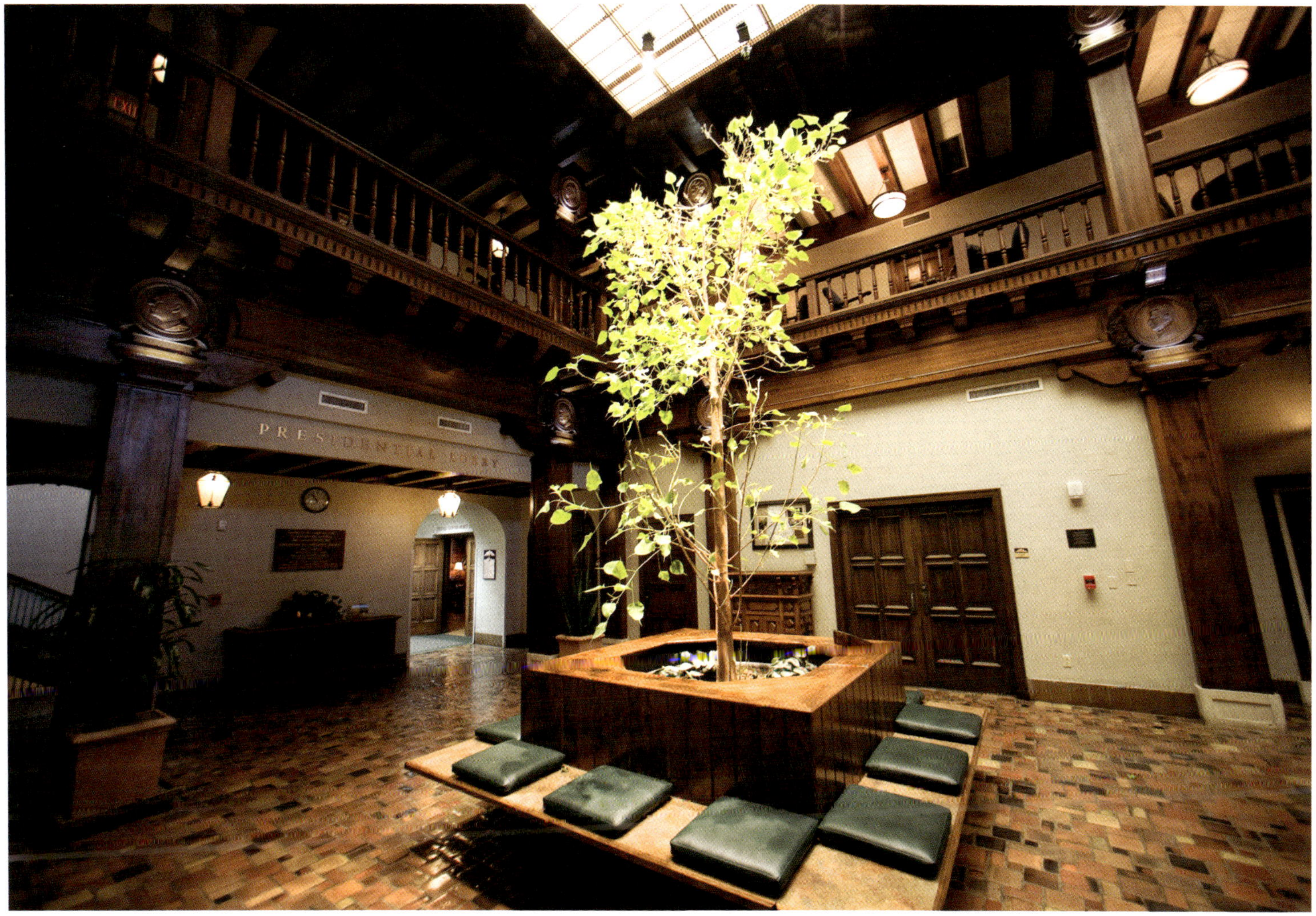

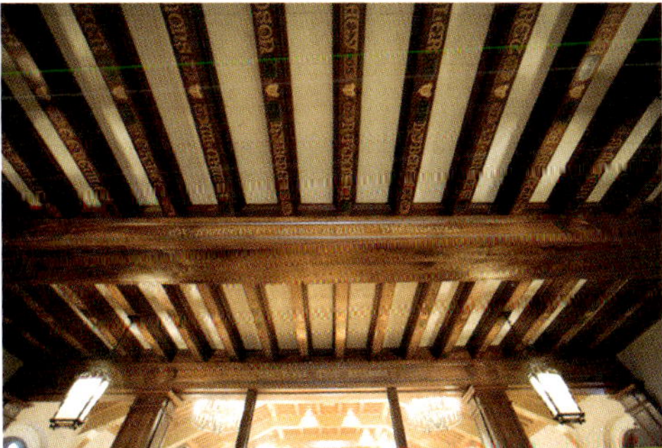

For more than two decades, the Union served as the headquarters of the Texas Exes. Names of alumni association presidents are painted on the beams of the lobby and are still kept current.

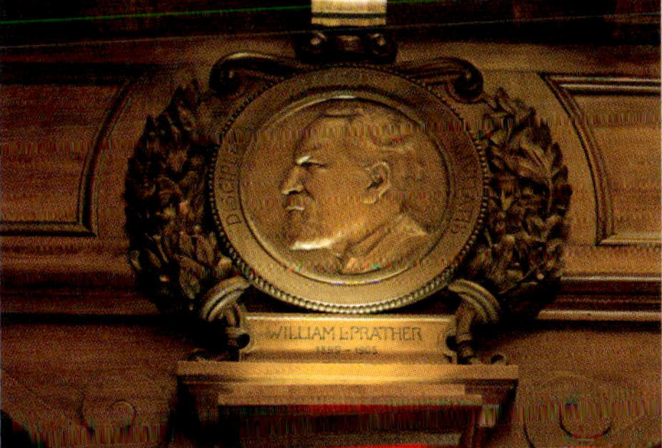

The defining feature of the Presidential Lobby is the collection of hand-carved oak portraits of University presidents. Pictured is William Prather, whose frequent use of the phrase "The eyes of Texas are upon you" inspired the song "The Eyes of Texas" in 1903.

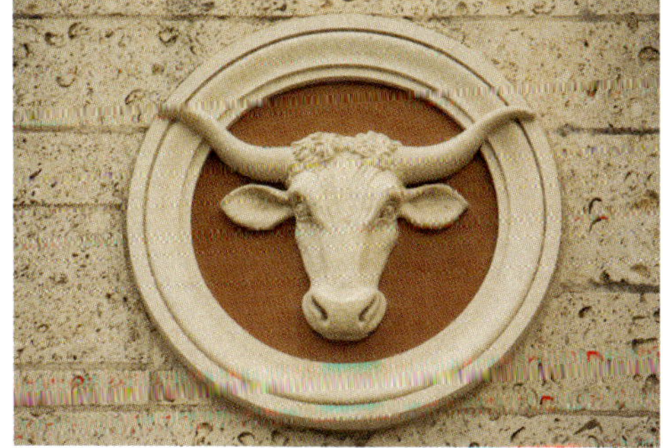

A longhorn medallion on the north side of the Texas Union. University athletic squads have been known as the Longhorns since 1904.

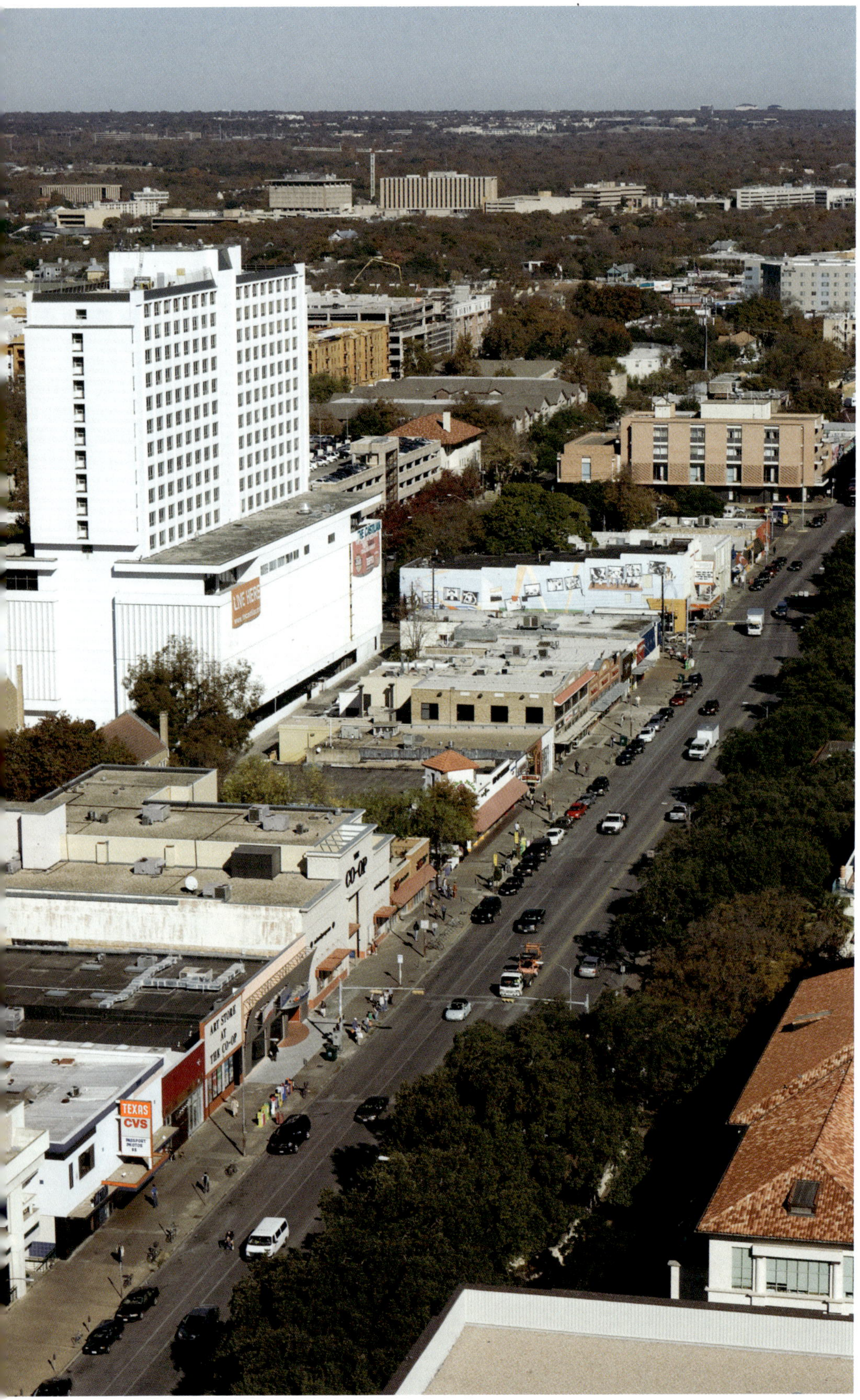

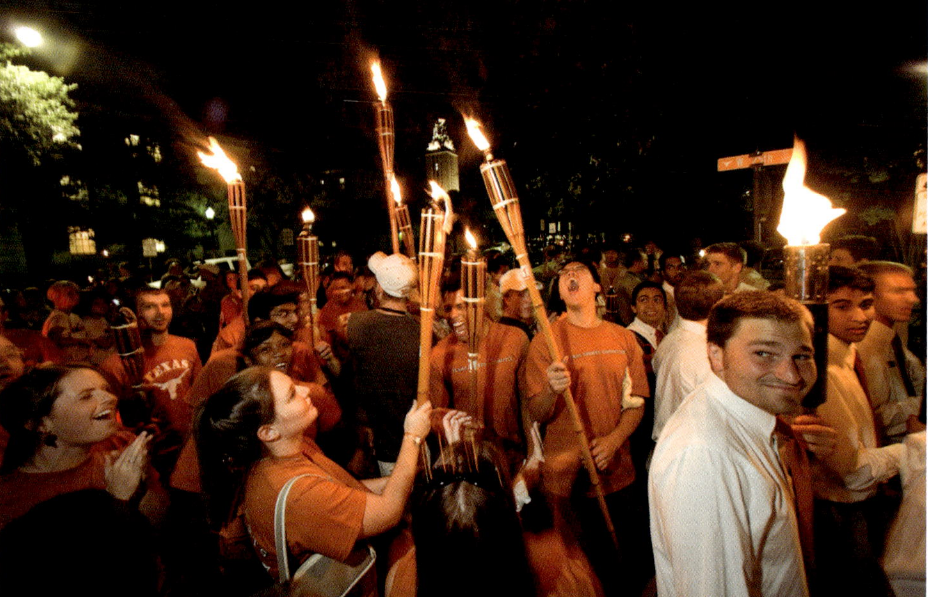

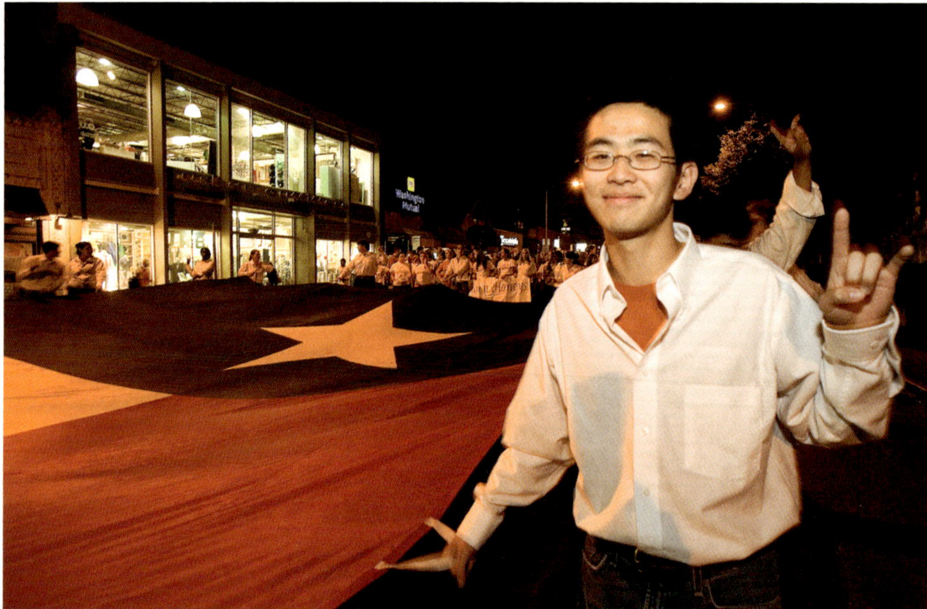

Left The bookstores, coffee shops, and other stores along Guadalupe Street, or "The Drag," are a lively part of University life. When UT opened in 1883, the street boasted two grocery stores, a dry goods shop, and a saloon. The Drag has been the site of jubilant celebrations for UT athletic victories, spring Round-up Parades, and protest marches.

Top Each October, the week of the Texas vs. Oklahoma football game is marked by the annual "Beat OU Torchlight Parade and Rally" down Guadalupe Street. Torchlight parades were common in the 1940s and 1950s but disappeared in the late 1960s. The tradition was revived in 1987 and regularly attracts thousands of UT fans.

Above Members of the Alpha Phi Omega service fraternity carry the "World's Largest Texas Flag" in the Torchlight Parade.

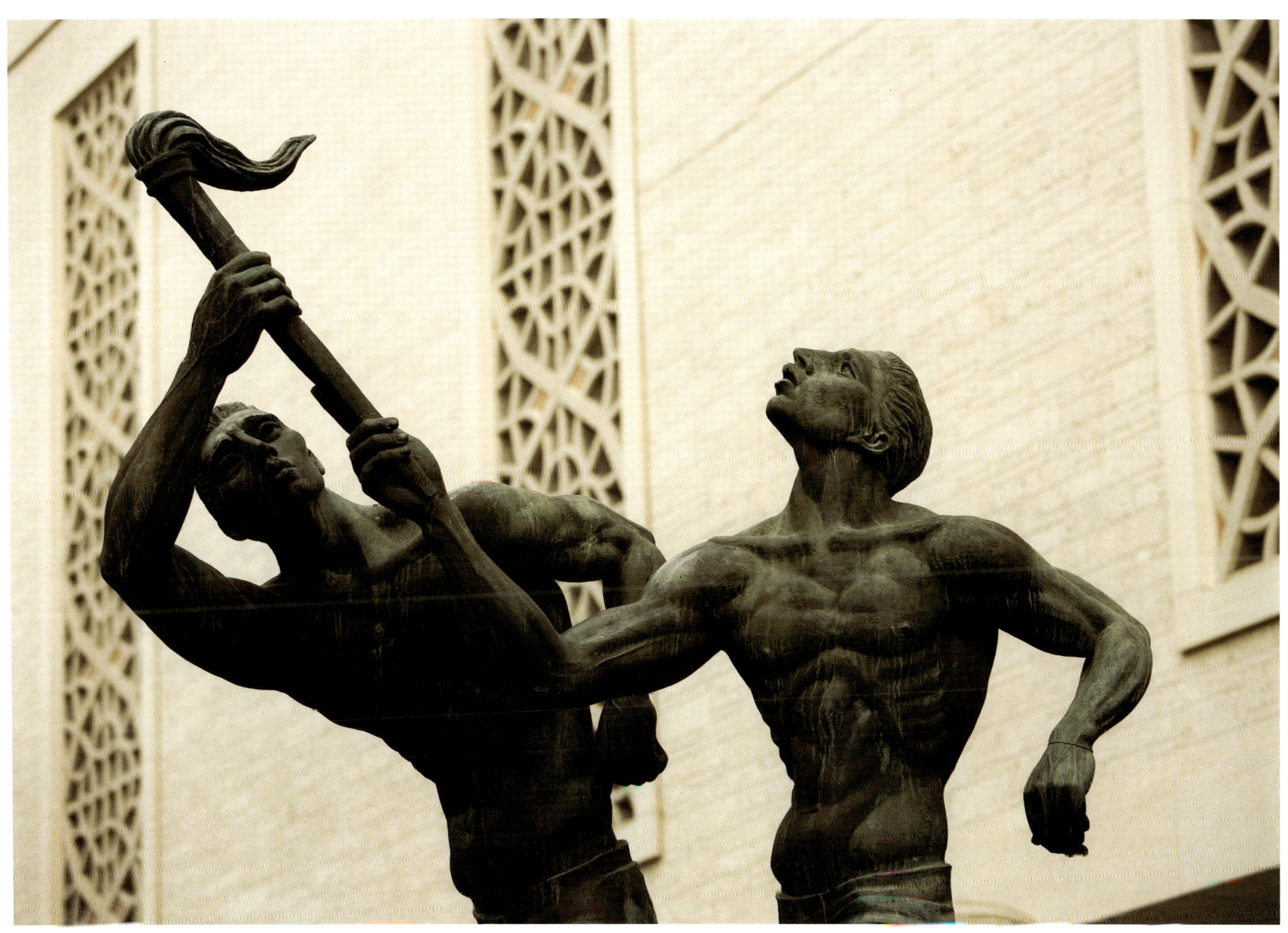

In front of the Flawn Academic Center, "The Torch Bearers," a 12 1/2 -foot bronze statue by Charles Umlauf, symbolizes the passing of knowledge from one generation to the next.

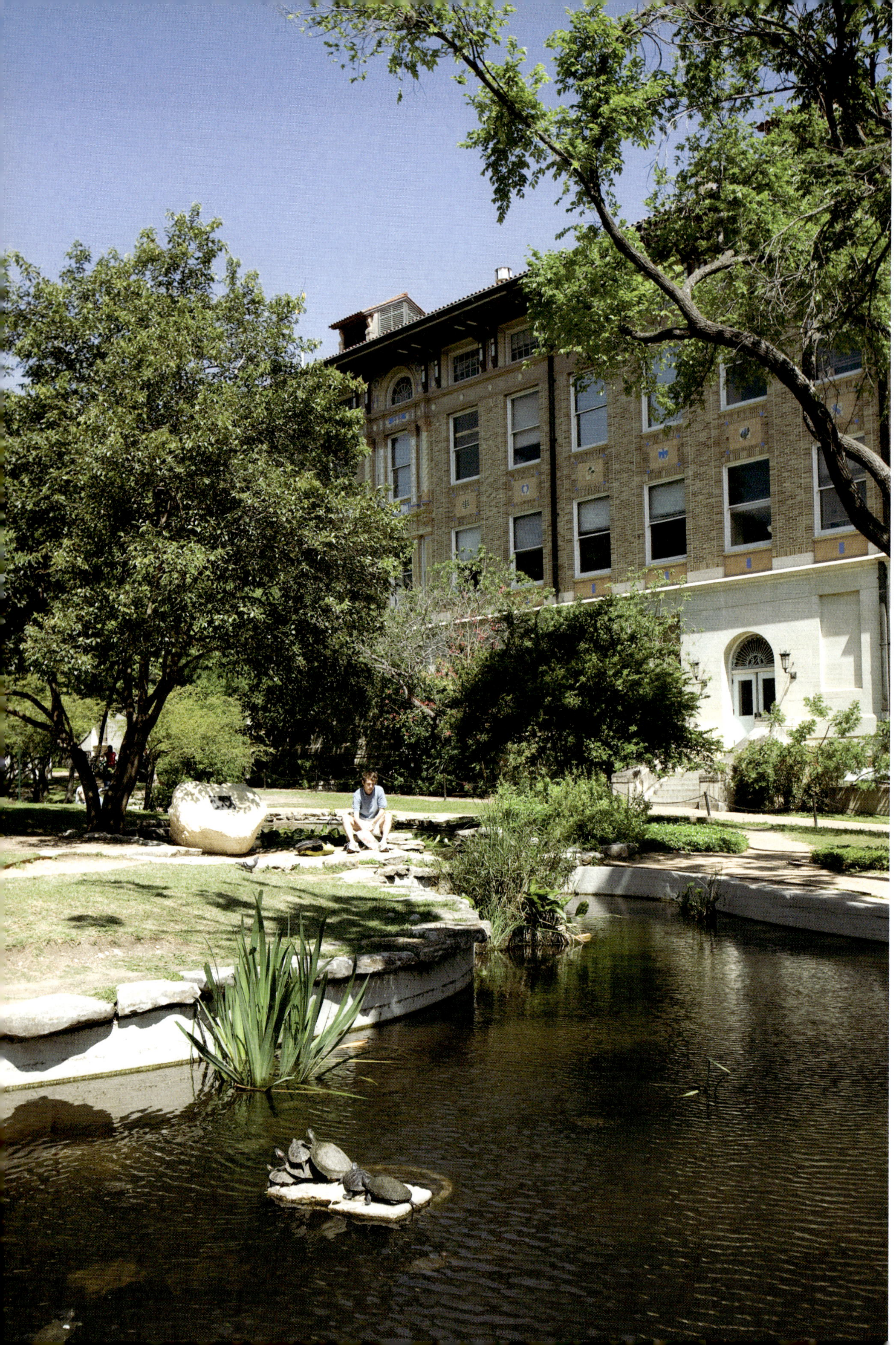

Left Just northeast of the Texas Union is the Biological Laboratories Building. Built in 1925 and now home to the Botany Department, its labs have been used for notable early research in genetics.

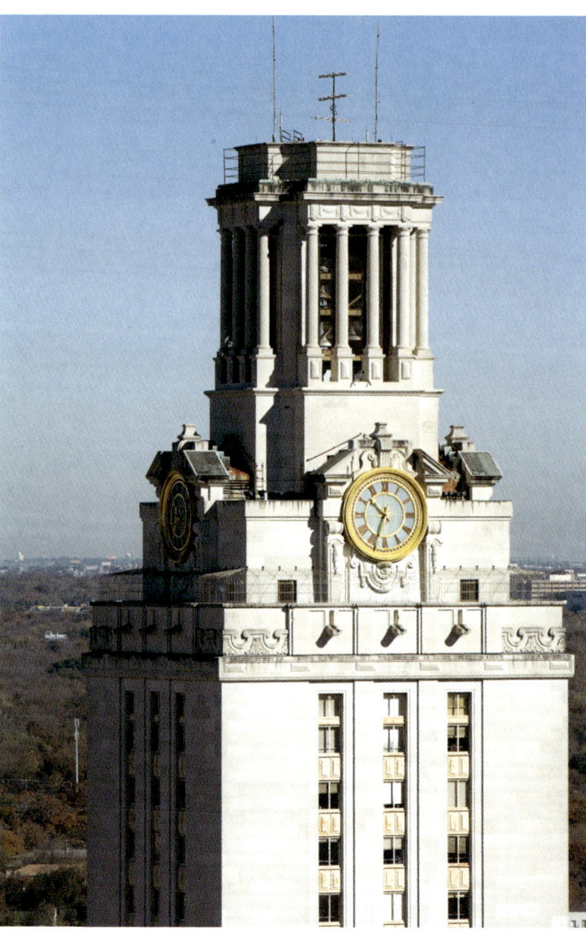

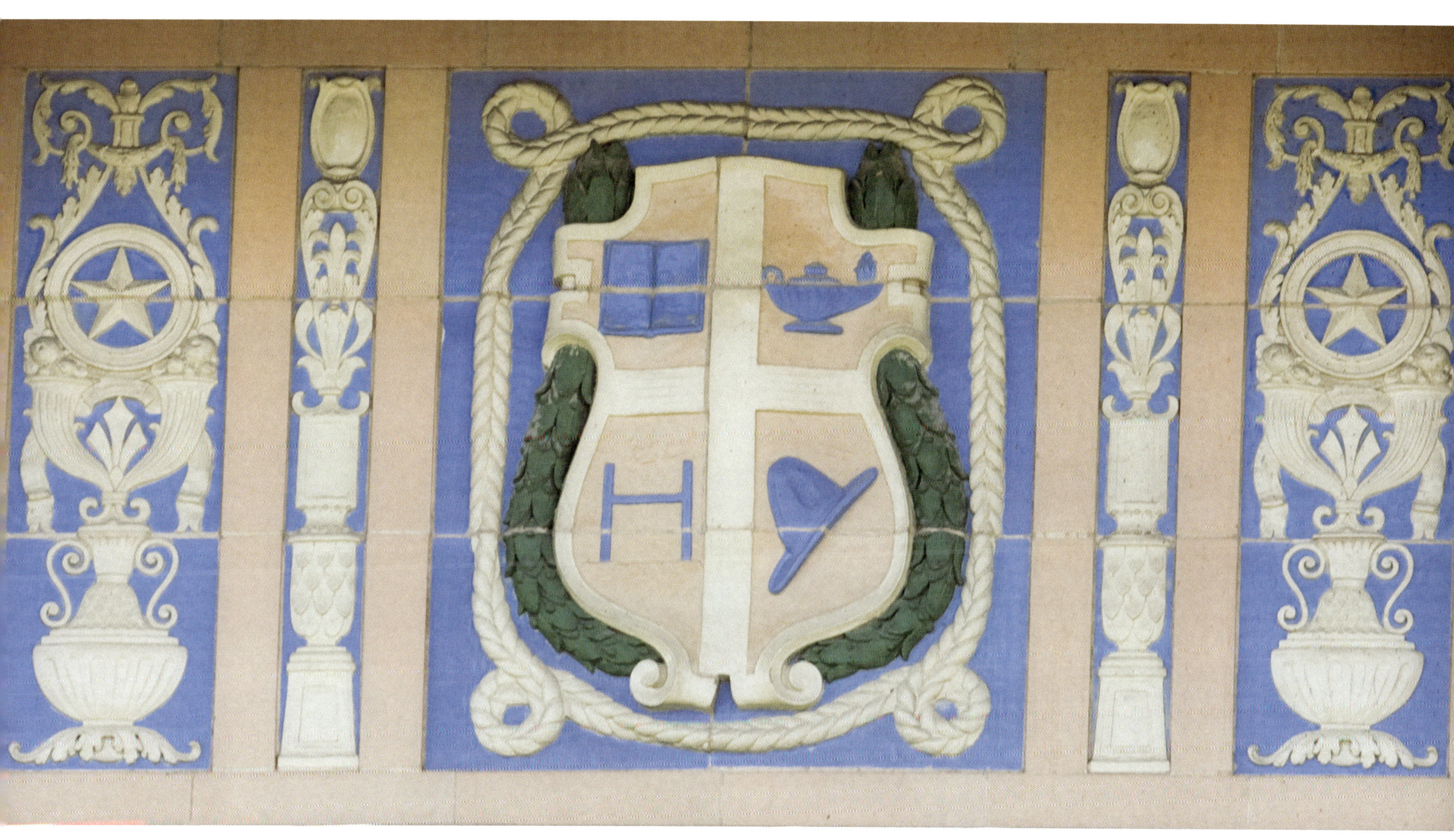

Designed by the Herbert Greene firm of Dallas, the Biological Laboratories Building is a departure from the classical look of Battle and Sutton Halls. Texas-themed icons can be found on the building, including stars, longhorn skulls and bluebonnets. This terra cotta shield, which appears under the eaves, relates four aspects of college life in Austin: an open book of knowledge, the lamp of wisdom; a ten-gallon hat, symbolic of a unique Texas culture; and a football goal post to indicate athletics and extracurricular activities.

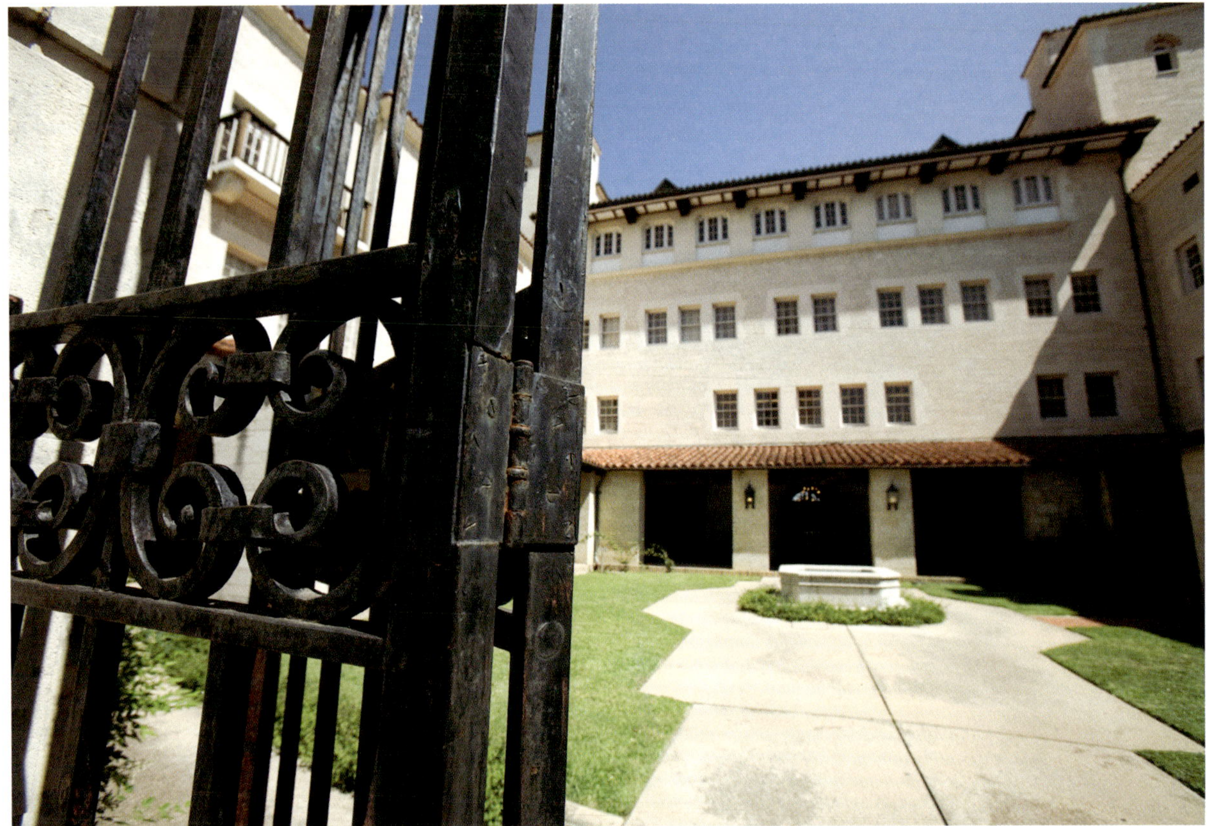

Northeast of the Biological Laboratories stands Mary Gearing Hall, home to the Department of Human Ecology. Opened in 1933 as the Home Economics Building, it was renamed in 1976 for Mary Gearing, the first chair of the department.

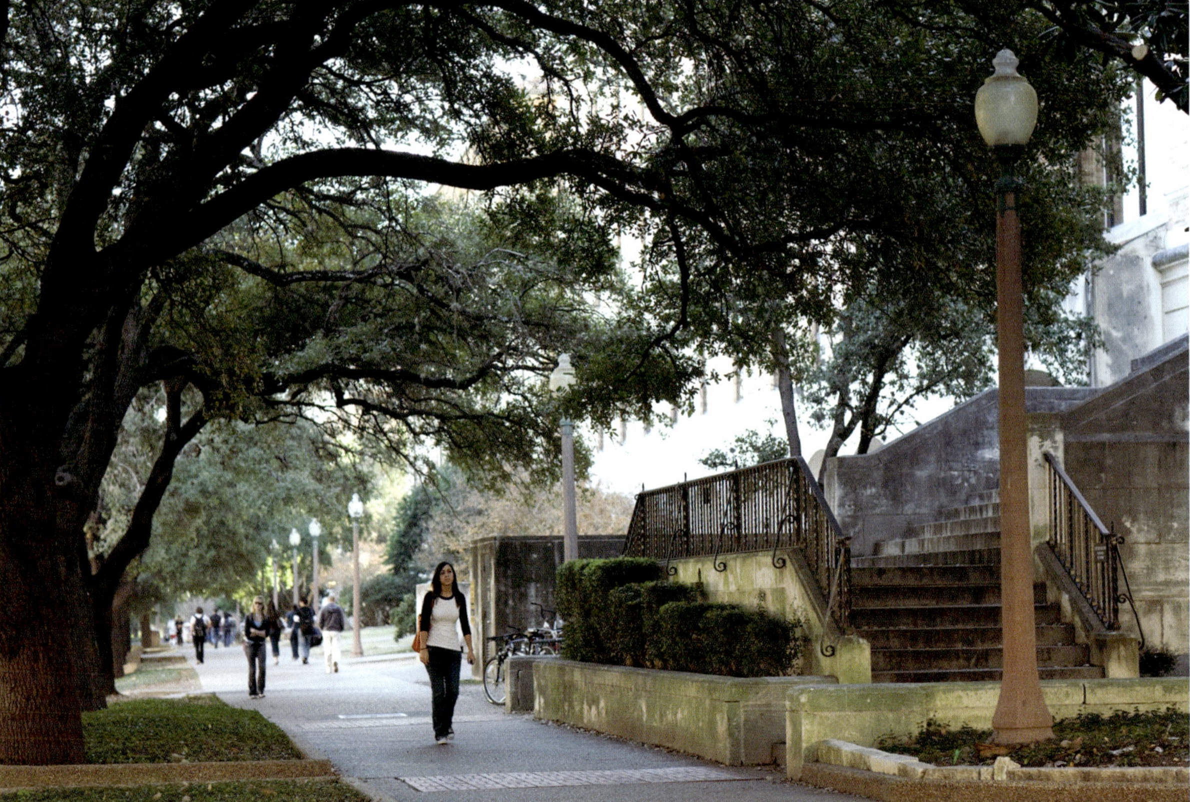

Despite the intense Texas sun, students traversing the walks around the campus are sheltered under expansive live oak trees.

Right Completed in 1937 as the University's central library, the Main Building and Tower is the iconic landmark of the campus. While it still contains a Life Sciences Library, the Main Building is primarily used by the University administration.

Below The four faces of the Tower clock are more than 12 feet in diameter and covered in gold leaf. The Knicker Carillon at the top of the Tower is comprised of 56 bells, the largest in Texas.

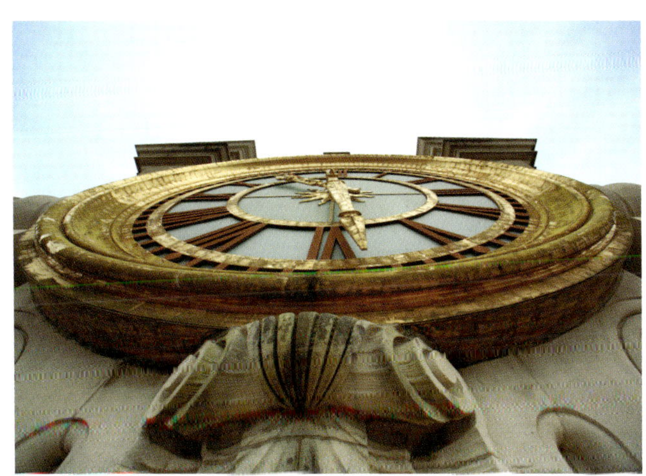

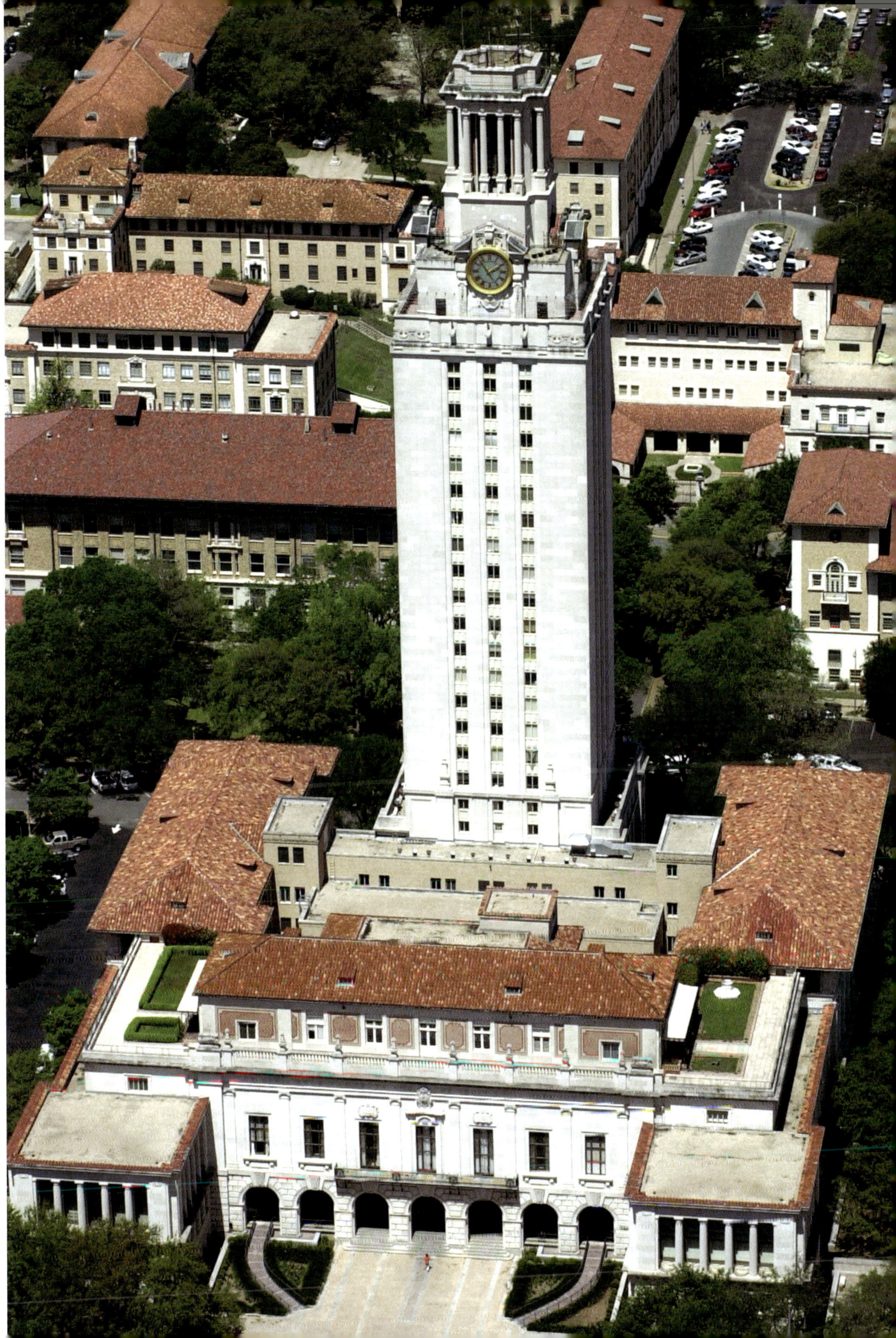

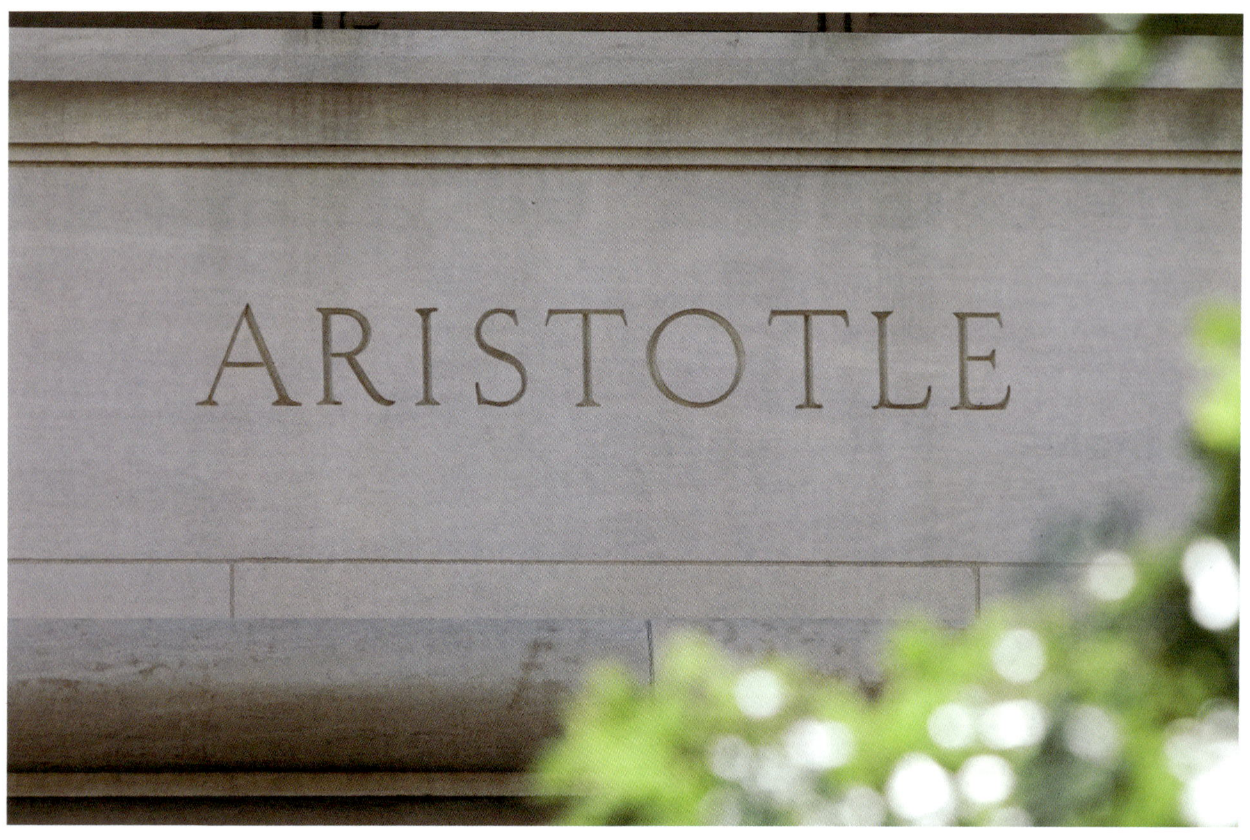

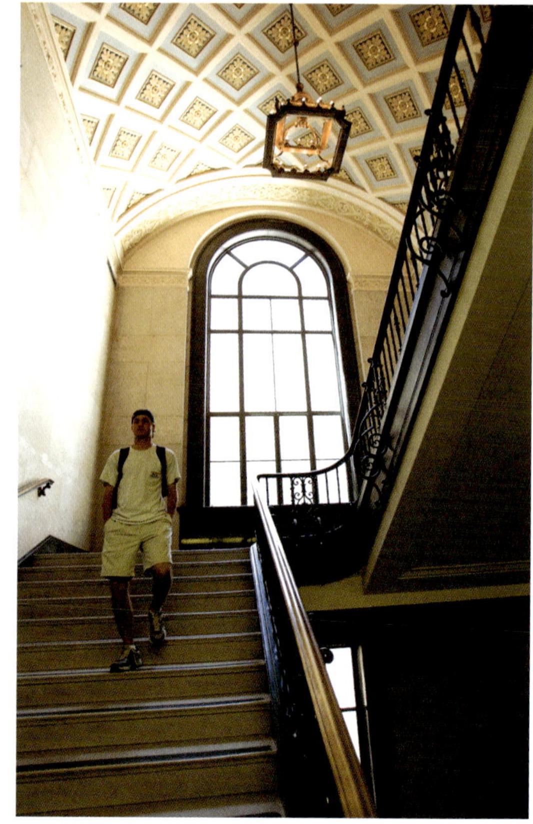

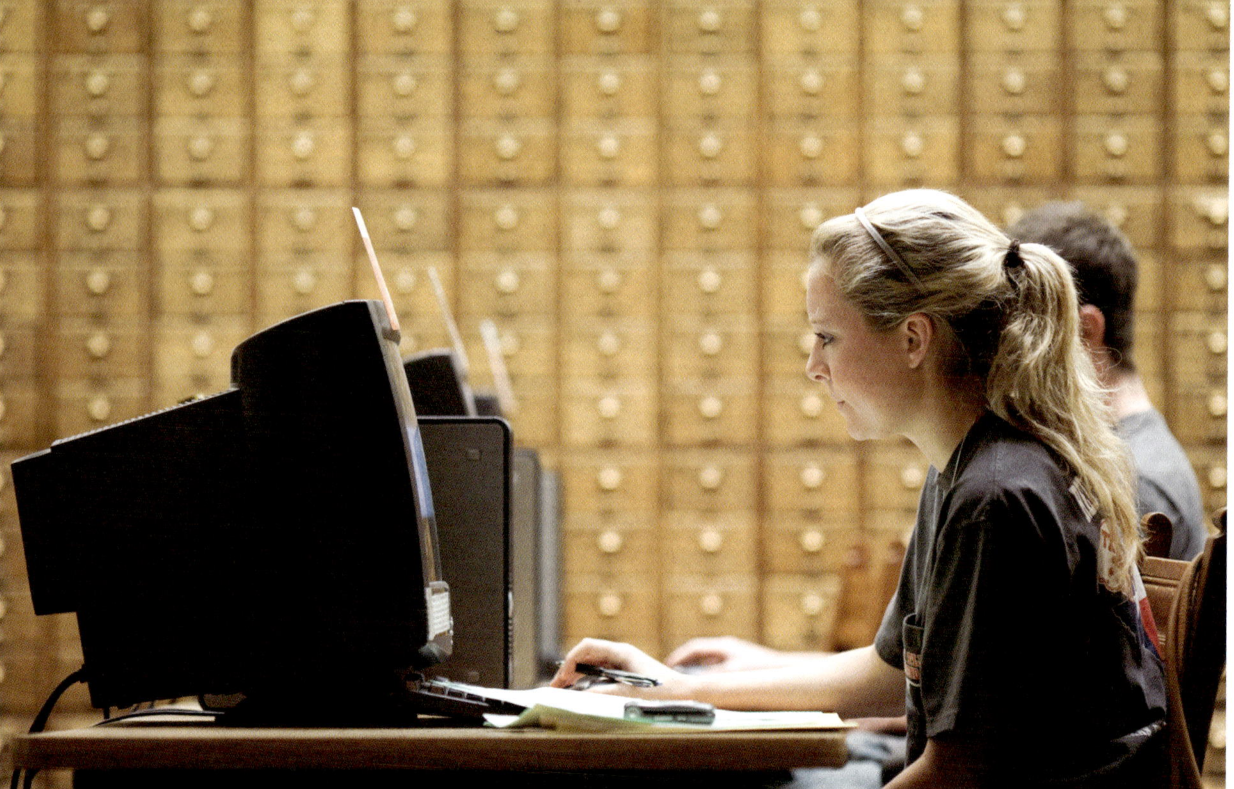

Above Left Inscribed under the tall windows along the east and west sides of the Main Building are 14 names distinguished in literature, including Aristotle, Dante, Cervantes, and Mark Twain. Above the windows are the seals of 12 universities significant in the development of higher education, among them Paris, Oxford, Harvard, and Vassar. On the north side of the building, displayed in gold leaf, are letters and hieroglyphs of languages from which English evolved: Egyptian, Phoenician, Hebrew, Greek, and Latin.

Above A student traverses the grand stairway of the Main Building that leads to the second floor library.

Left Changing with the times. The Main Building's old card catalog is a backdrop to the more modern online resources.

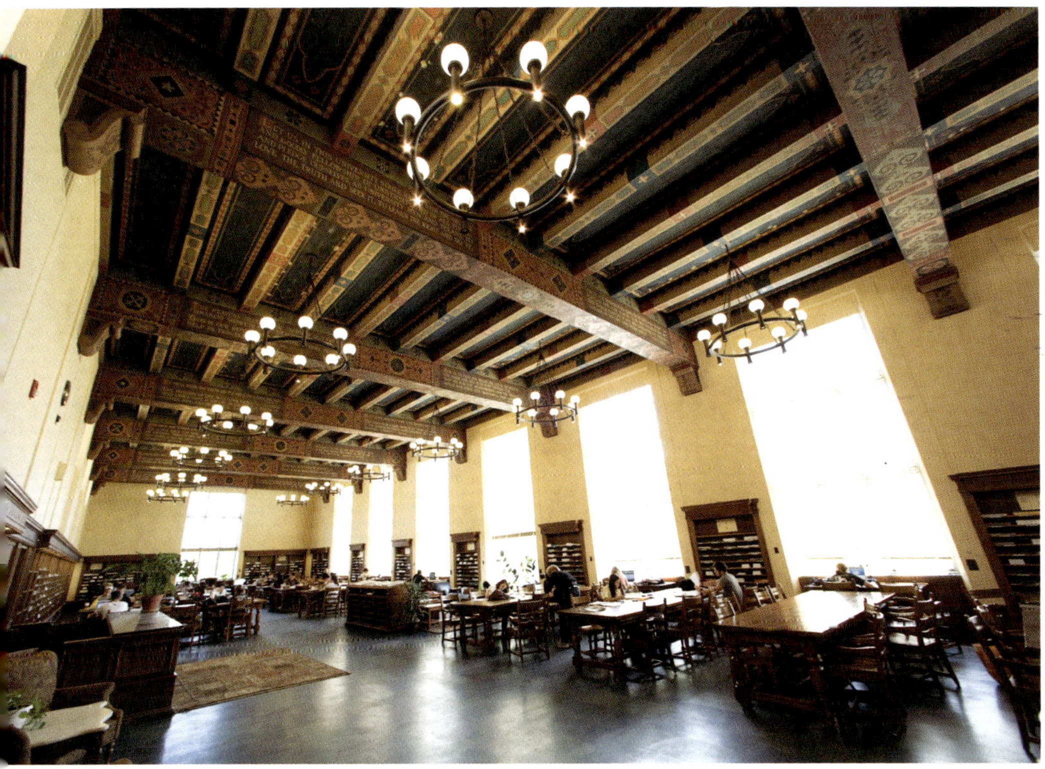

One of a pair of cavernous reading rooms, the Hall of Noble Words spans the east side of the Main Building. On the west side, the Hall of Texas houses part of the University's extensive Plant Resources Center.

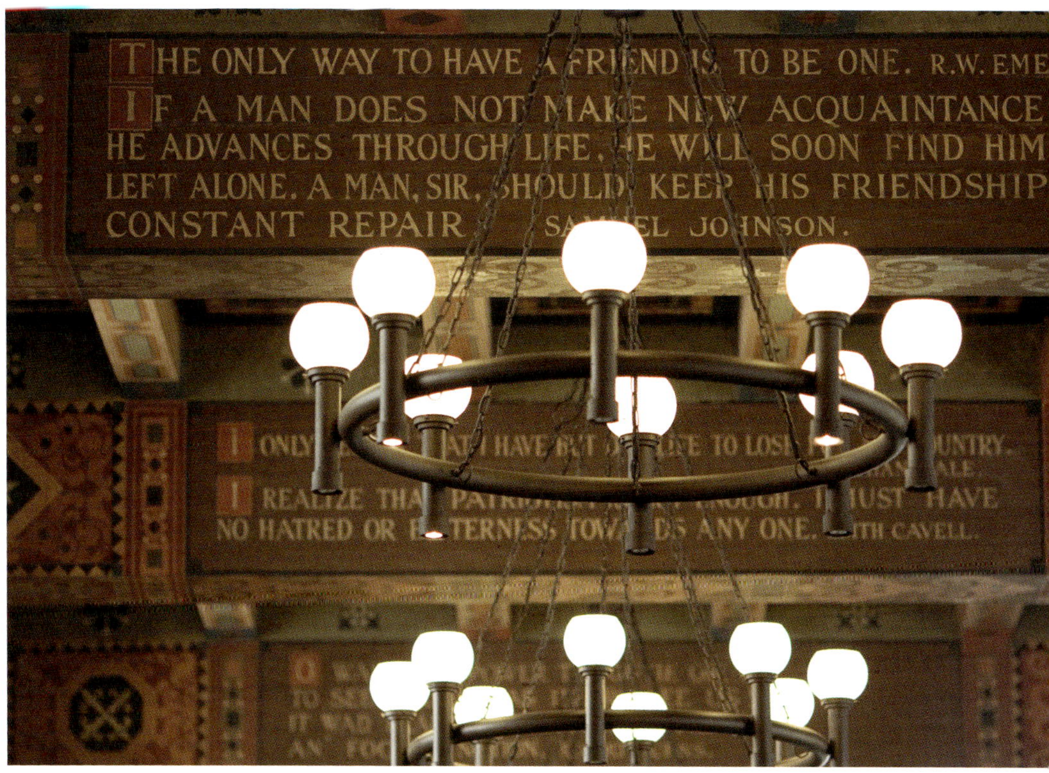

In the Hall of Noble Words, each side of a ceiling beam is decorated with quotes and exhortations within a specific theme. Displayed here from the top of the image are friendship, patriotism, and good judgment. The supporting brackets of the beams are embossed with the signature marks of famous printers in the 15th and 16th centuries.

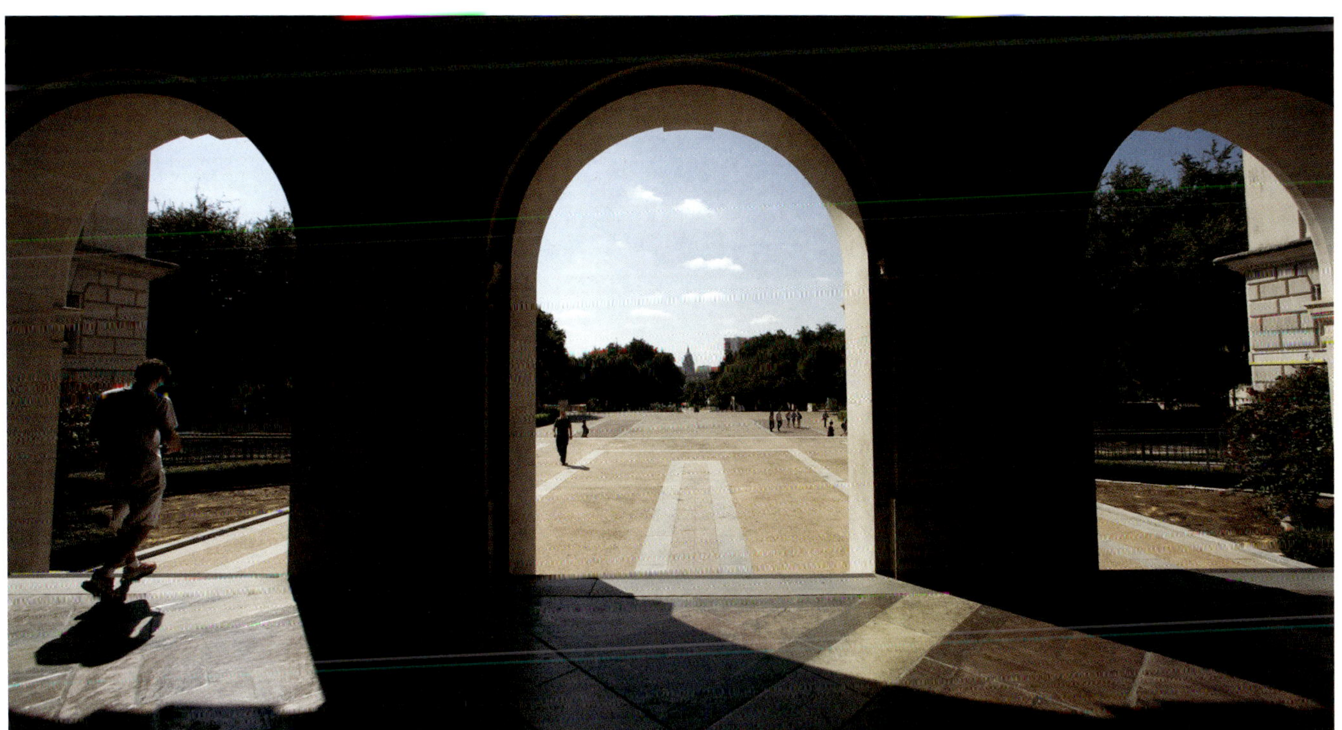

The spacious loggia of the Main Building, sometimes considered the "front porch" of the University, possesses a commanding view of the Main Mall and the dome of the Texas Capitol beyond.

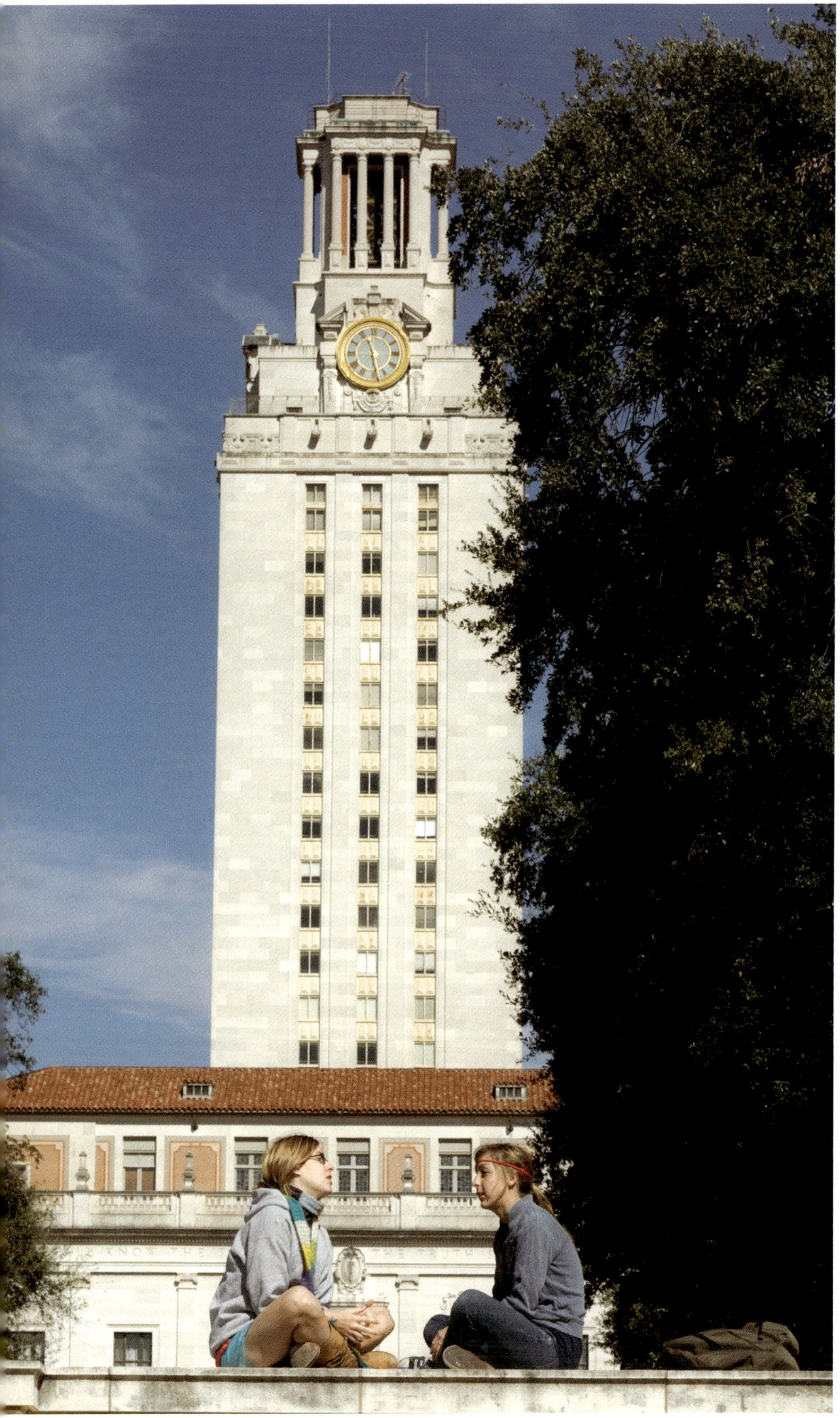

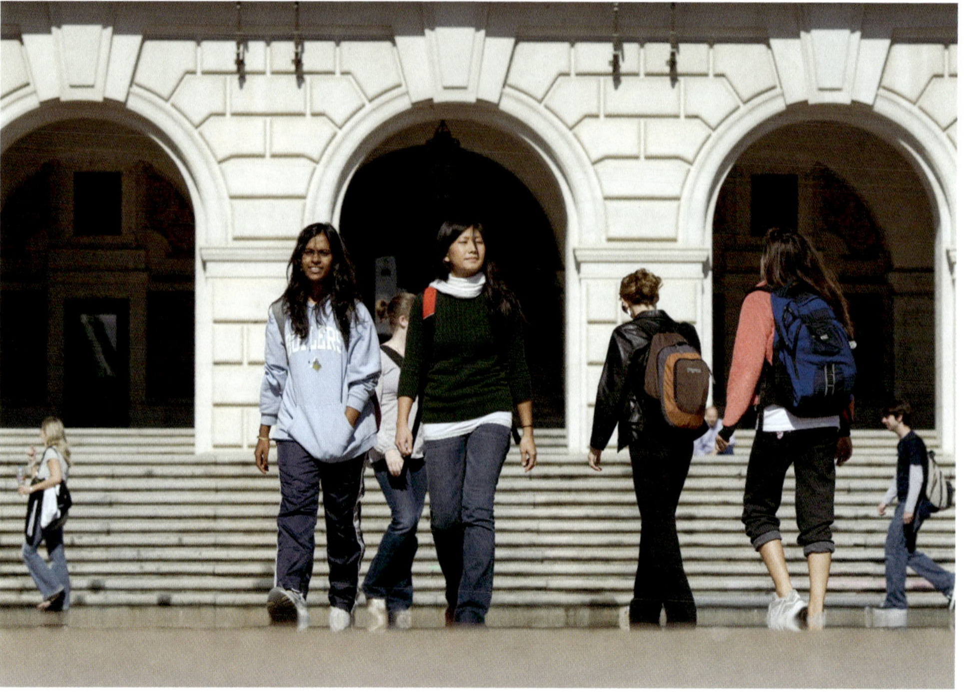

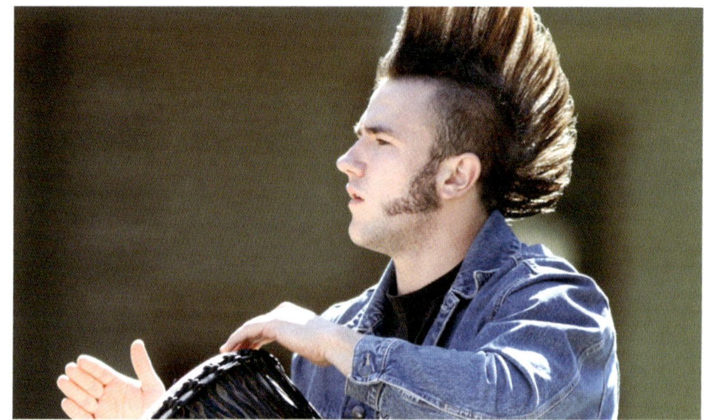

Left The Main Mall, directly in front of the Tower, is the heart of the campus. Ever since the University opened in 1883, the area in front of the Main Building (whether it was the Victorian-Gothic Old Main, or the current Main Building and Tower) has served as a stage for countless rallies, protests and celebrations.

Top Students walk the Main Mall between classes.

Facing Page In 1941, students consulted Madame Augusta Hipple, a local fortune teller, as to the best way to defeat Texas A&M on the football field. She advised burning red candles the week before the game to unite the Longhorn spirit. The trick worked, and red candles have been employed for various big games through the years. The tradition was absent in the late 1960s and 1970s, but returned in 1986 in the form of the annual Texas Hex Rally.

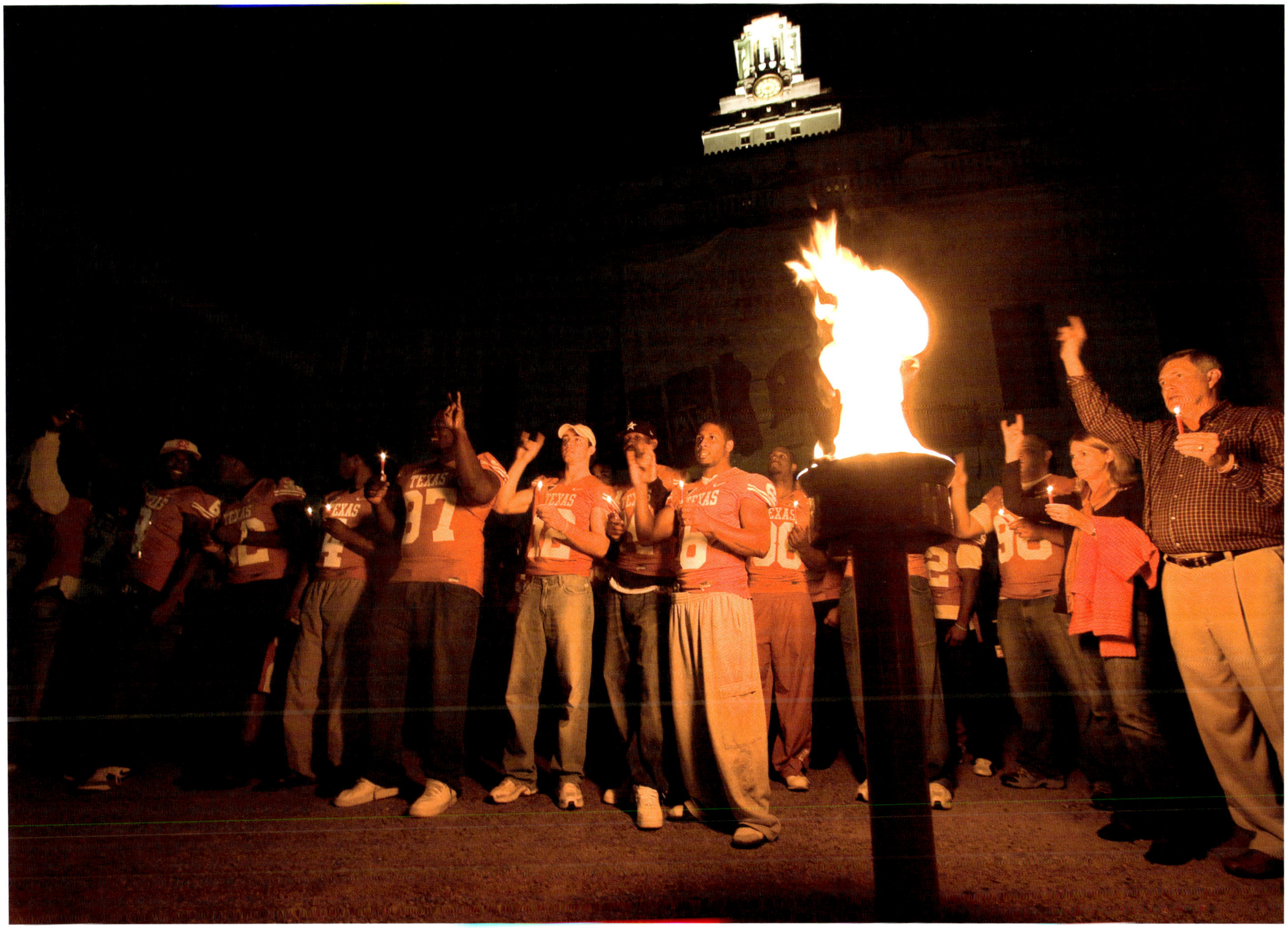

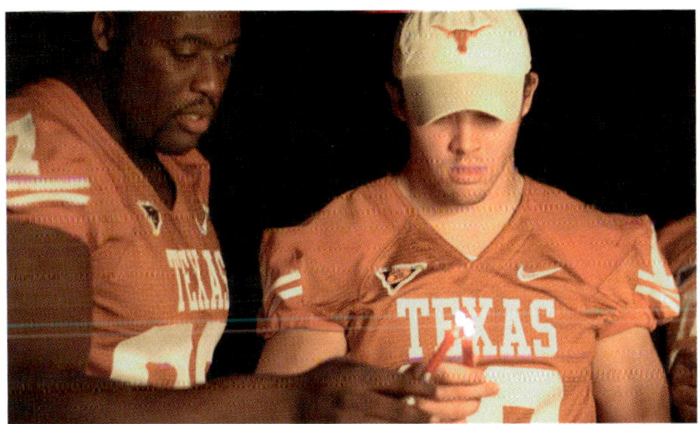
TEXAS

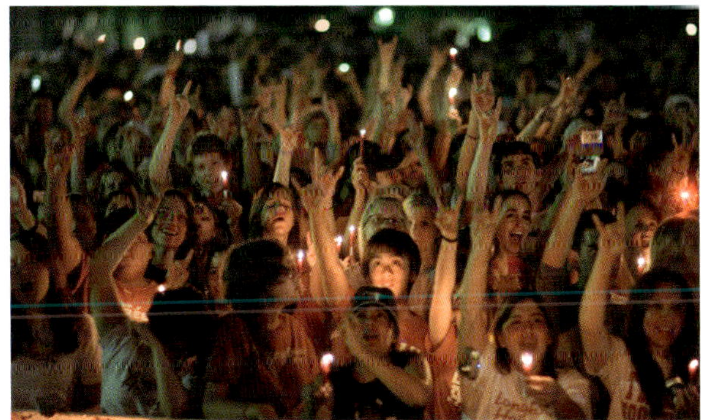

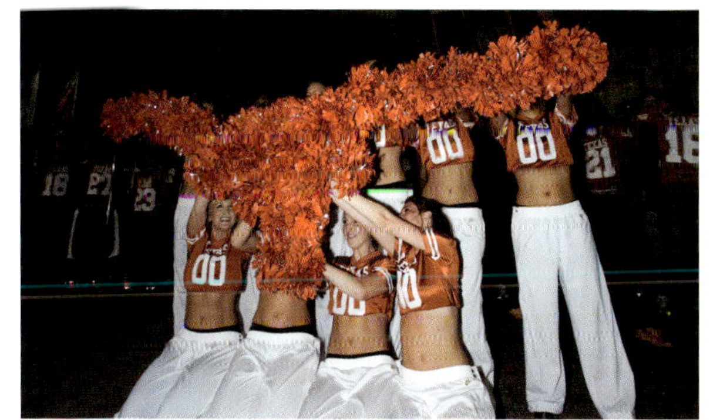

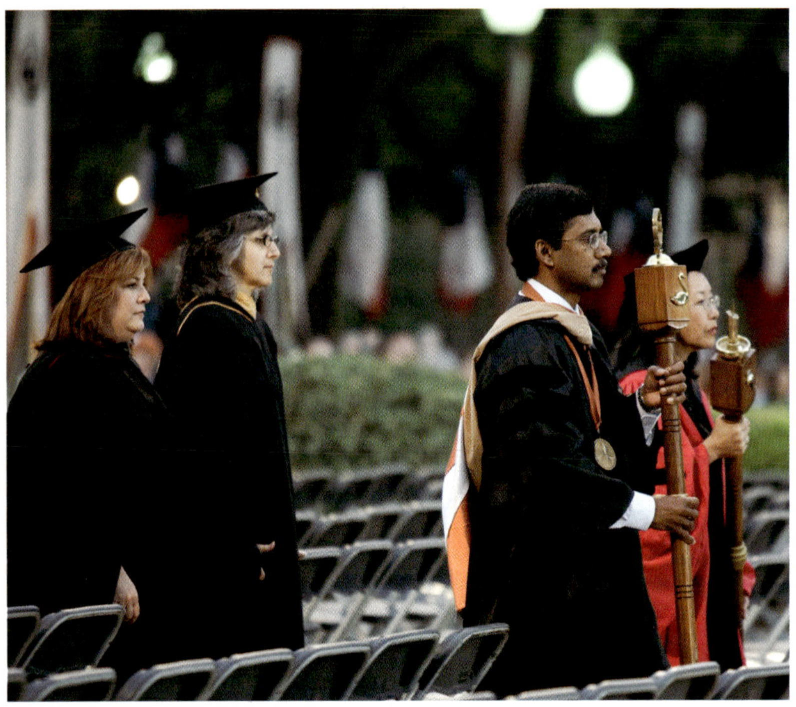

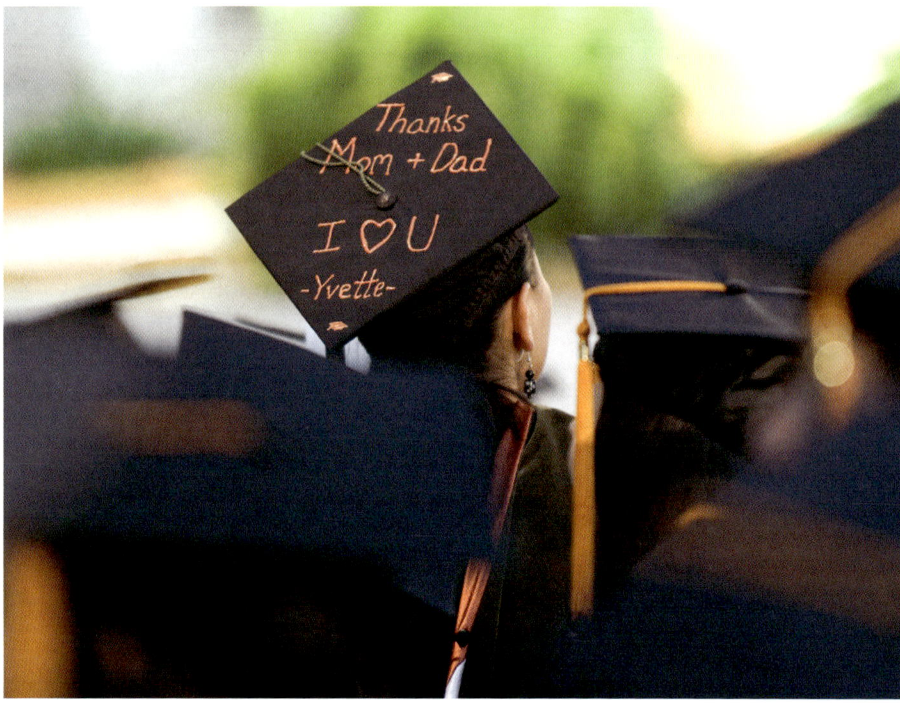

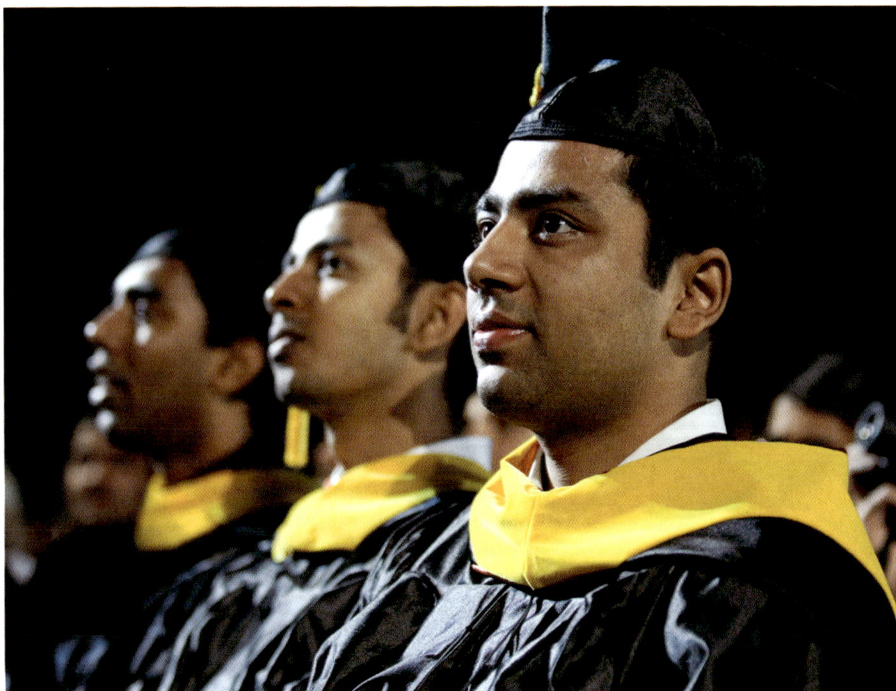

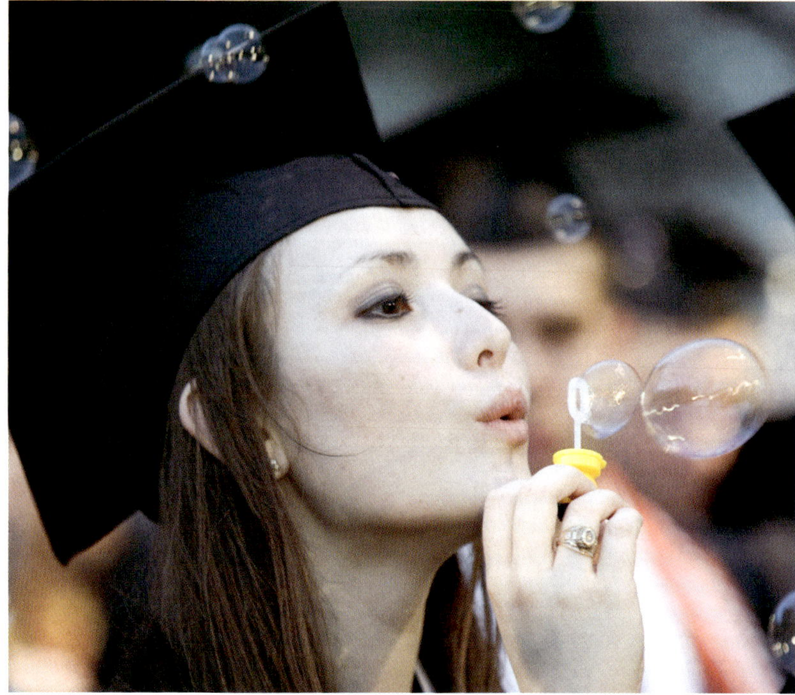

Spring Commencement has always been the capstone event of the academic year. On June 14, 1884, thirteen law degrees were presented at the first ceremony in Millet's Opera House in downtown Austin. Today, more than 11,000 degrees from fifteen schools and colleges are awarded annually, and the grand ceremony on the Main Mall has become an elaborate production, complete with special lighting, colorful banners and fireworks.

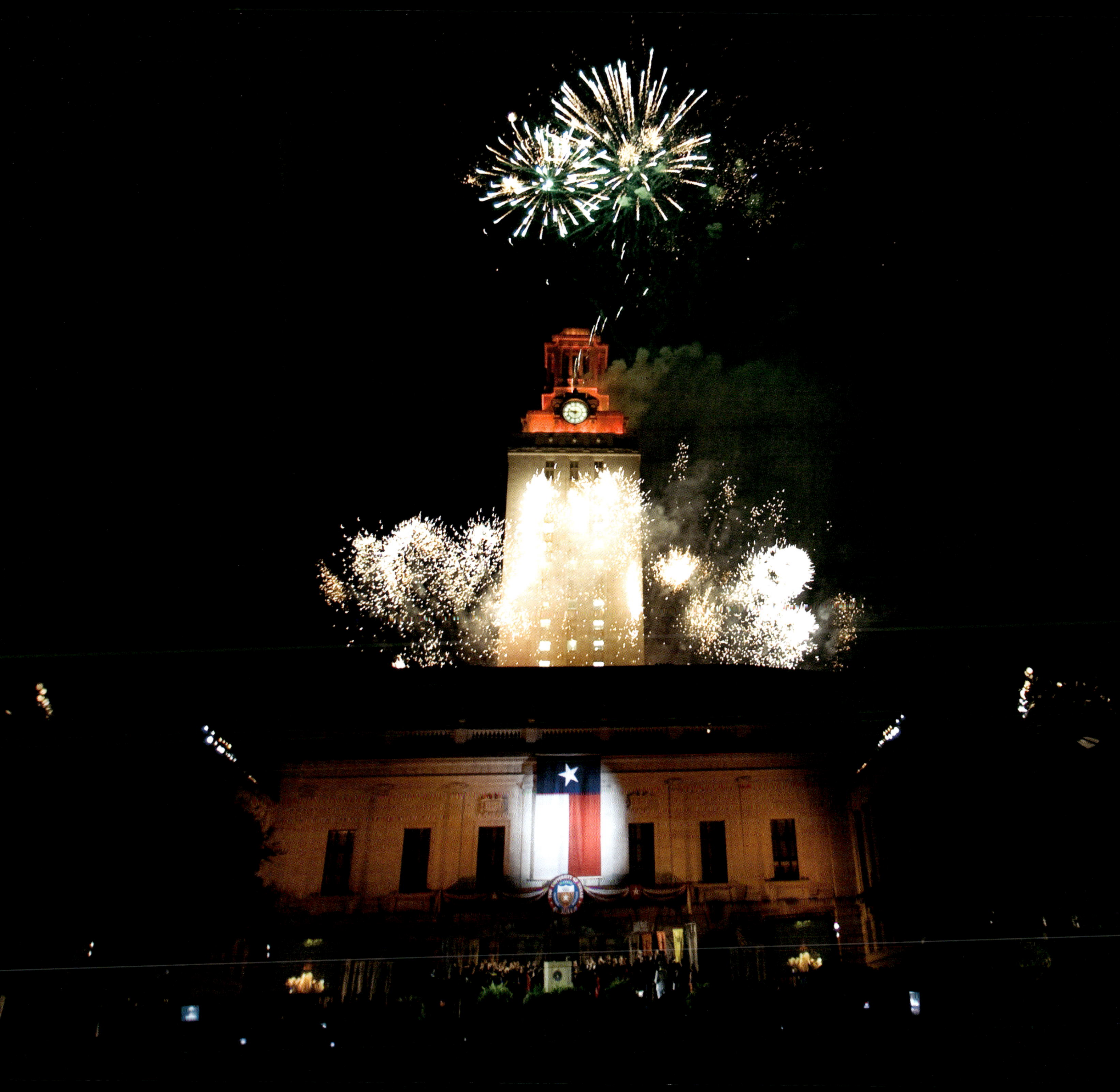

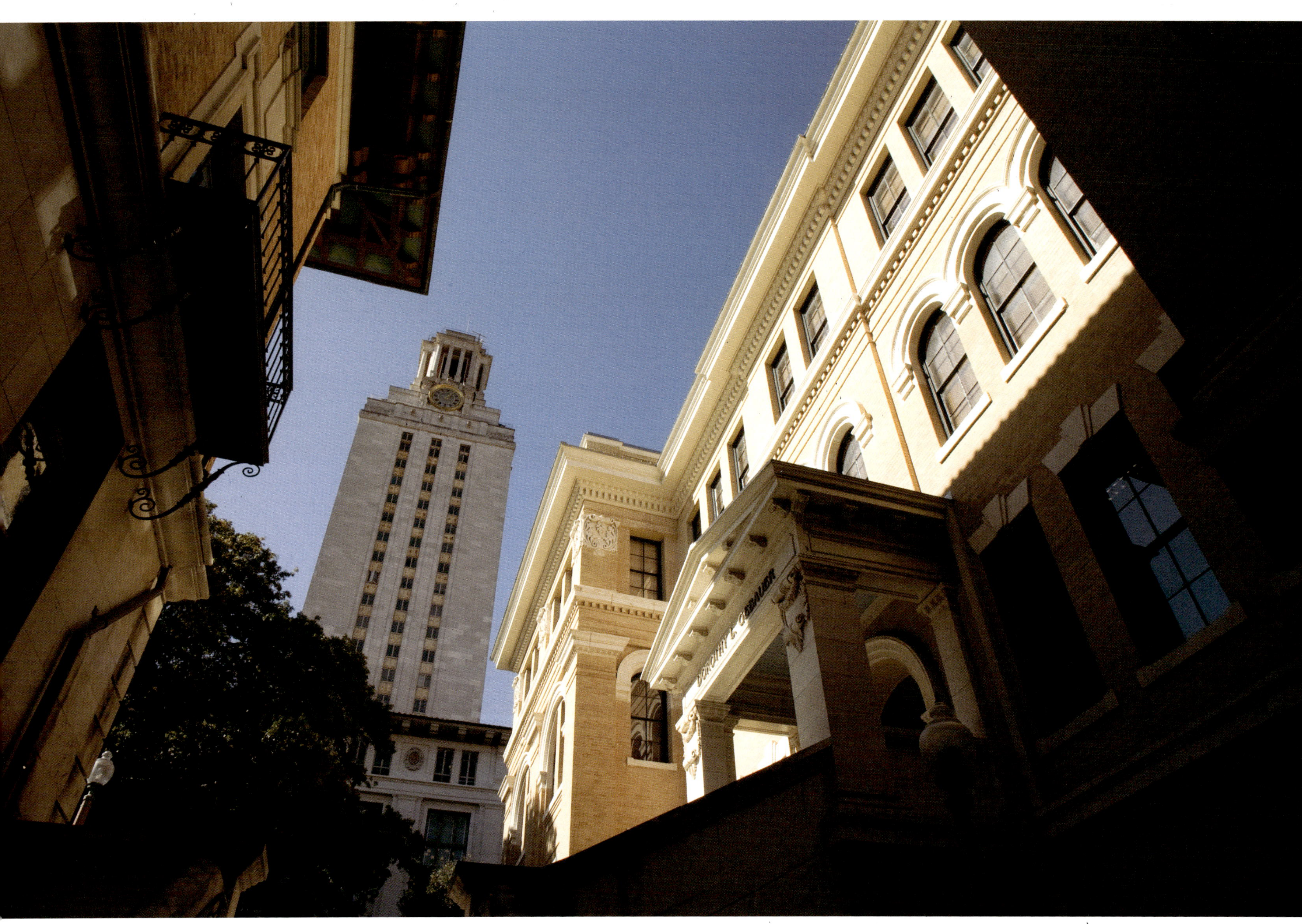

A view of the Tower framed by the W.C. Hogg Building on the left and the Gebauer Building on the right. Opened in 1904 for what was then the Engineering Department, Gebauer is the oldest surviving University building and is today the headquarters for the College of Liberal Arts.

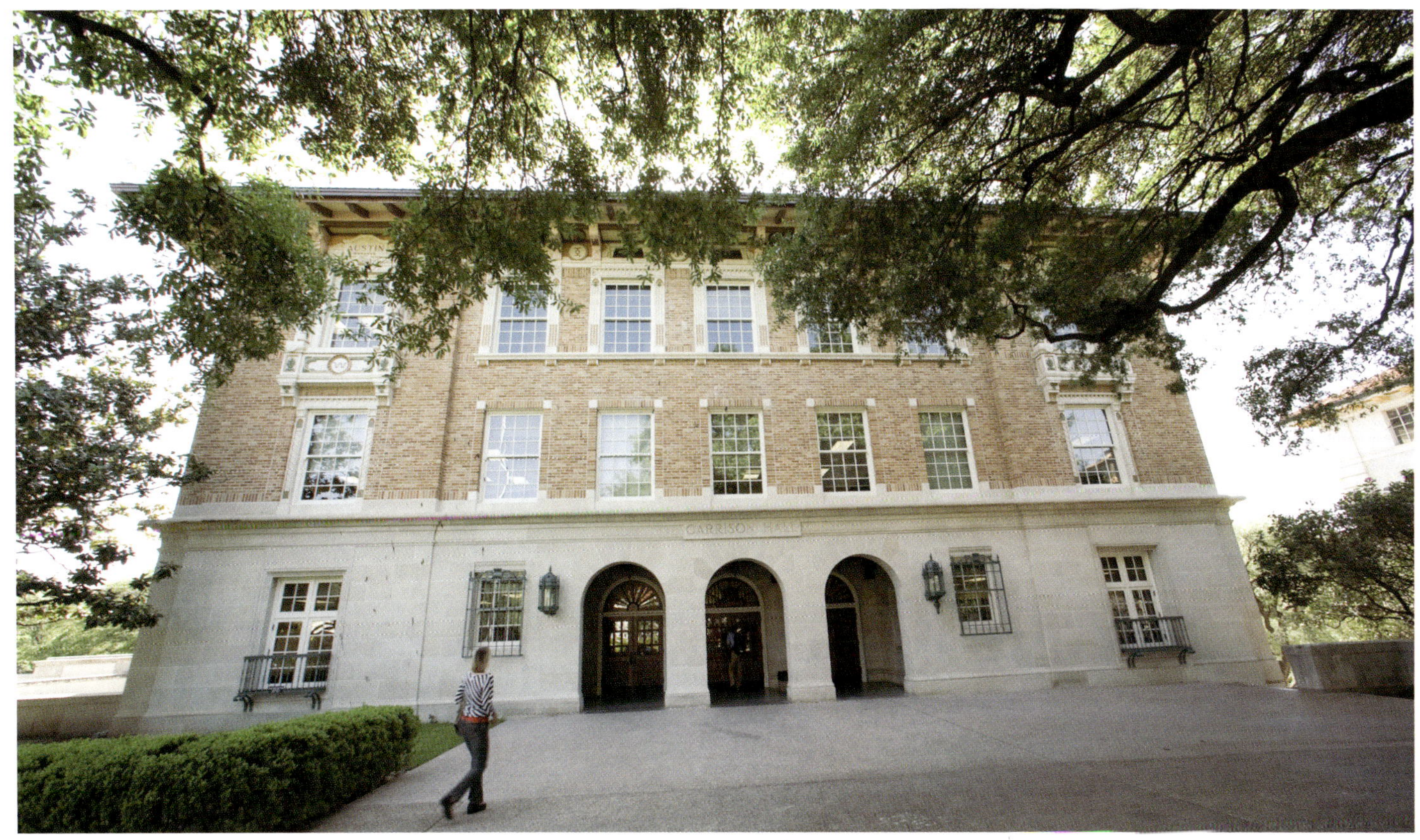

Southeast of the Main Building stands Garrison Hall, used by the Department of History. It was opened in 1926 and named for George Garrison, one of UT's earliest professors and the first chair of the history department.

Like the Biological Laboratories, Garrison Hall's ornamentation is unmistakably Texan. Limestone carvings of longhorn skulls, cacti, and bluebonnets decorate the entrances. Imprinted below the eaves are the names of statesmen from the Republic of Texas, among them Houston, Austin, Travis, and Lamar. And 32 terra cotta cattle brands adorn the building, carefully chosen to represent various periods in the development of Texas. Pictured is the wavy W brand of the King Ranch.

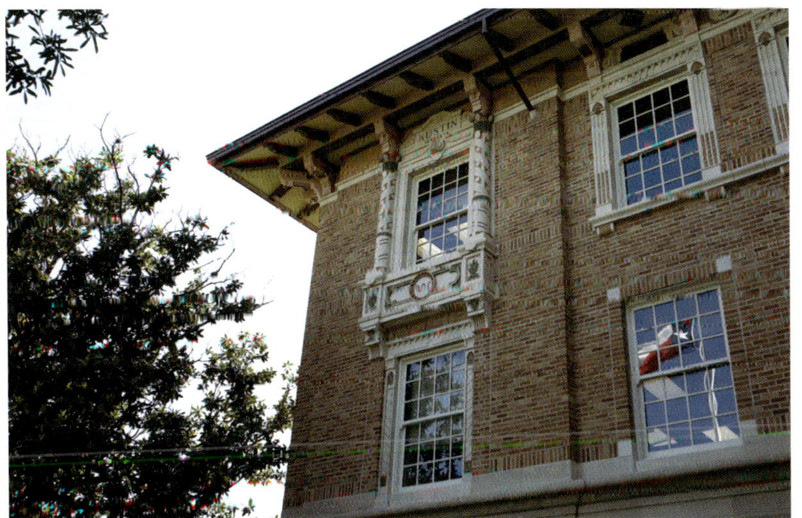

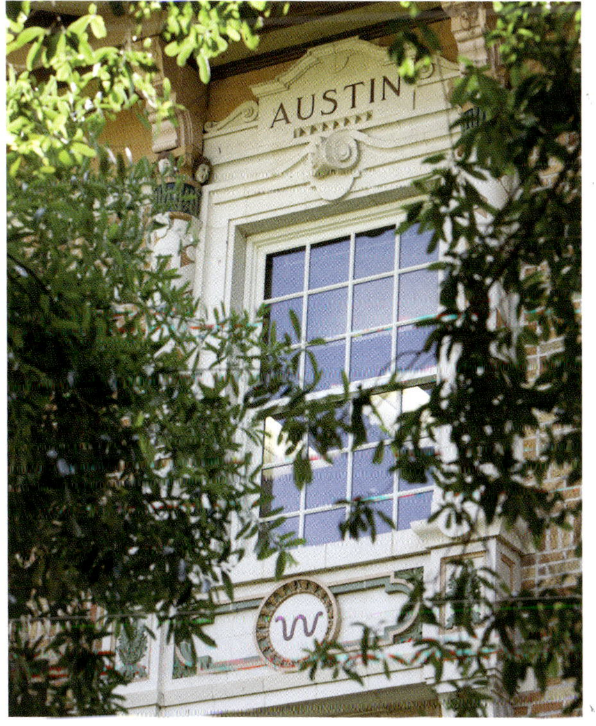

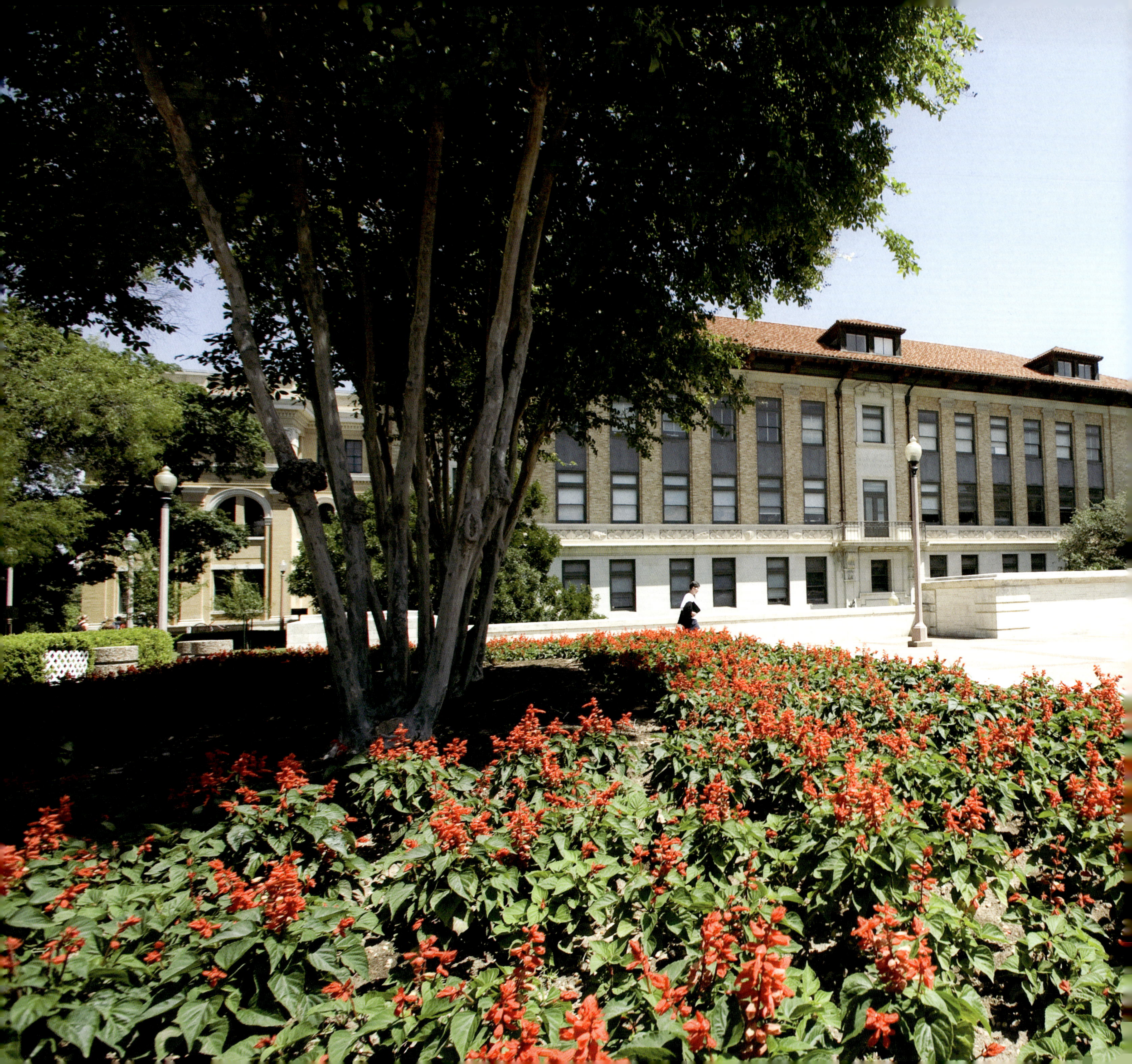

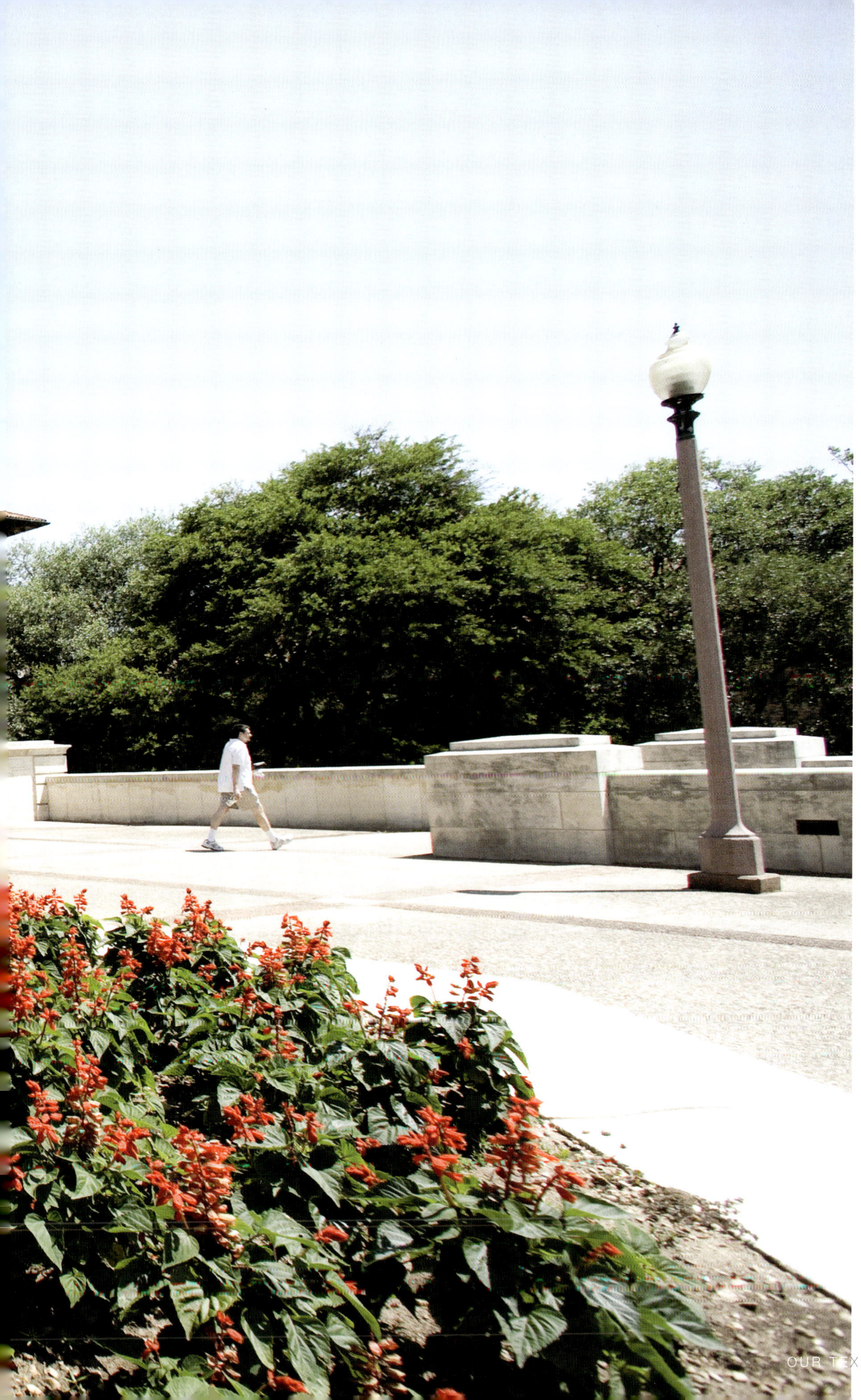

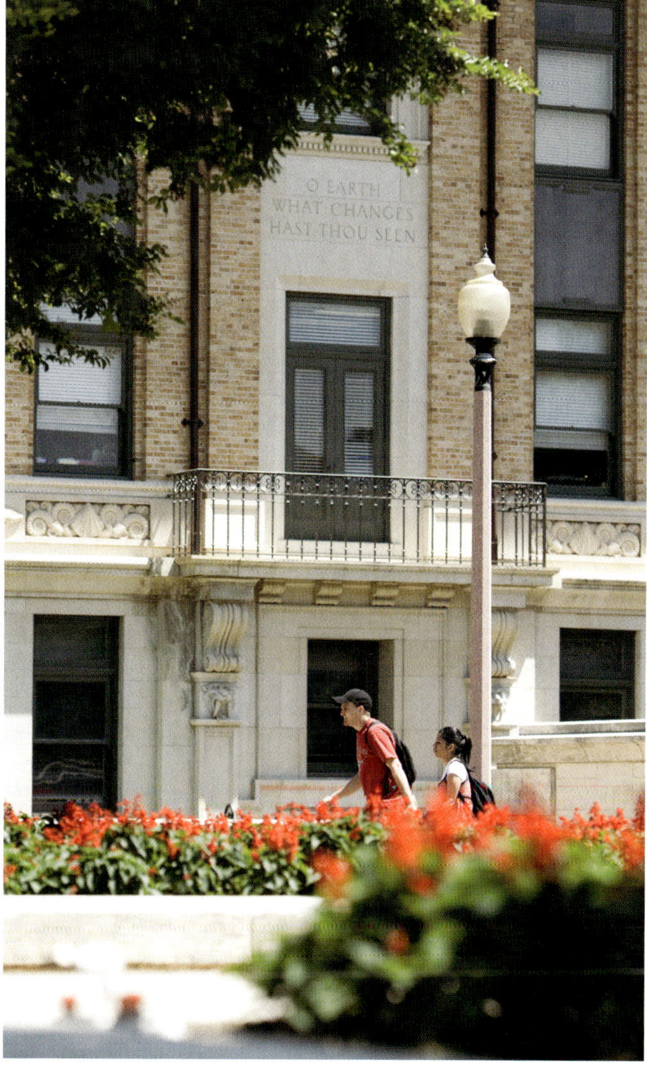

Left Due north of Garrison Hall, across the East Mall, is the W.C. Hogg Building, home of the College of Natural Sciences. Will C. Hogg was a law graduate of the University, served on the Board of Regents, and was an important benefactor.

Above Dedicated in 1933 and initially used by the geology department, the exterior of the Hogg Building is girded by a series of limestone friezes featuring ancient life, fossils, crystals, and ores. On the south side is a quote from Tennyson: "Ô Earth, what changes hast thou seen."

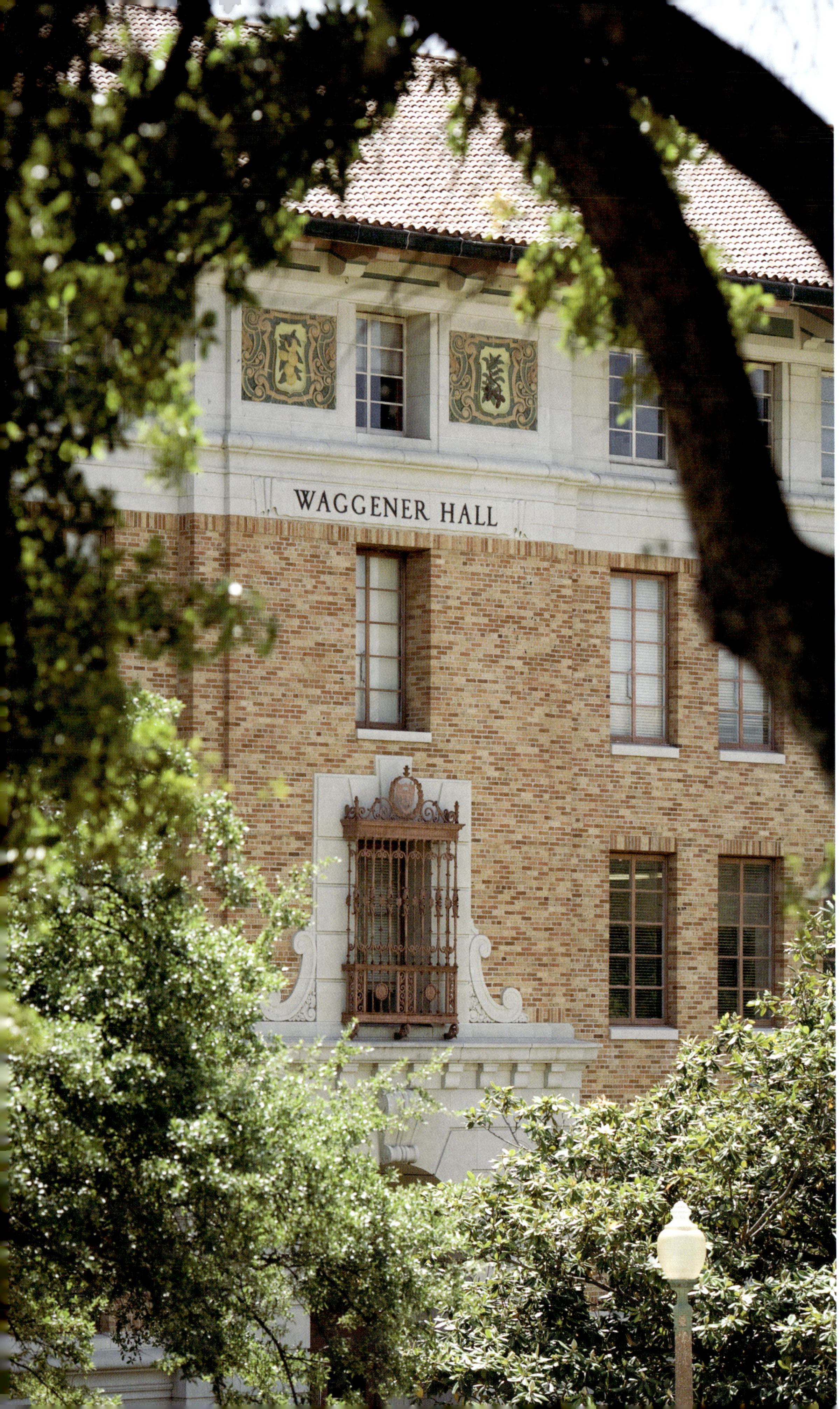

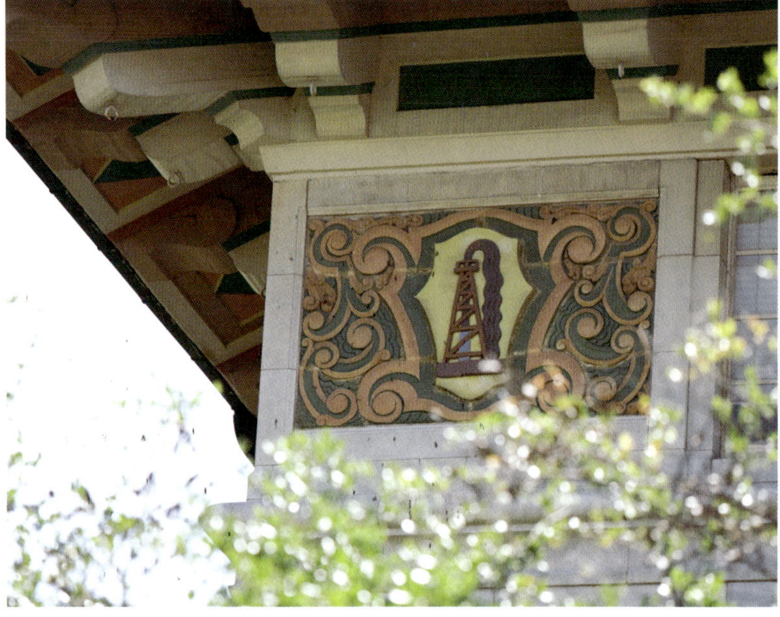

Left Named for Leslie Waggener, UT's first president, and constructed in 1931, Waggener Hall was initially used by the business school. It is now home for the classics and philosophy departments.

Above As with many other campus buildings, Waggener Hall's ornamentation indicates its original use. In this case, the terra cotta decoration displays exports of Texas, including cotton, citrus, pecans, cattle, and oil (pictured).

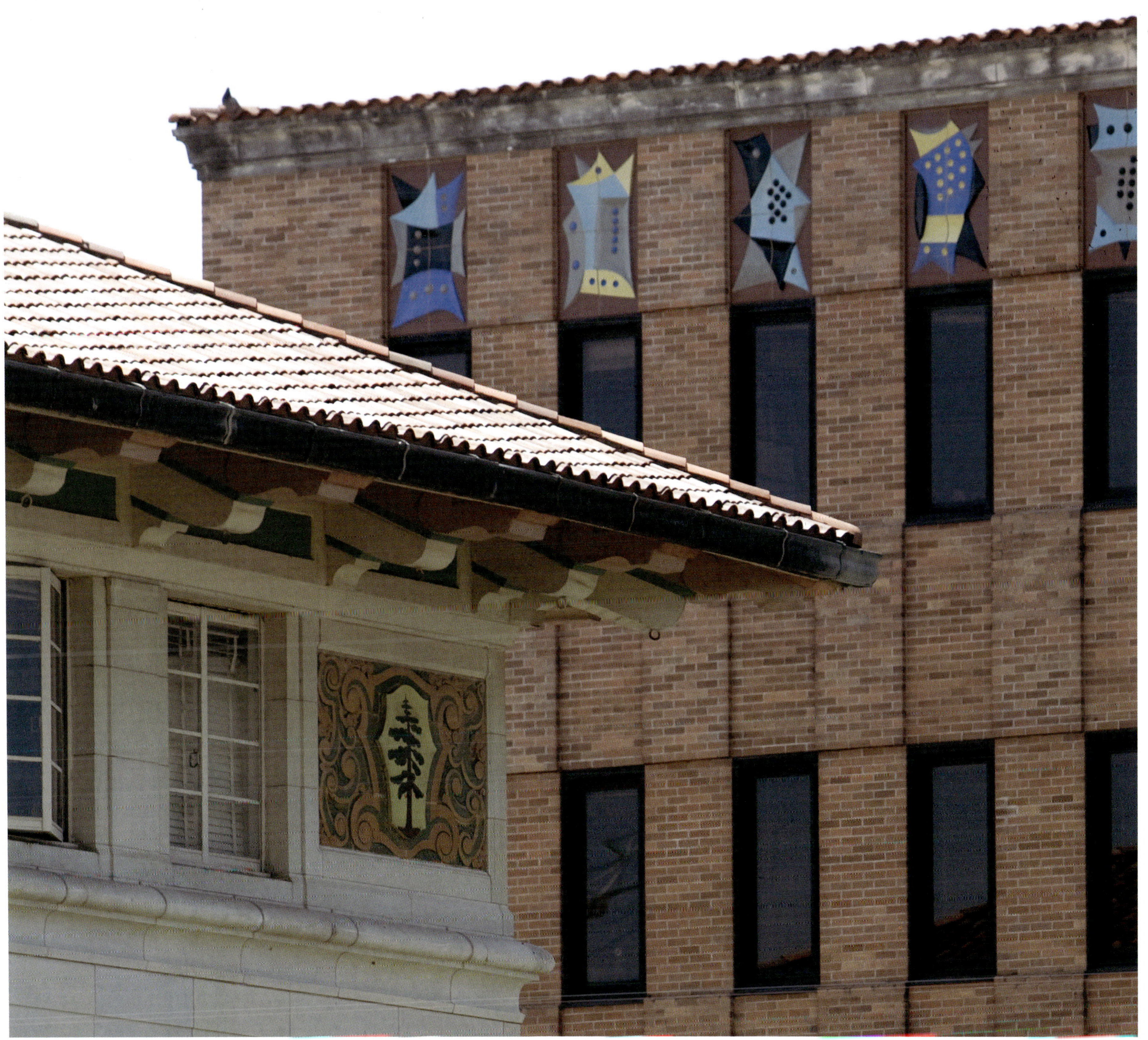

A look at the old and new. With Waggener Hall on the left, the business school moved into what was then called the Business Economics Building in 1962, the first campus structure with an escalator. It is now the Kozmetsky Center for Business Education. To brighten the building, 50 ceramic reliefs were installed above the top floor windows, designed by UT art professor Paul Hatgil.

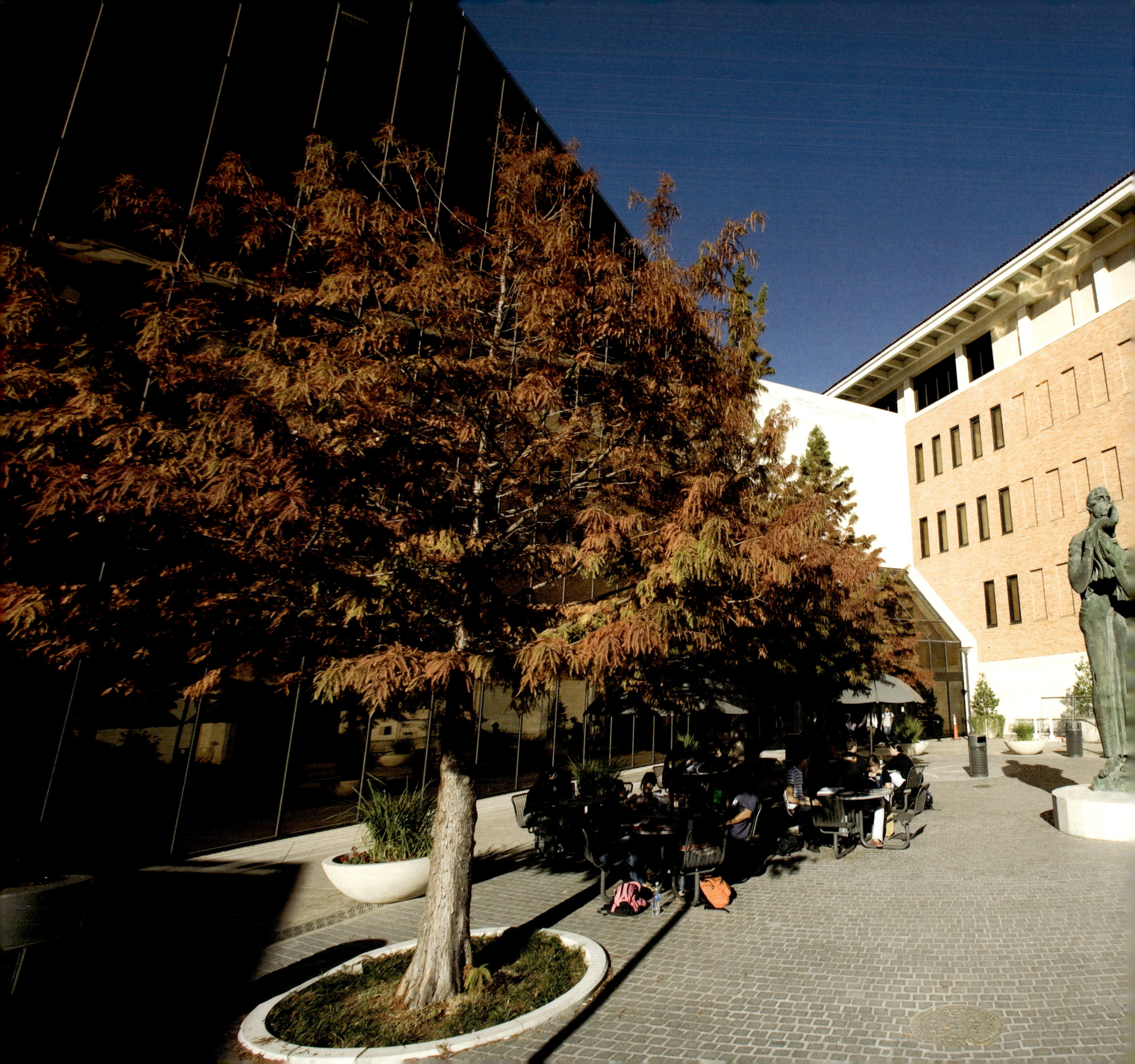

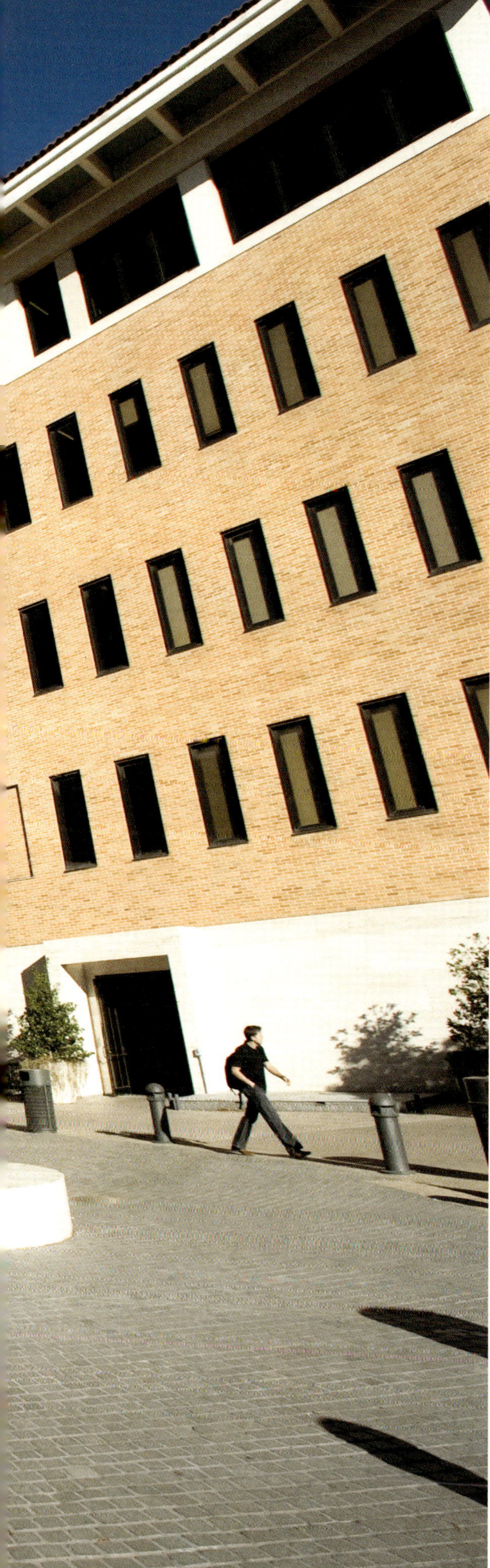

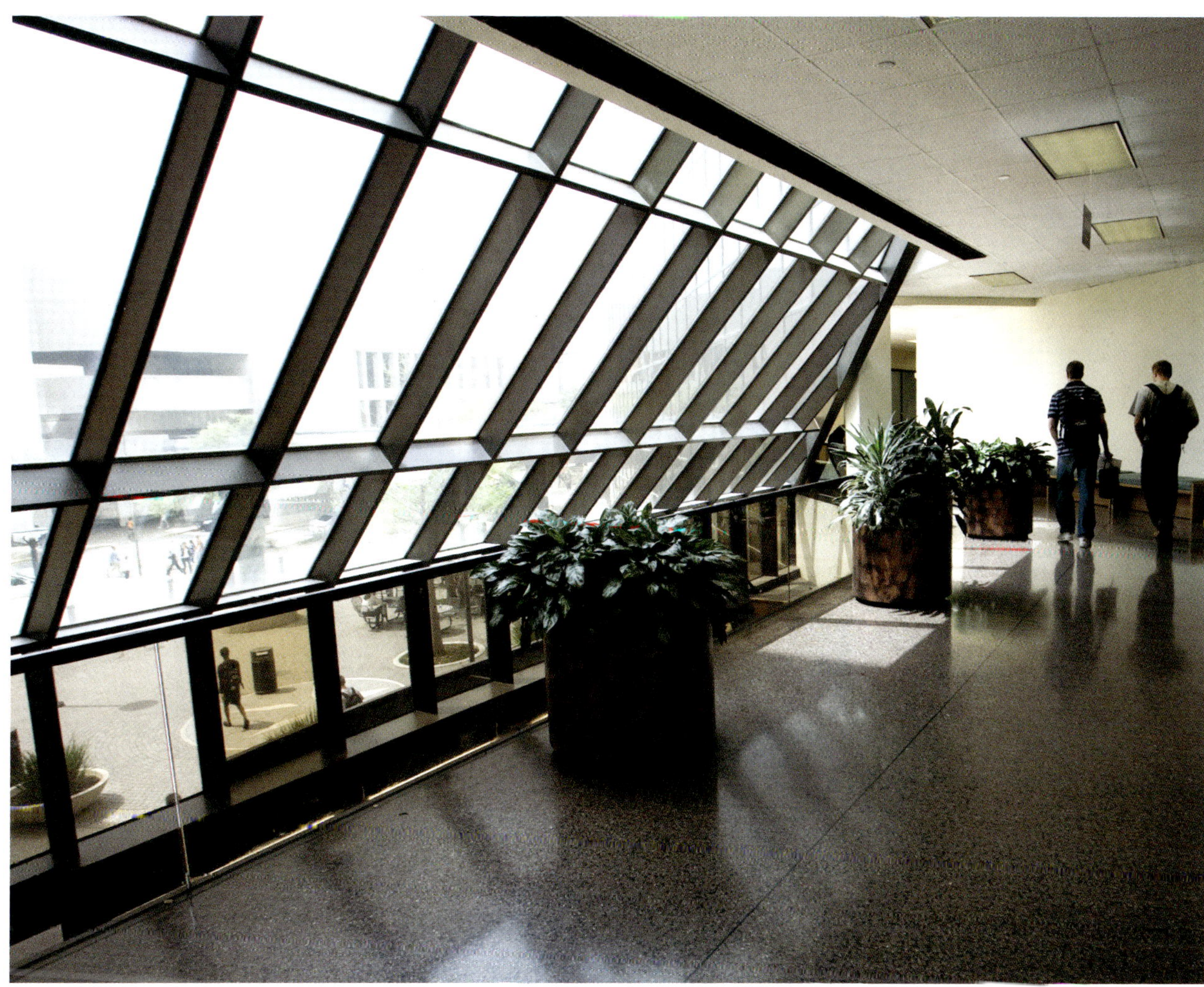

Above Business classes were first offered in 1912. In 2000, the University's College of Business Administration was renamed due to the generous support of Billy J. "Red" McCombs. The McCombs School offers degrees in accounting, marketing, management, finance, and information management.

Left At the front entrance to the McCombs School of Business stands "The Family," a Charles Umlauf portrayal of the basic economic unit.

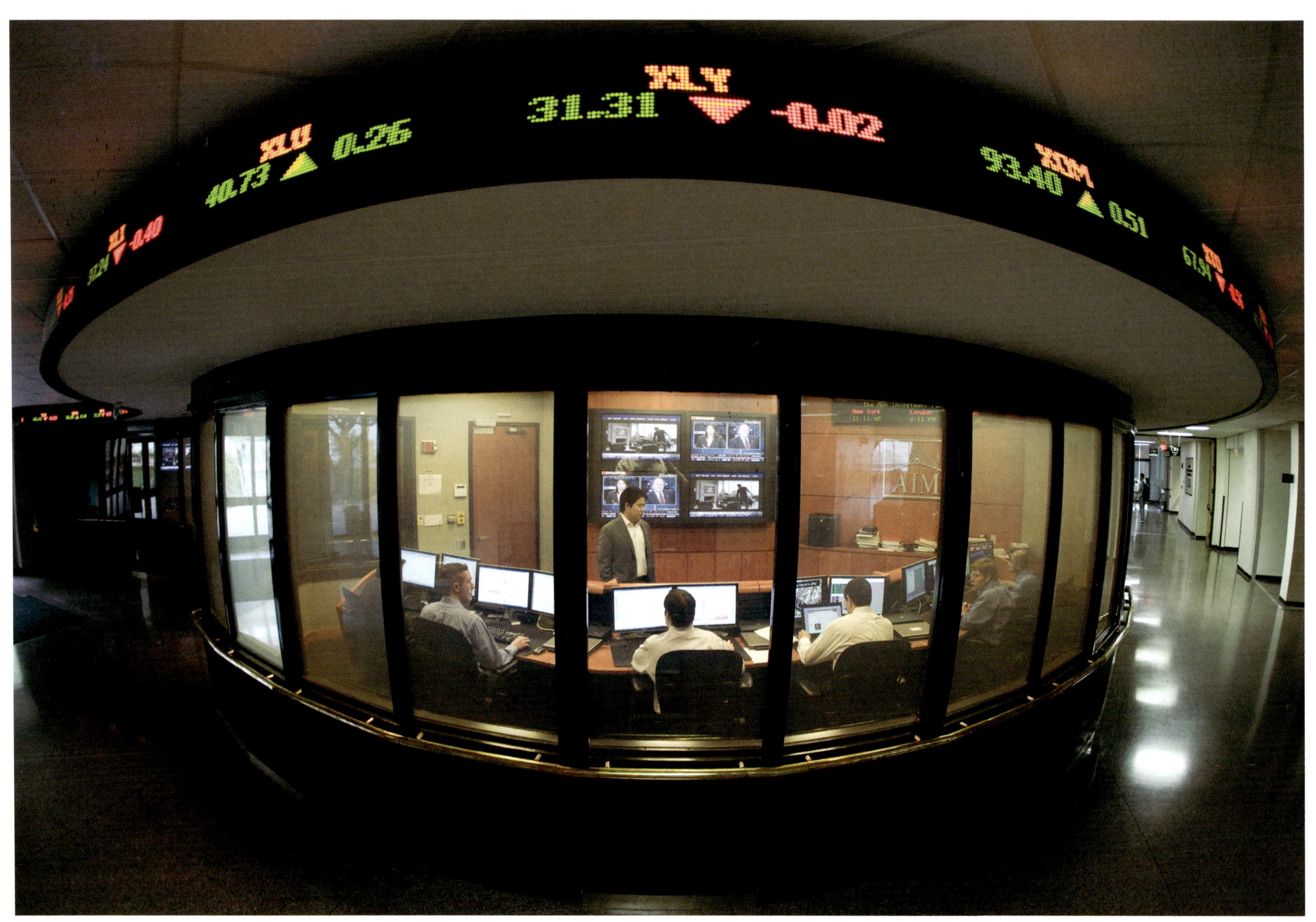

When it opened in 1996, the McCombs School's Financial Trading and Technology Center was the first of its kind on a college campus. The facility helps students and faculty to understand the increasing flow of financial data and its impact on markets, as well as develop new applications of information technology to finance.

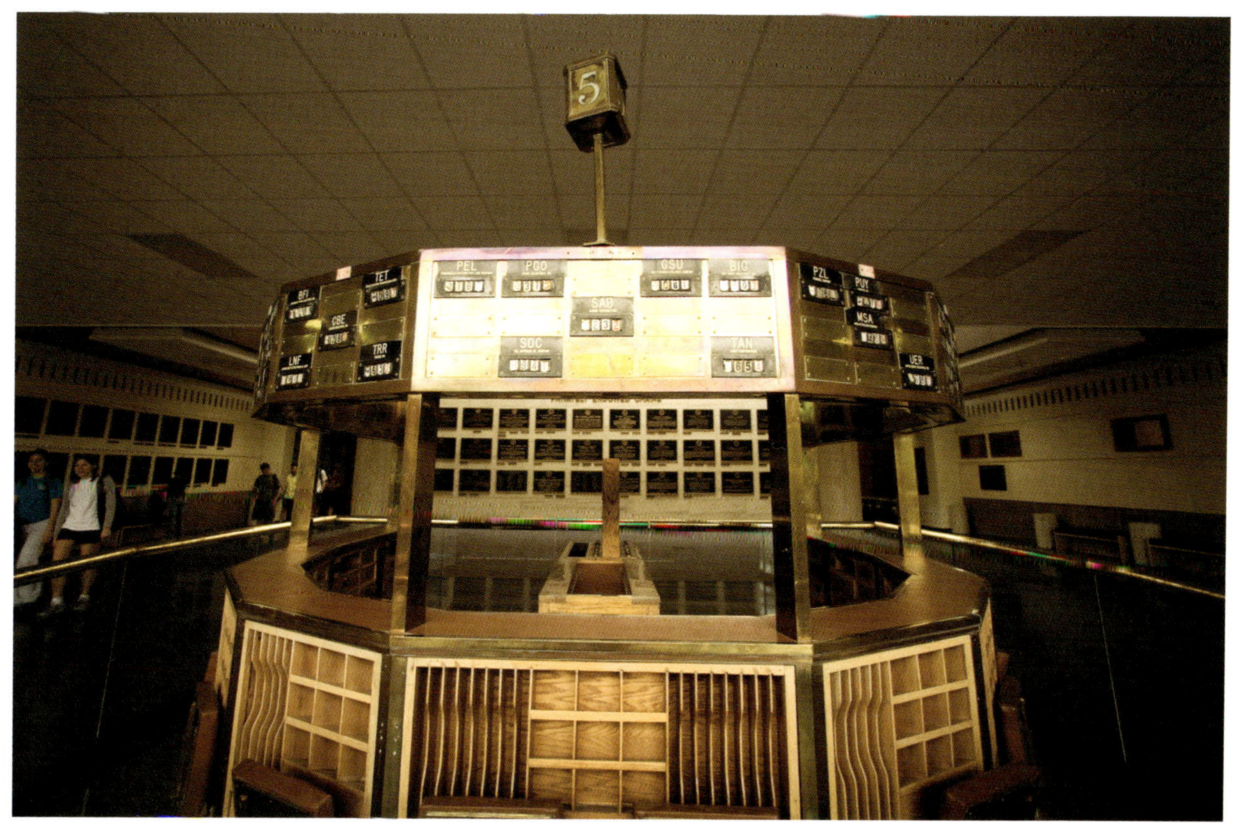

"Old Number 5," an early trading booth from the New York Stock Exchange, is the centerpiece for the McCombs School's front lobby.

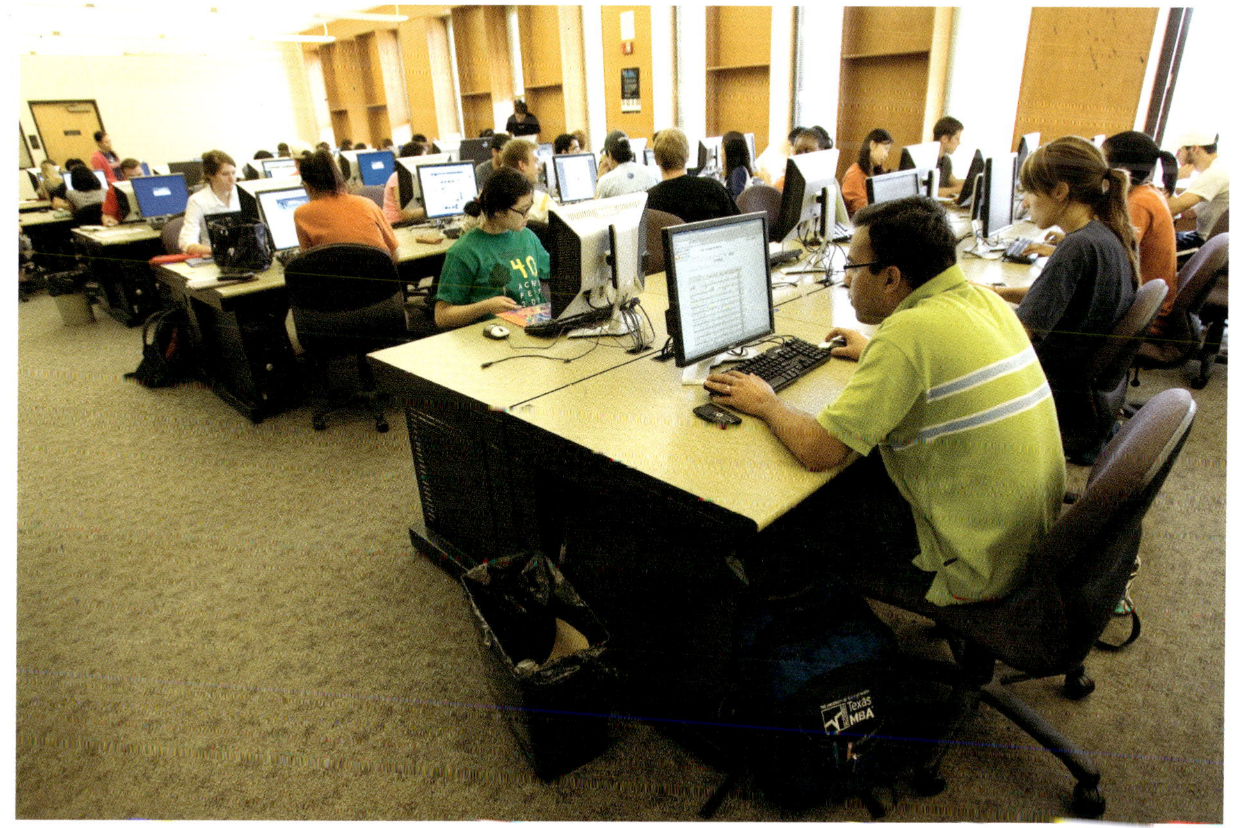

A sign of the 21st century: Crowded computer labs are a regular feature on the University campus.

Across the street from the McCombs School of Business is Gregory Gymnasium, the headquarters of the Division of Recreation Sports. When it was opened in 1930, Gregory Gym hosted the University basketball games. It is now home court of women's volleyball.

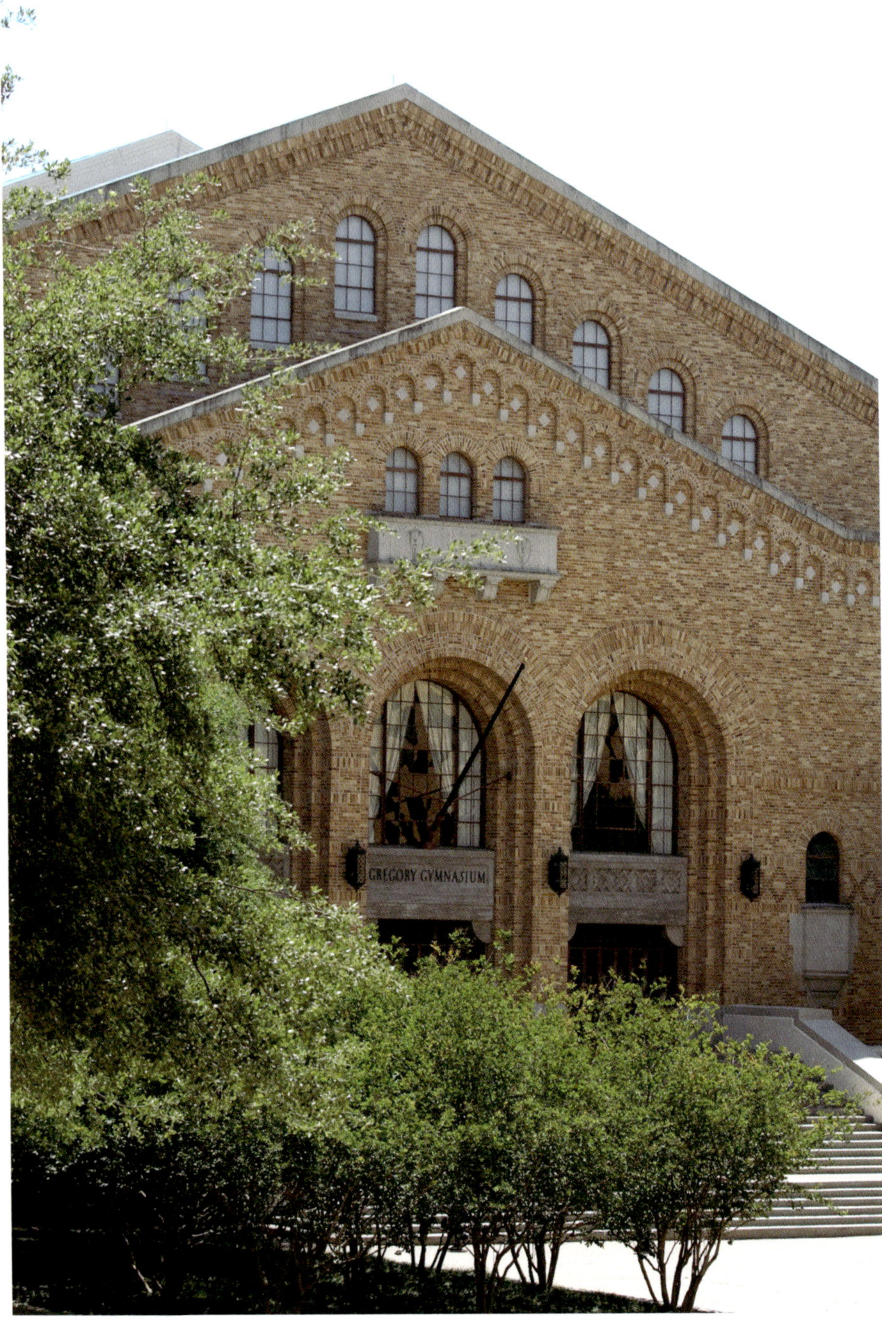

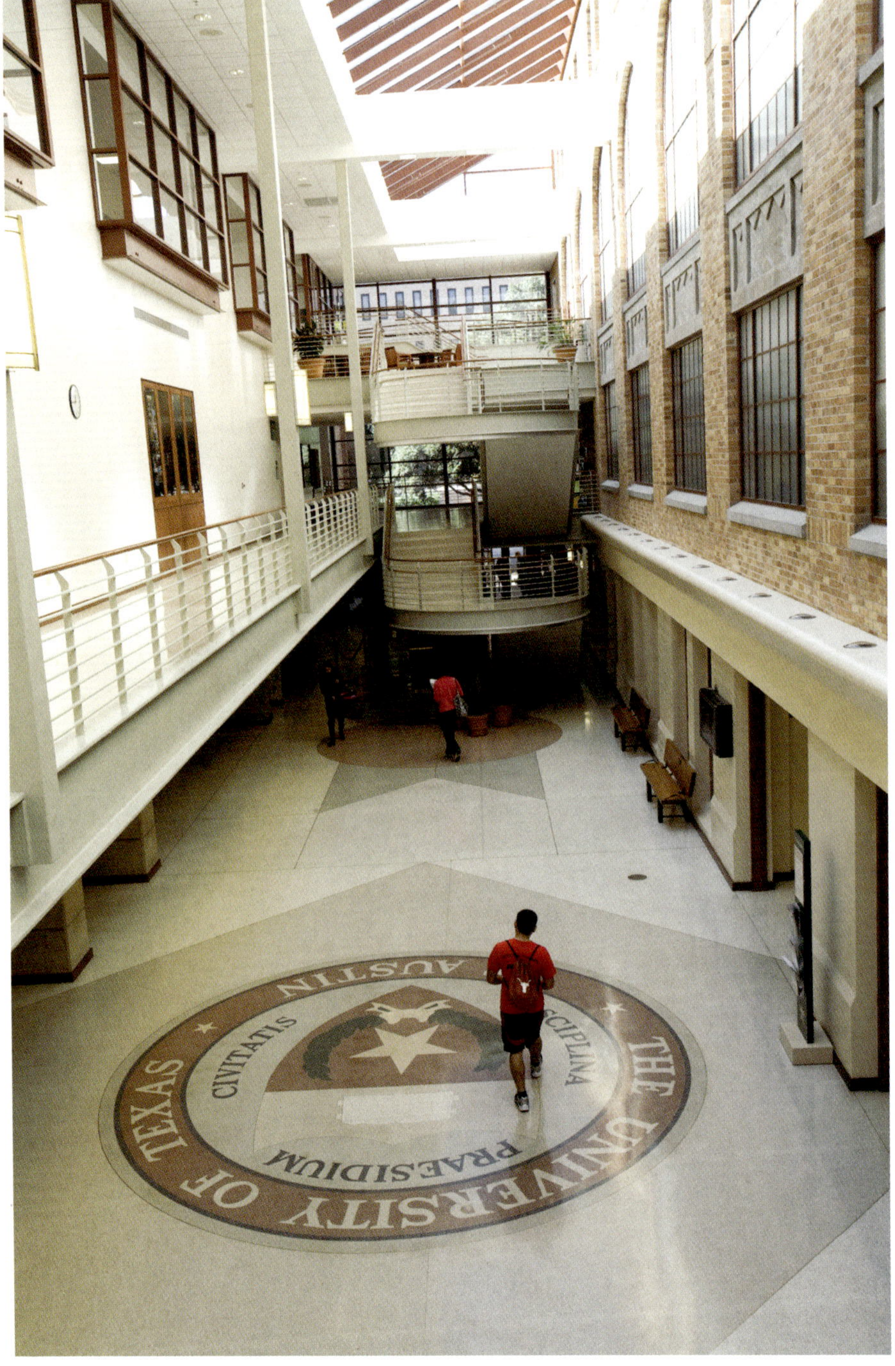

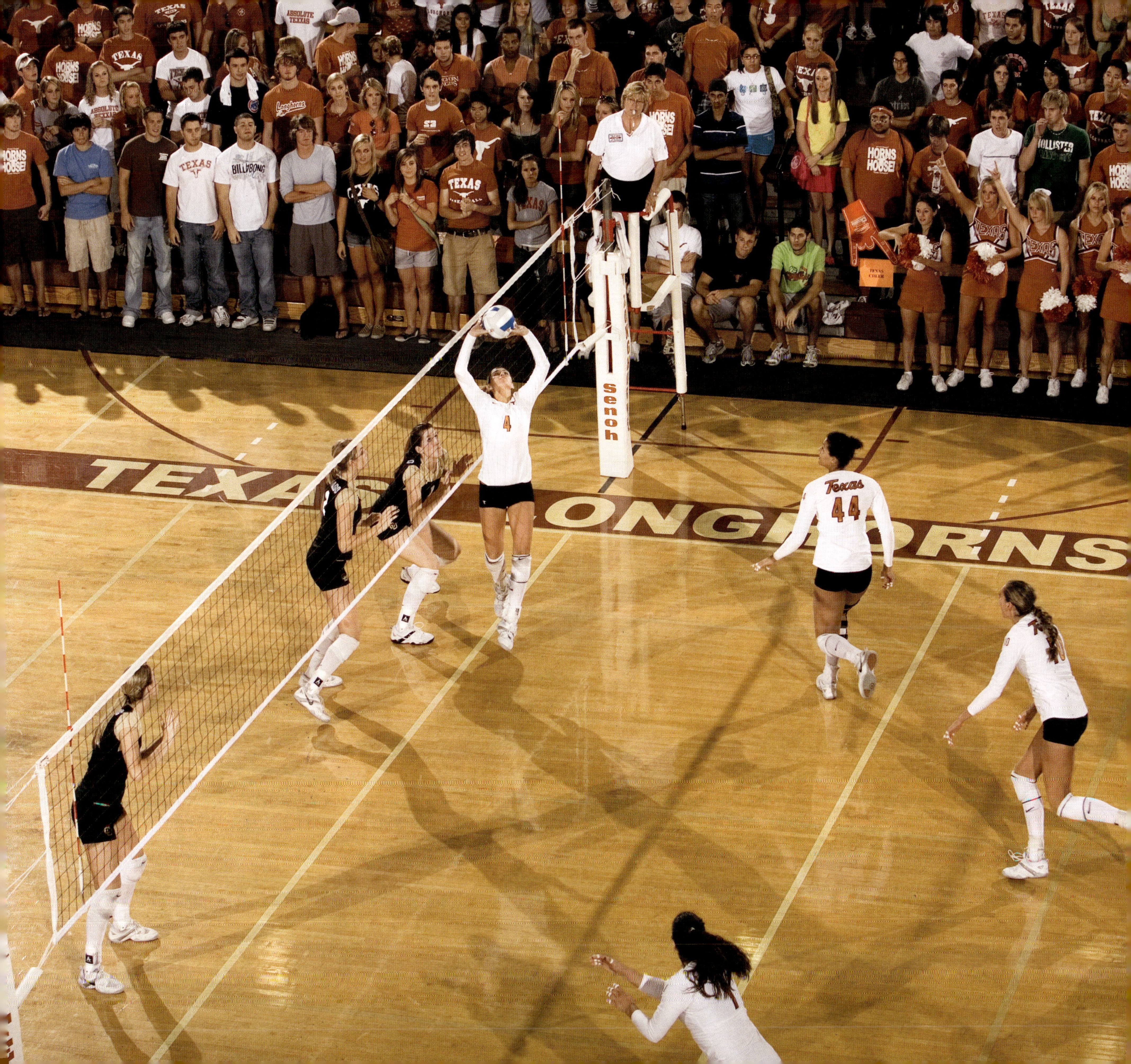

Senoh
Texas
44

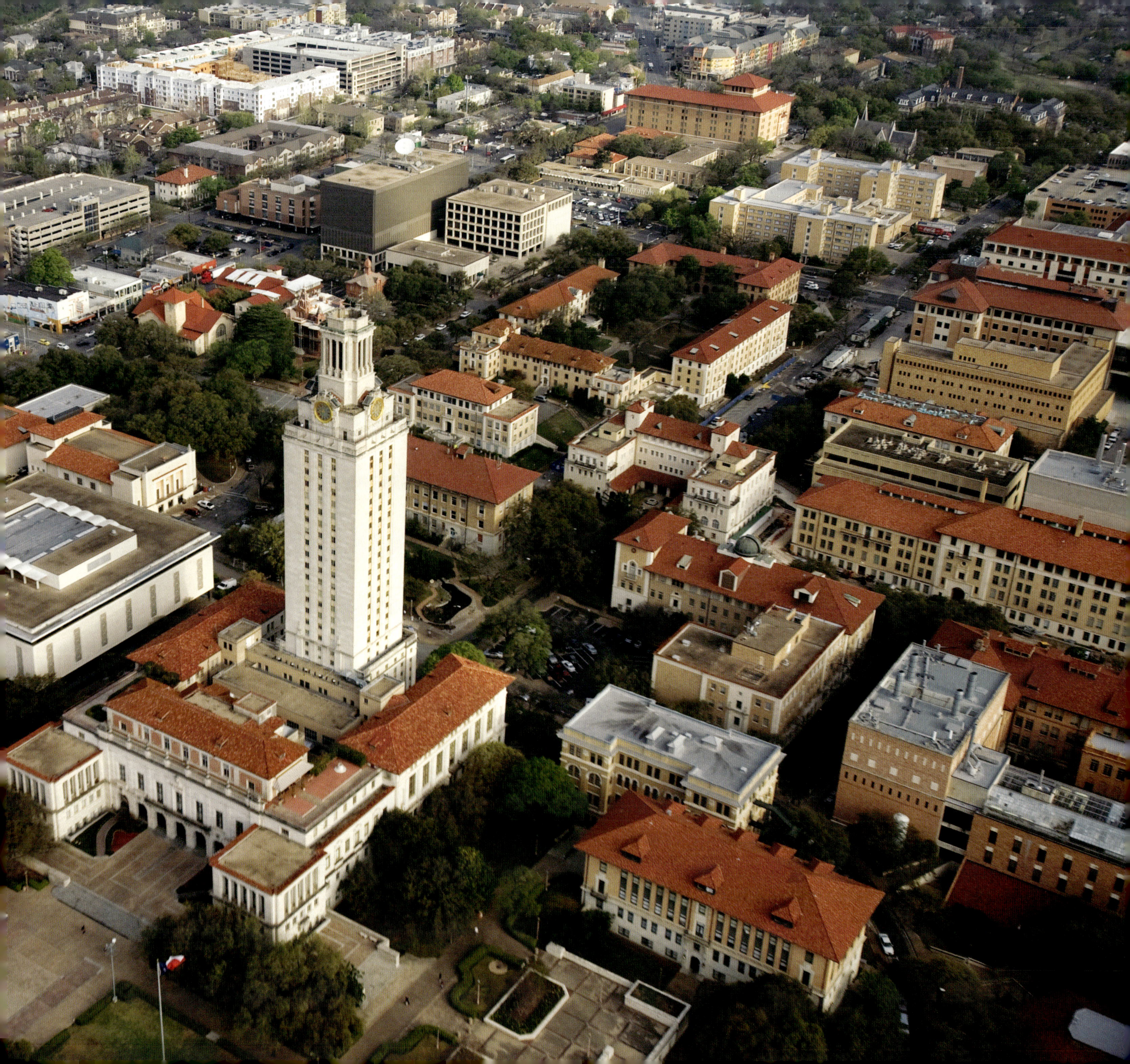

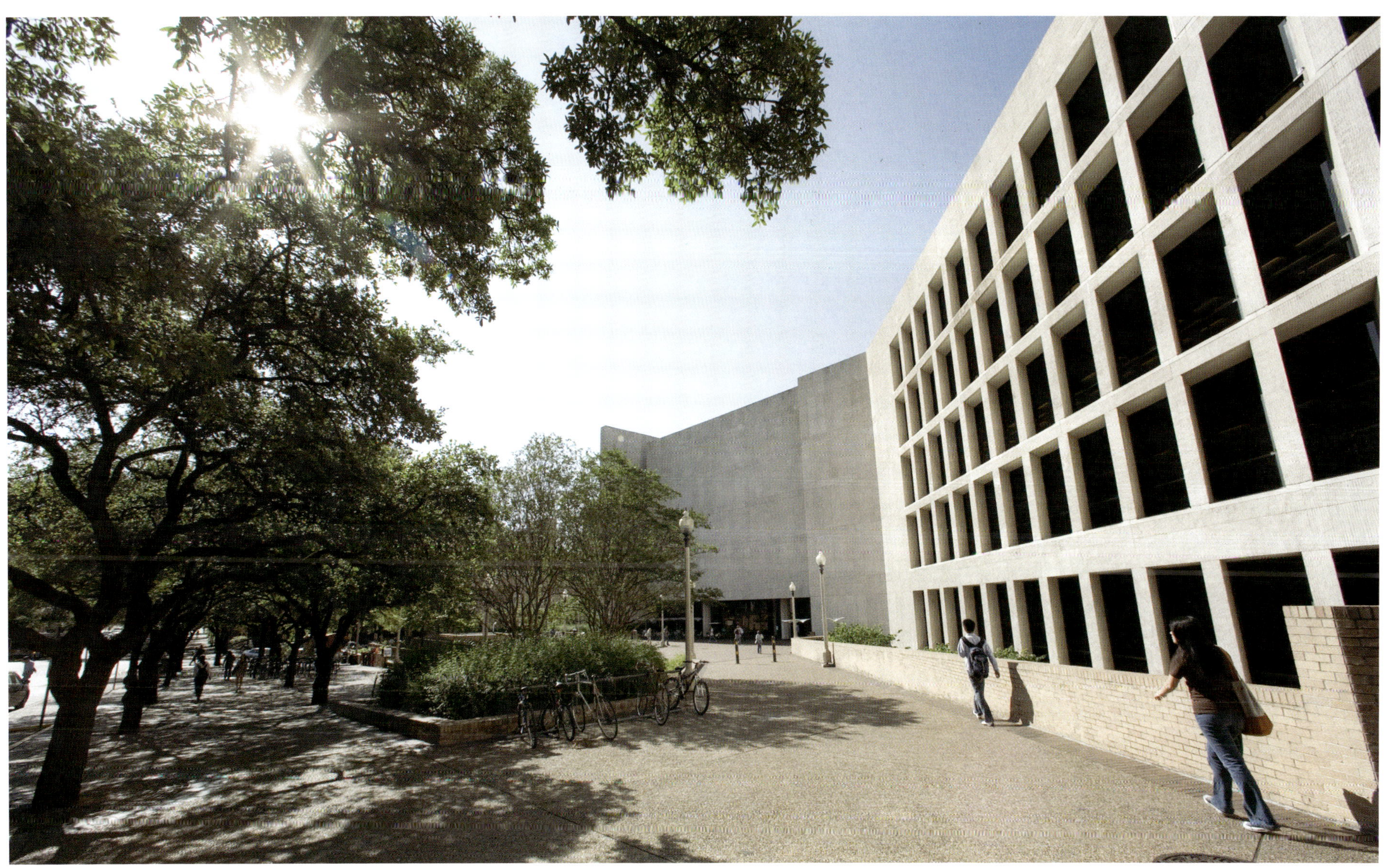

Completed in 1977, the Perry-Castañeda Library is the main library on the campus. In all, the University's 15 libraries hold more than 9 million volumes.

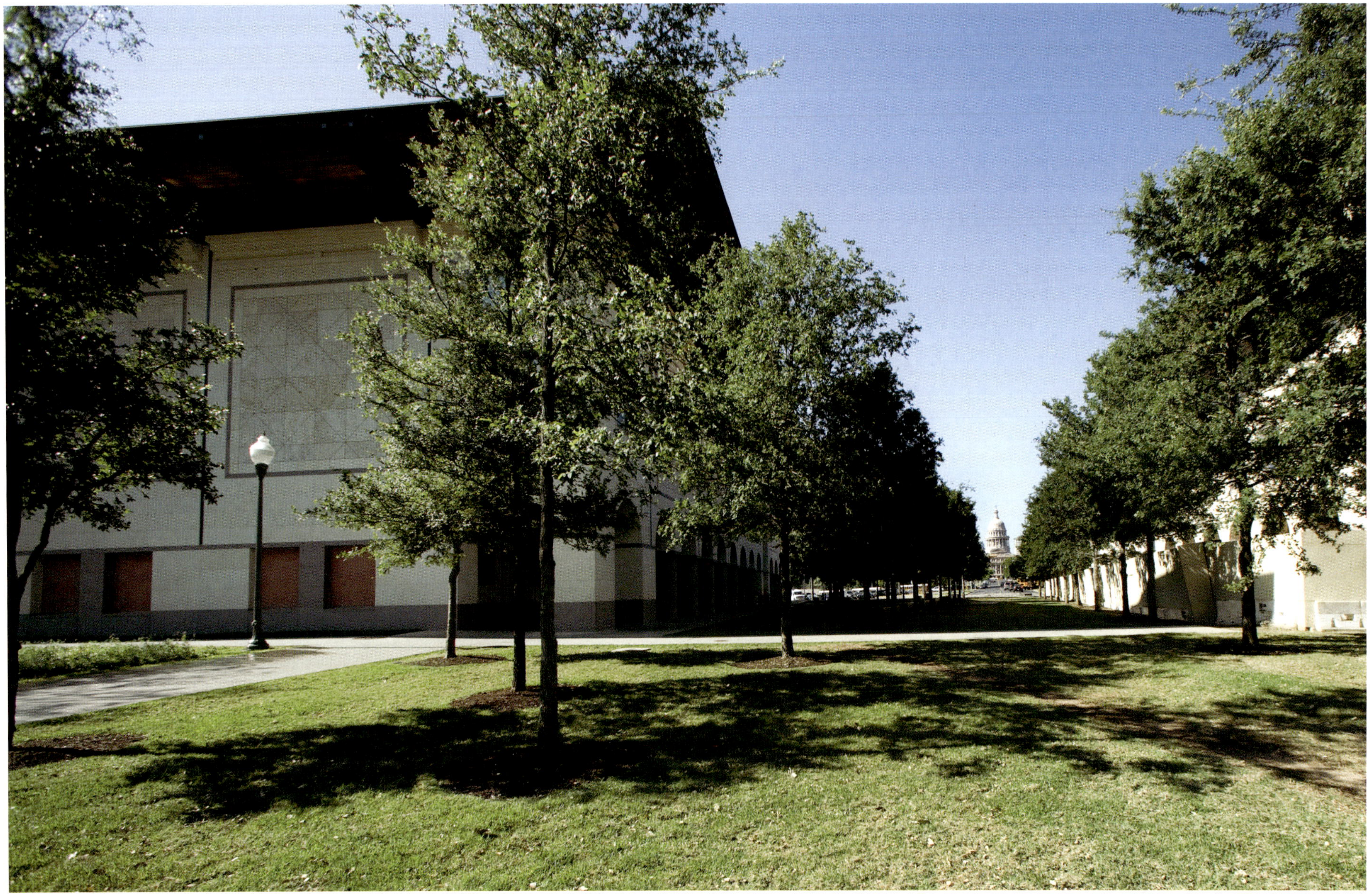

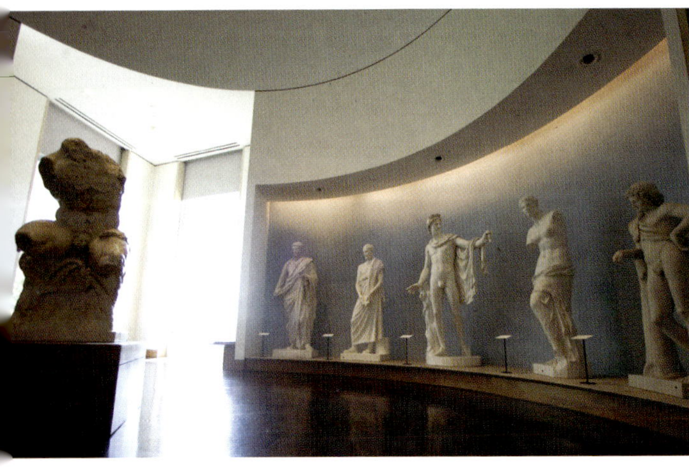

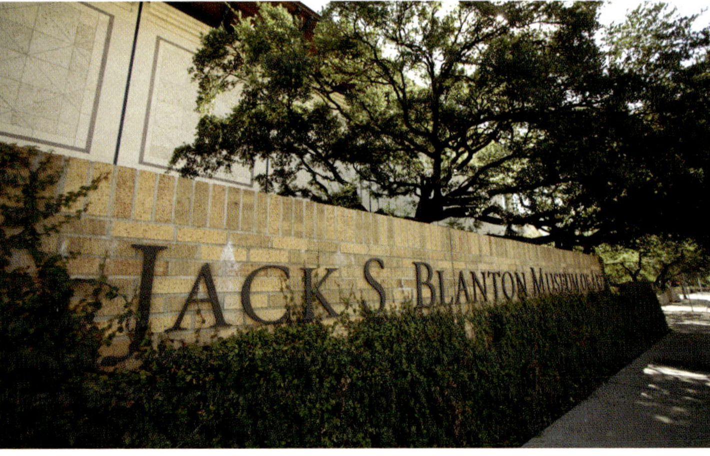
JACK S. BLANTON

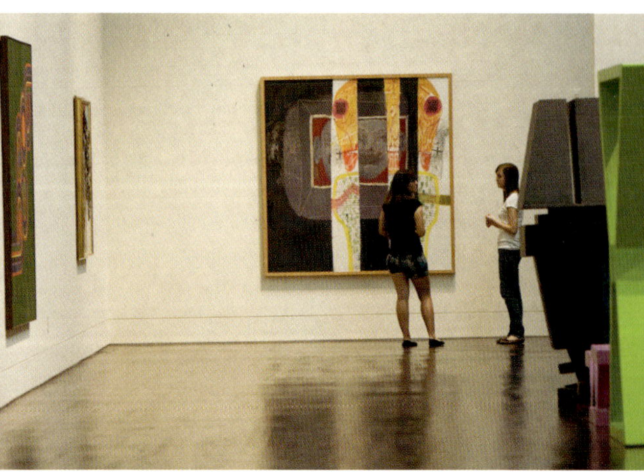

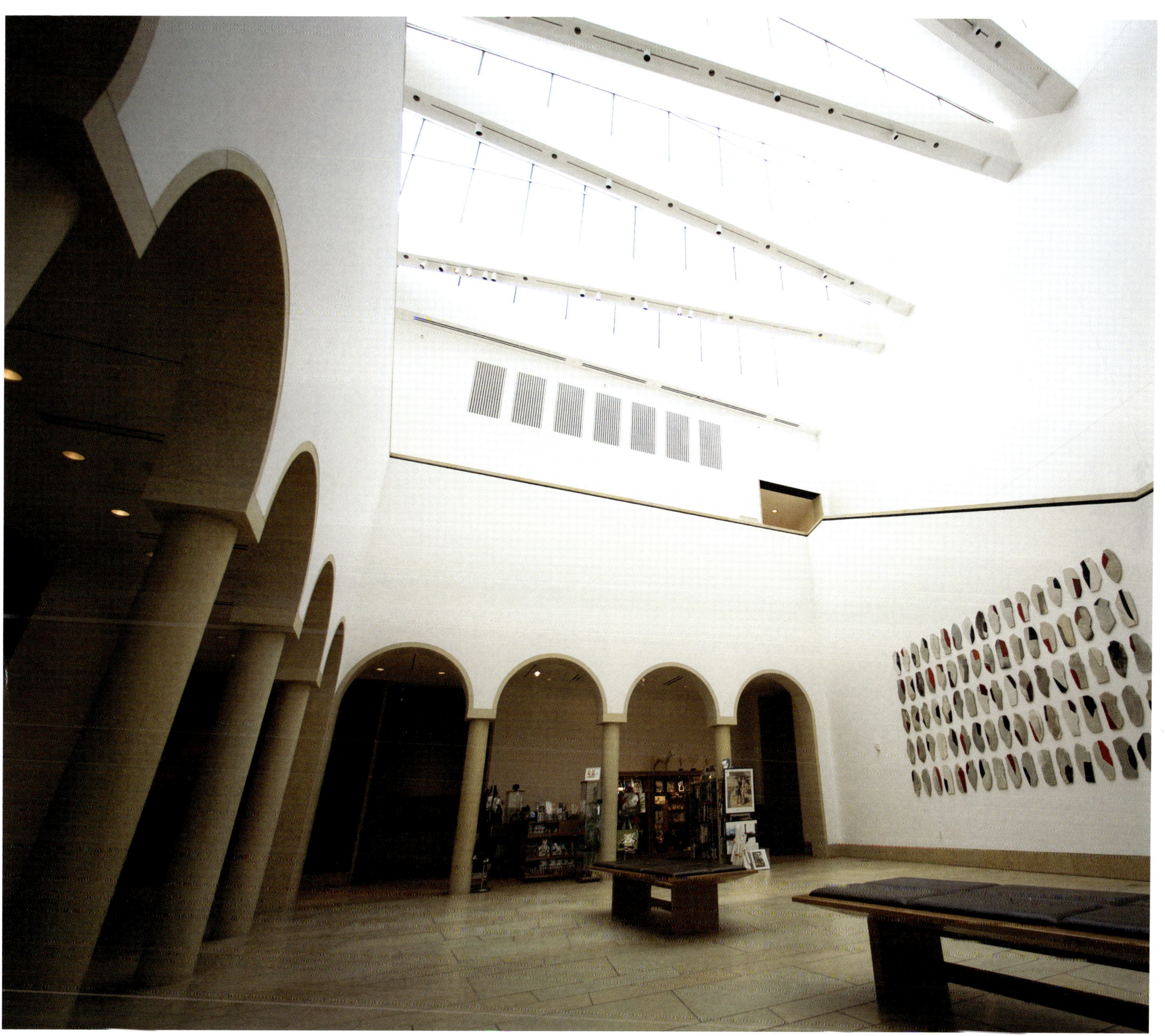

The Jack S. Blanton Museum of Art opened in spring 2006 and is the largest art museum on a college campus. Situated at the southern end of the University grounds, just across the street from the Bob Bullock Texas State History Museum, the Blanton Museum boasts extensive collections in American, European, Latin American, and contemporary art.

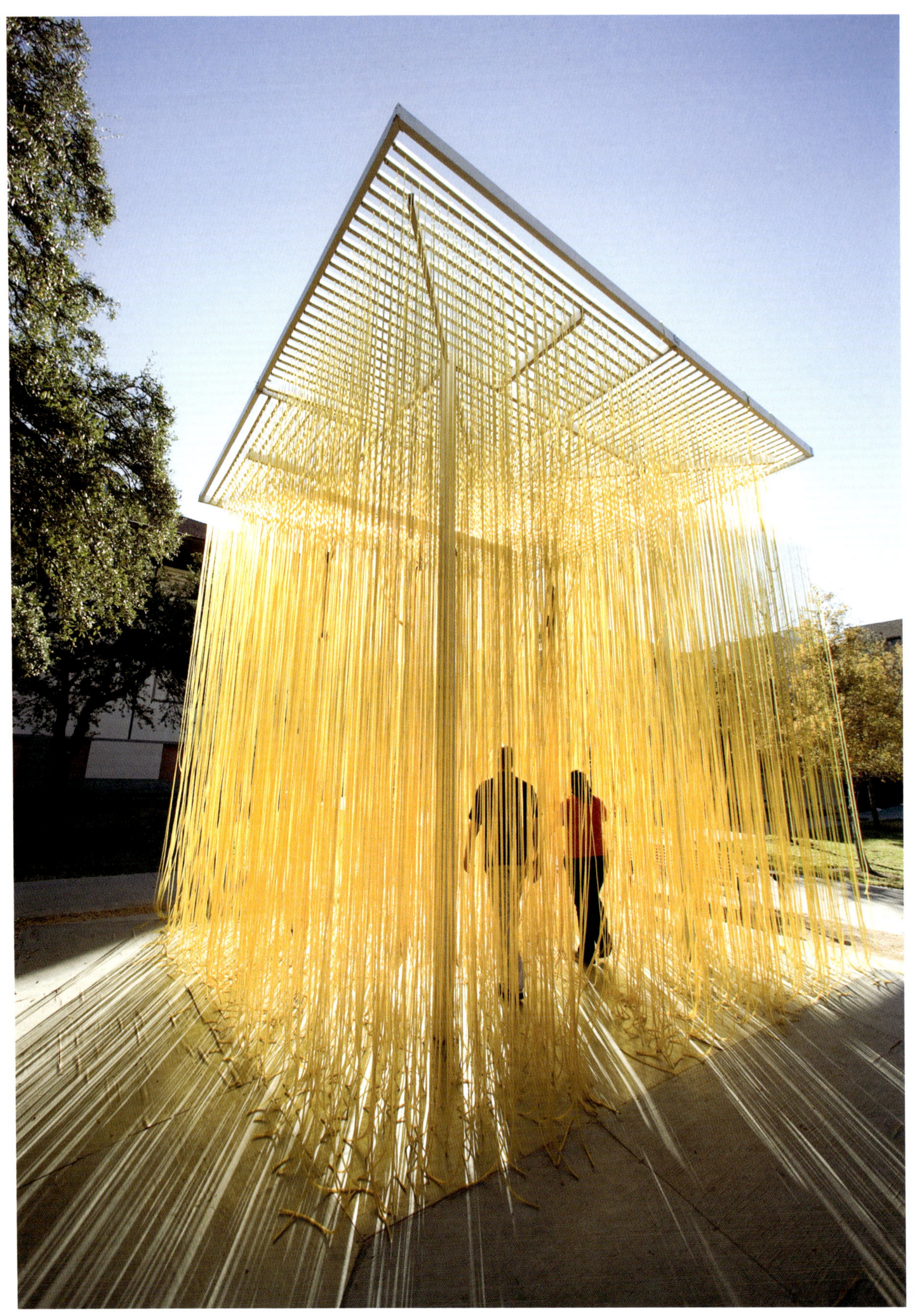

Outside of the Blanton Museum is "Penetrable," a piece created by Jesus Rafael Soto in 1990. Created from the artist's experiments with the dynamics of space and form and the physical experience of the spectator, viewers are encouraged to walk through the work.

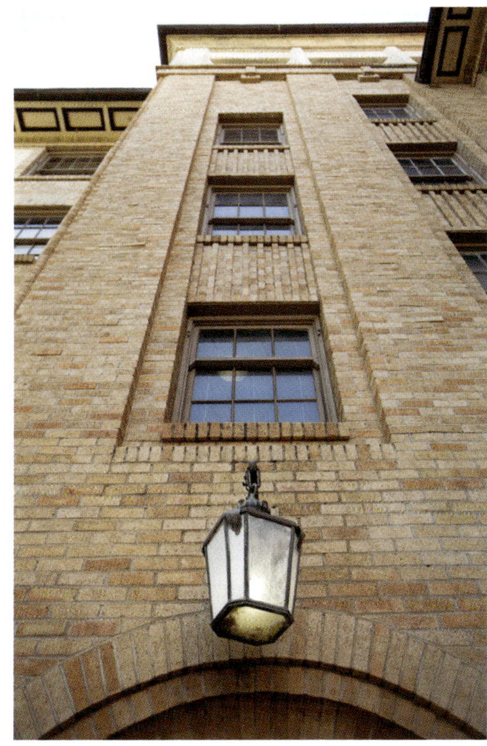

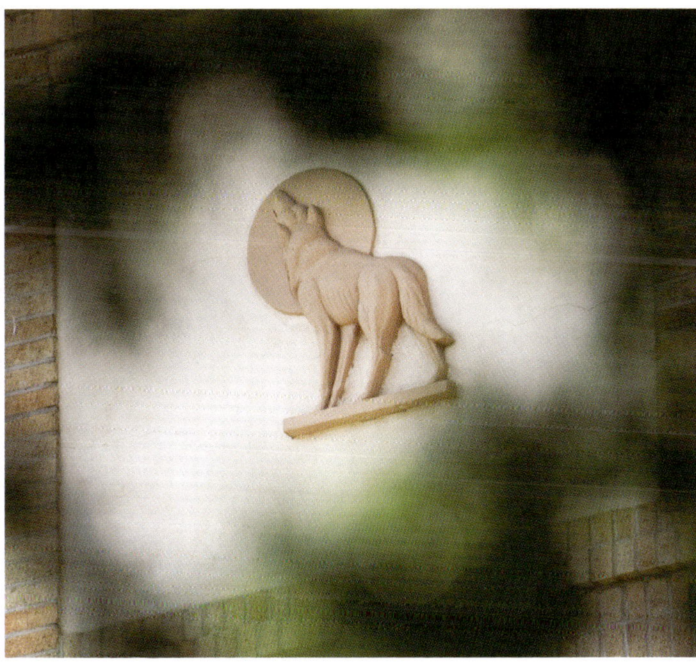

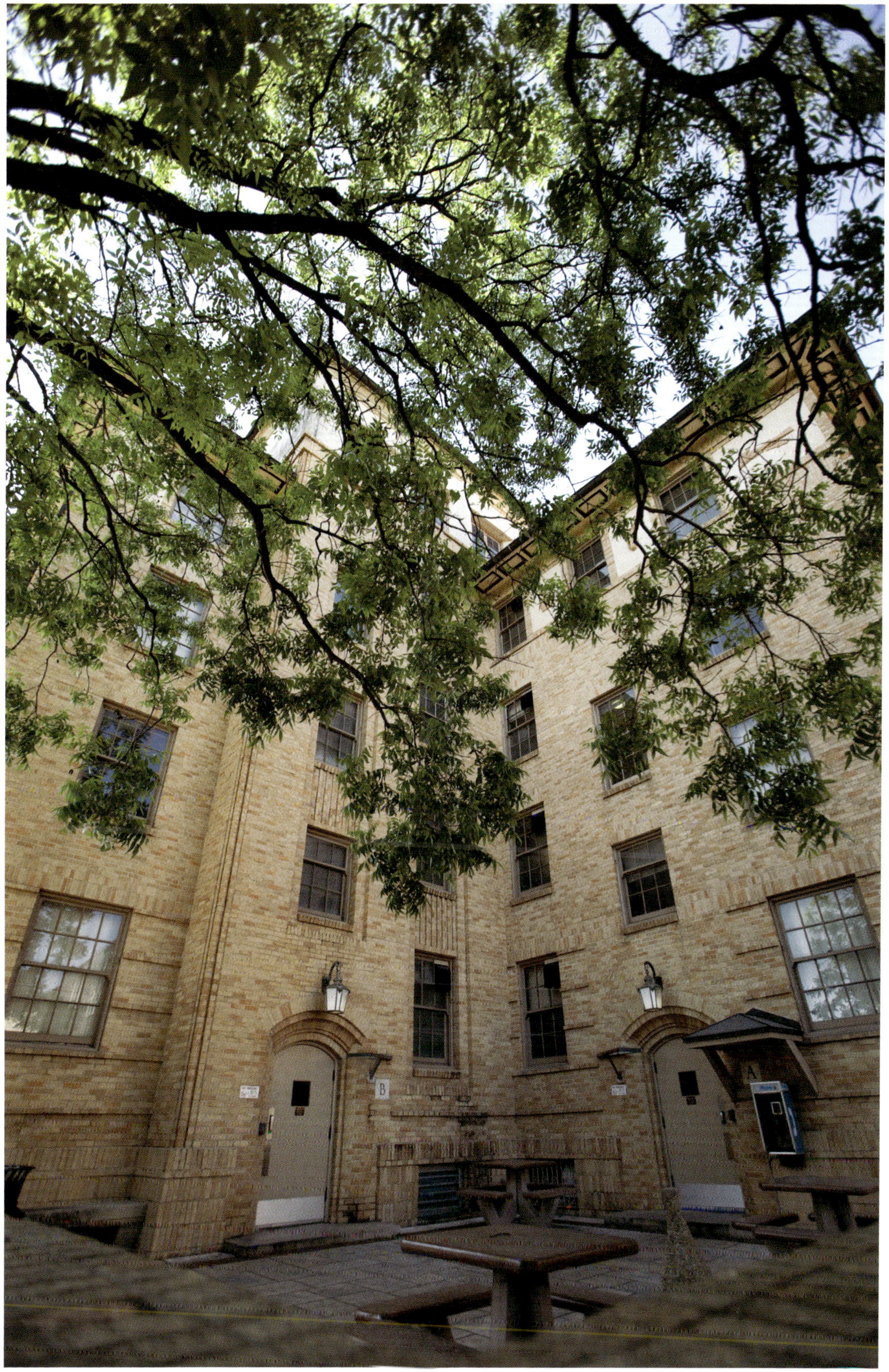

Brackenridge Hall was opened in 1932 as a dormitory for men, but has since been renovated as a coed residence hall. The building is named for George Brackenridge, a University benefactor from San Antonio who served on the Board of Regents for 27 years. When Brackenridge Hall was being designed, UT student Bob Wilson suggested that terra cotta friezes on the building depict scenes and symbols of ranch life in the southwest.

The University seal decorates a corner of Roberts Hall. The seal was created by Greek professor William Battle and officially approved in 1905. Its central feature is a shield, divided into two fields, the upper white and the lower orange. In the lower field are the historic wreath and star of the Seal of the State of Texas; the upper contains an open book as a symbol of an institution of learning. The shield rests within a circle of blue, the color of sincerity, and contains the motto: *Disciplina Praesidium Civitatis*, a Latin translation of Mirabeau Lamar's quote, "A cultivated mind is the guardian of democracy." Around the disc of blue is a larger one of red, the color of strength, bearing the words, "The University of Texas at Austin."

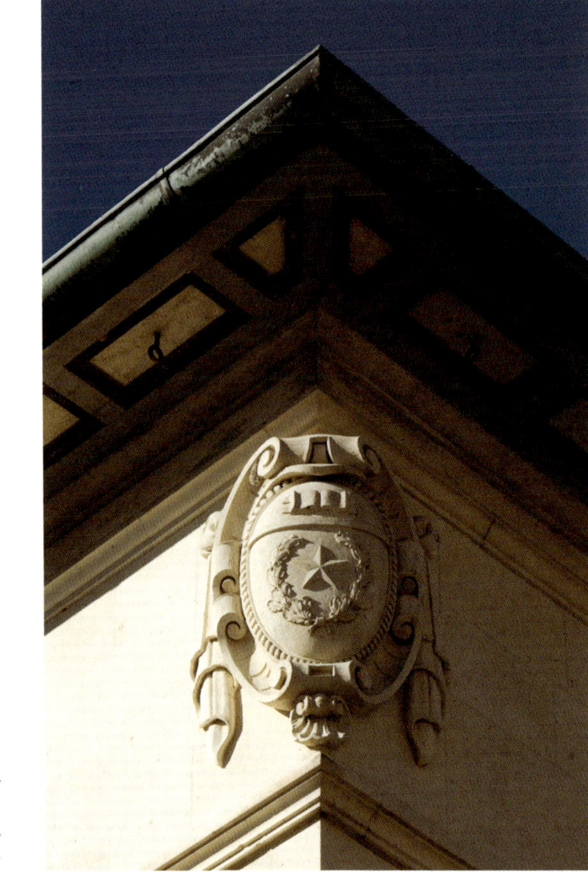

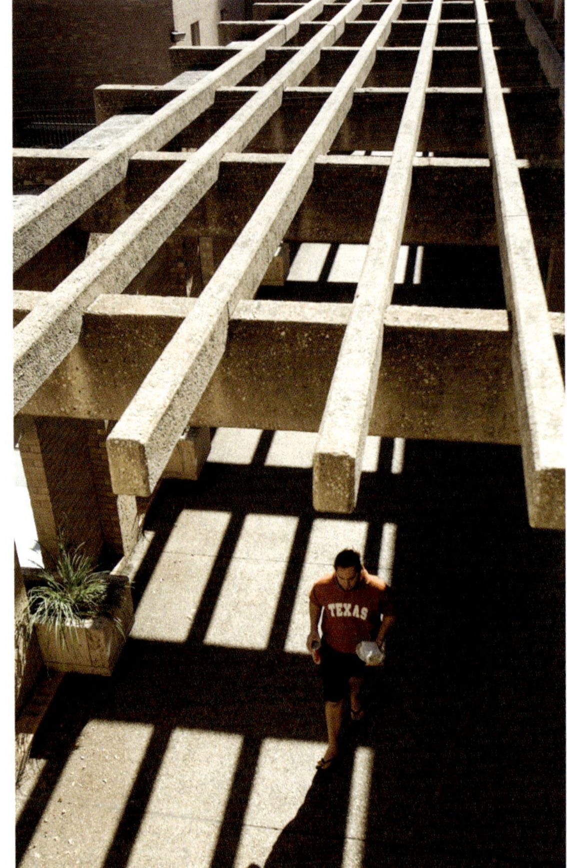

Left and Right

The courtyard of Jester Center. Opened in 1969 and named for Beauford Jester, a UT graduate who served as chairman of the Board of Regents and governor of Texas, Jester Center is one of the largest college residence halls in the nation. With a capacity of about 3,000 students, at one time Jester Center had its own zip code.

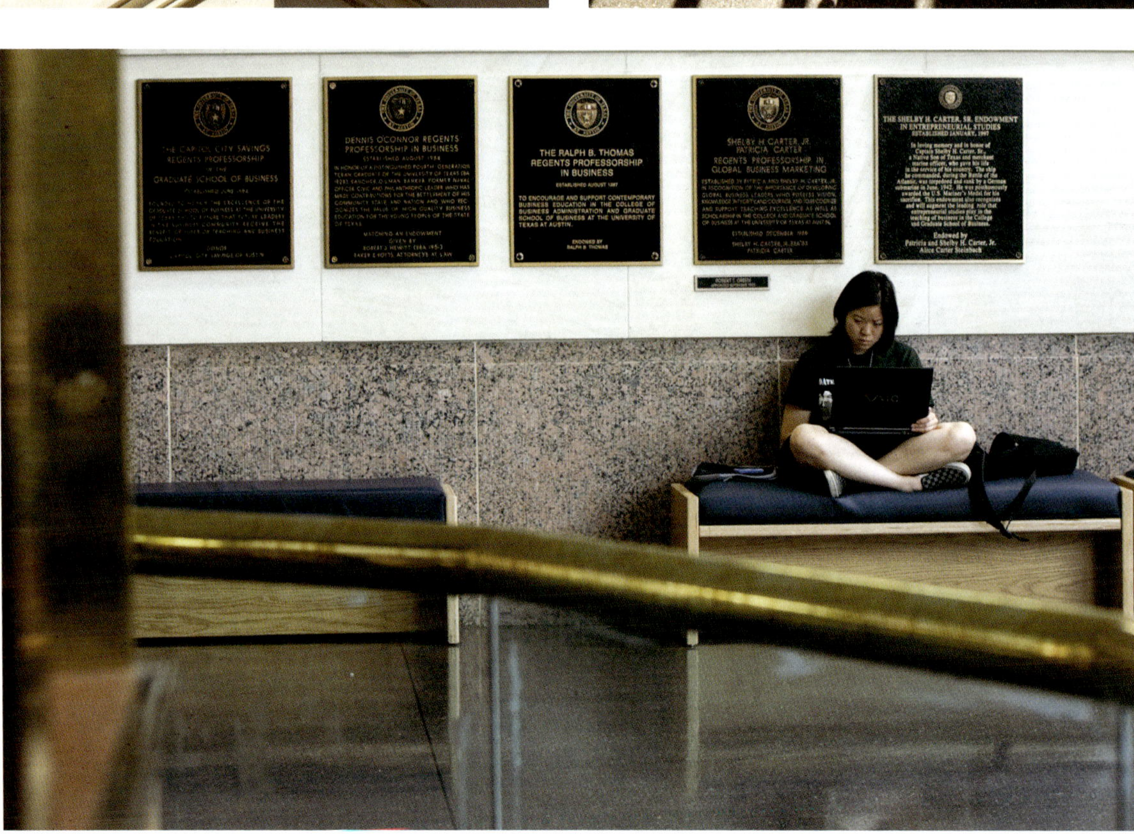

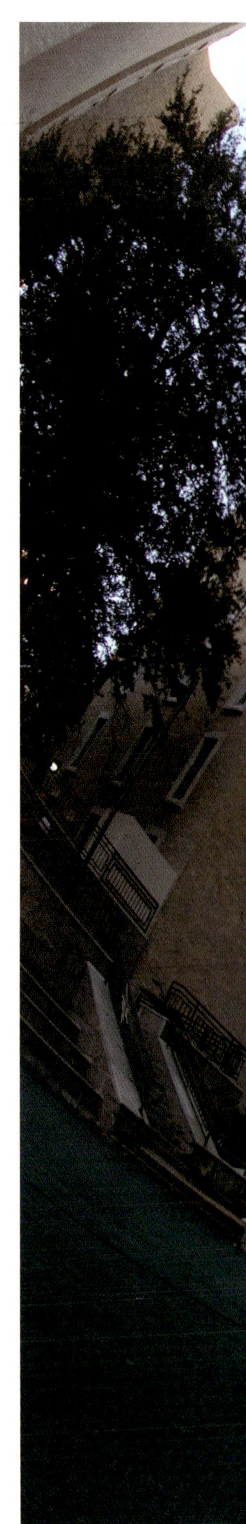

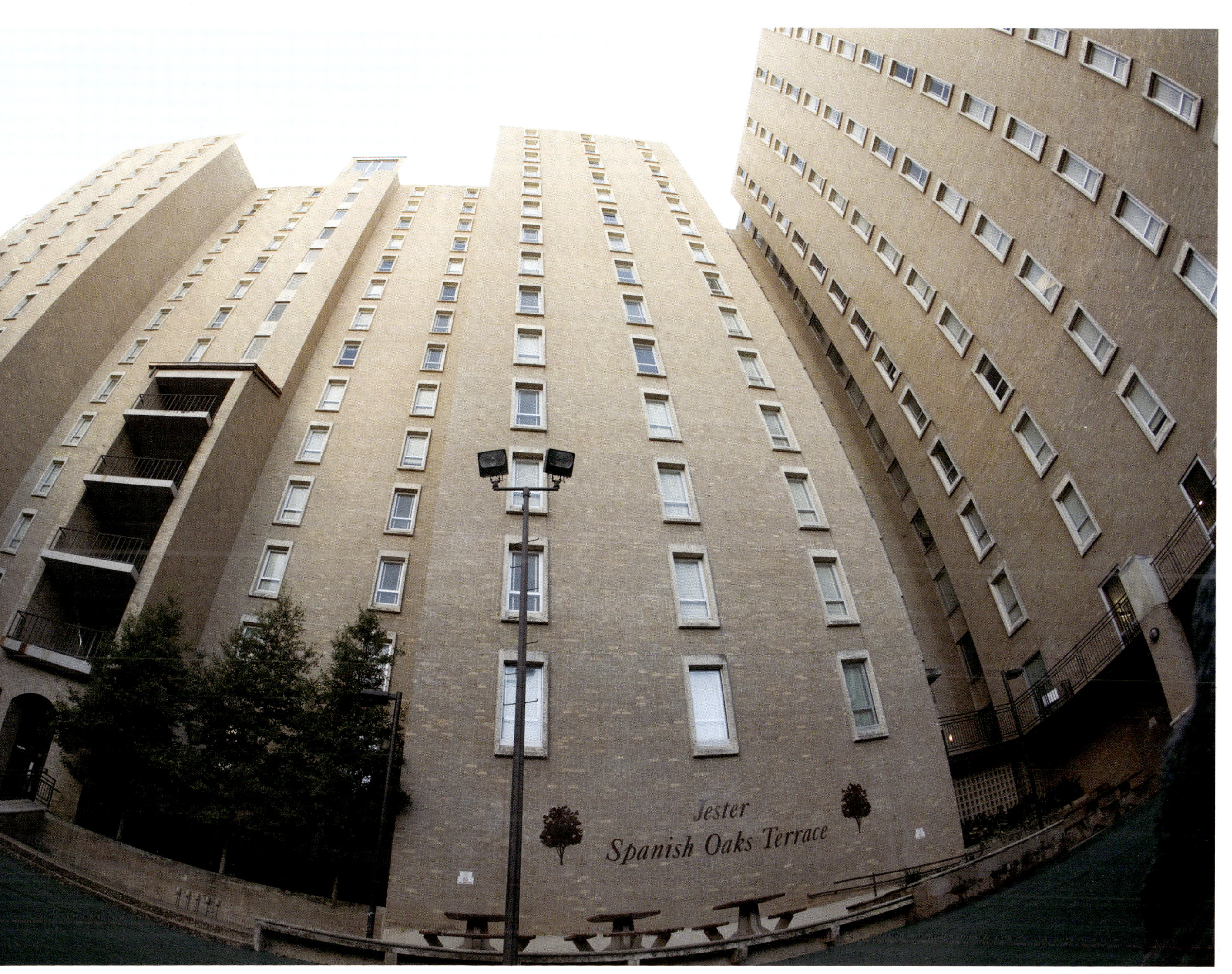
Jester
Spanish Oaks Terrace

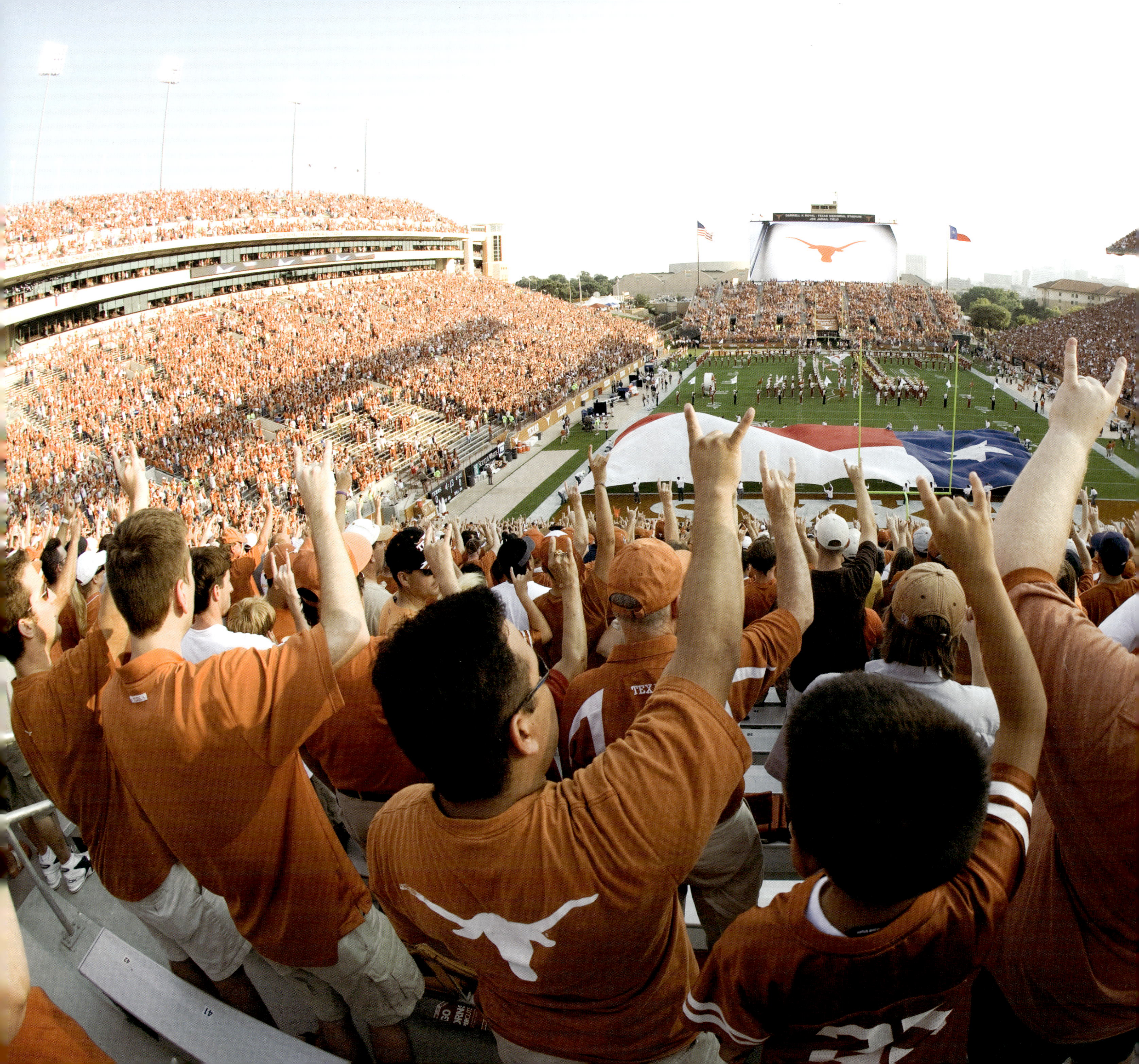

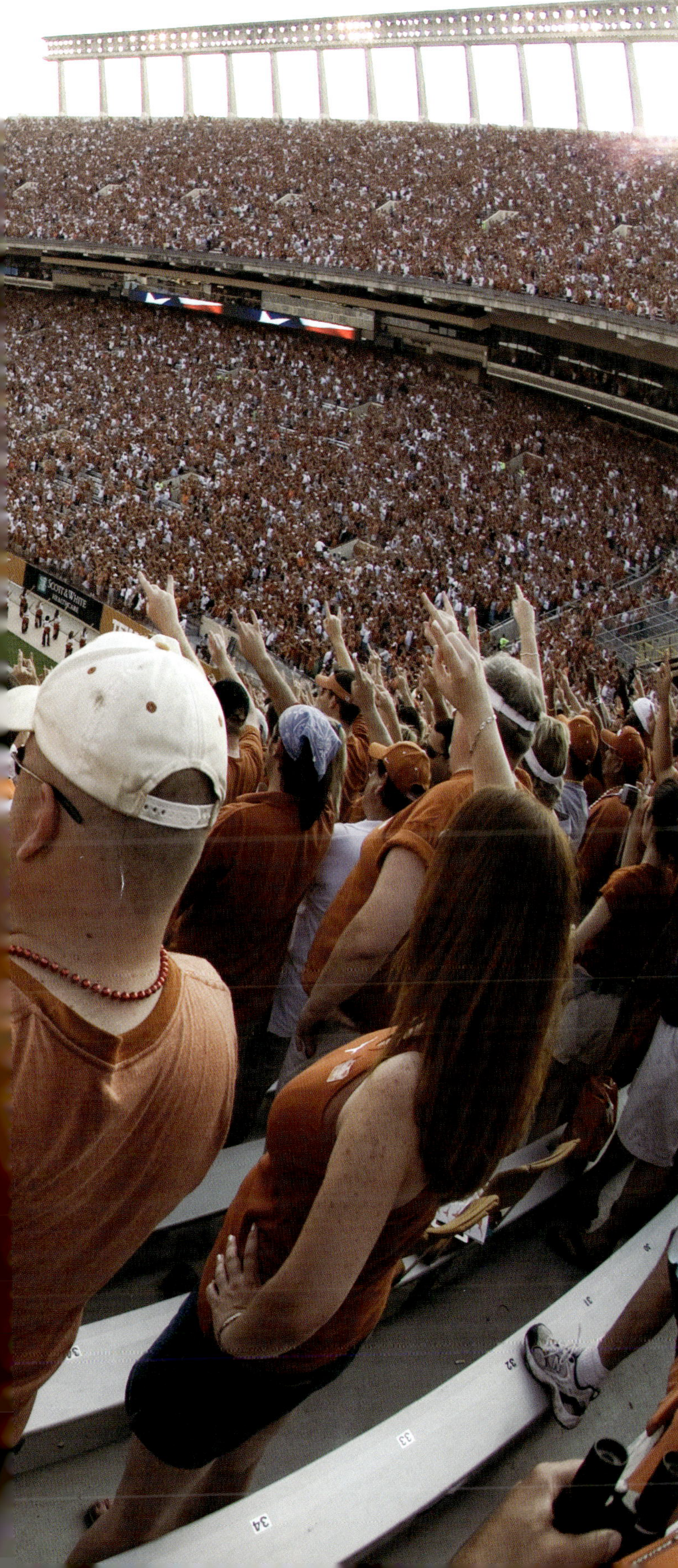

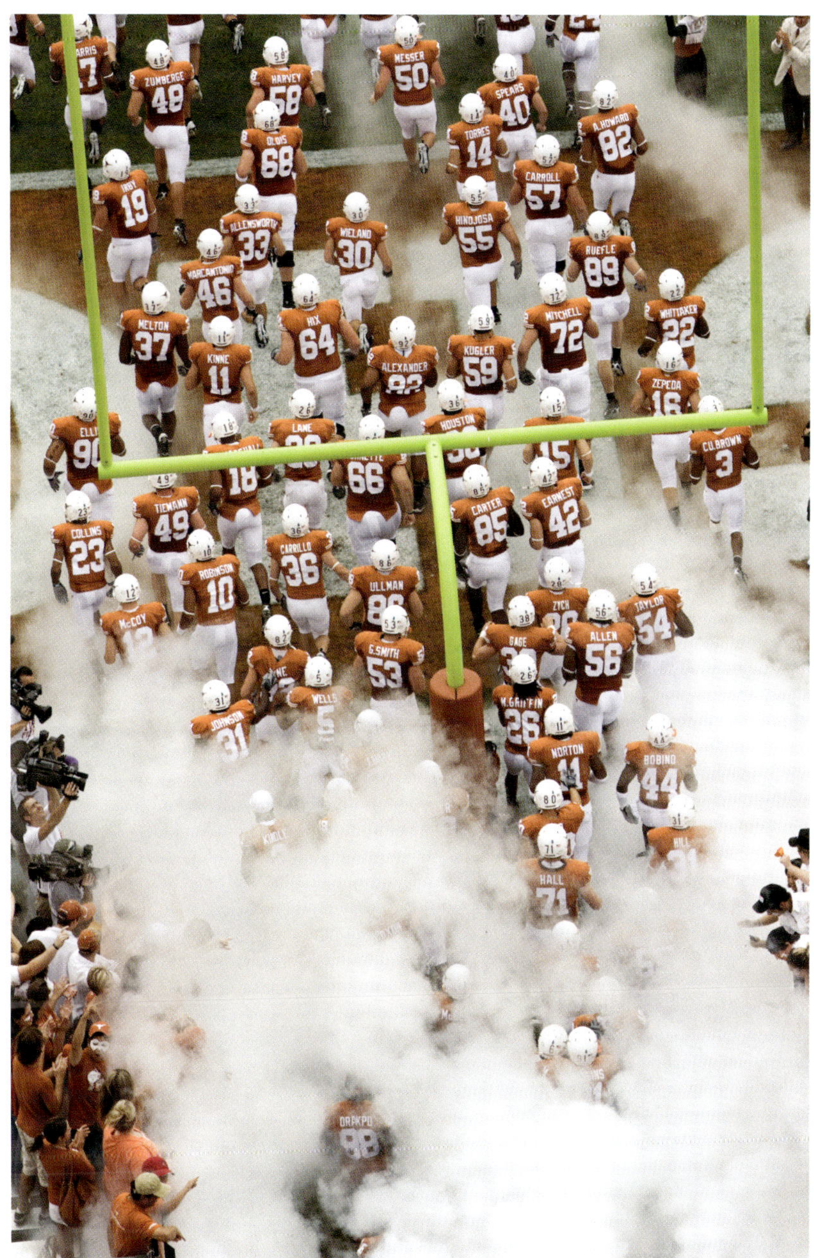

The Longhorn football team makes a grand entrance onto the field at Darrell K Royal – Texas Memorial Stadium.

With Alpha Phi Omega's Texas Flag unfurled on the field, UT fans hold their horns high and sing "The Eyes of Texas."

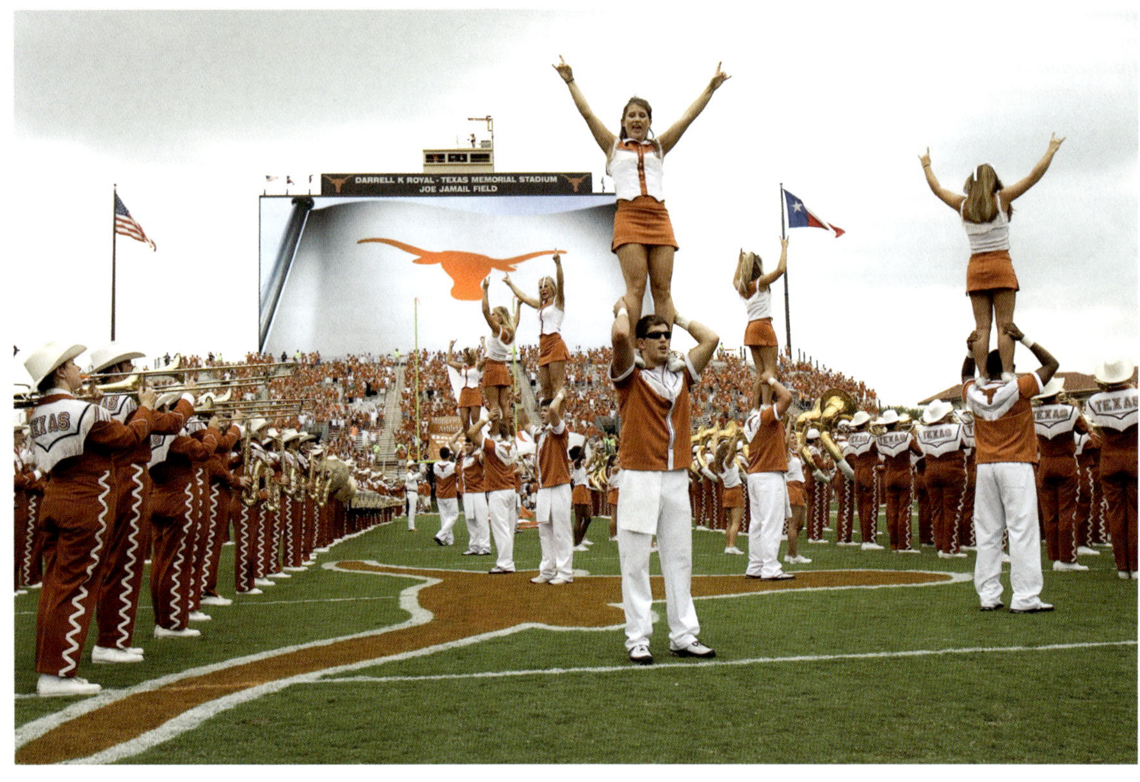

Left In the midst of a sea of burnt orange, the Longhorn Band and UT cheerleaders rally the Texas fans before the game begins.

Below UT's high-definition jumbotron dwarfs fans in south end zone stands.

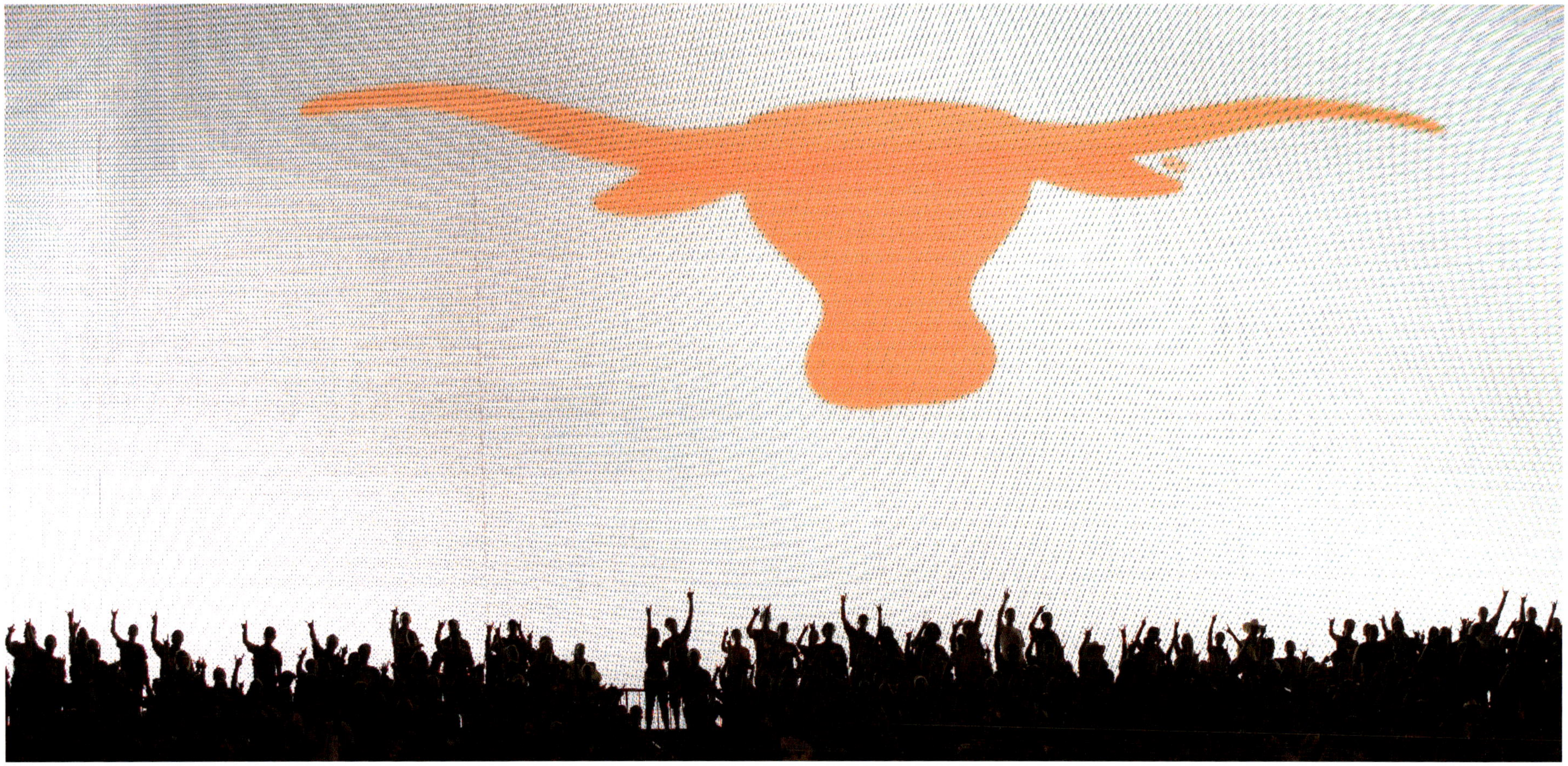

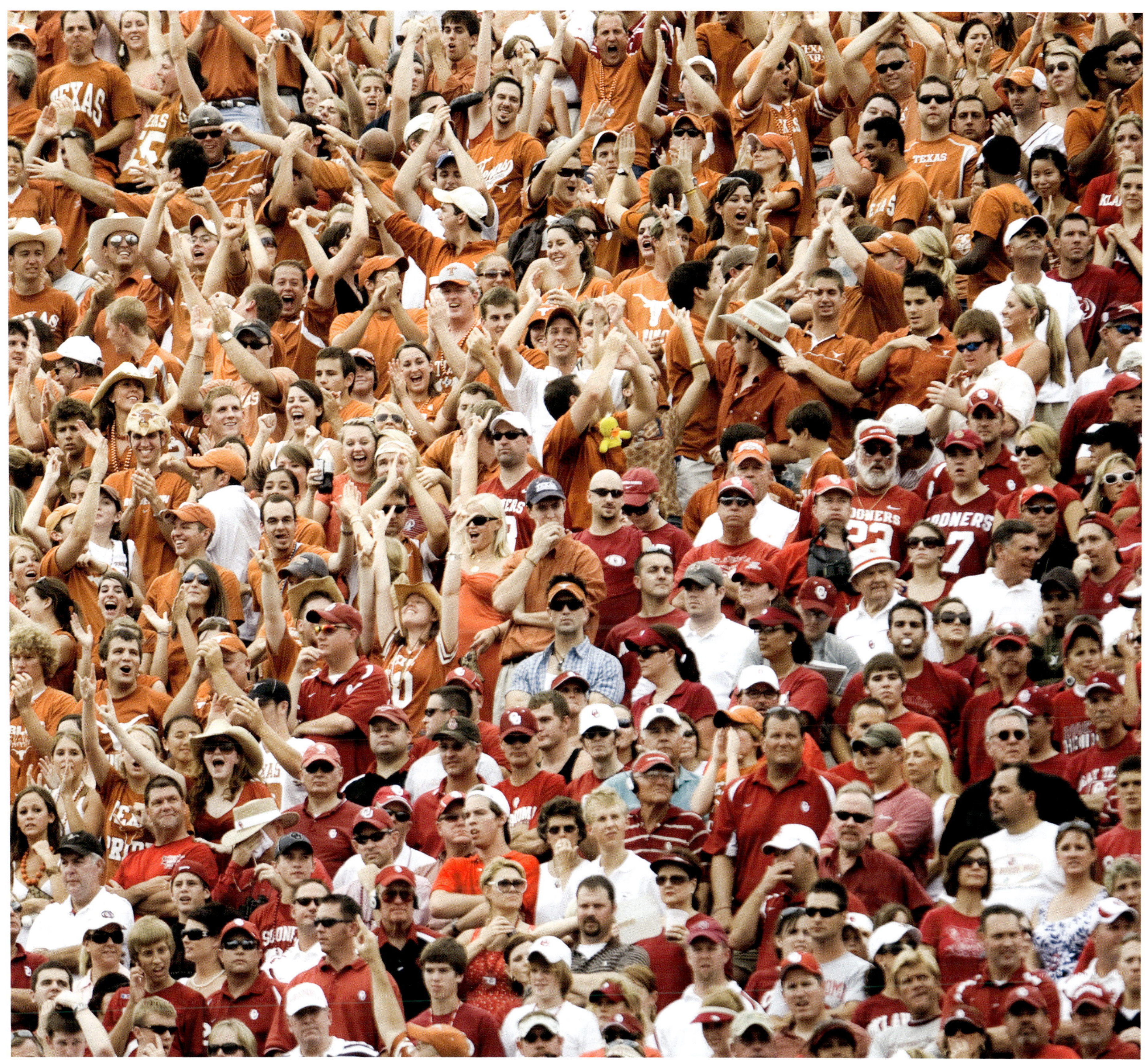

Above Every October, Texas and Oklahoma football fans show their true colors at the Red River Rivalry in Dallas. Here, Longhorn fans celebrate a score while the OU faithful look on in stunned silence.

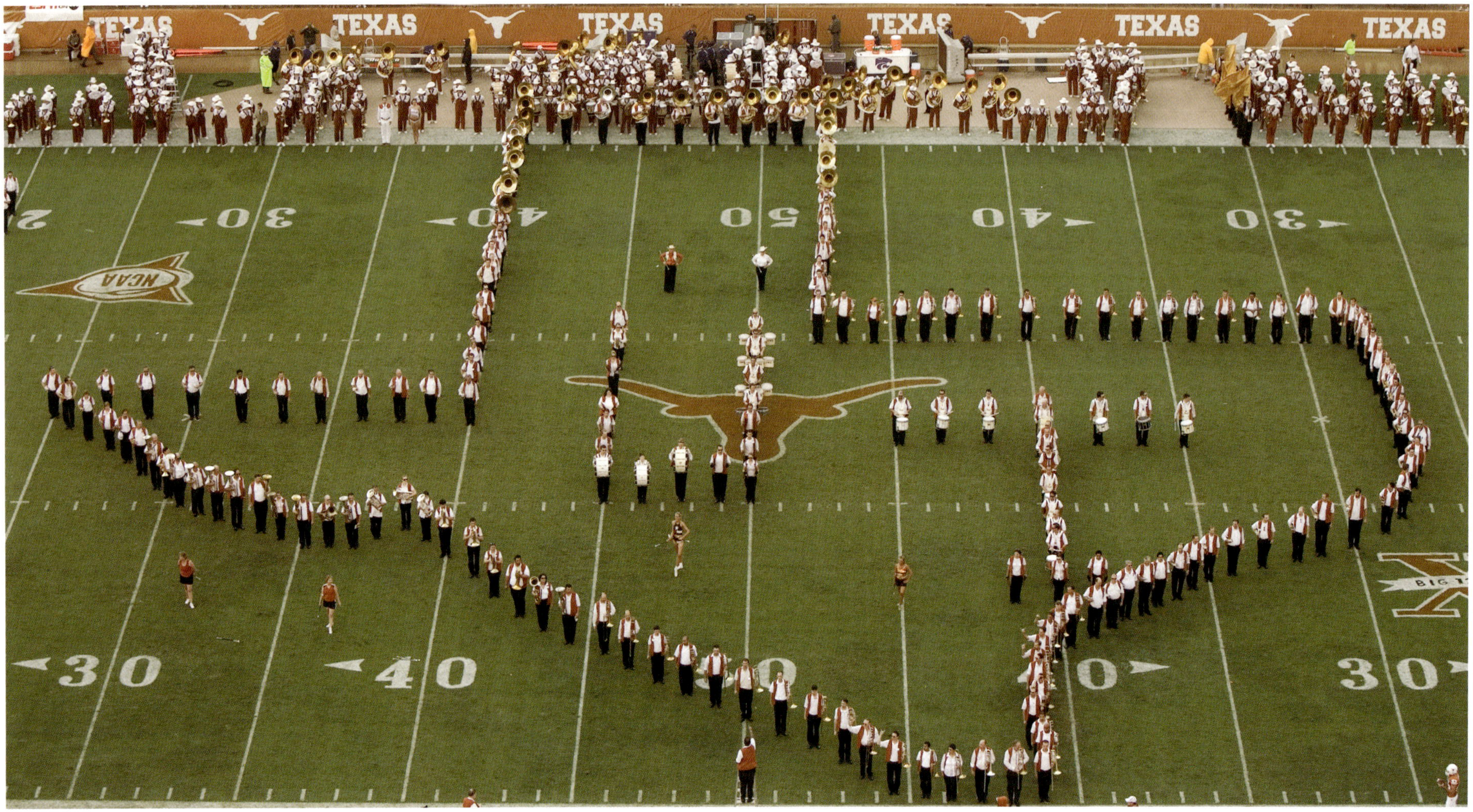

Above The revered University of Texas Alumni Band annually performs a halftime show as part of the Longhorn Band's reunion weekend.

Below Eight feet in diameter and about 500 pounds, "Big Bertha" made its first appearance with the Longhorn Band in 1955.

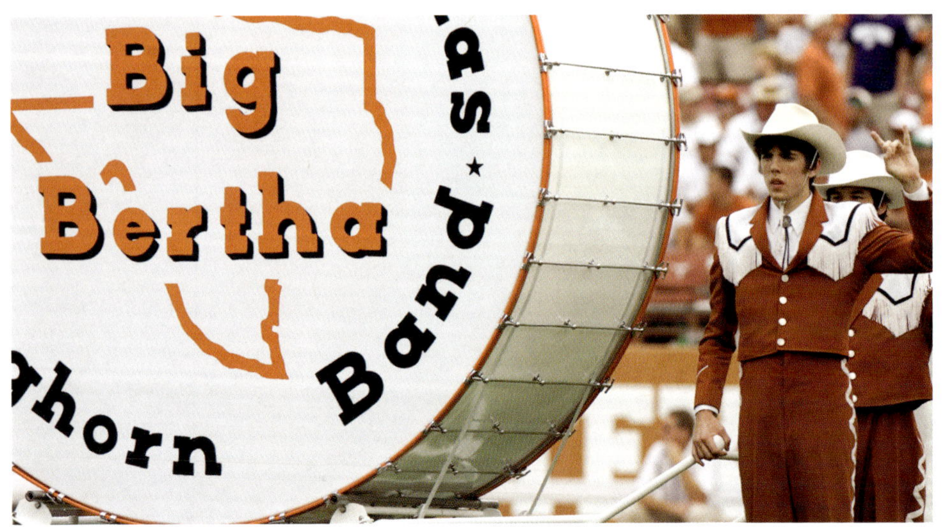

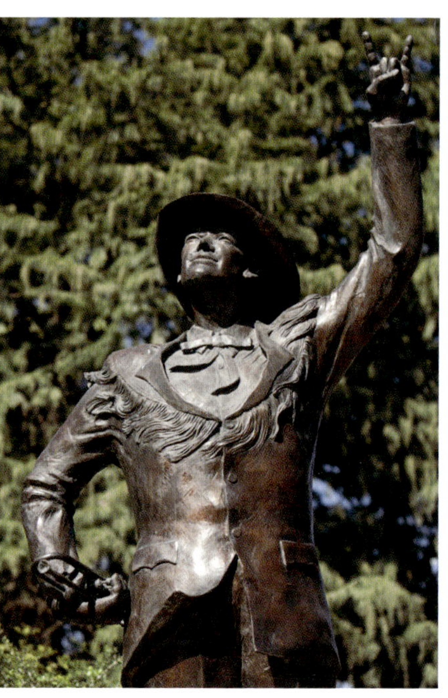

Right On the corner of 23rd Street and San Jacinto Boulevard is a statue dedicated as part of the Longhorn Band's centennial year in 2000. Originally called the University Band, the group was founded in 1900 by chemistry professor Eugene Schoch, who recruited 16 students, visited Jackson's Pawn Shop in downtown Austin, and spent $150 of his own money for musical instruments.

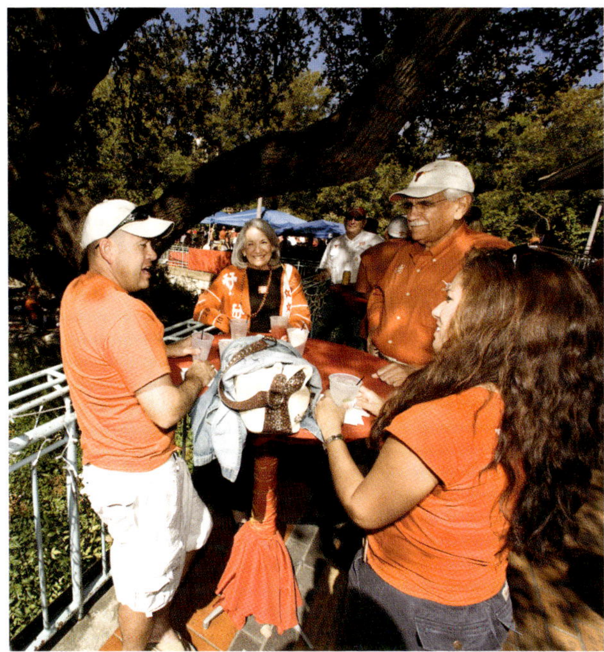

Before every home football game, thousands of UT alumni revel on the Etter-Harbin Alumni Center grounds as part of the Texas Exes Tailgate.

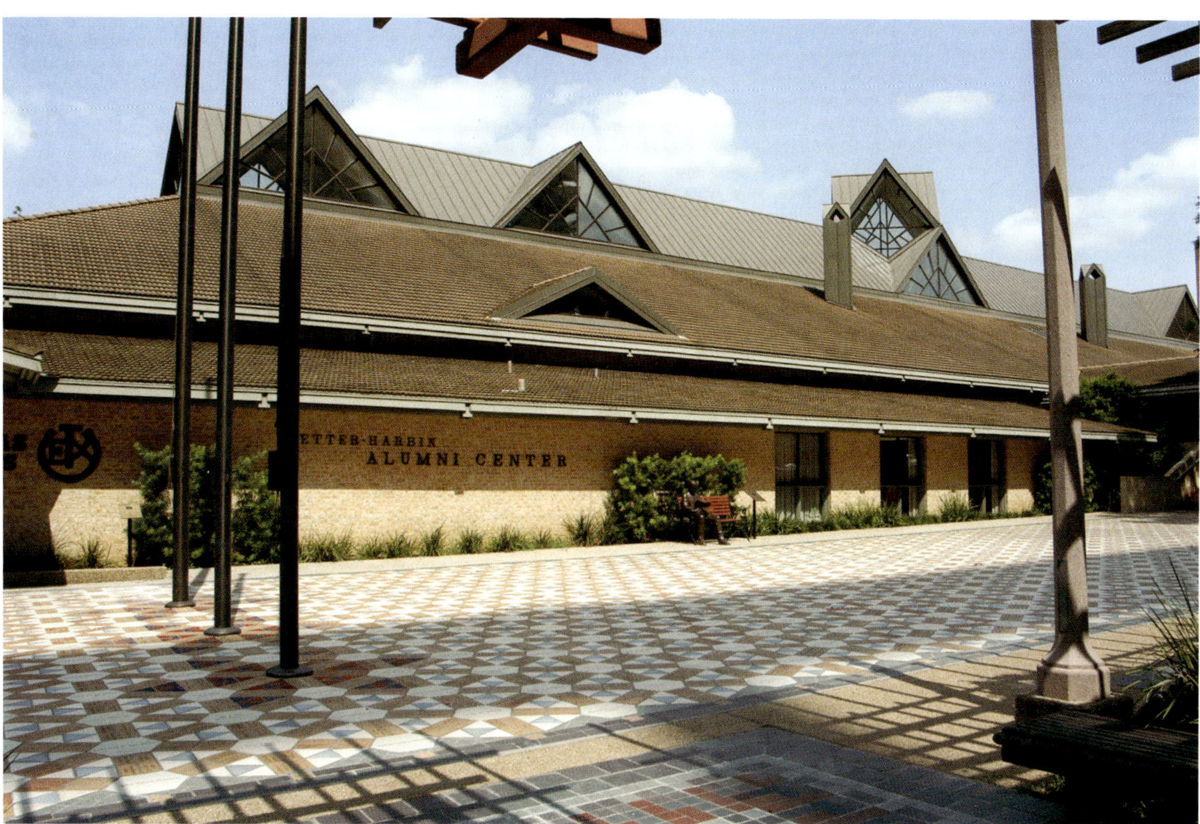

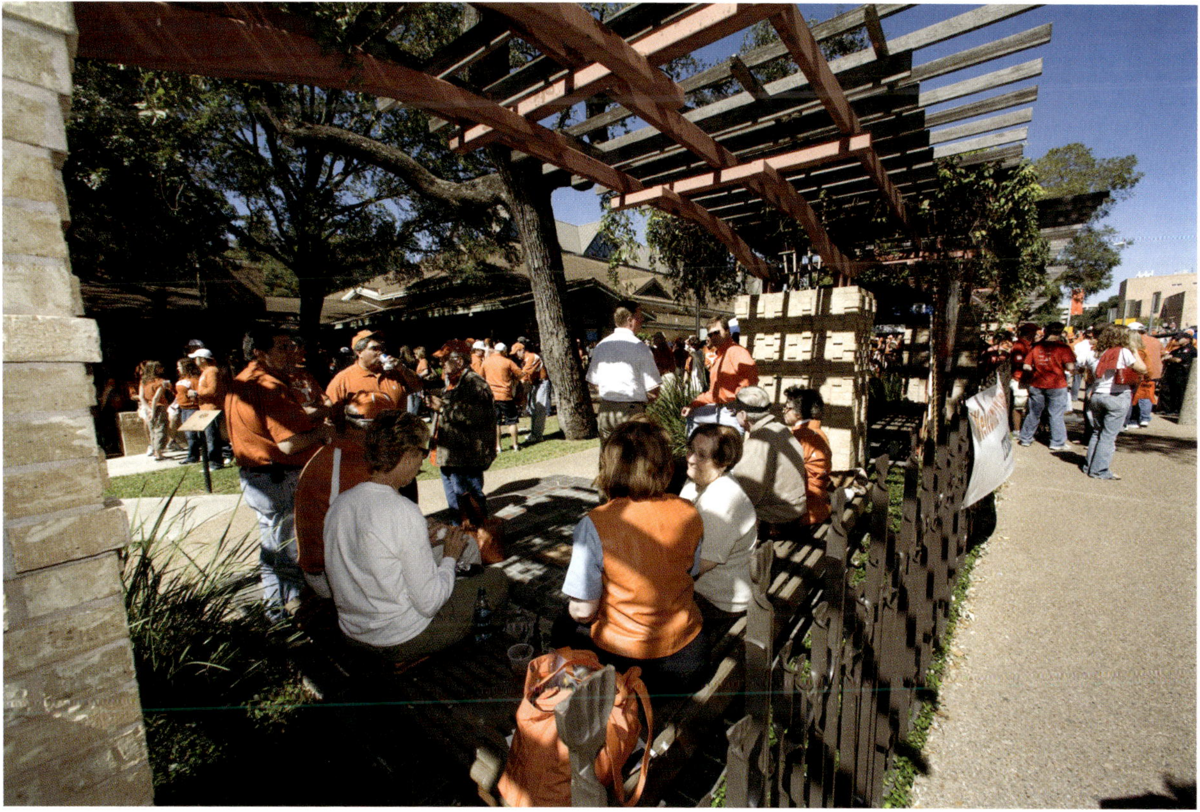

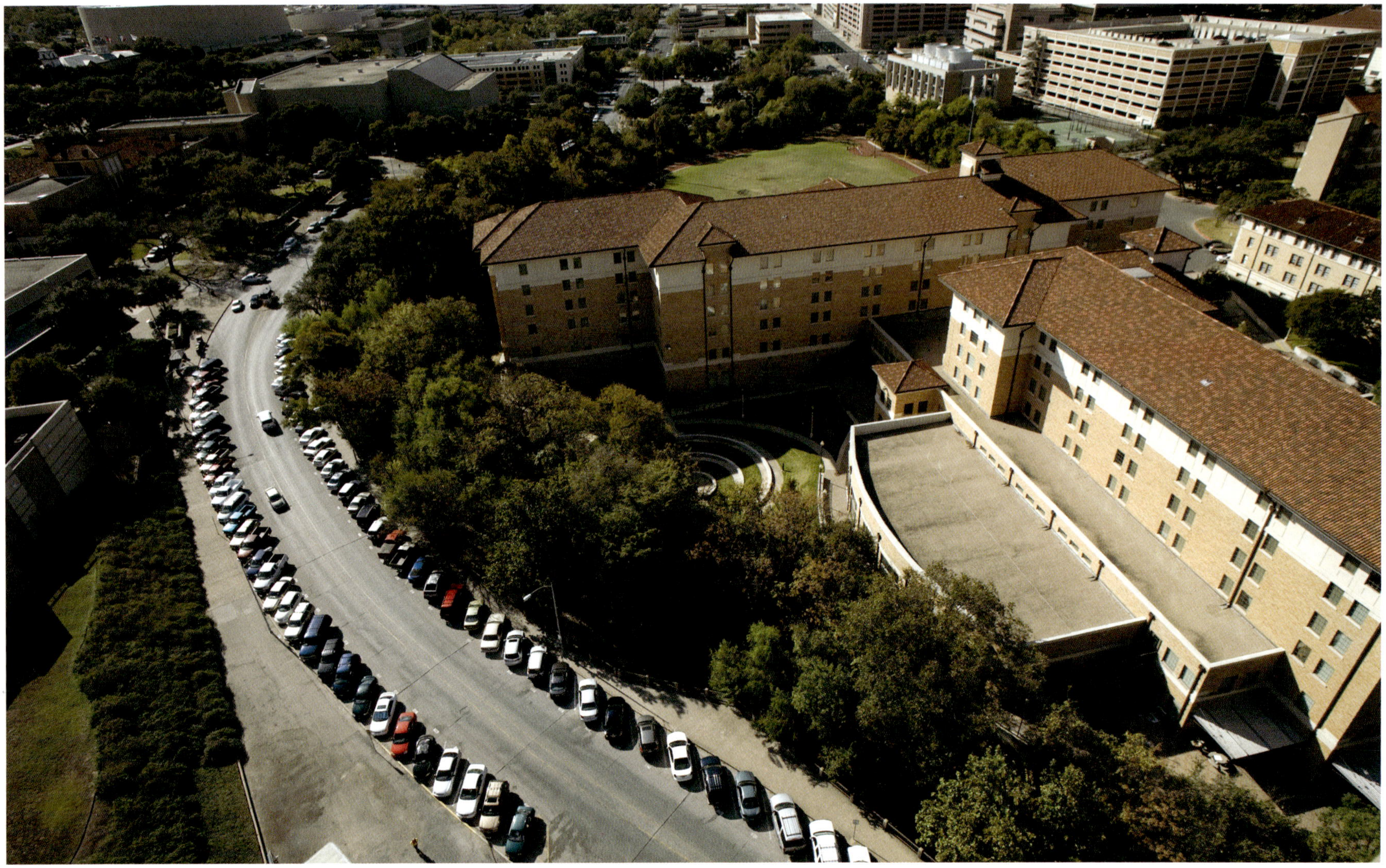

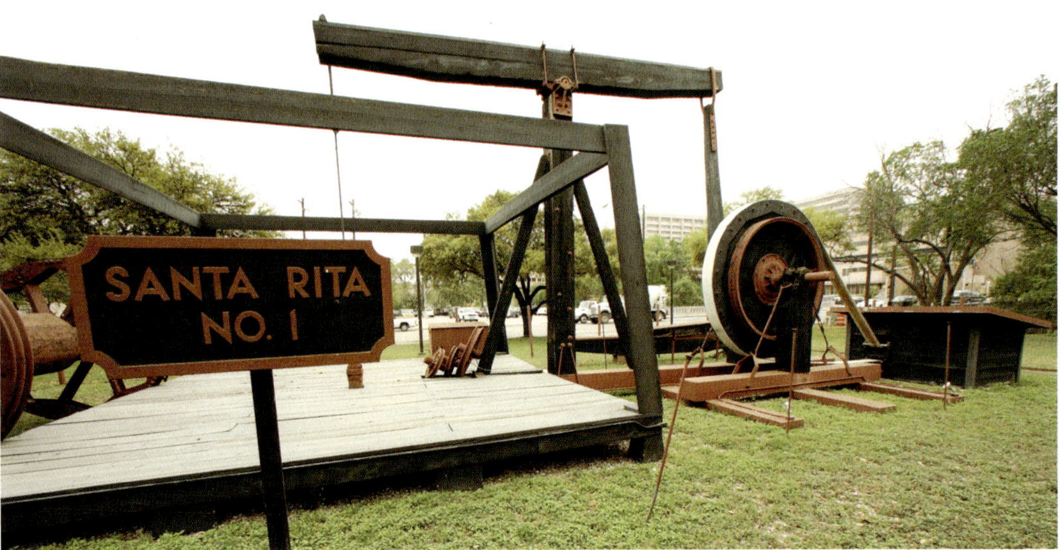

Above A view of the San Jacinto Residence Hall and Clark Field just beyond.

Left On May 28, 1923, the Santa Rita oil well "blew in," and the discovery of oil on UT lands in West Texas forever changed the University. The original rig was transported to Austin and installed on the campus in 1958.

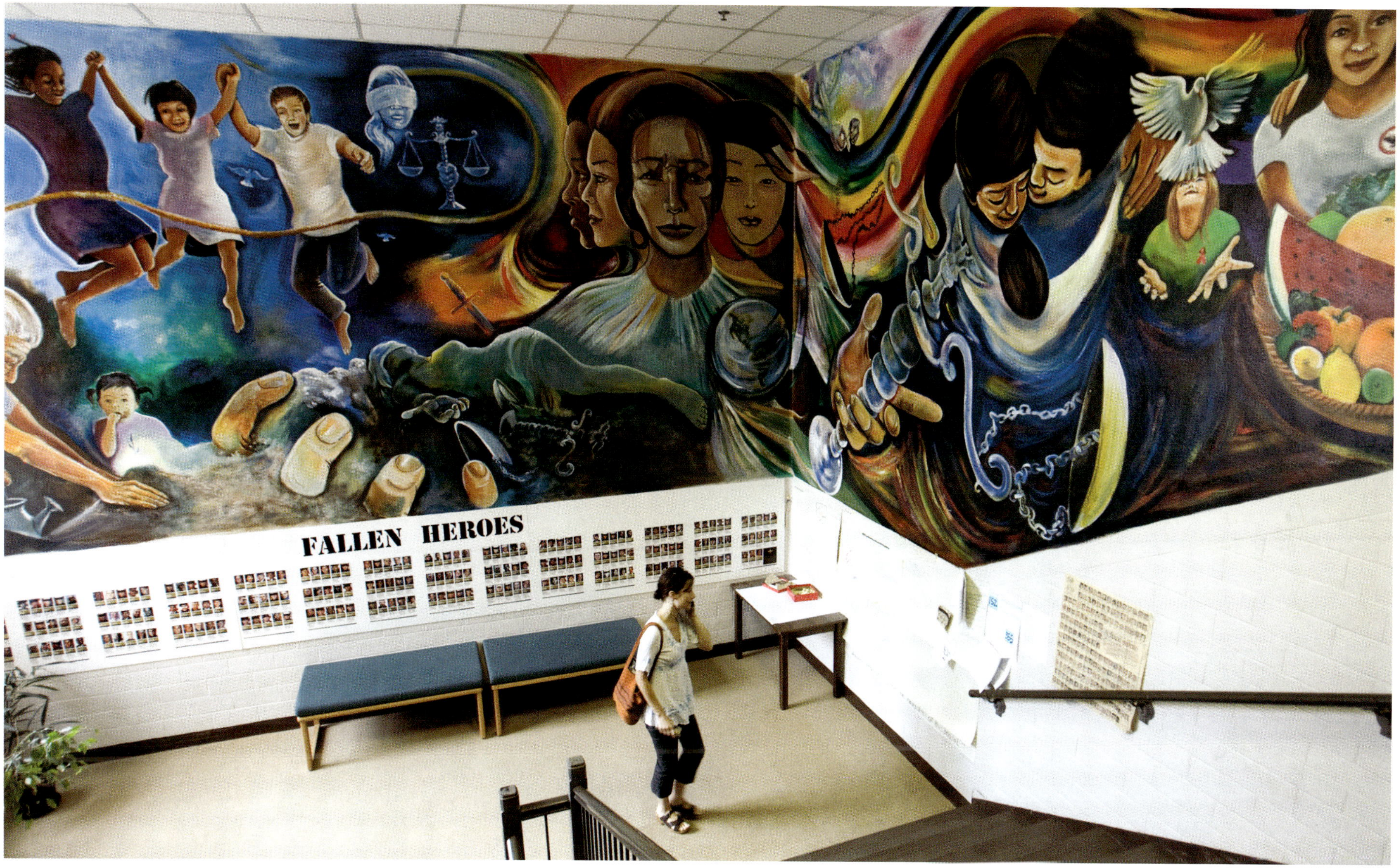

One of the highlights of the School of Social Work Building is a mural painted by Raul Valdez in April 1996. After soliciting suggestions from students and faculty on the meaning and impact of social work on society, the artist produced this colorful work. It reflects social issues ranging from violence and poverty to education and positive community spirit. Those at the dedication, including then-president Robert Berdahl, were invited to add their handprints.

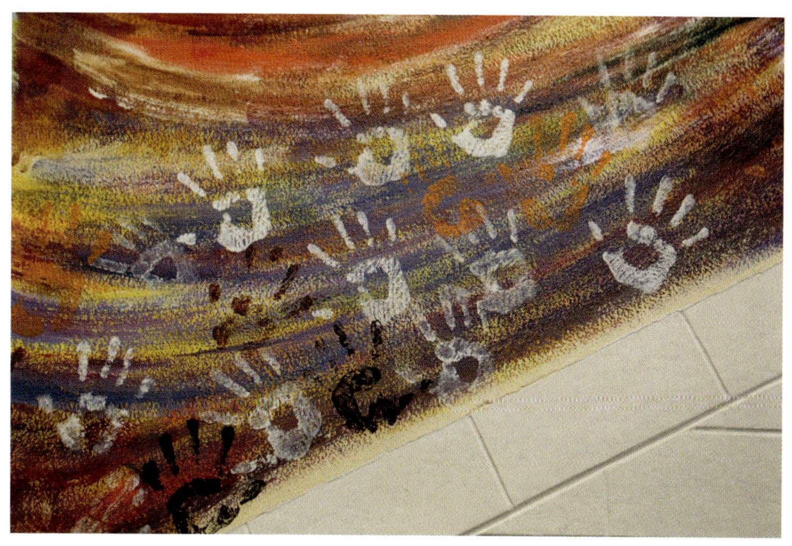

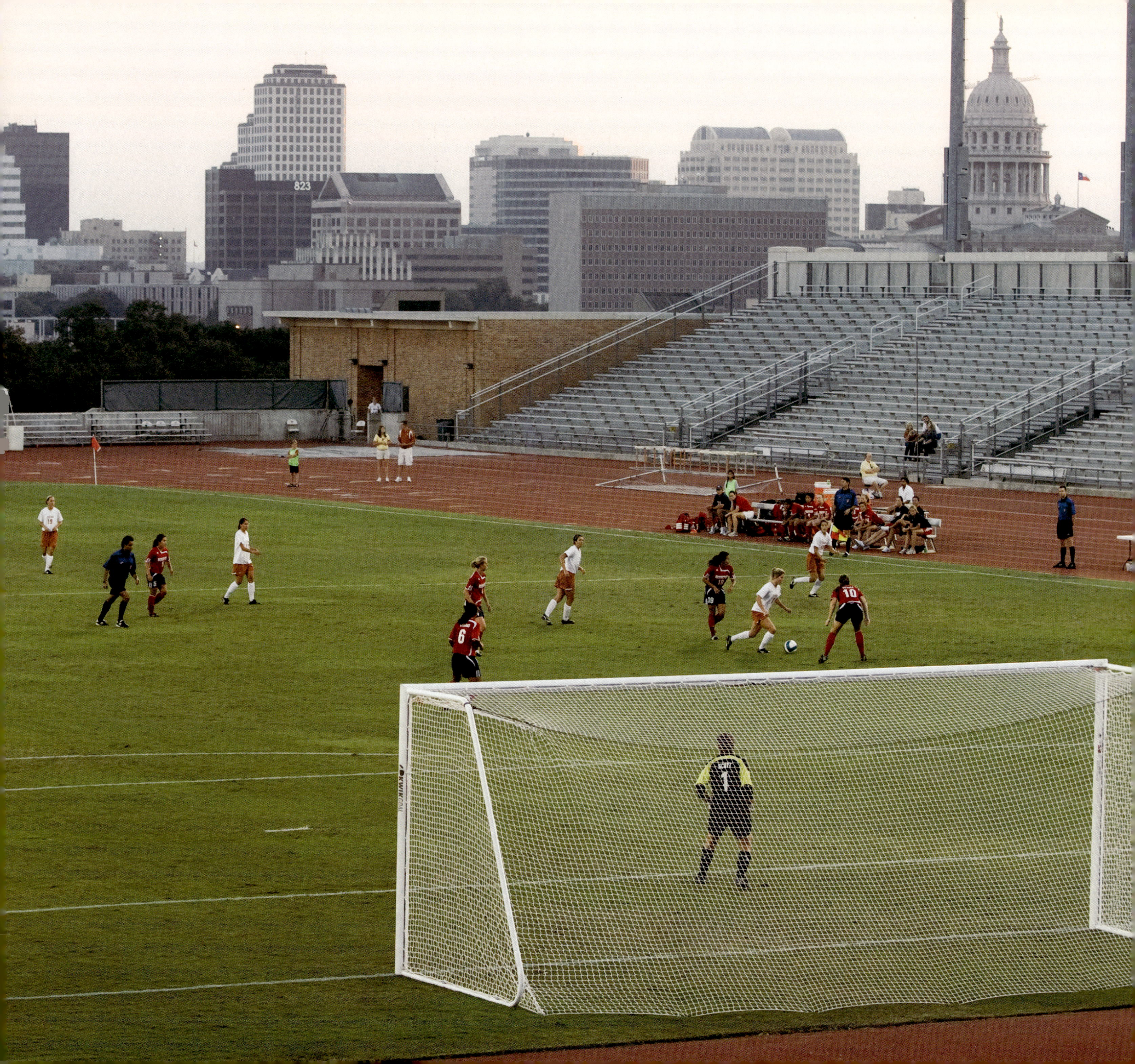
823

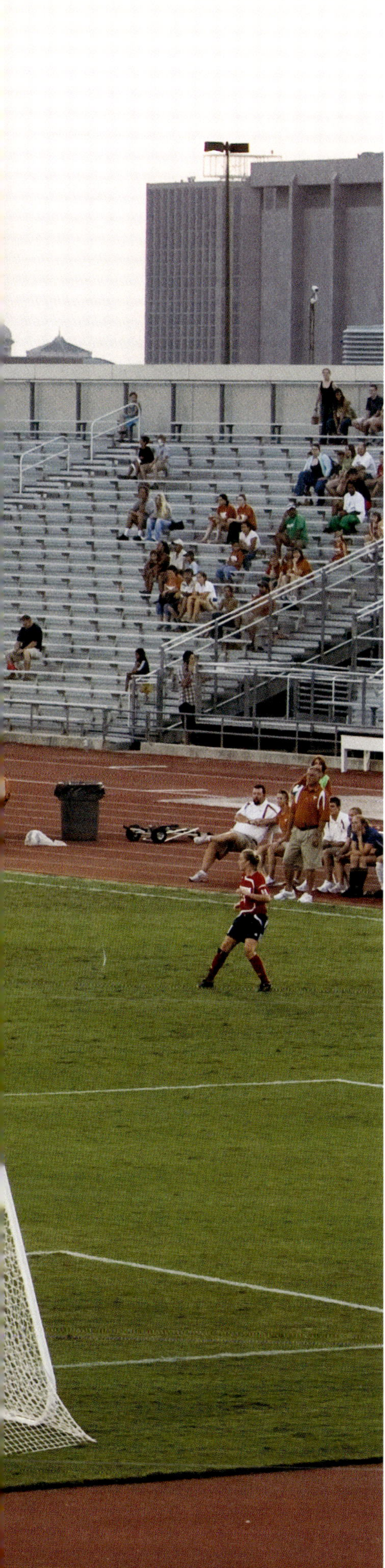

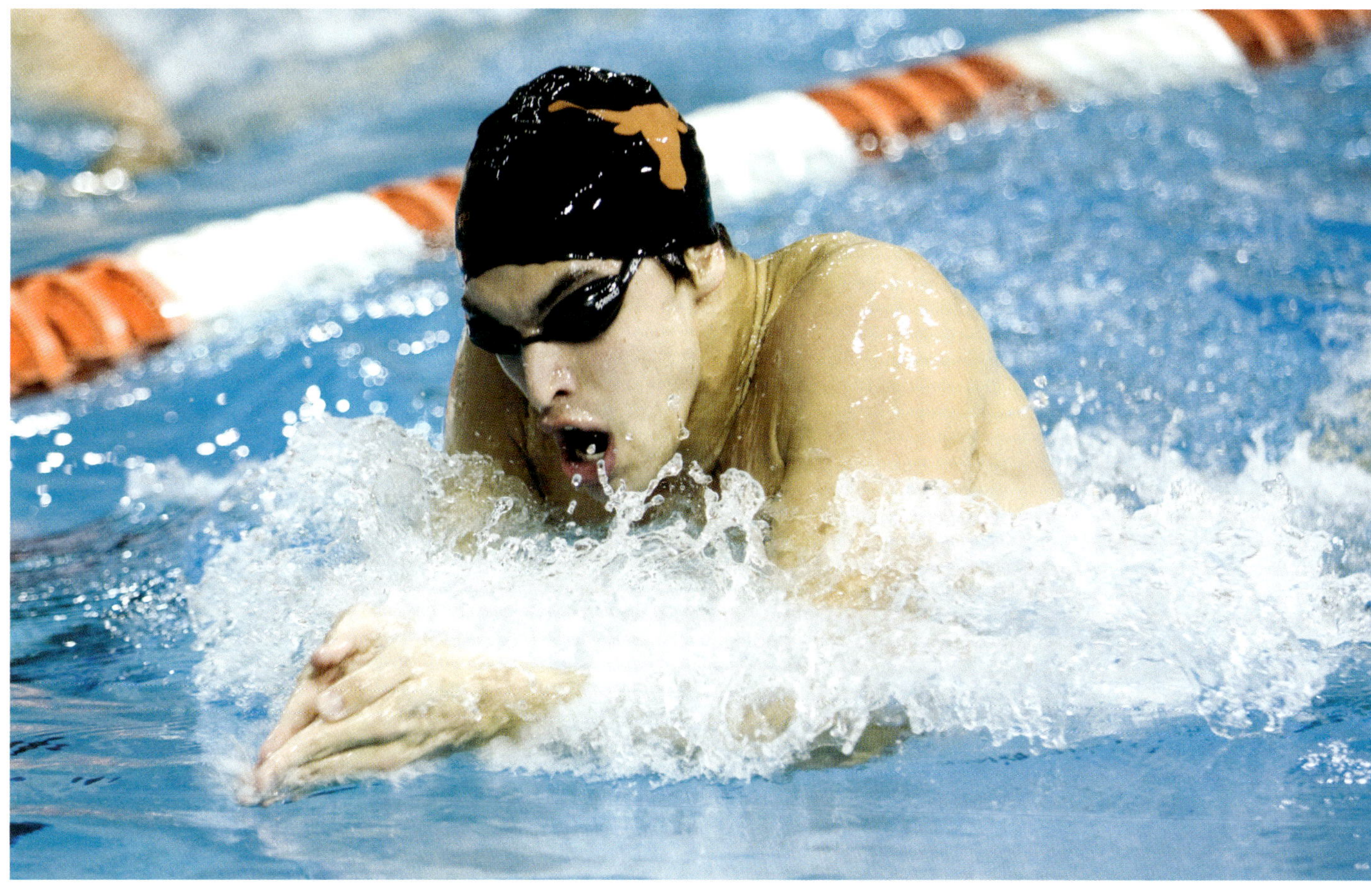

Left With a panoramic view of downtown Austin, the women's soccer team competes at Mike A. Myers Stadium, as do the track teams.

Above The Lee and Joe Jamail Texas Swimming Center was opened in 1977 and was modeled after the facilities used for the 1972 Olympic Games in Munich. The men's and women's swim teams have won multiple national championships.

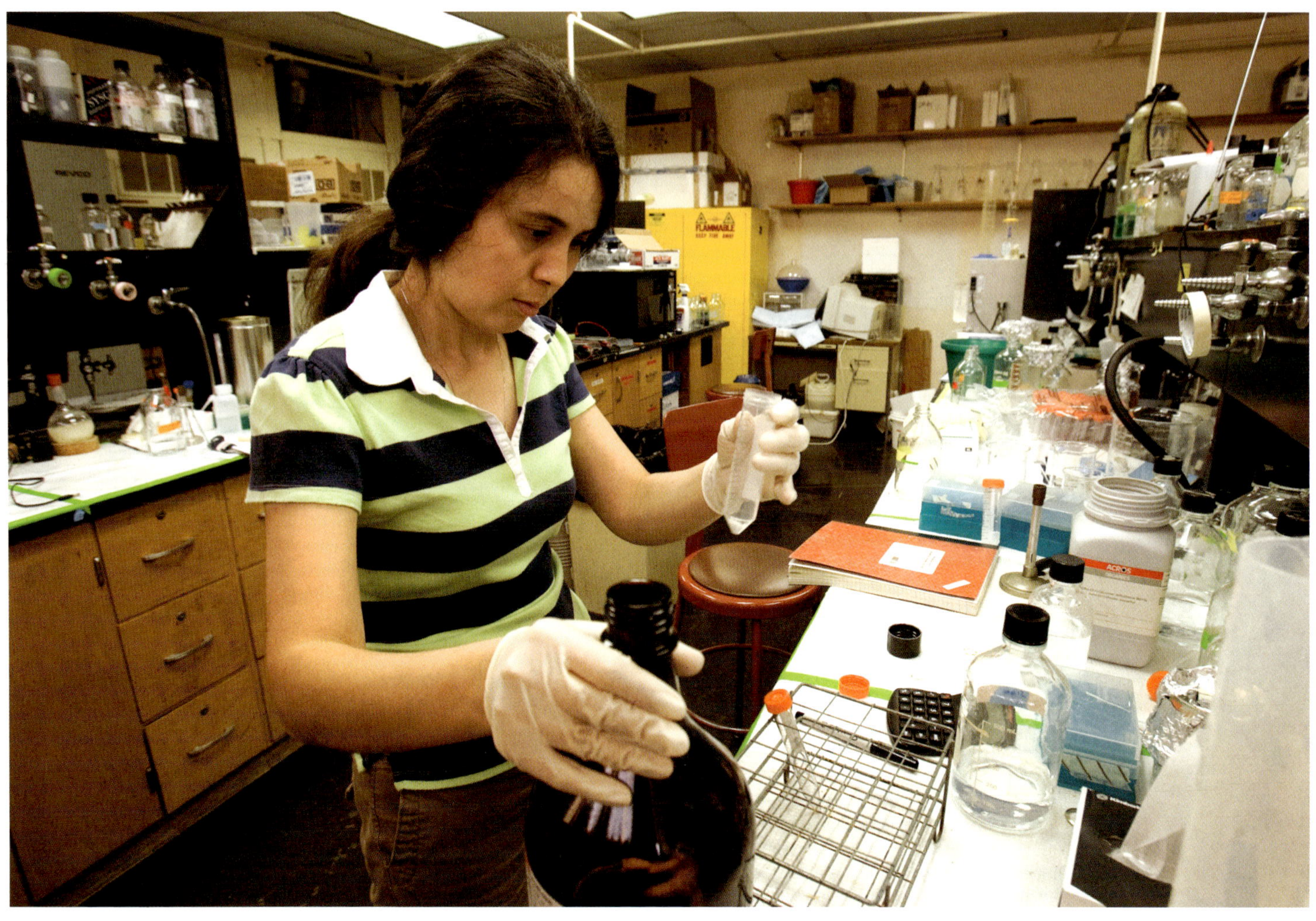

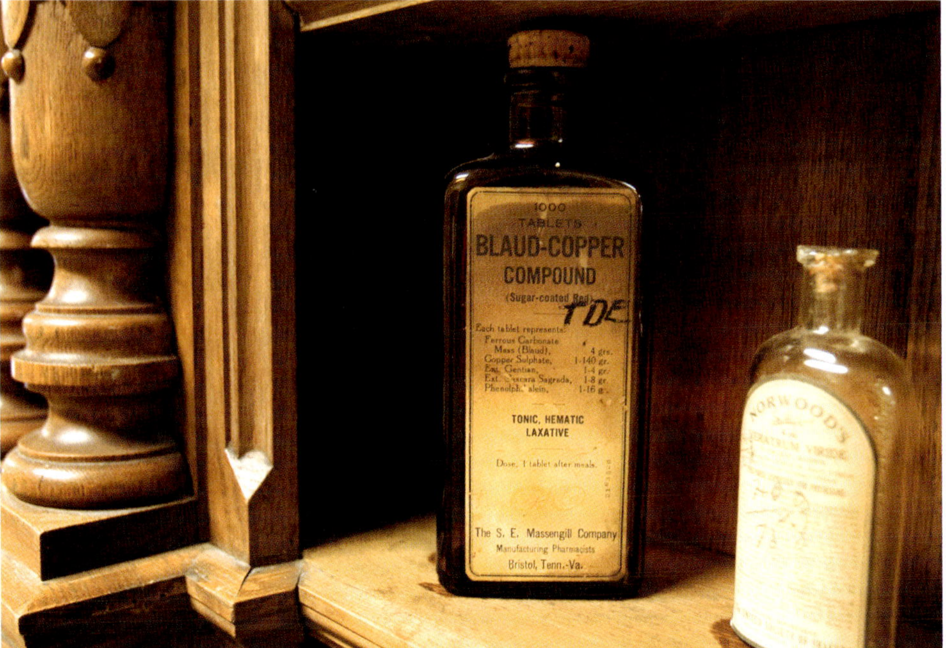

Above A busy student works in a laboratory at the College of Pharmacy.

Left Since 1977, the College of Pharmacy has been acquiring antique drug store items, which are on display throughout the college's two buildings.

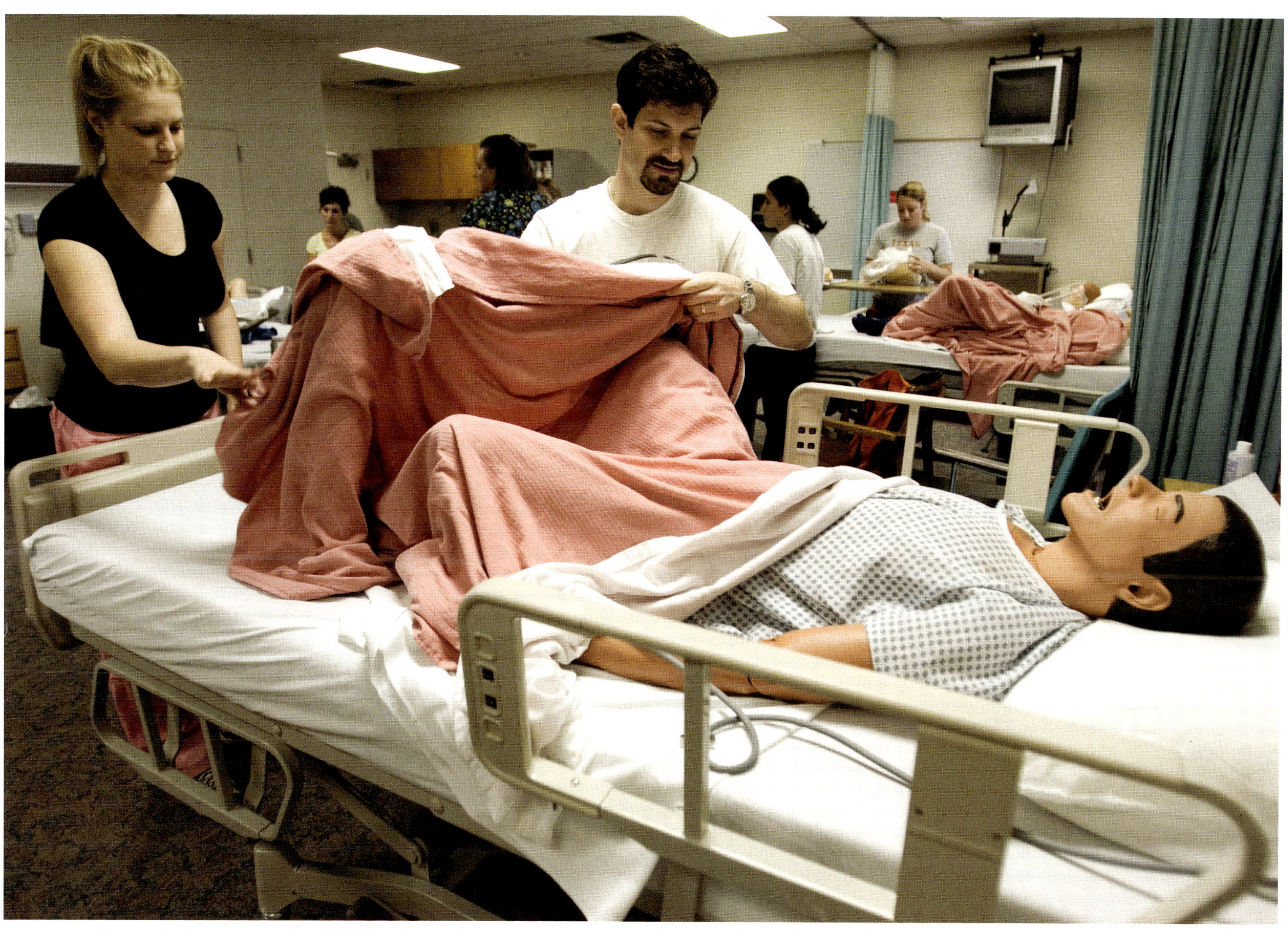

Students at the School of Nursing study their profession in a laboratory class. An important learning tool at the nursing school is a realistic virtual patient that can be fitted with a variety of wounds or programmed to reflect different medical conditions.

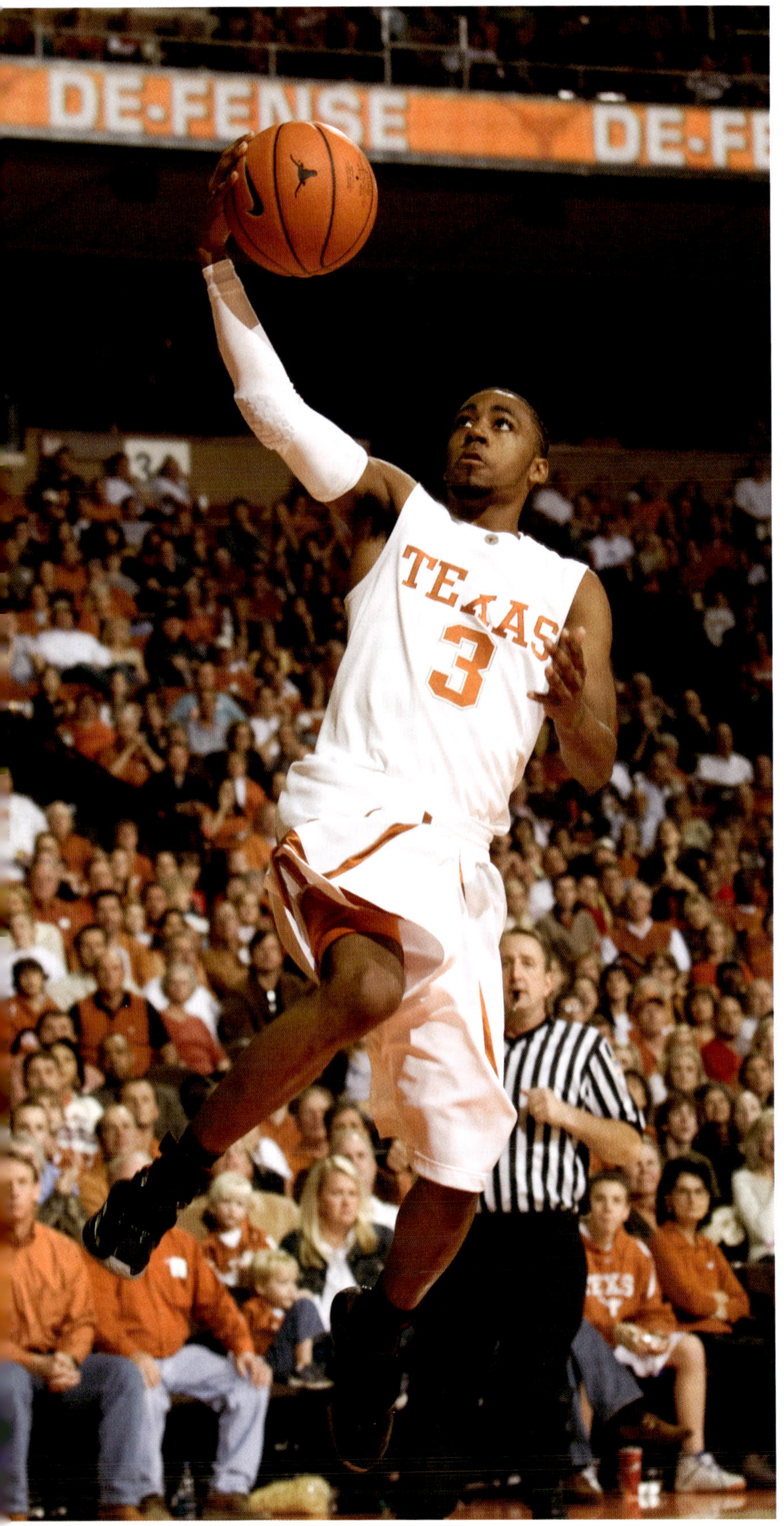

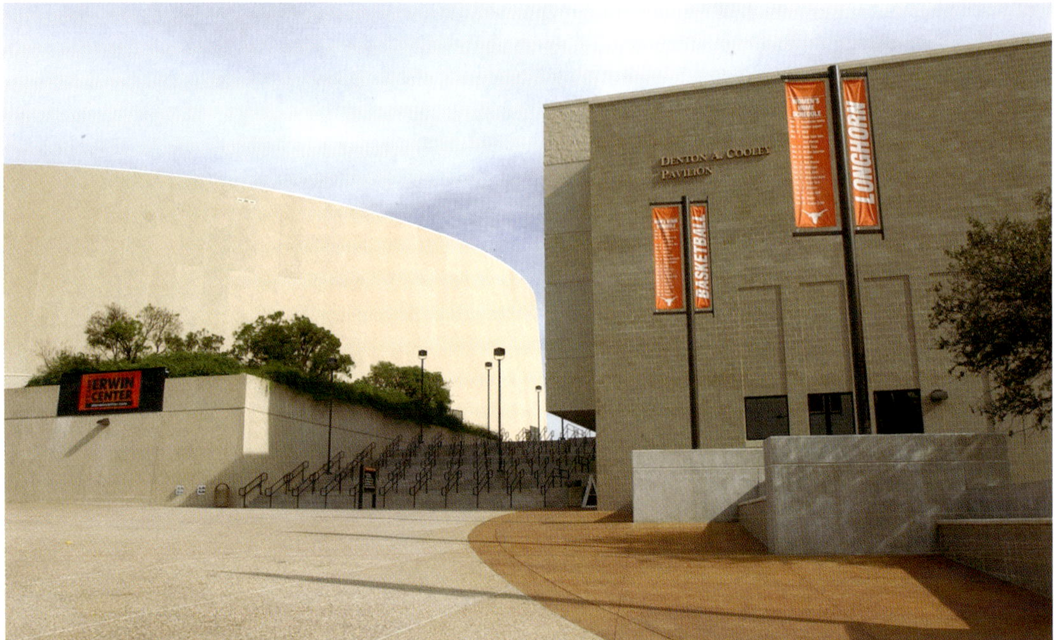

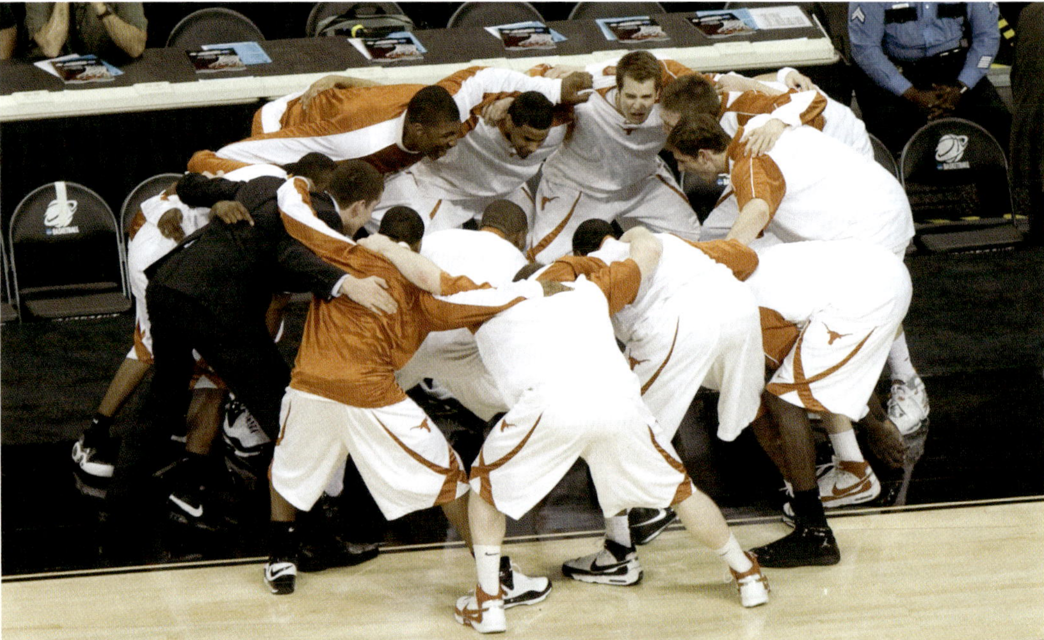

The Frank Erwin Center, along with the Denton Cooley Pavilion practice facility, is headquarters for the men's and women's basketball squads, including A.J. Abrams at left. The Erwin Center holds about 18,000 spectators.

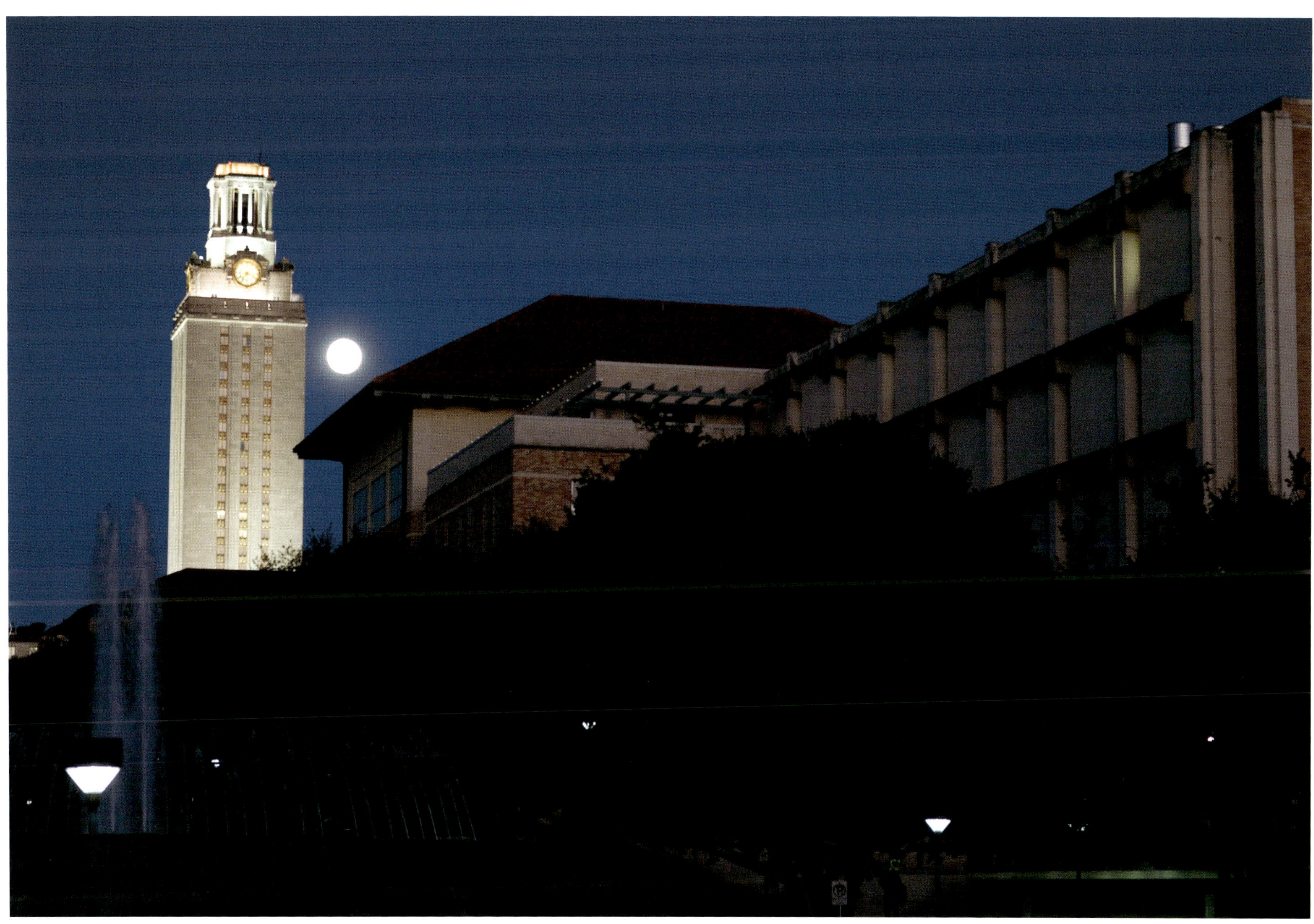

A moonlight view of the East Mall and the Jackson School of Geosciences building. Uniting the Department of Geology, the Bureau of Economic Geology, and the Institute of Geophysics, the Jackson School was designated a separate college in 2005.

Facing Page After a 12-year effort by students, a bronze statue of Martin Luther King Jr. was unveiled on the East Mall in September 1999. The likeness of the civil rights leader was one of the first on a U.S. college campus.

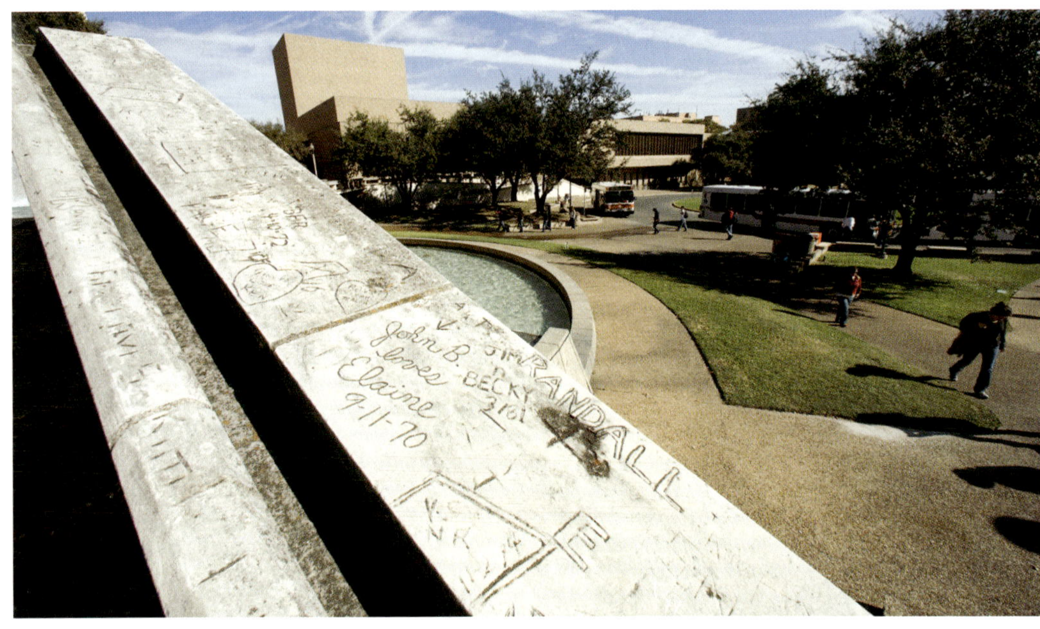

Turned on for the first time in 1970, the East Mall Fountain is 80 feet in diameter and presents a familiar backdrop to students on their way to class. The fountain is bracketed by a pair of stairways made from soft limestone. Through the years, students have carved initials and class years in the railings.

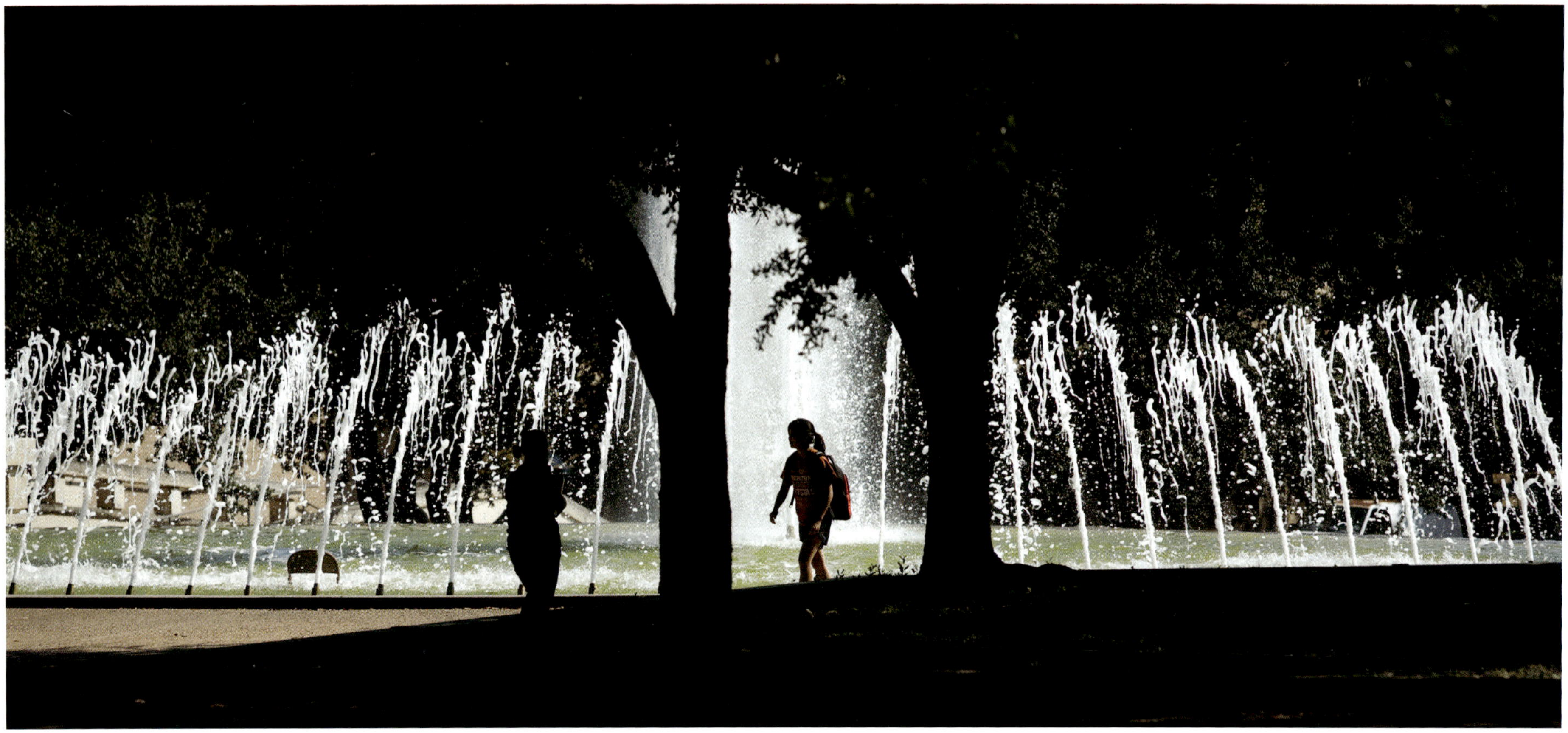

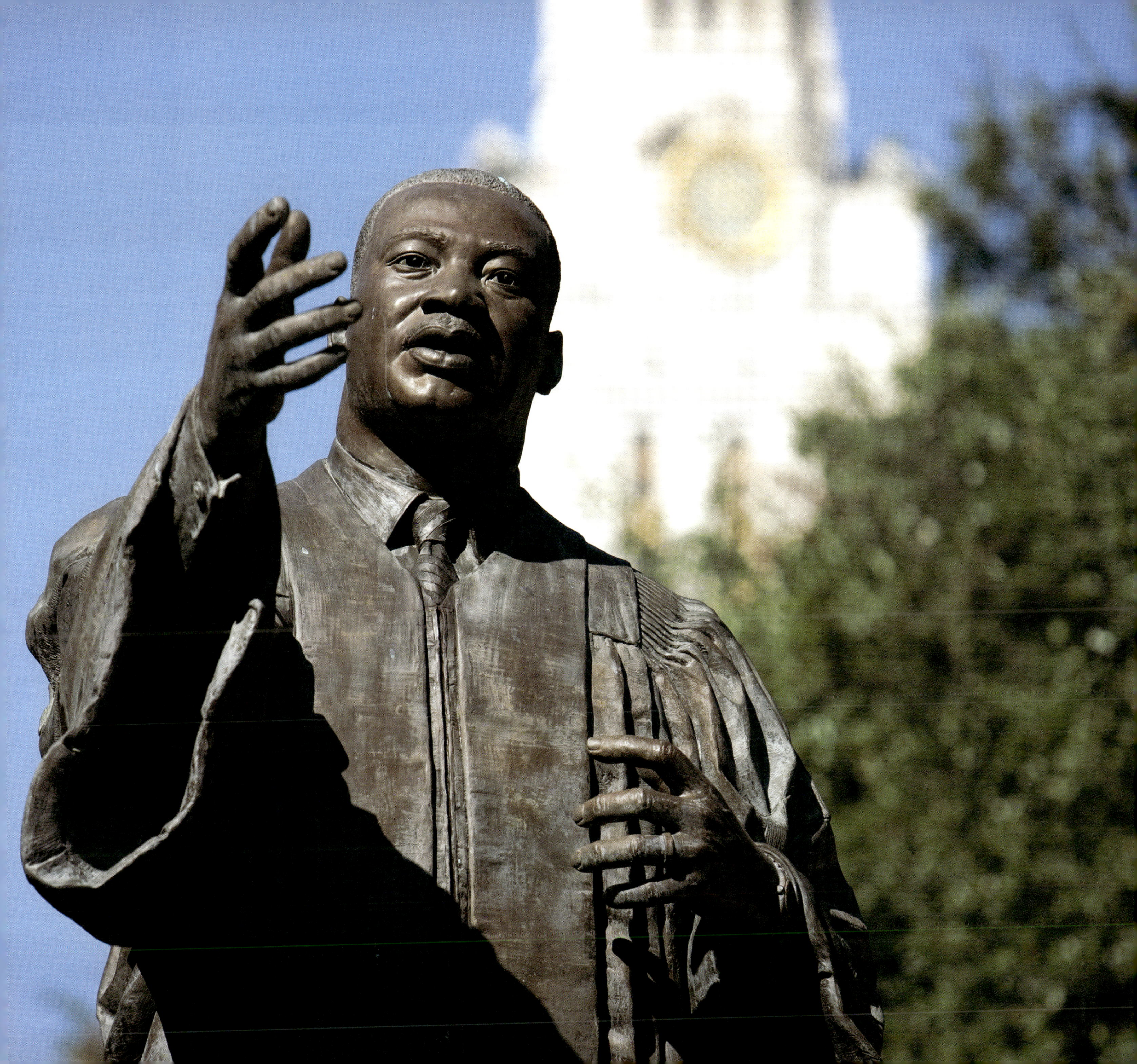

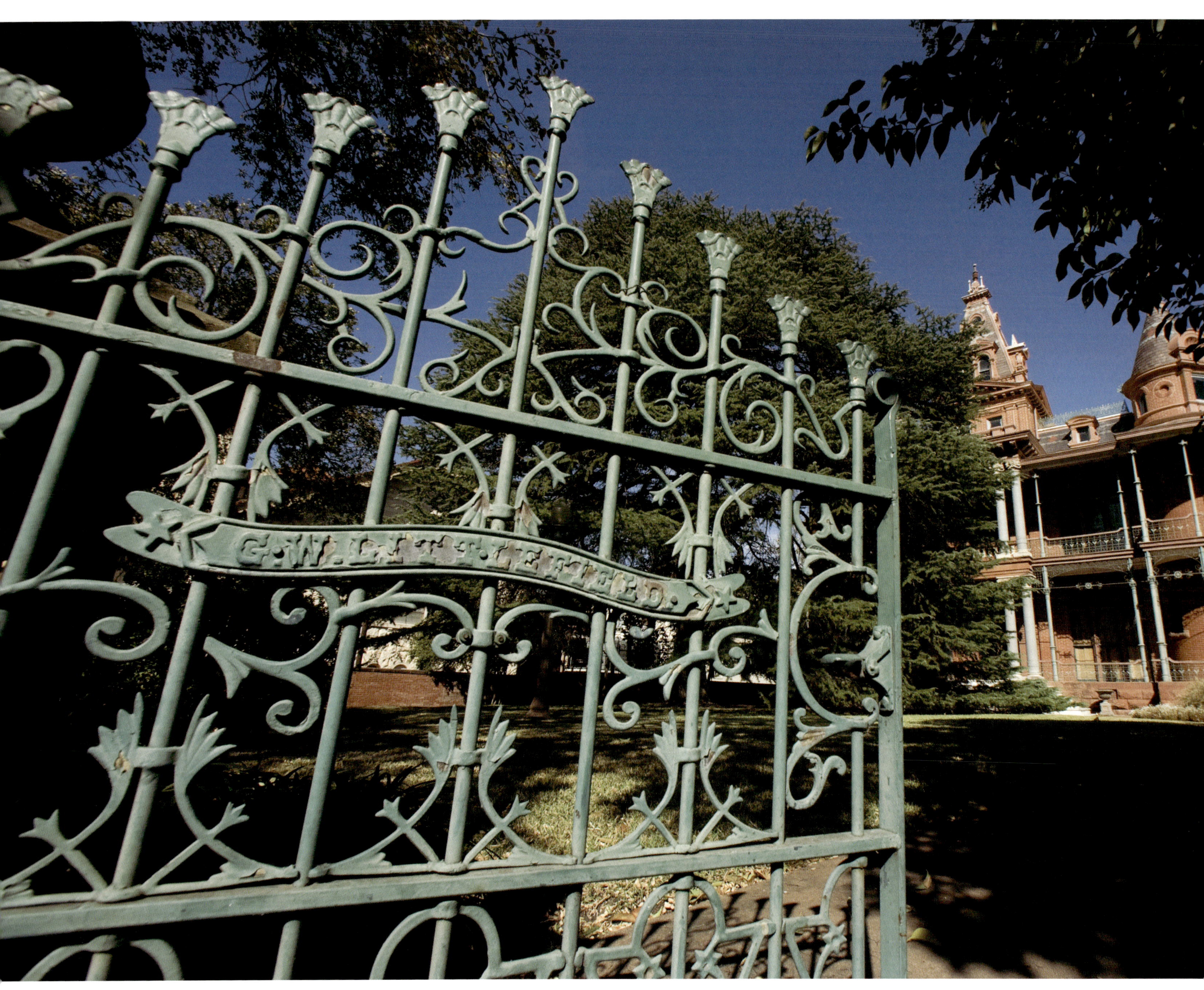
G.W.LITTLEFIELD.

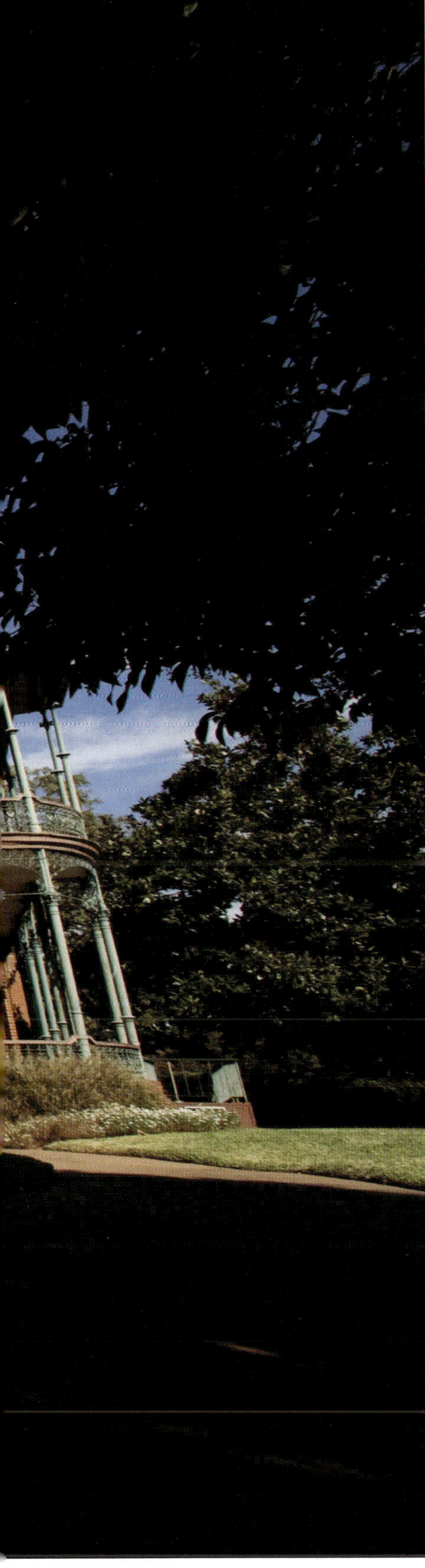

The Littlefield Home and its carriage house were bequeathed to the University in 1920 and belonged to George W. Littlefield, an Austin banker and cattleman who served on the Board of Regents and was a UT benefactor. The Victorian-style mansion was completed in 1894 at a cost of about $50,000, and was constructed of red-brown brick from St. Louis, with sandstone trim. In the late 1930s it was used by the music department for practice rooms, and in World War II the mansion served as the headquarters for Navy ROTC, with a pair of anti-aircraft guns placed on the front lawn and a firing range in the attic. Today, the Littlefield Home contains a portion of the University's Development Office.

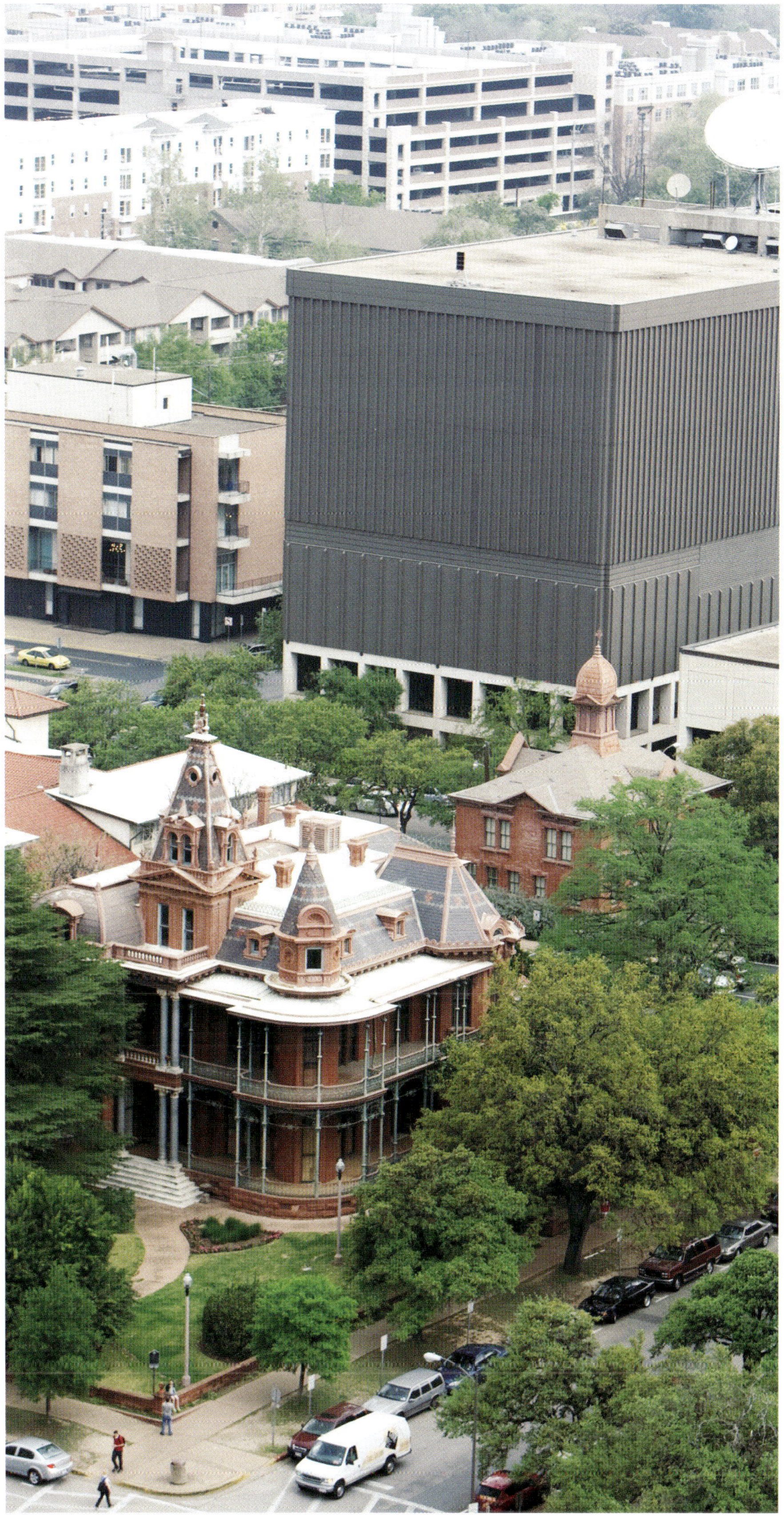

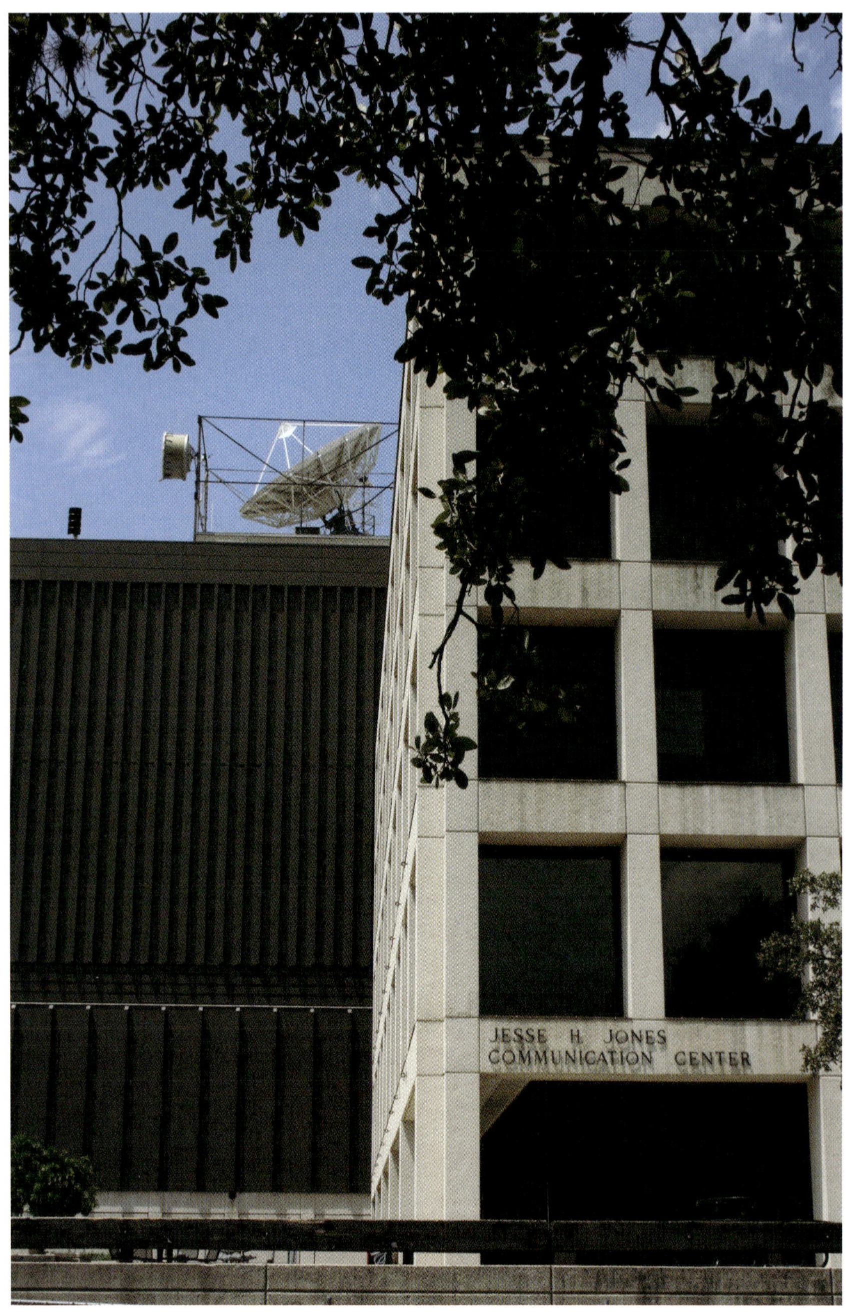

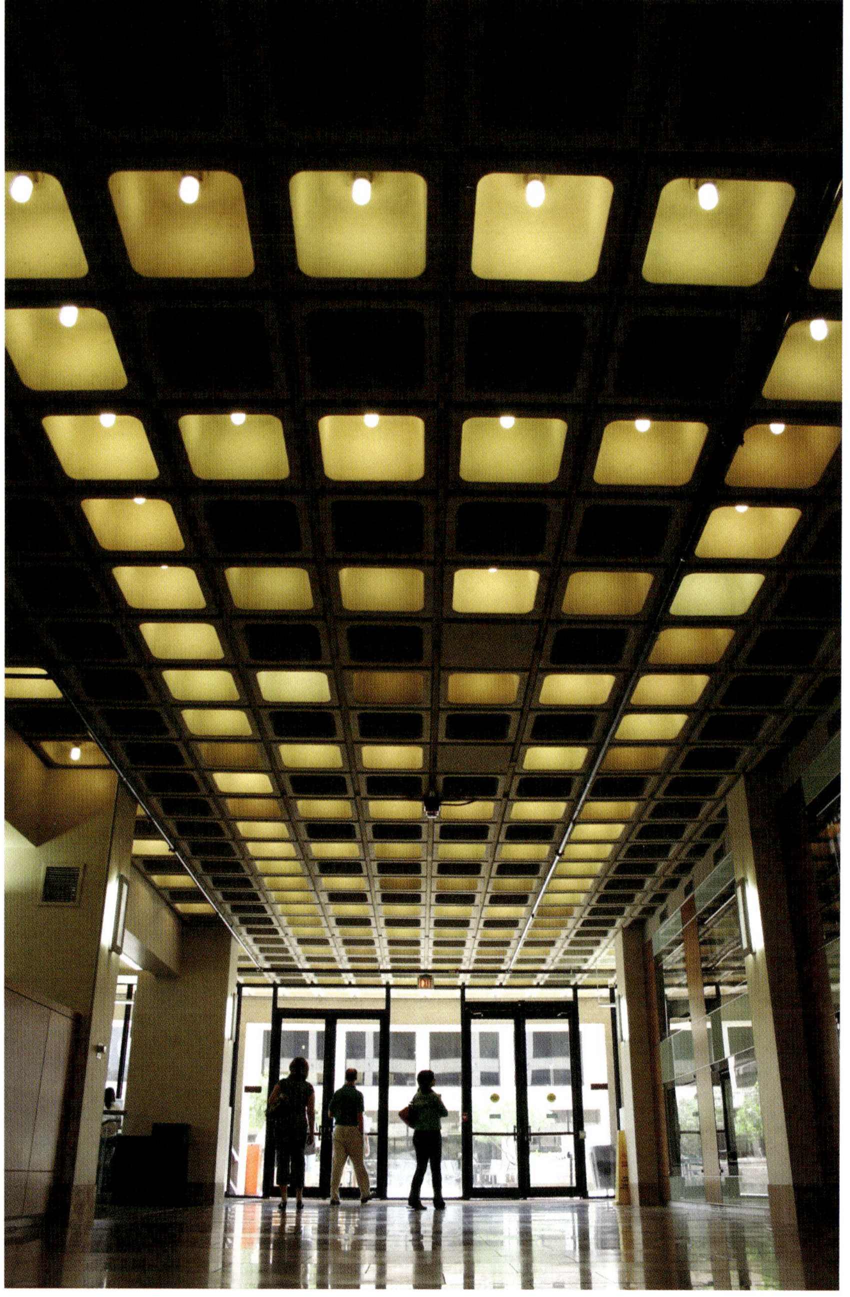

The Jesse H. Jones Communication Center houses the College of Communication. Comprised of three buildings surrounding a central plaza, the college offers programs in advertising, communication sciences and disorders, communication studies, public relations, radio-tv-film, and journalism. One building houses KUT-FM radio and KLRU-TV public television, including the studio used for the well-known music program *Austin City Limits*. The Communication Center also contains Texas Student Media, which produces *The Daily Texan* newspaper and the *Cactus* yearbook.

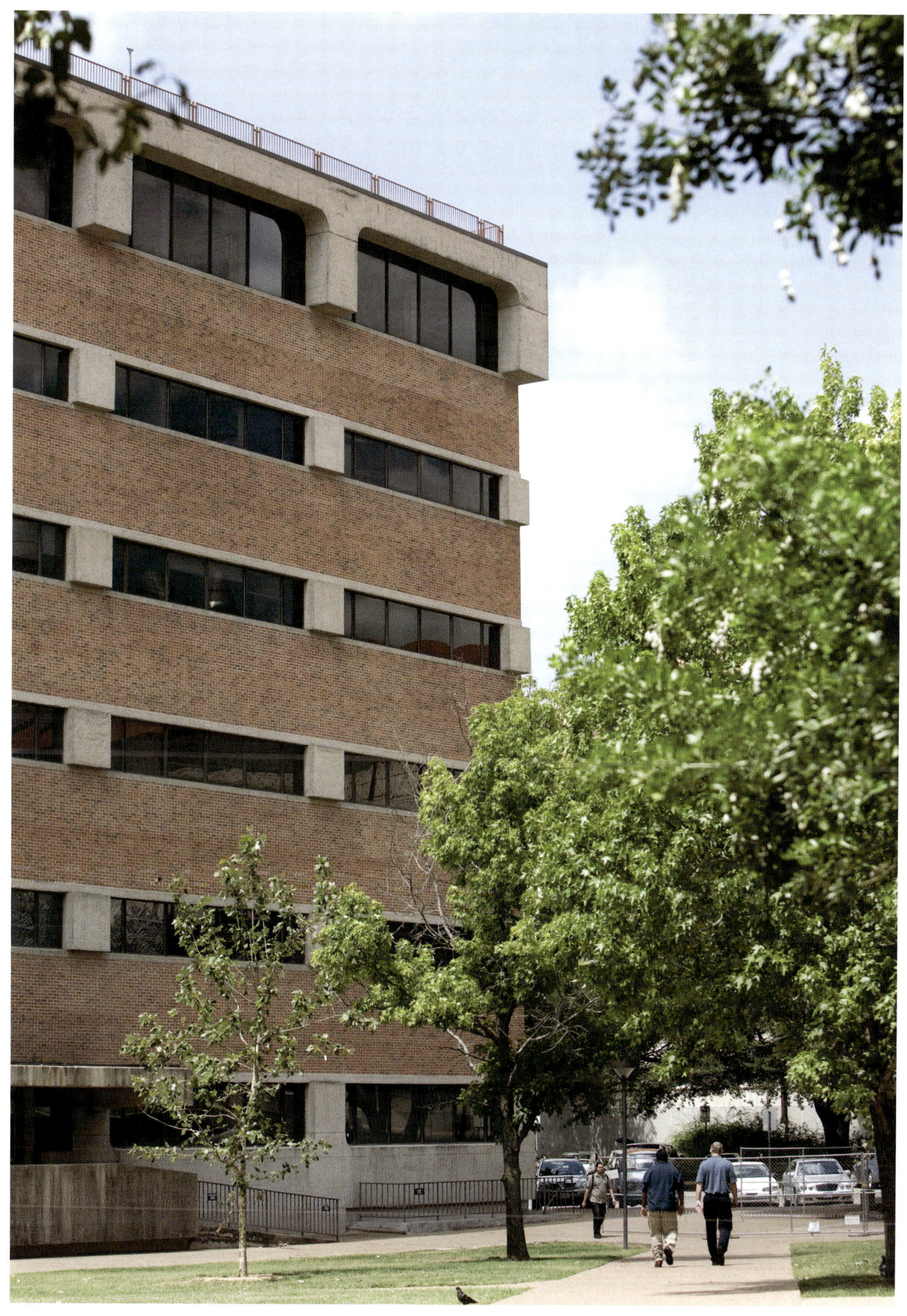

Completed in the spring of 1969, the Patterson Laboratories Building houses the Department of Zoology and is named for distinguished UT professor John T. Patterson, who served on the faculty from 1908 – 1955.

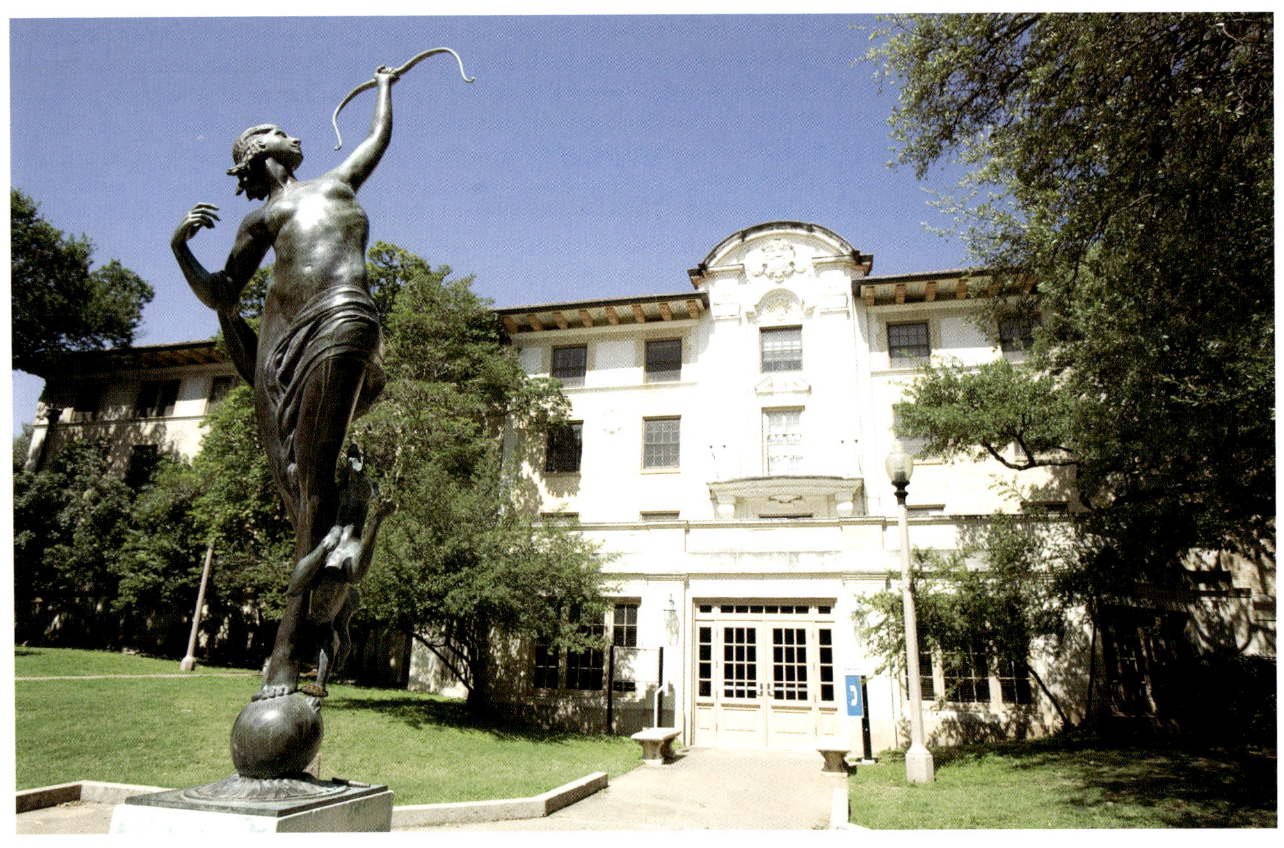

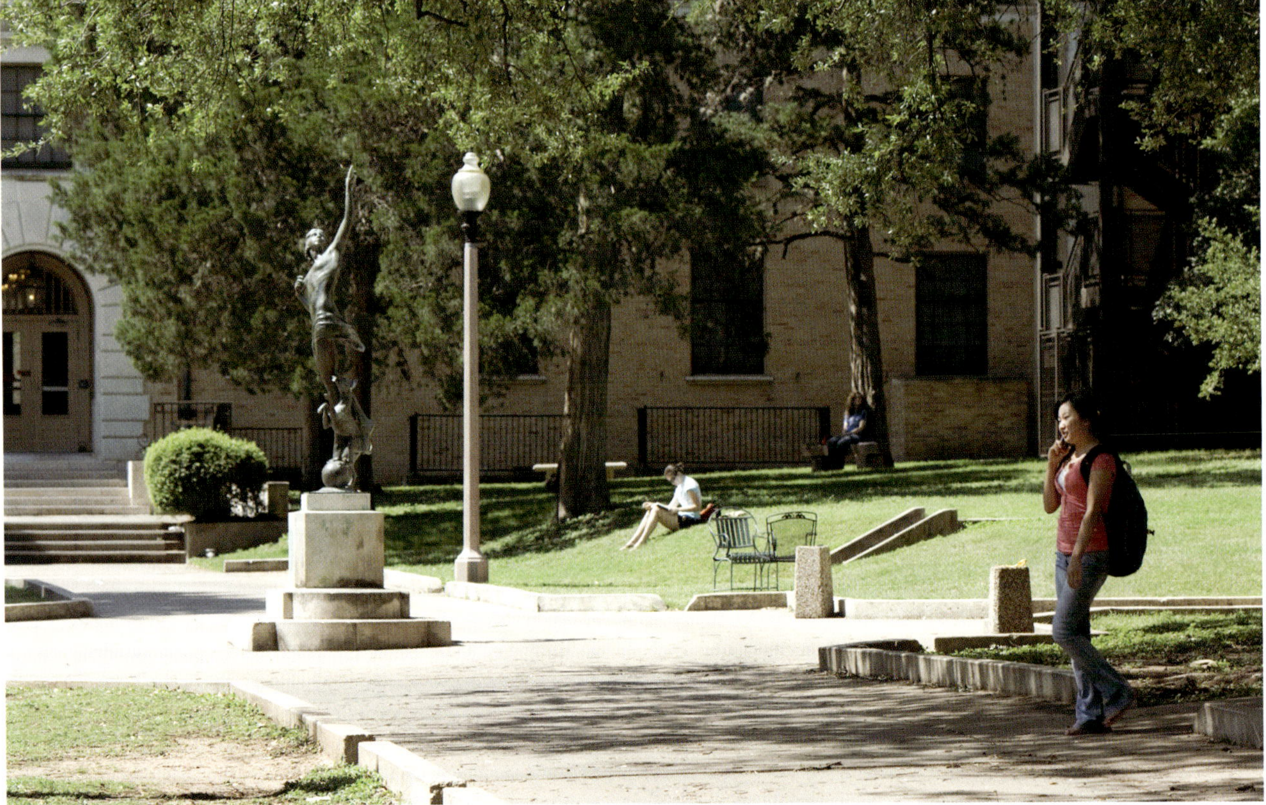

Across the street from the Communication Center is a quadrangle of residence halls: Littlefield, Andrews, Blanton, and Carothers. Initially, all were women-only dorms. Today, three are coed, while Littlefield, built in 1929 and the oldest residence hall on the campus, is still reserved for freshmen women. In the center of the courtyard is a statue of Diana the Huntress. An 18-year-old Bette Davis is believed to have been the model.

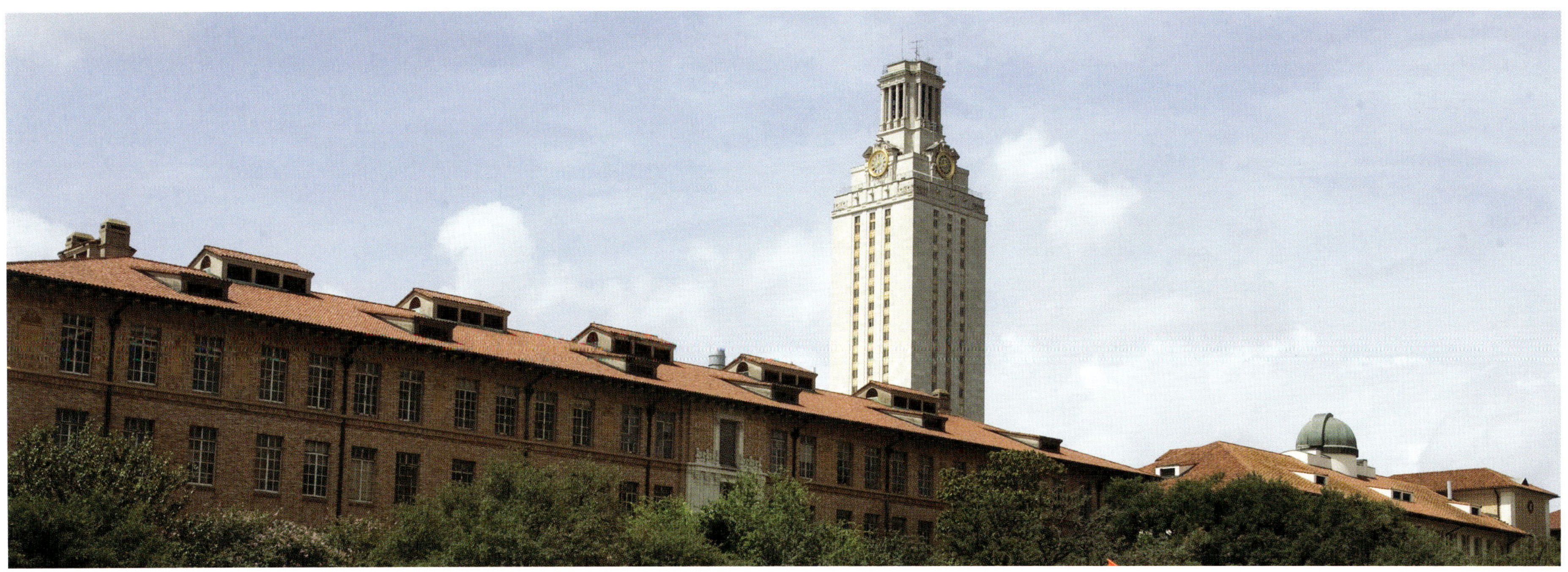

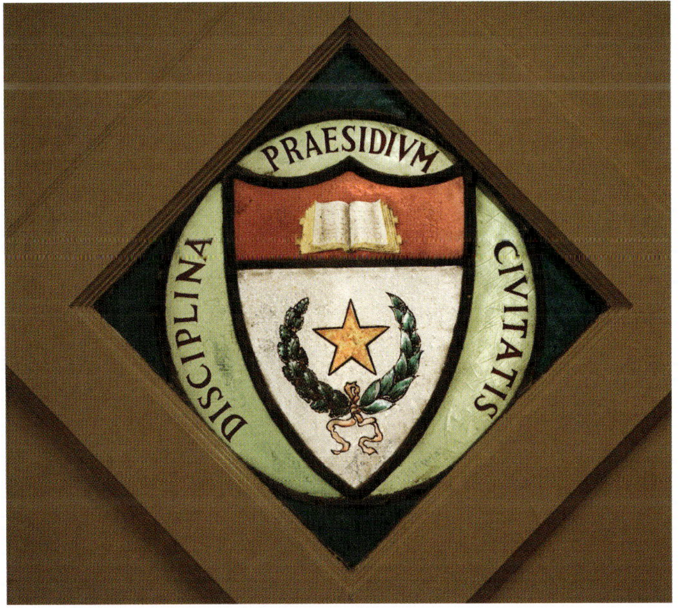

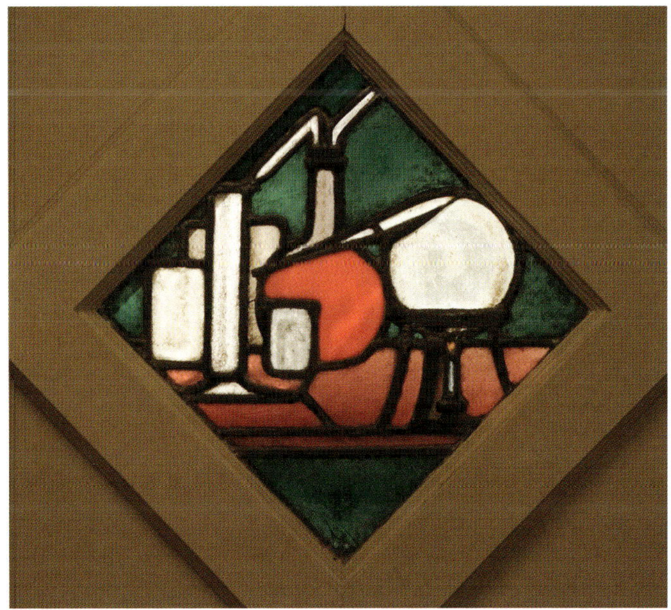

Above A view of science row. Along 24th Street is Welch Hall, home to the Department of Chemistry, and Painter Hall, used by the School of Biological Sciences. When it was opened in the 1930s, Painter Hall housed physics and astronomy, and it still has a 9-inch refracting telescope on its roof.

Left The stained glass windows greet visitors to the Mallet Chemistry Library. When the University opened in 1883, John Mallet was one of the University's inaugural eight professors and the first chairman of the faculty.

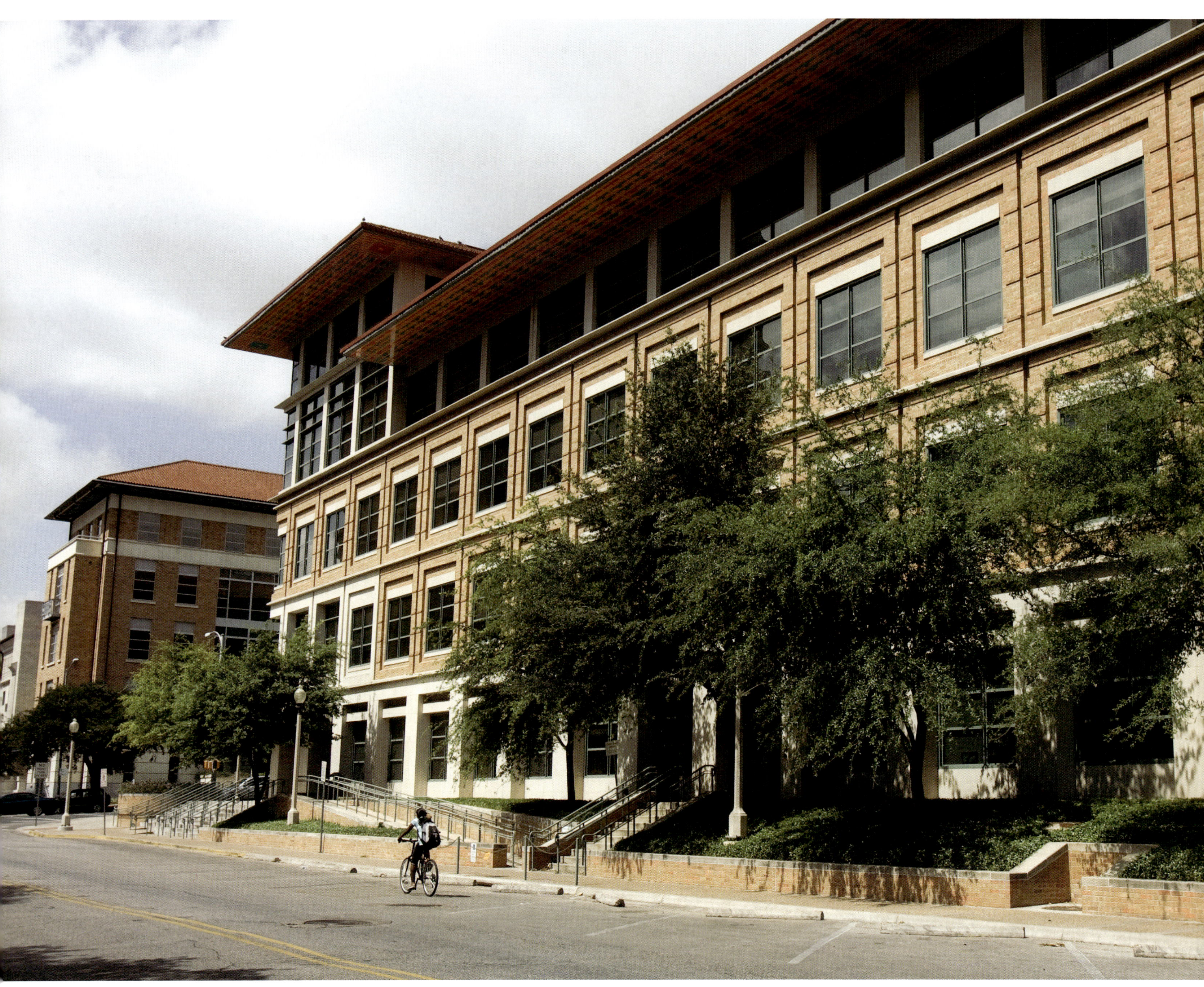

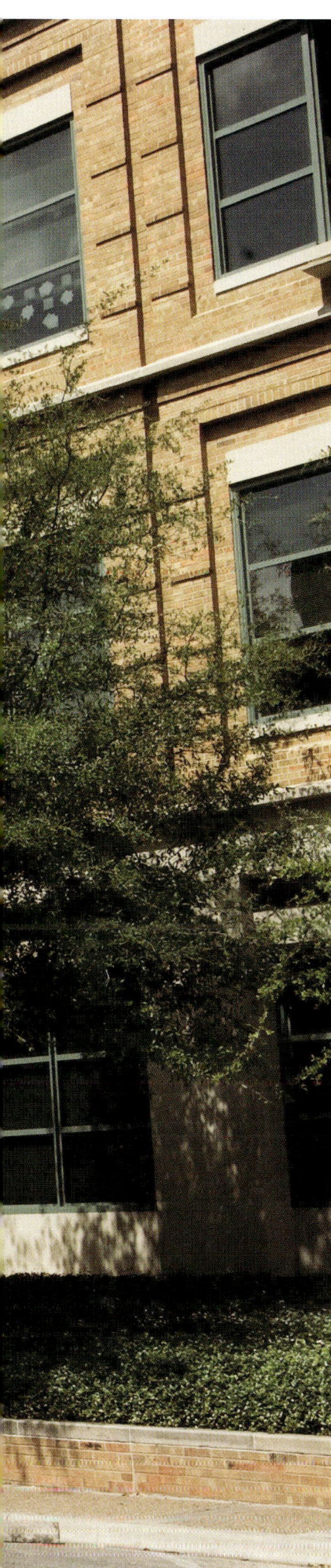

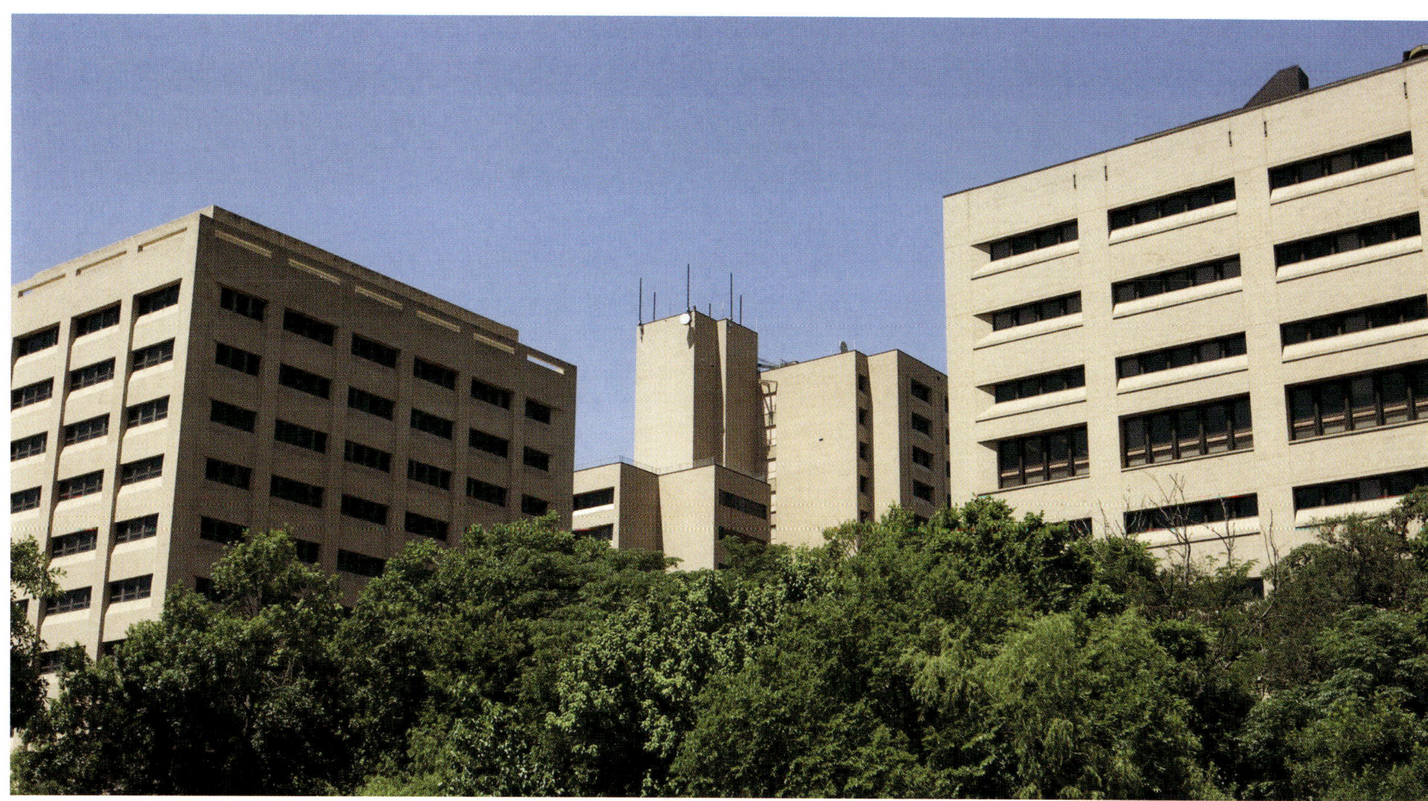

Left On the north side of campus, the spacious Sarah M. and Charles E. Seay Building houses the Department of Psychology. Among the largest academic units in the College of Liberal Arts, psychology was in dire need of space. It had been housed in eight locations on the campus before the Seay Building was completed in 2002 and placed the department under one roof.

Above In stark contrast to the limestone walls and red-tiled roofs, the science and engineering section of campus presents a formidable skyline. From left: Cockrell Hall (civil engineering), Robert Lee Moore Hall (physics, math, and astronomy), and the Engineering Teaching Center (mechanical engineering).

Right The key of Tau Beta Pi, a national engineering honor society, stands watch at the entrance to the Mechanical Engineering Building.

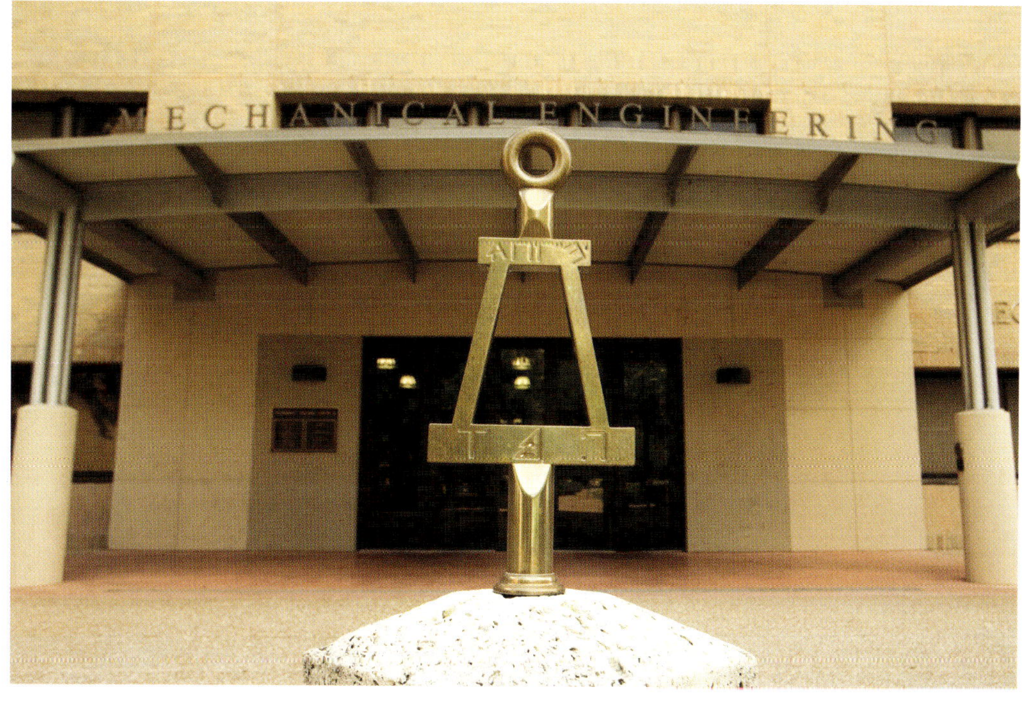

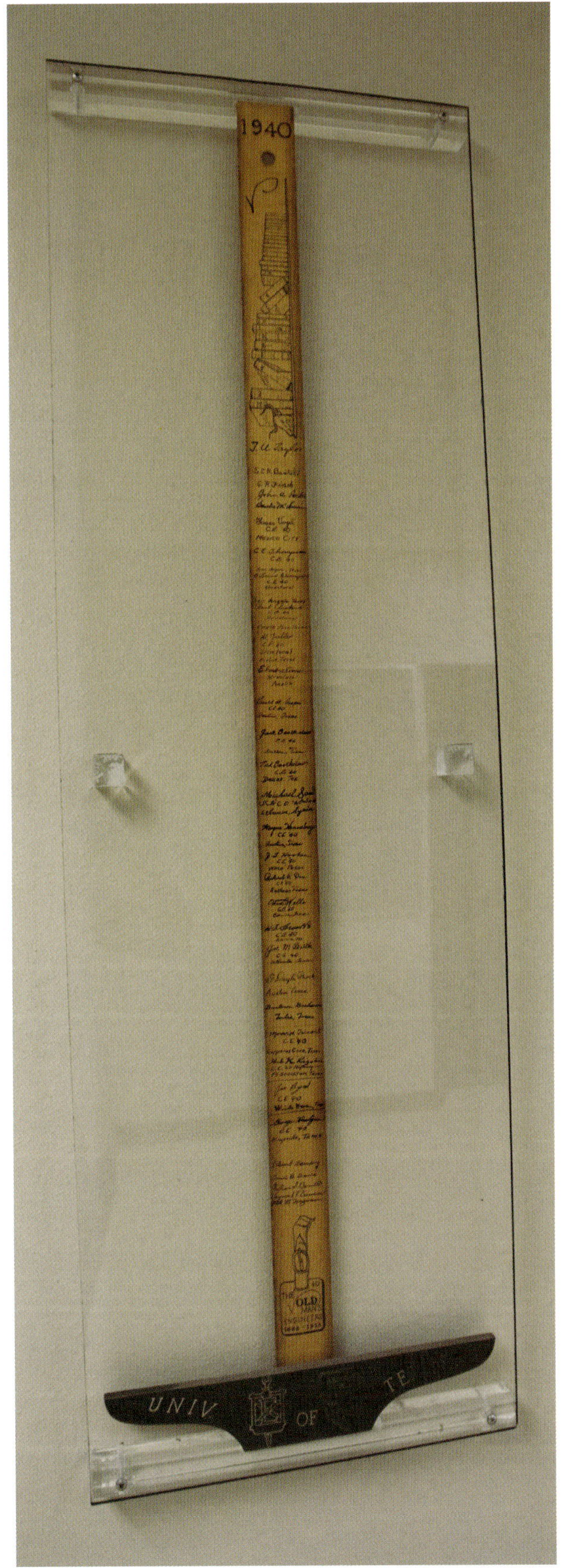

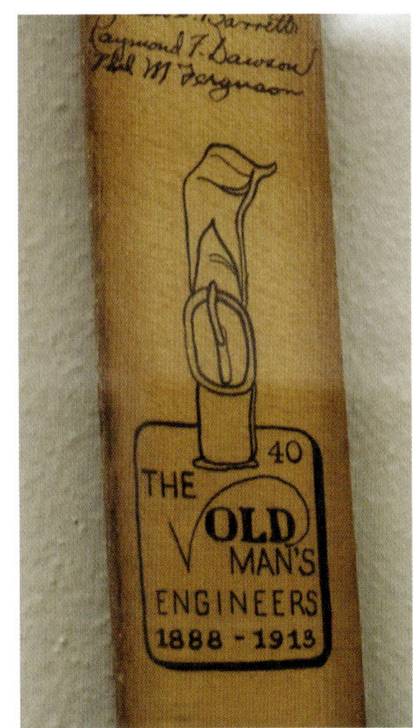

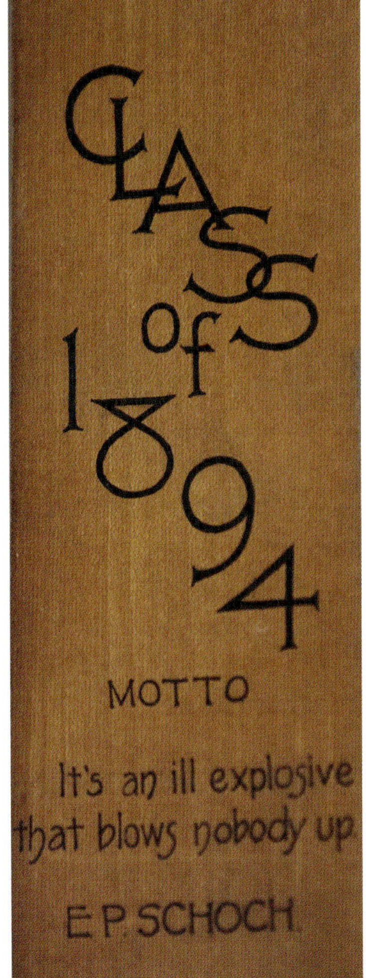

Far Left In a long-standing tradition, members of each engineering graduating class sign a T-square that is displayed on the walls of Cockrell Hall.

Above Left Many of the early T-squares are hand-decorated with images important to UT engineers. Pictured here is a watch fob once given to all engineering graduates by Thomas U. Taylor, the School's first dean. The elongated check mark, which Dean Taylor used to indicate a perfect grade on a test or research paper, was dubbed the "ramshorn" by engineering students, and is today the trademark logo of the Cockrell School.

Left Among the earliest engineering graduates was Eugene "E. P." Schoch, who went on to serve on the University faculty and won national recognition as the "Father of Chemical Engineering" in the South. He maintained a lifelong interest in music, and in 1900 founded what would become the Longhorn Band.

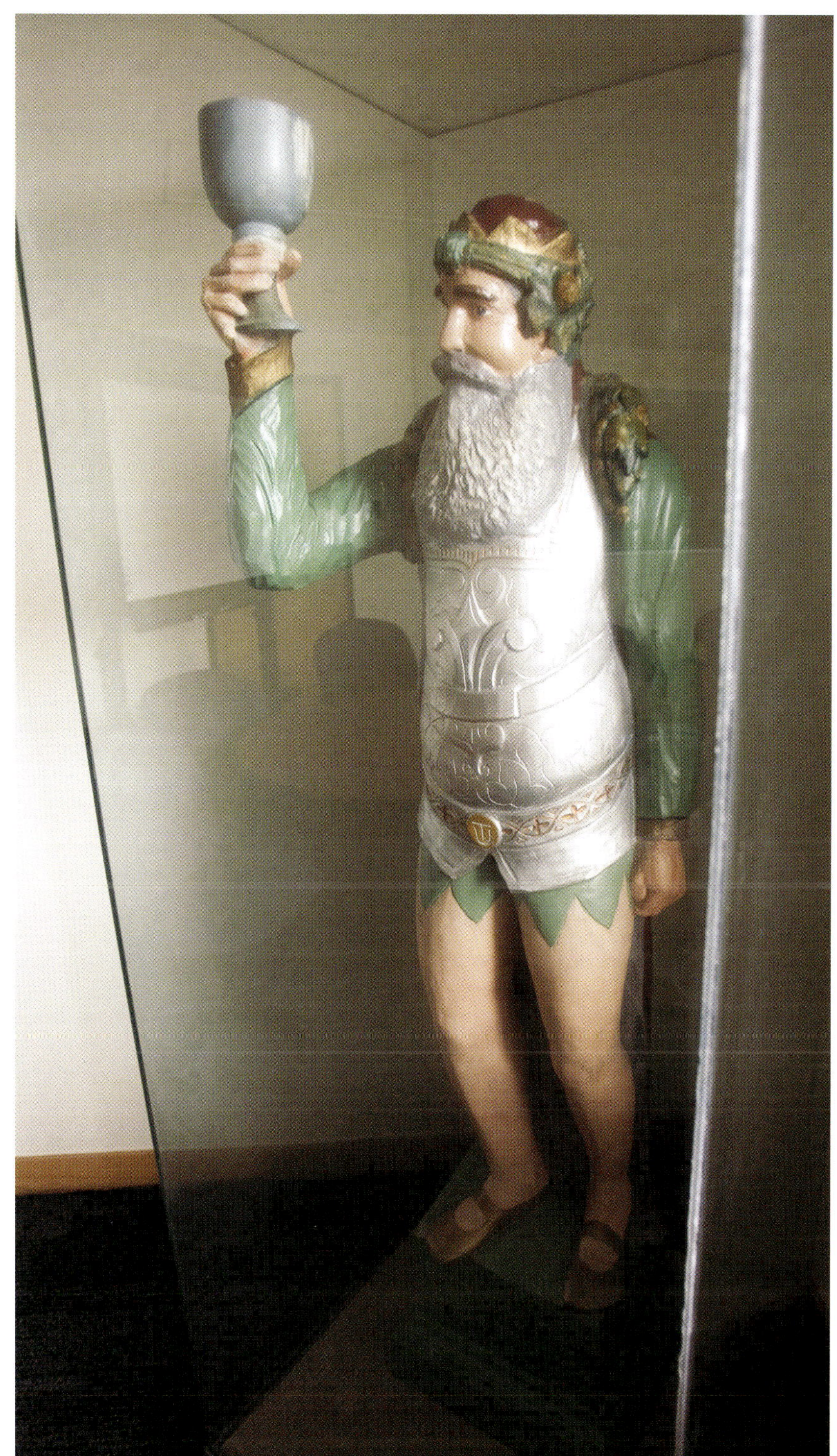

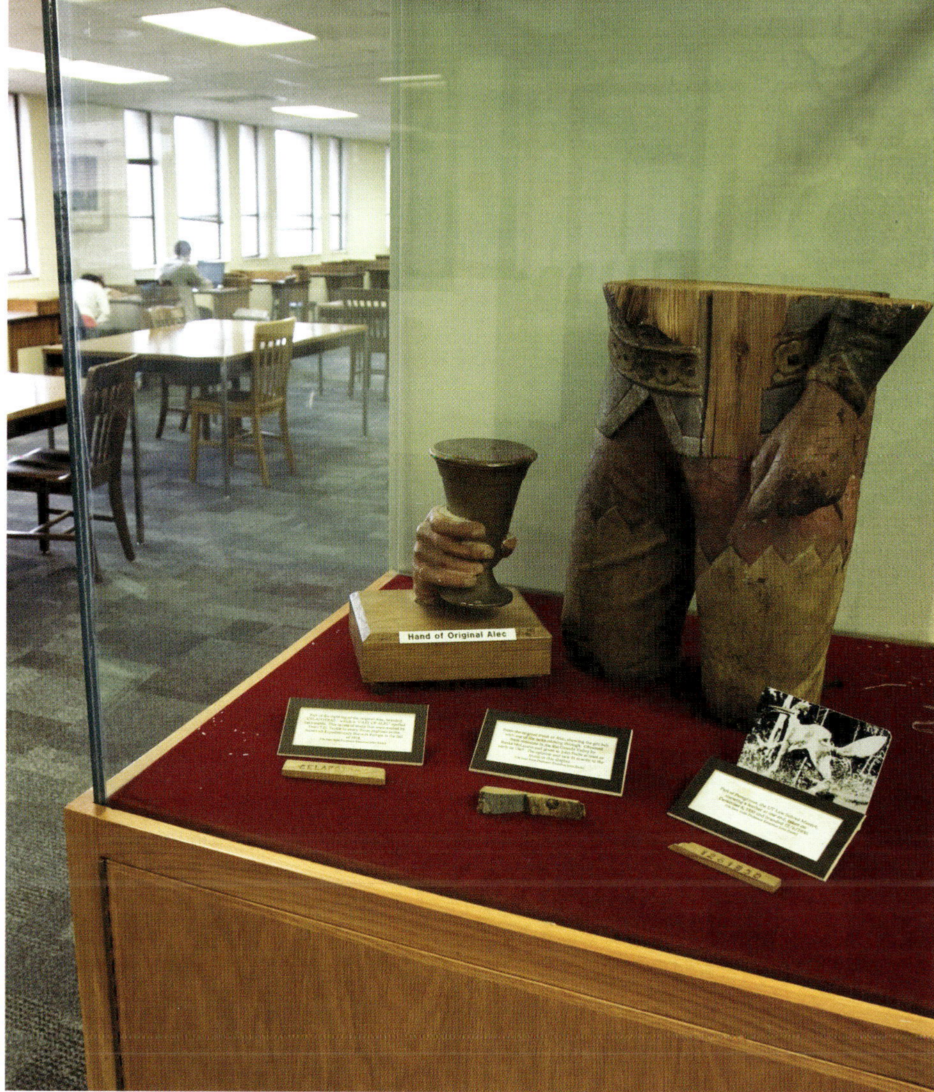

Left Among the University's schools and colleges, a few have taken on mascots, or "patron saints." The Law School boasts the famed Peregrinus, Business lauds the wily Hermes, and Architecture claims the mysterious Ptah. But the most recognized is Alexander Frederick Claire, or simply "Alec," the patron saint of the UT engineers, here, on display in the McKinney Engineering Library.

Above Skirmishes with rival law students have resulted in the destruction of the earliest renderings of Alec. Some pieces that have been salvaged are on display in the library.

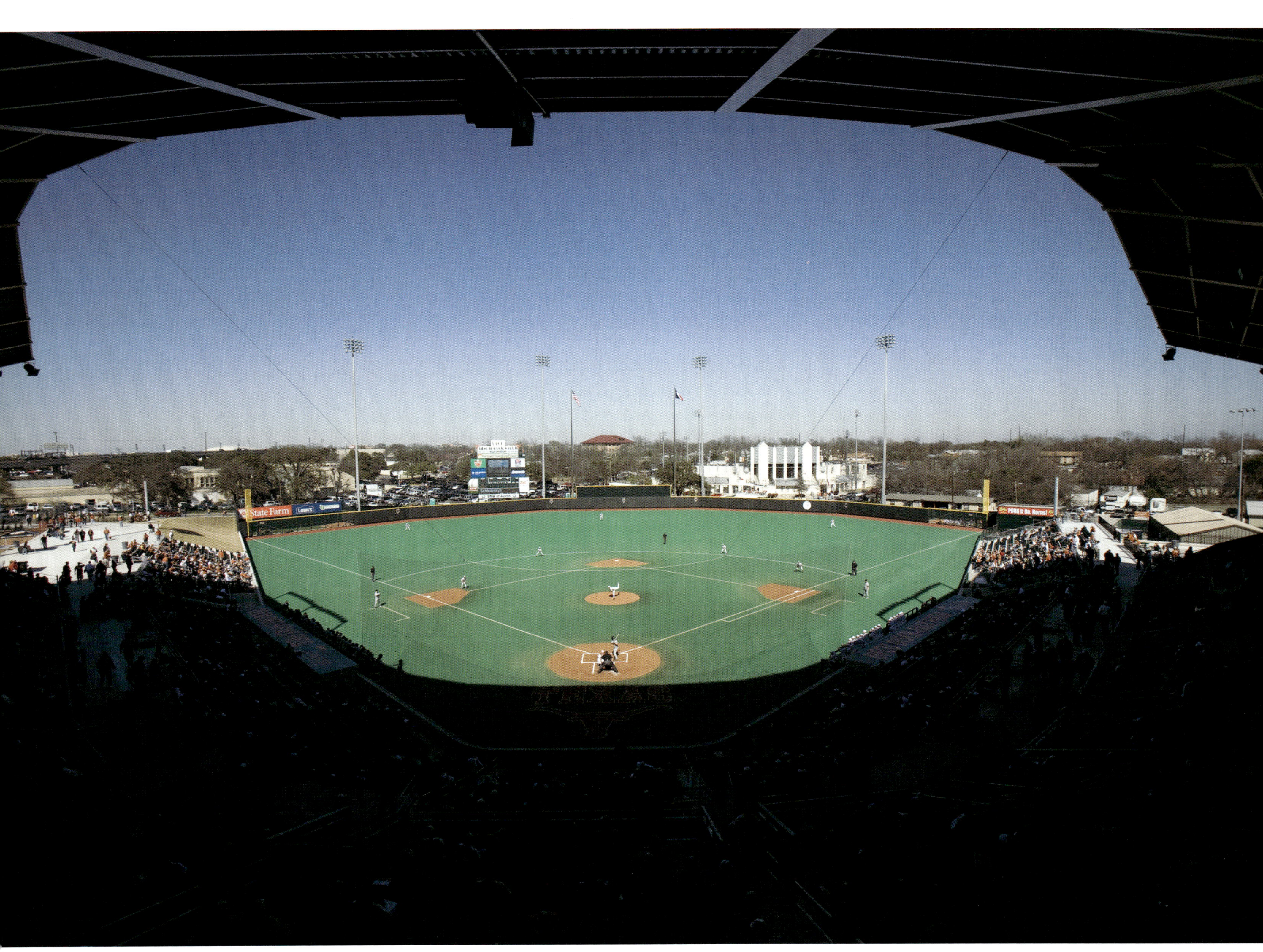

The newly renovated UFCU Disch-Falk Field is home to the baseball team. With the winningest program in college baseball history, the Longhorns hold the record for the most appearances at the College World Series and have won six national titles.

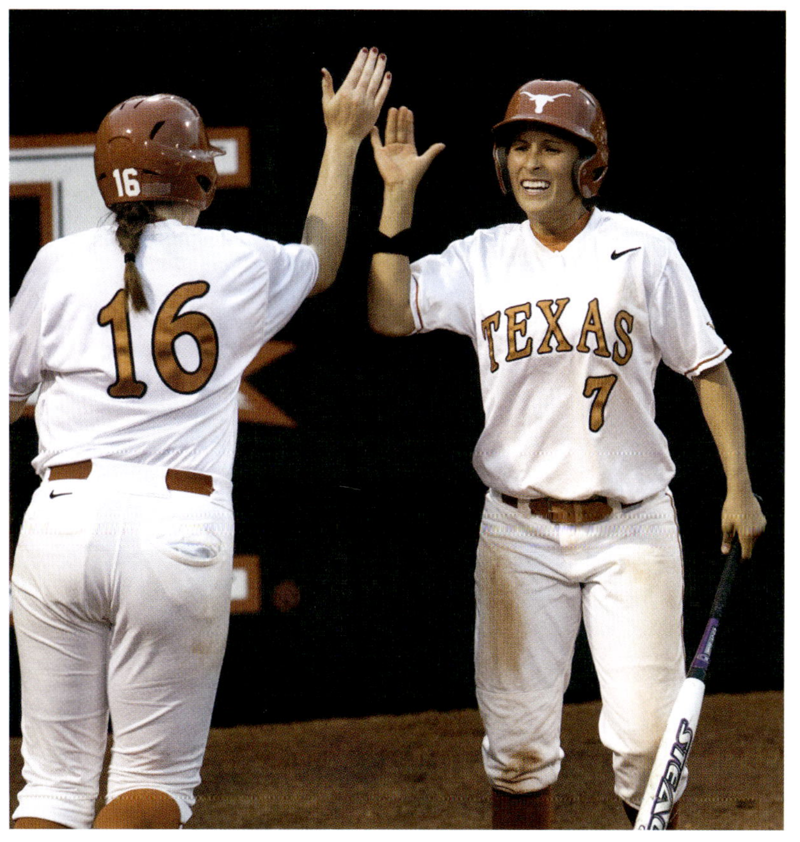

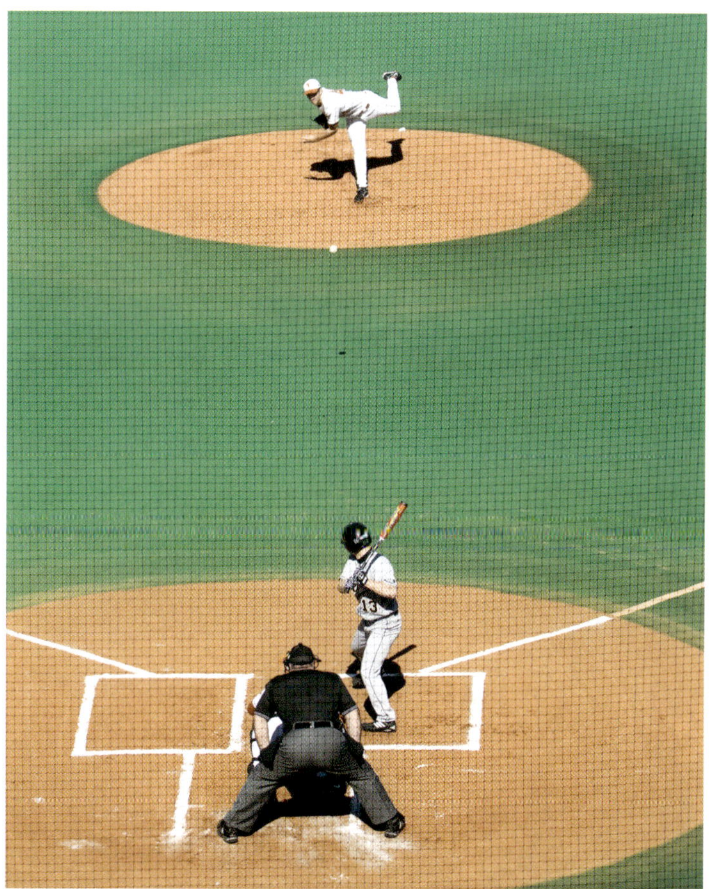

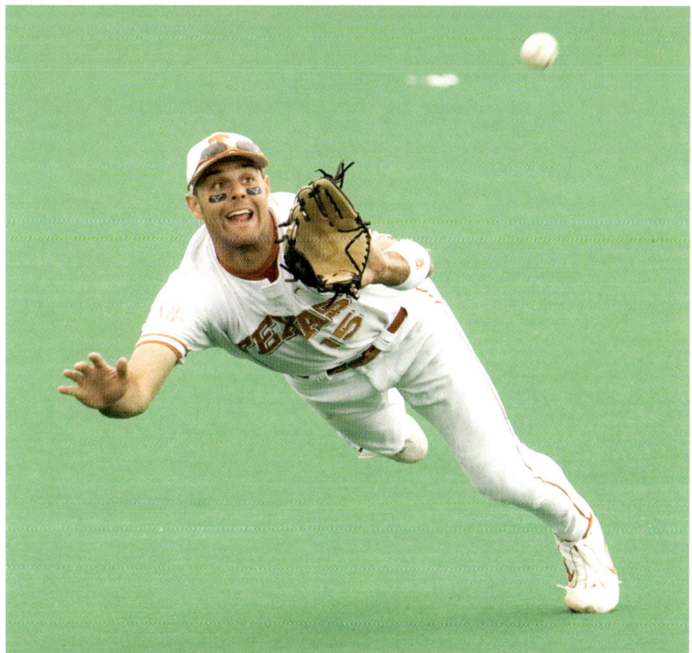

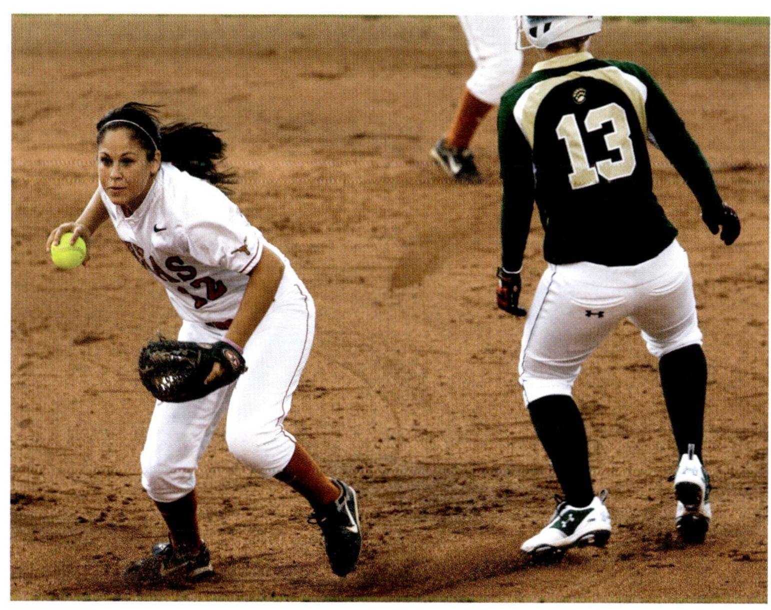

Top Left and Bottom Right The women's softball team debuted in 1996, and the squad already has qualified for the College World Series four times, a record for such a young program.

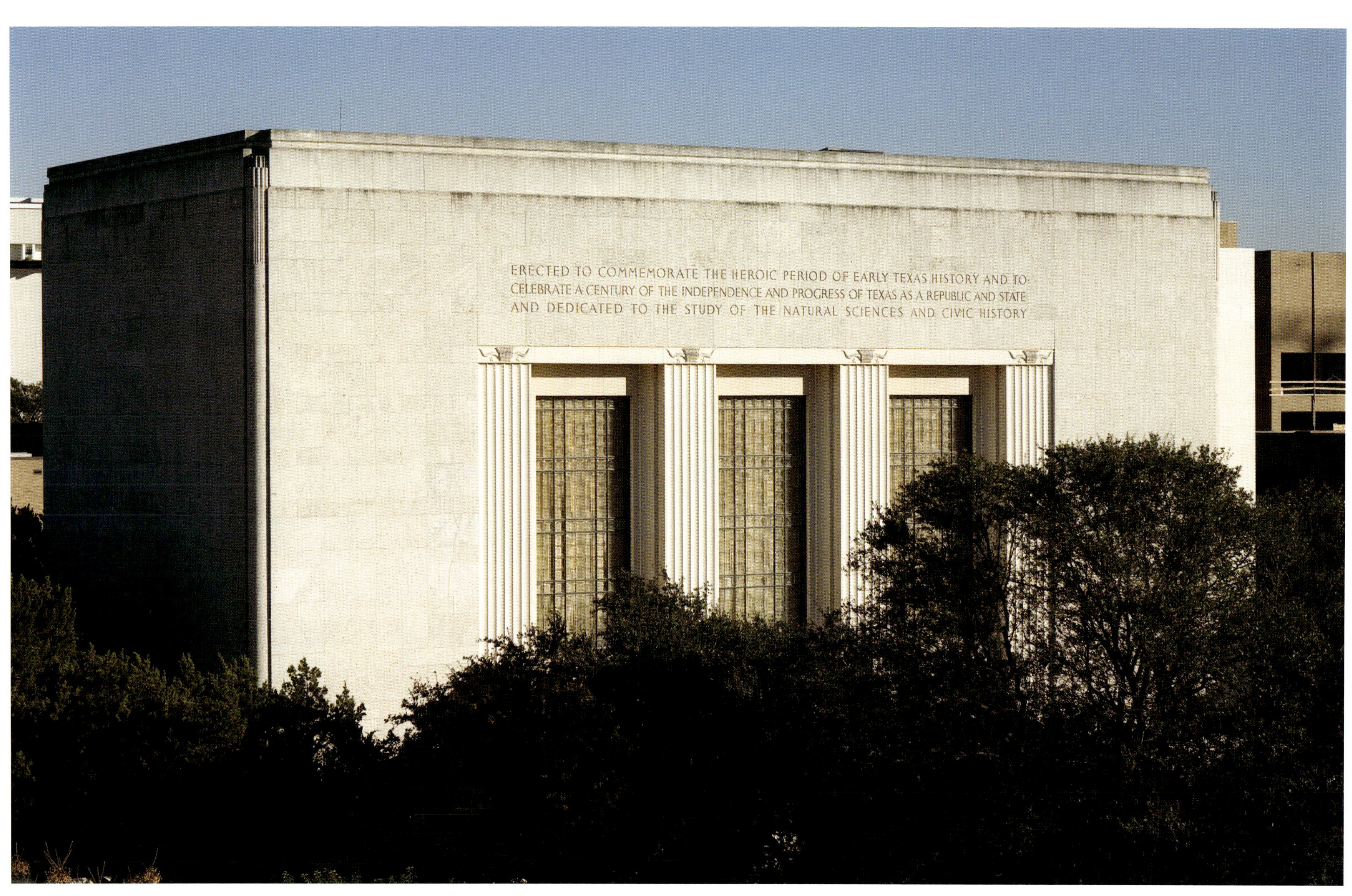

Peeking over the live oak tress, the Texas Memorial Museum is one of the most visited places on the campus. Built in honor of the 1936 Texas Centennial, ground was broken for the building by President Franklin Roosevelt during a whistle stop in Austin.

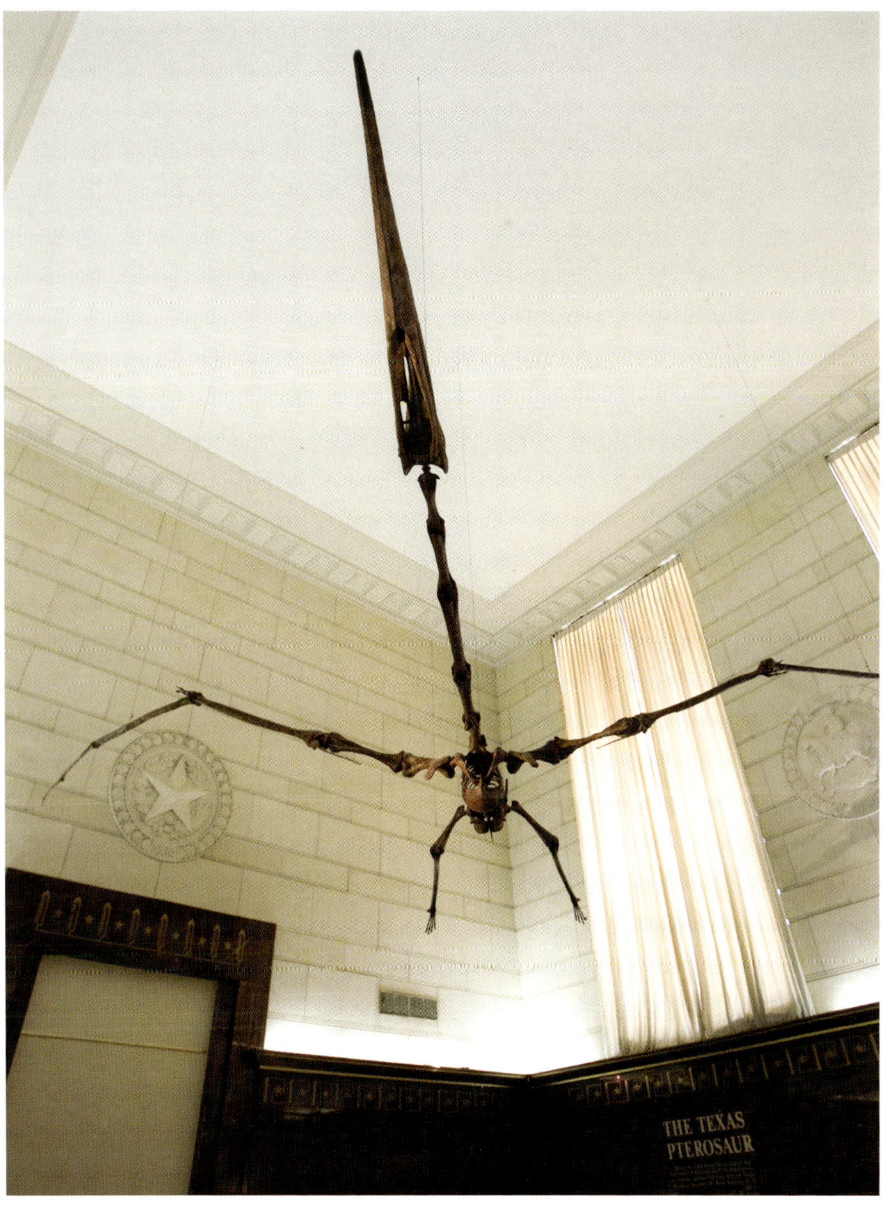

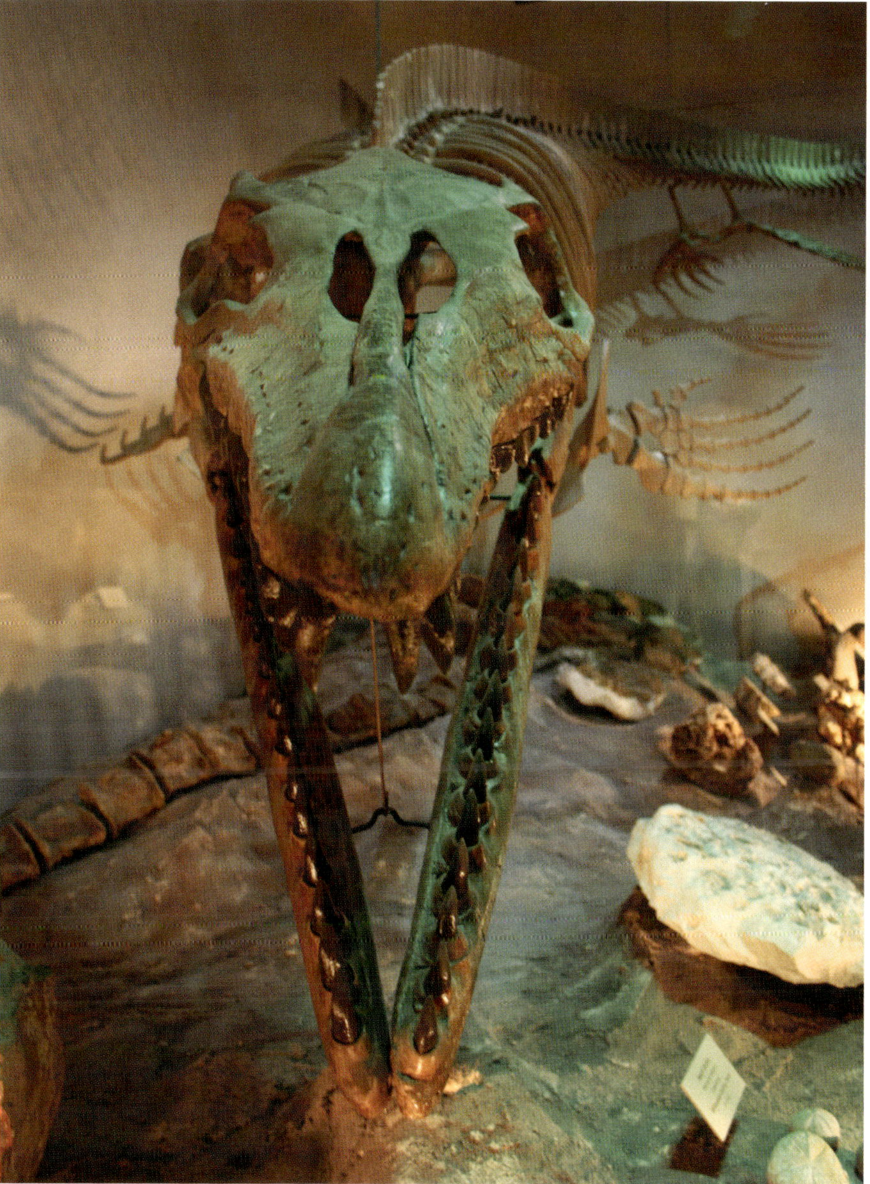

TMM is one of the premier museums preserving Texas' natural history. At left, the Texas Pterosaur, or *Quetzalcoatlus*, a life-size model of the Earth's largest ever flying creature, lords over the Great Hall. At right, the enormous, alligator-like Onion Creek Mososaur, discovered in South Austin, shows how different a place Texas used to be.

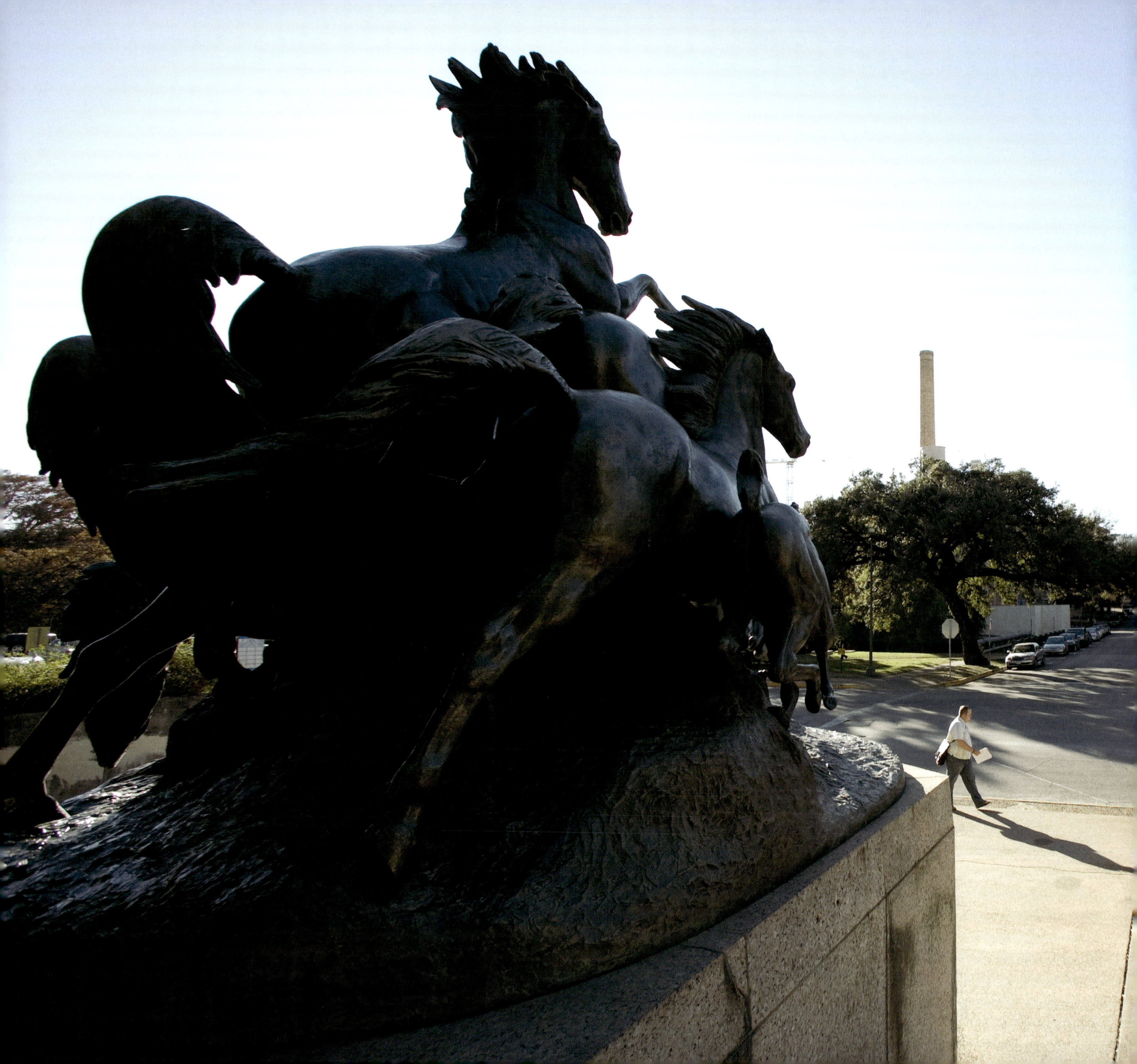

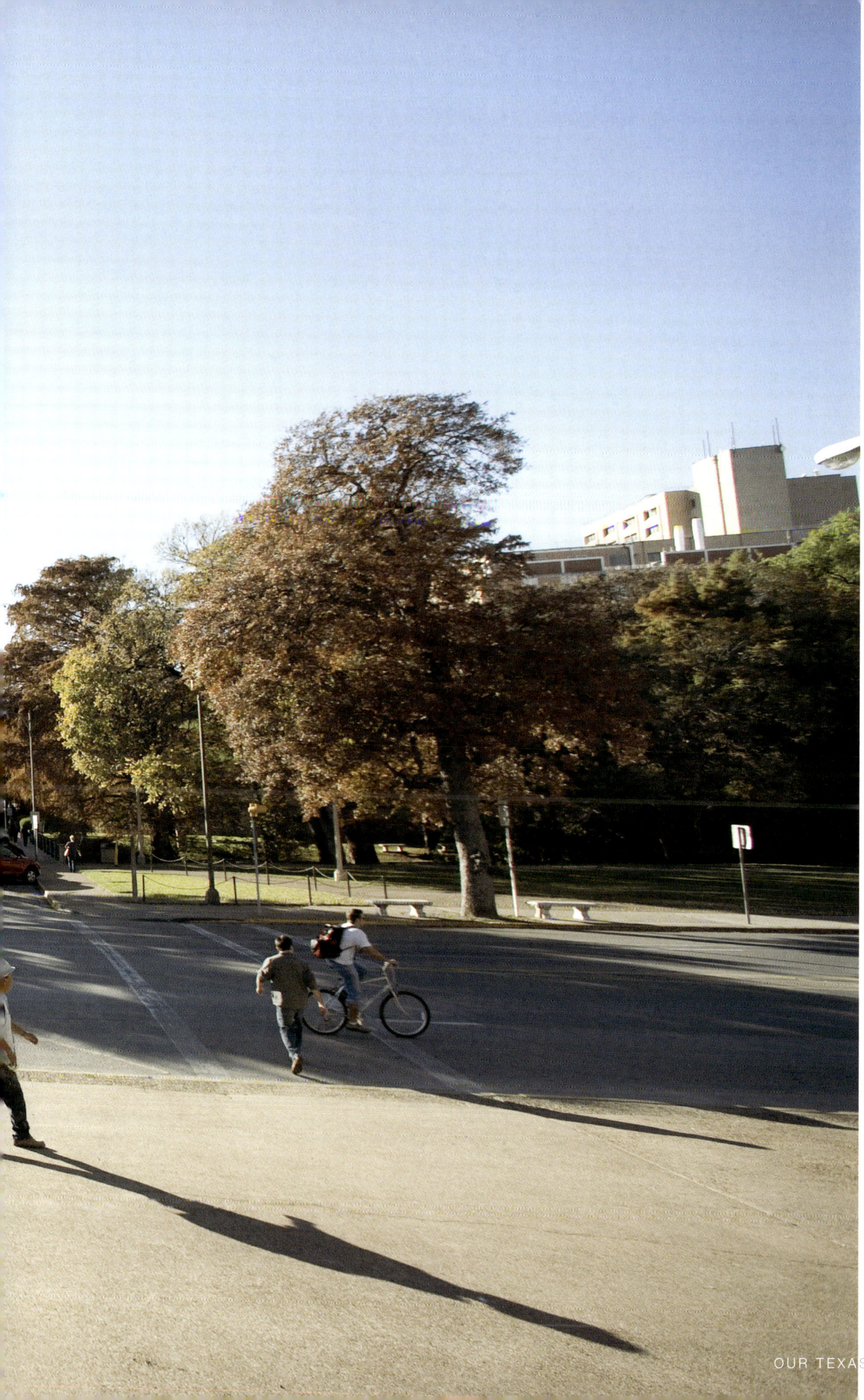

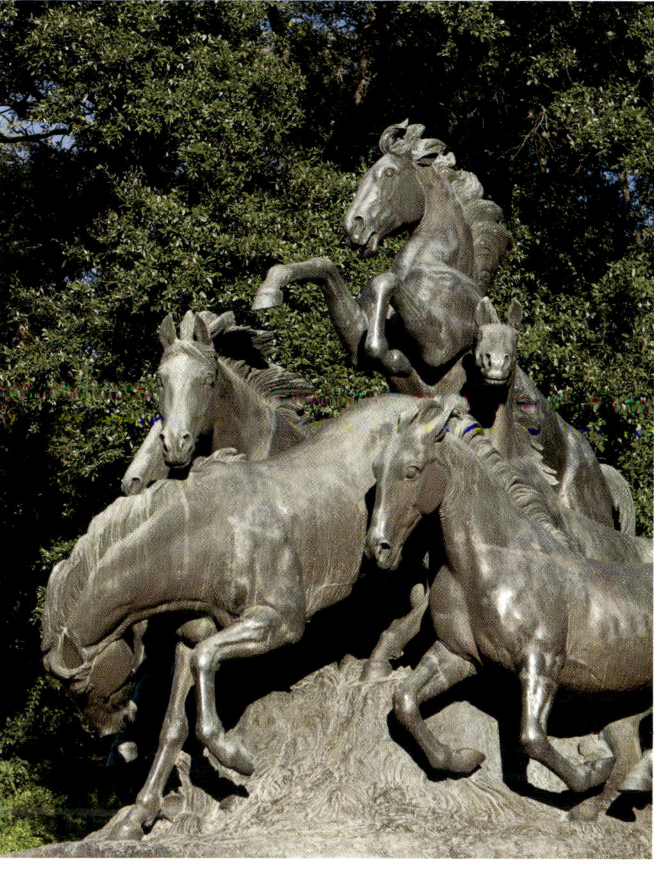

The Mustangs look out on the campus from the lawn in front of the Texas Memorial Museum. The statue was a gift from Ralph Ogden, an Austin oilman and rancher, and unveiled in 1948.

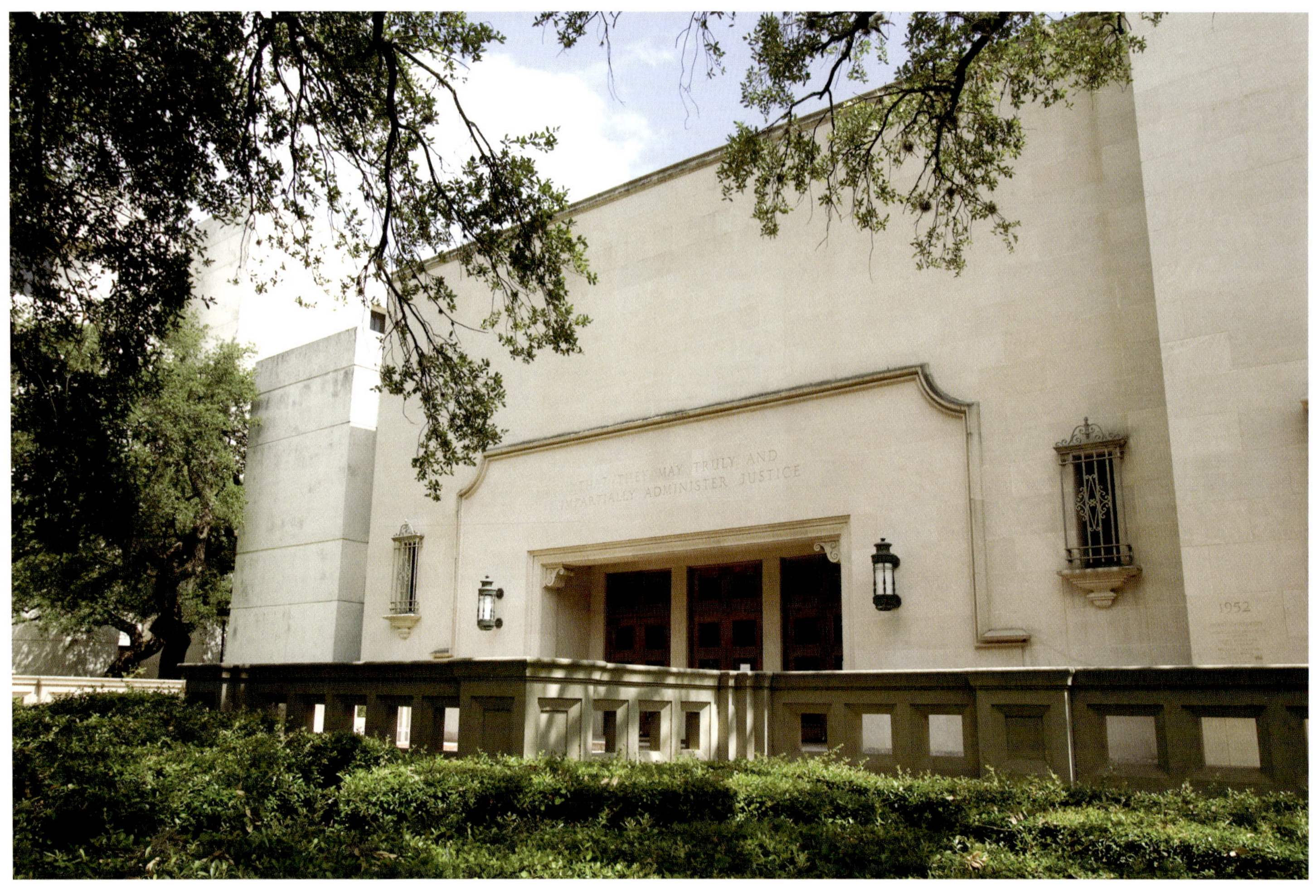

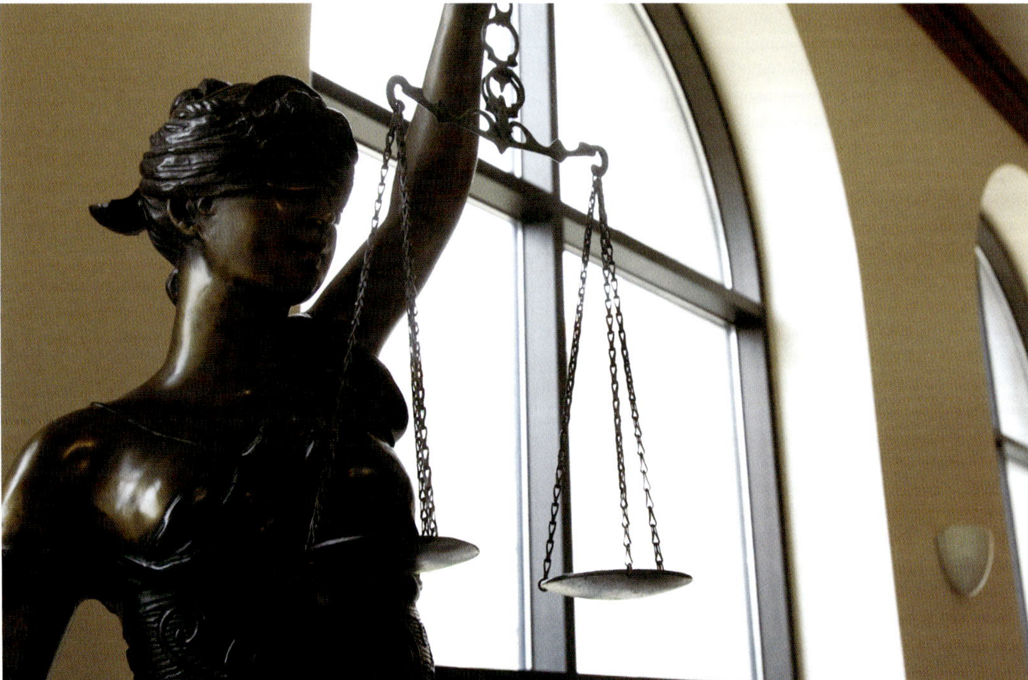

Dedicated in 1953, Townes Hall houses the School of Law. It is named for Judge John Townes, a well-loved dean of the law school in the early 1900s. The School of Law was one of the original academic departments when the University opened in 1883.

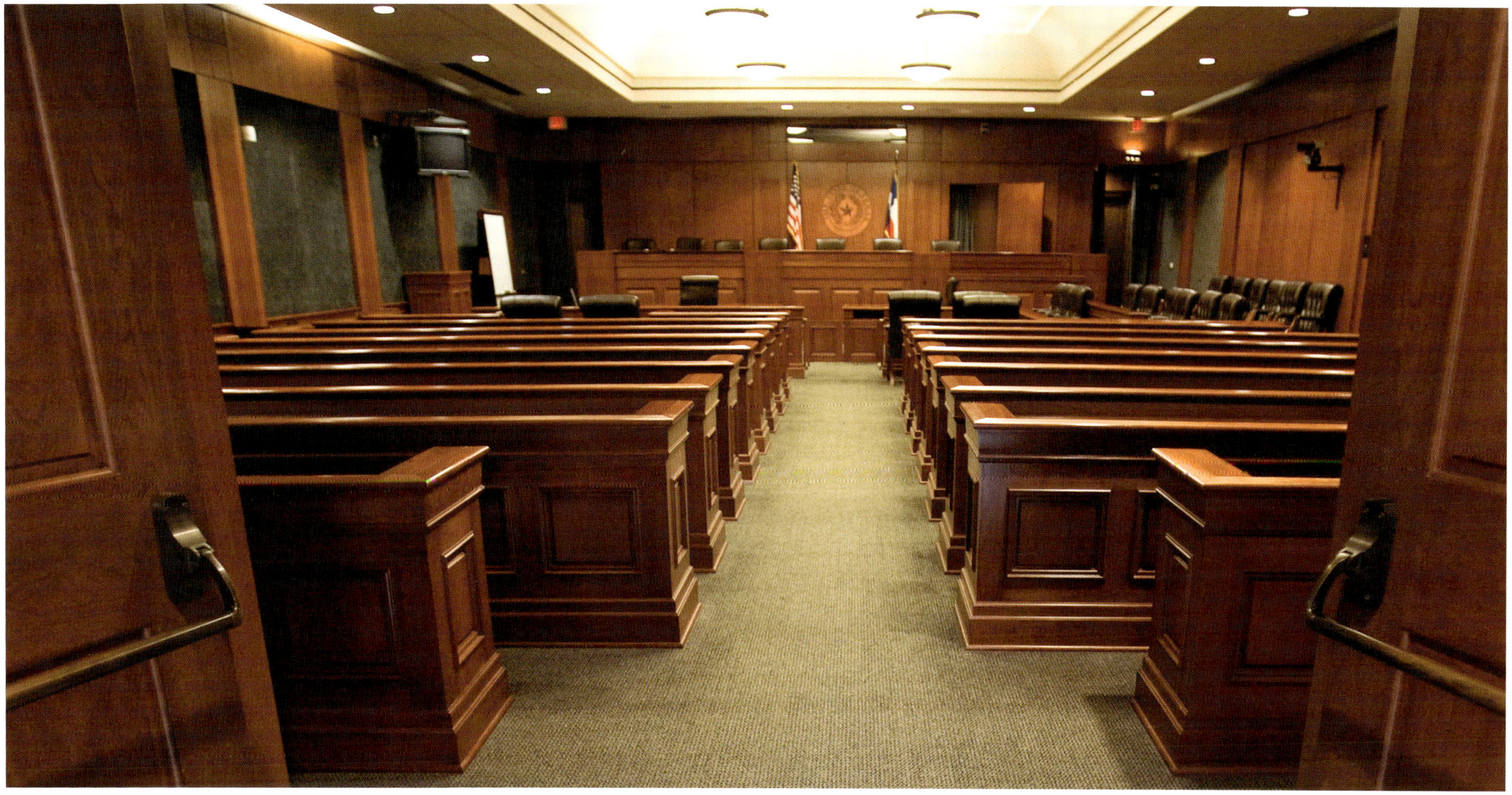

Above The Eidman Courtroom is used for mock trials, lectures, and symposiums.

Right The Peregrinus, patron saint of the law school, was invented by student Russell Savage in 1901. This mythic creature was intended to symbolize, both in limb and attitude, the maxims of equity. It wears Irish ditcher boots on its front feet to indicate the law's protection to the poor of society, while the boxing clubs on its hind legs show that even the most wealthy and influential must fear the law's power. The Peregrinus has an arched back, ever ready to spring into action to protect right or prevent wrong, and its sharp beak implies its power to penetrate the mysteries of the law, which the true student must obtain by study.

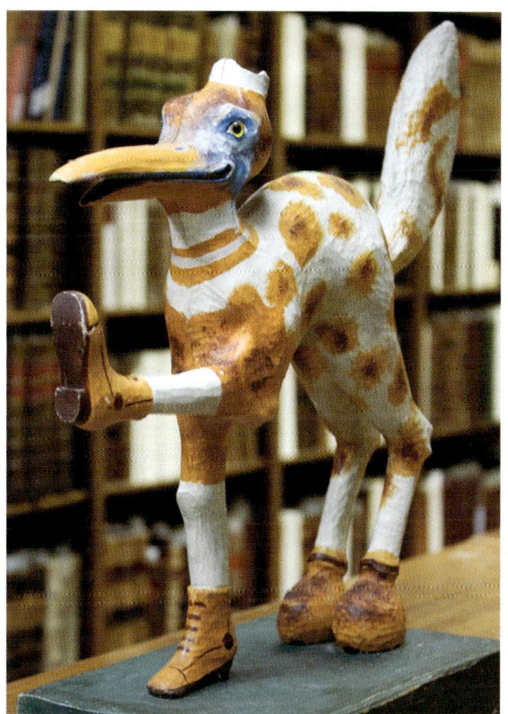

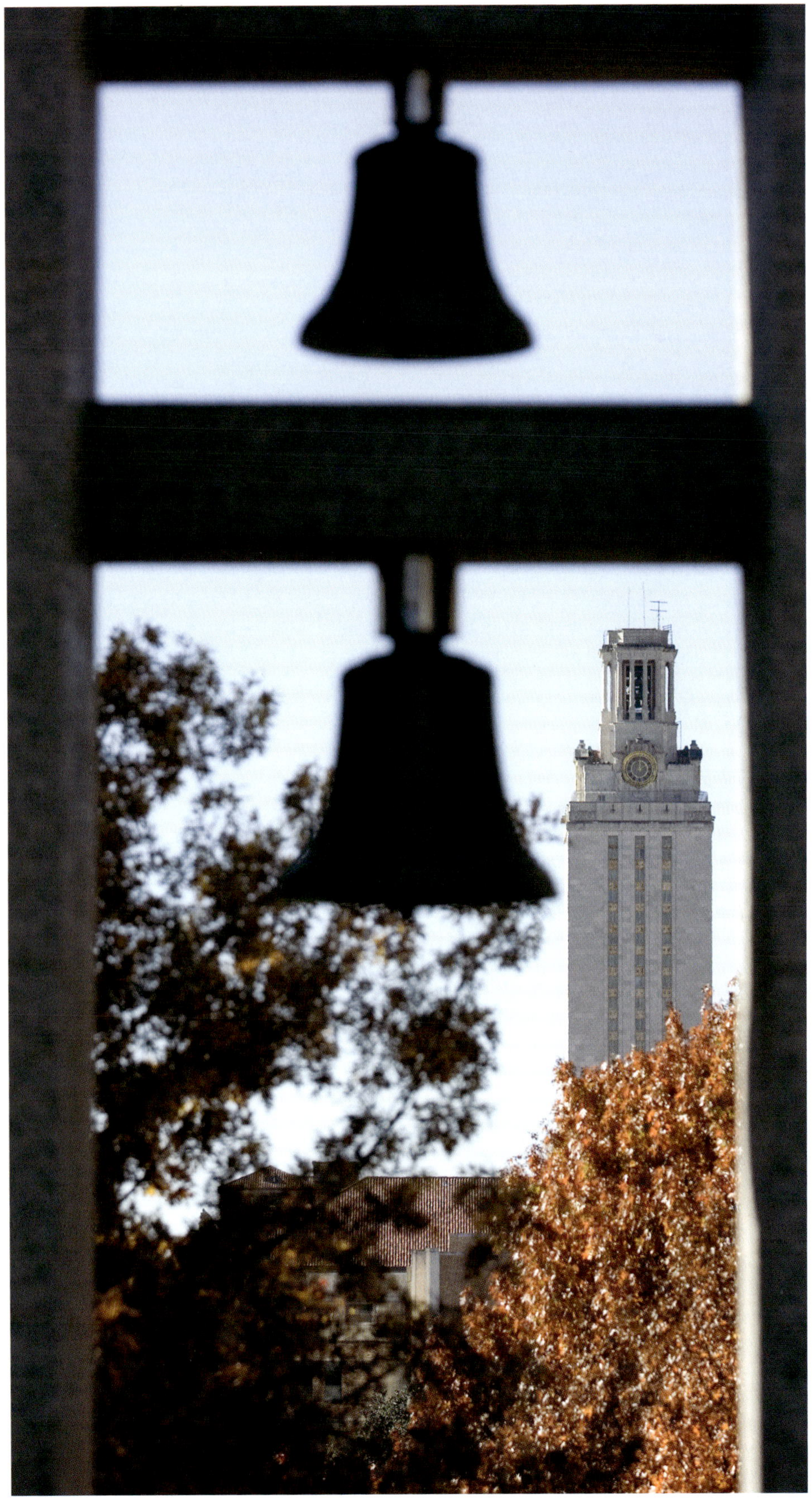

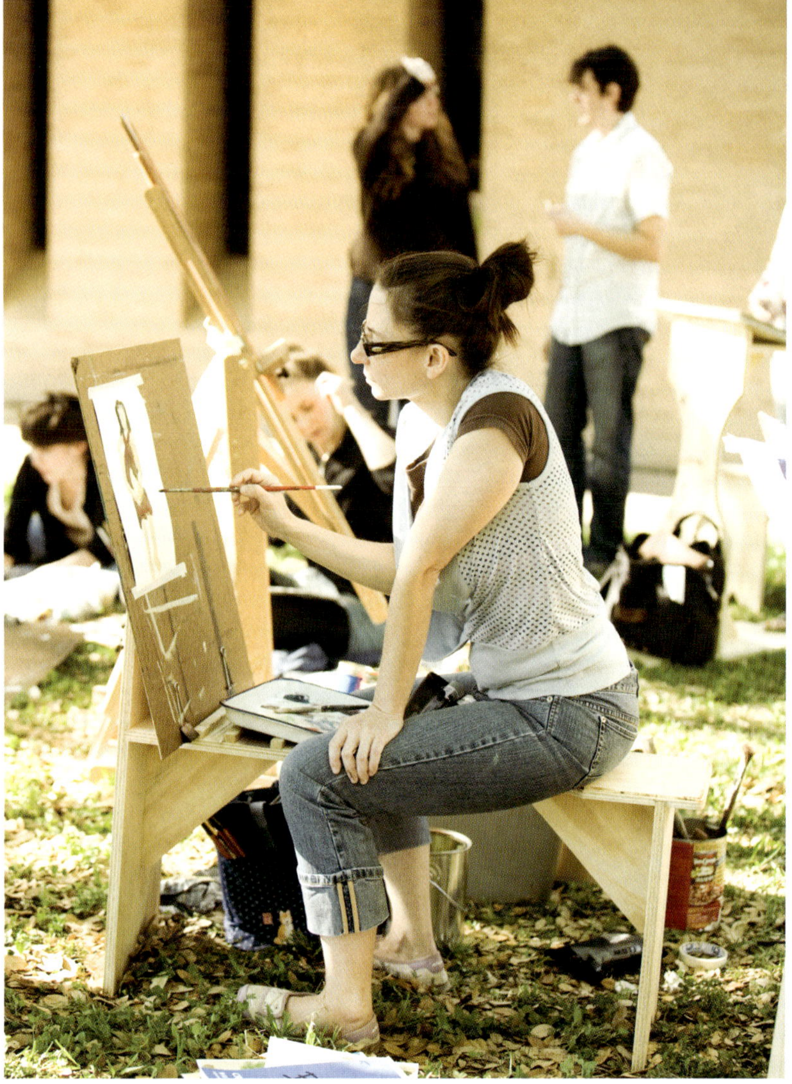

Left The Burleson Bells were a gift from Albert S. Burleson, a member of UT's inaugural graduating class of 1884 and U.S. Postmaster under President Woodrow Wilson. The bells were first used in the Old Main Building and are now displayed outside the Performing Arts Center.

Above and Facing Page With more than 200 faculty and departments in art and art history, theater and dance, and the newly created Butler School of Music, the University's nationally recognized College of Fine Arts seeks to prepare its students for the creation, practice, study, and teaching of the arts.

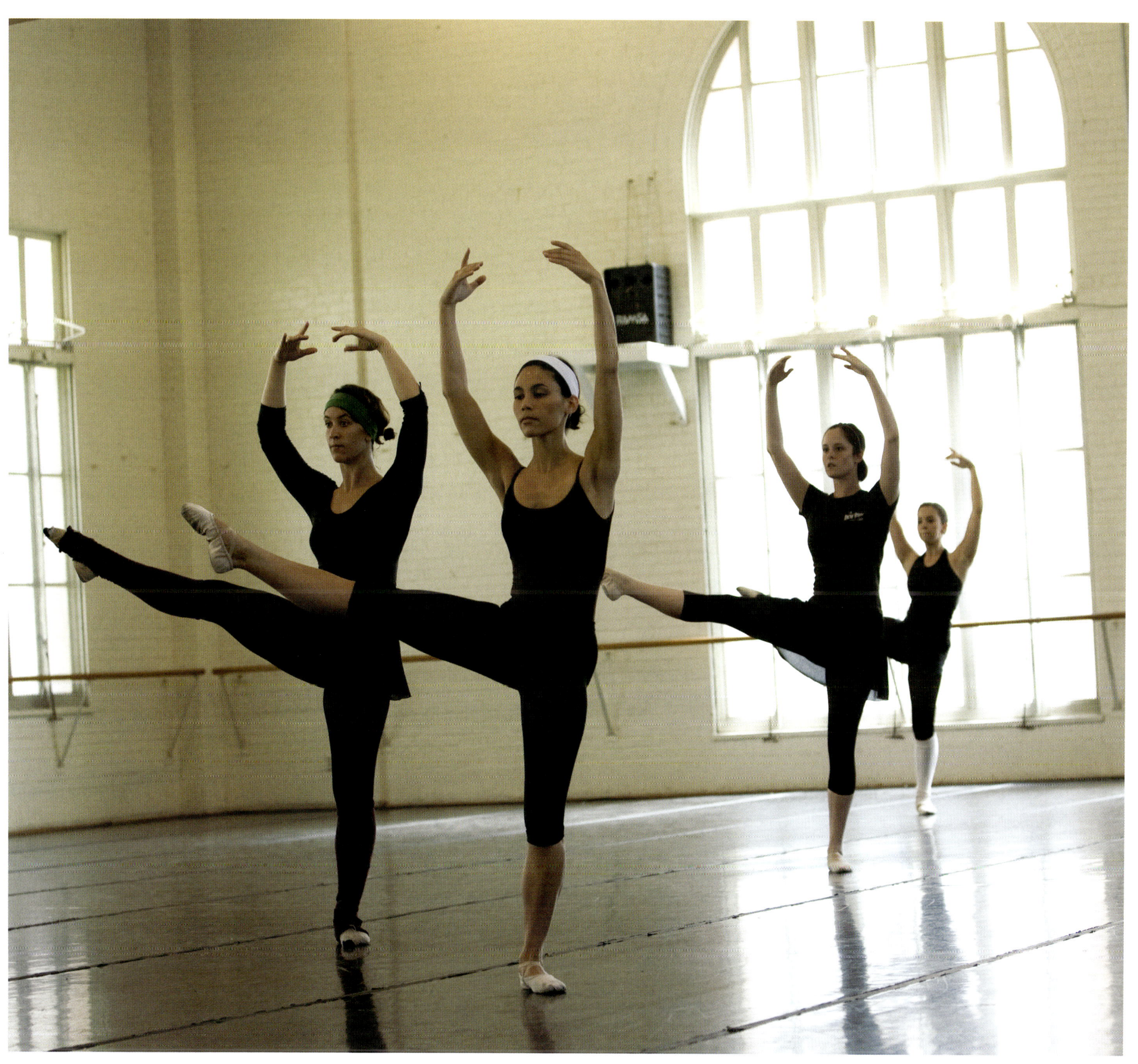

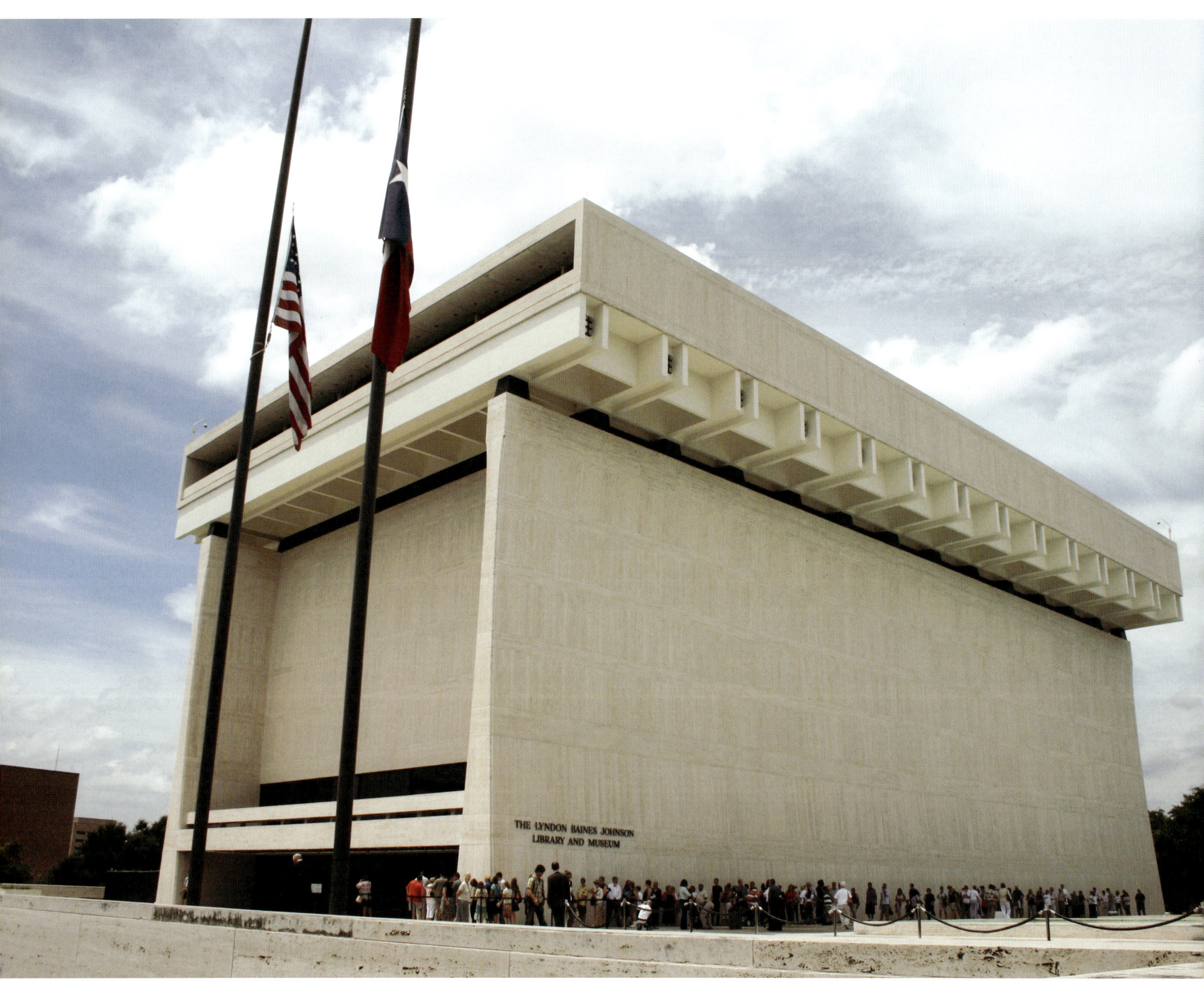
THE LYNDON BAINES JOHNSON
LIBRARY AND MUSEUM

Left Dedicated in 1971 with a nationally televised ceremony, the Lyndon Baines Johnson Presidential Library and Museum was the first such library to be located on a university campus. Here, visitors stand in line to pay their respects as Lady Bird Johnson lies in repose inside the monumental building.

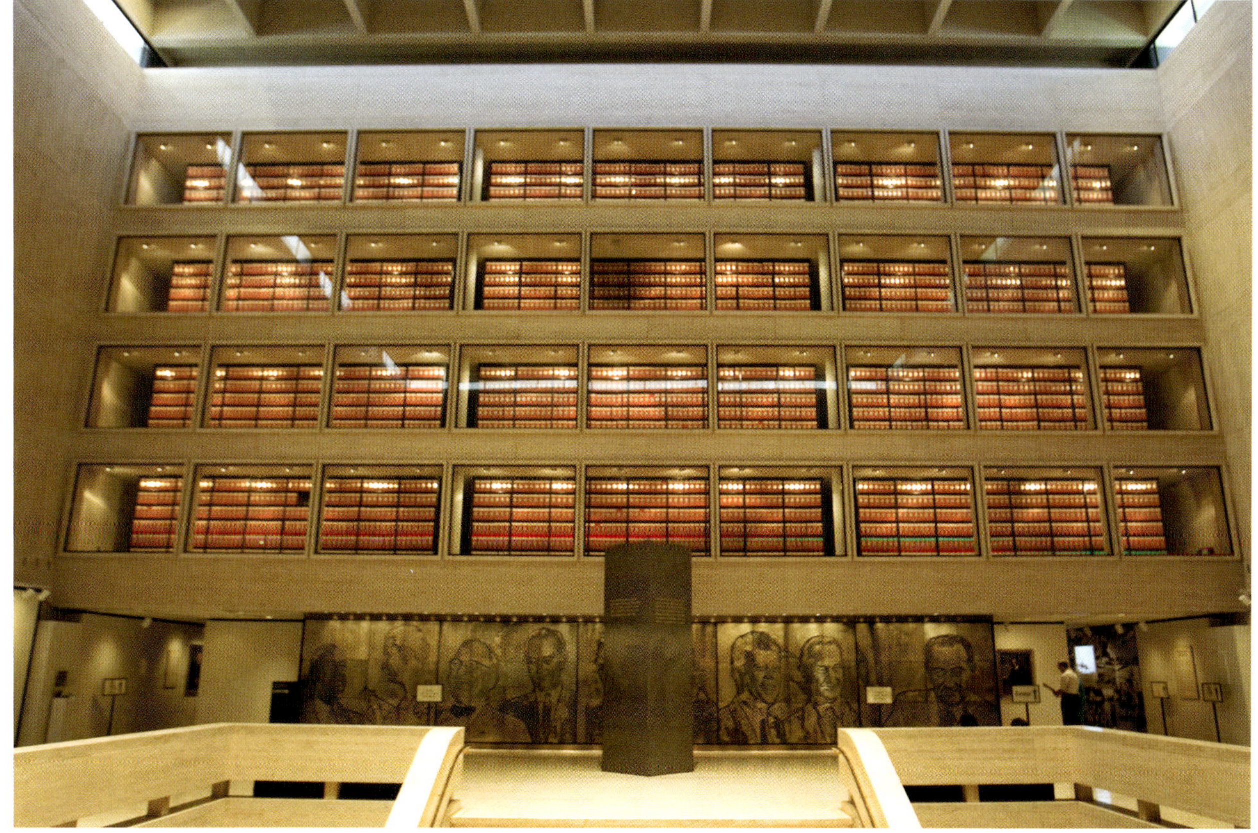

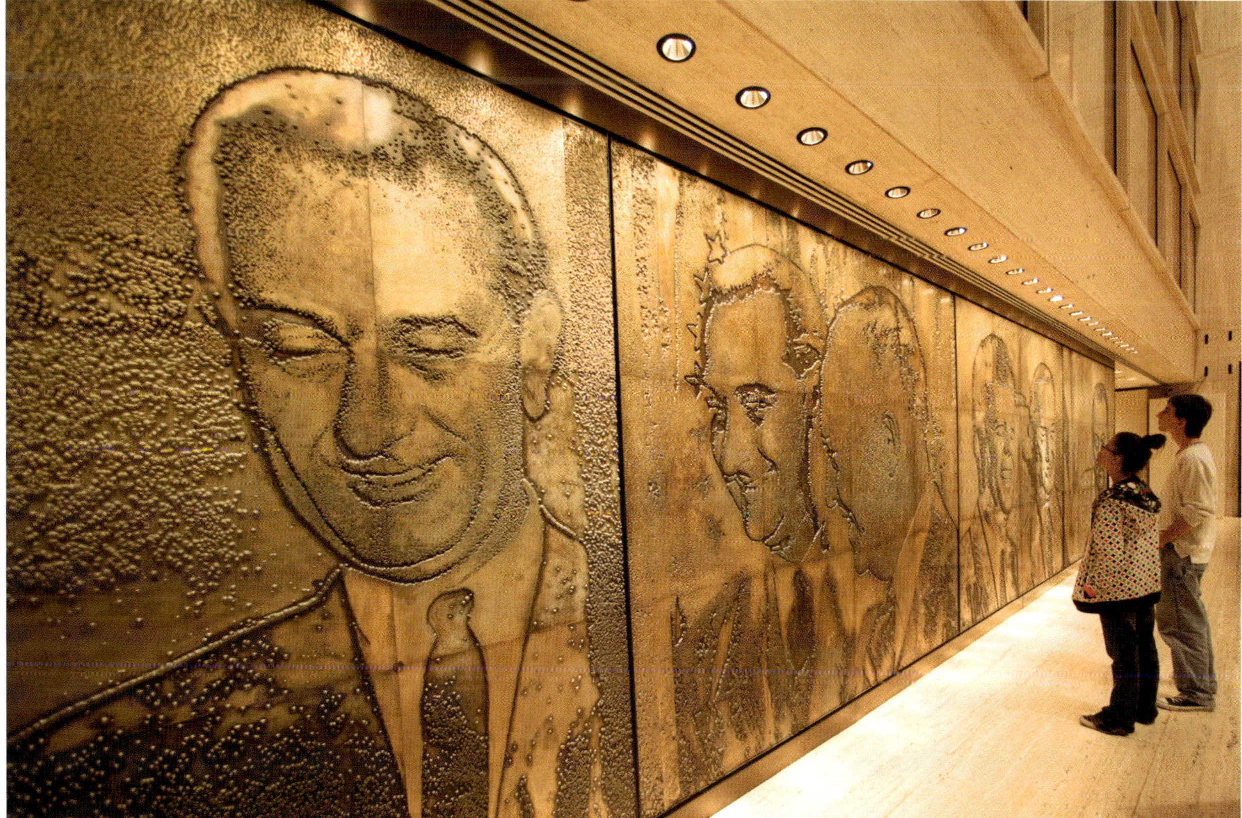

Above and Right In the Great Hall of the LBJ Presidential Library, four of the five floors of archives are visible as shelves stacked with red buckram-covered boxes embossed with gold presidential seals. The archives contain more than 3 million separate documents, almost 600,000 photographs, and recordings of President Johnson's White House conversations.

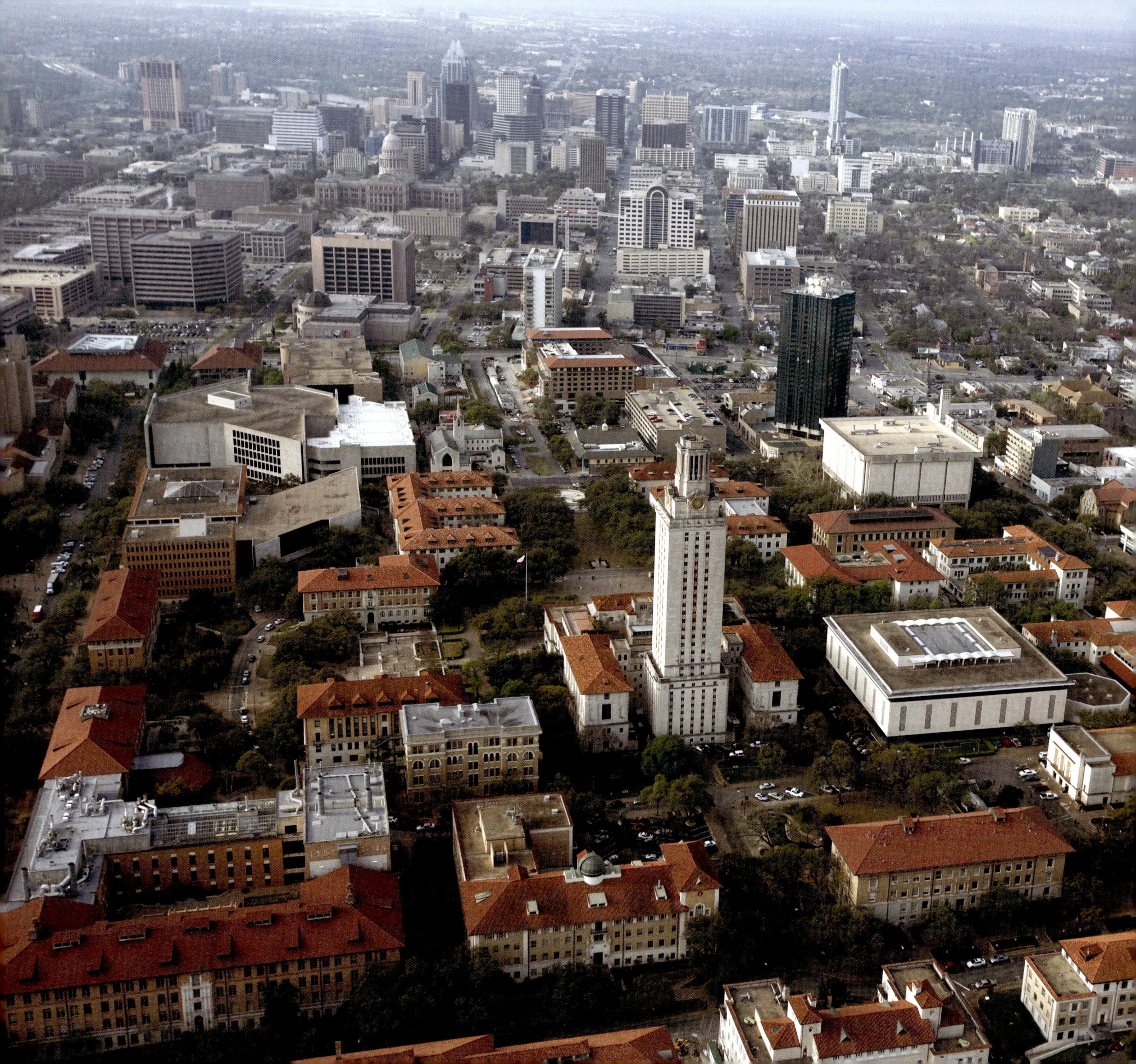

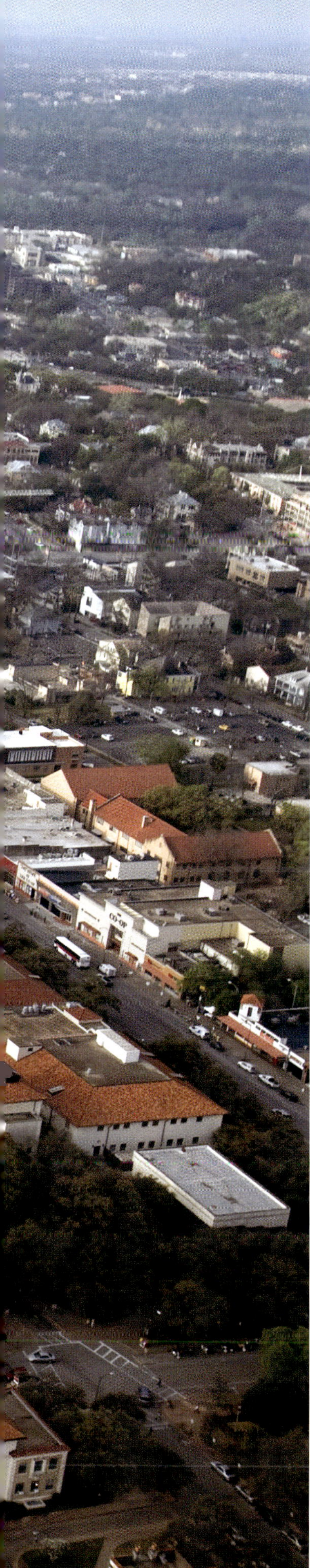

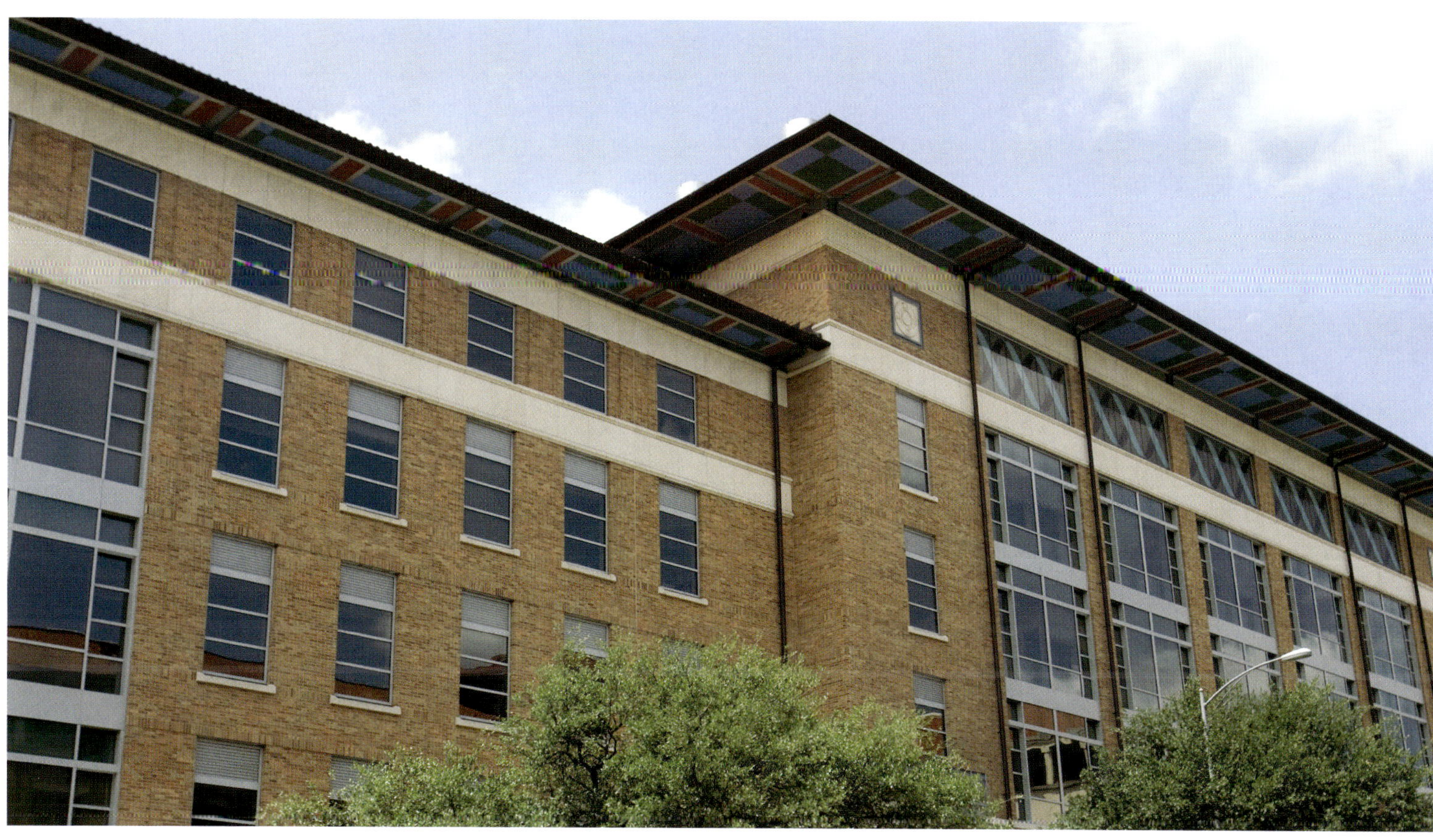

One of the newest buildings on the campus is the Neural and Molecular Biology Building, a research facility used by the School of Biological Sciences. The double-helix of DNA decorates the building just below the eaves.

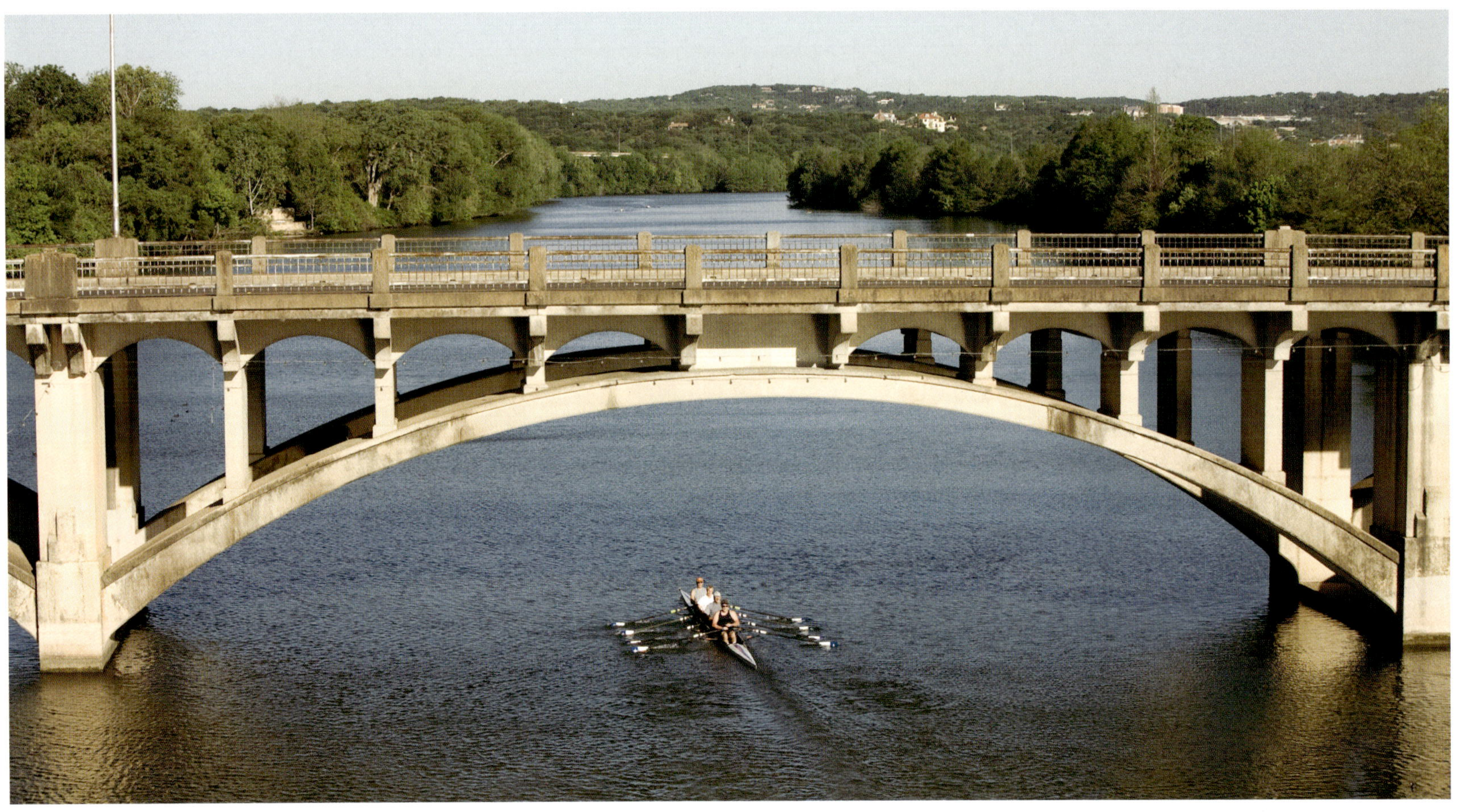

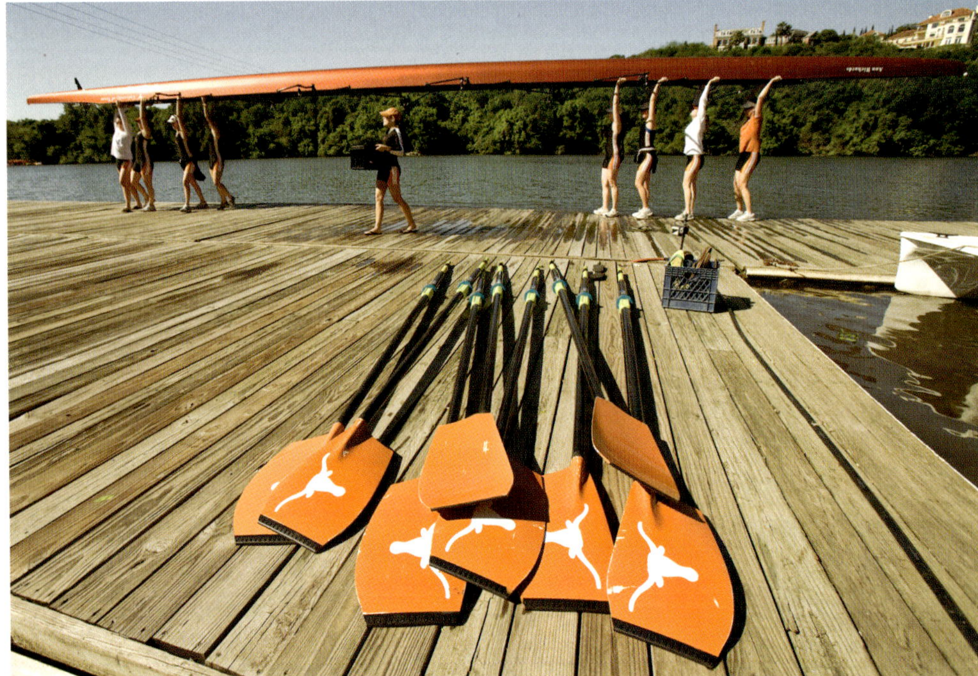

The women's rowing team practices on Lady Bird Lake in downtown Austin. An NCAA program since 1996, the team has won seven consecutive Big 12 Conference titles.

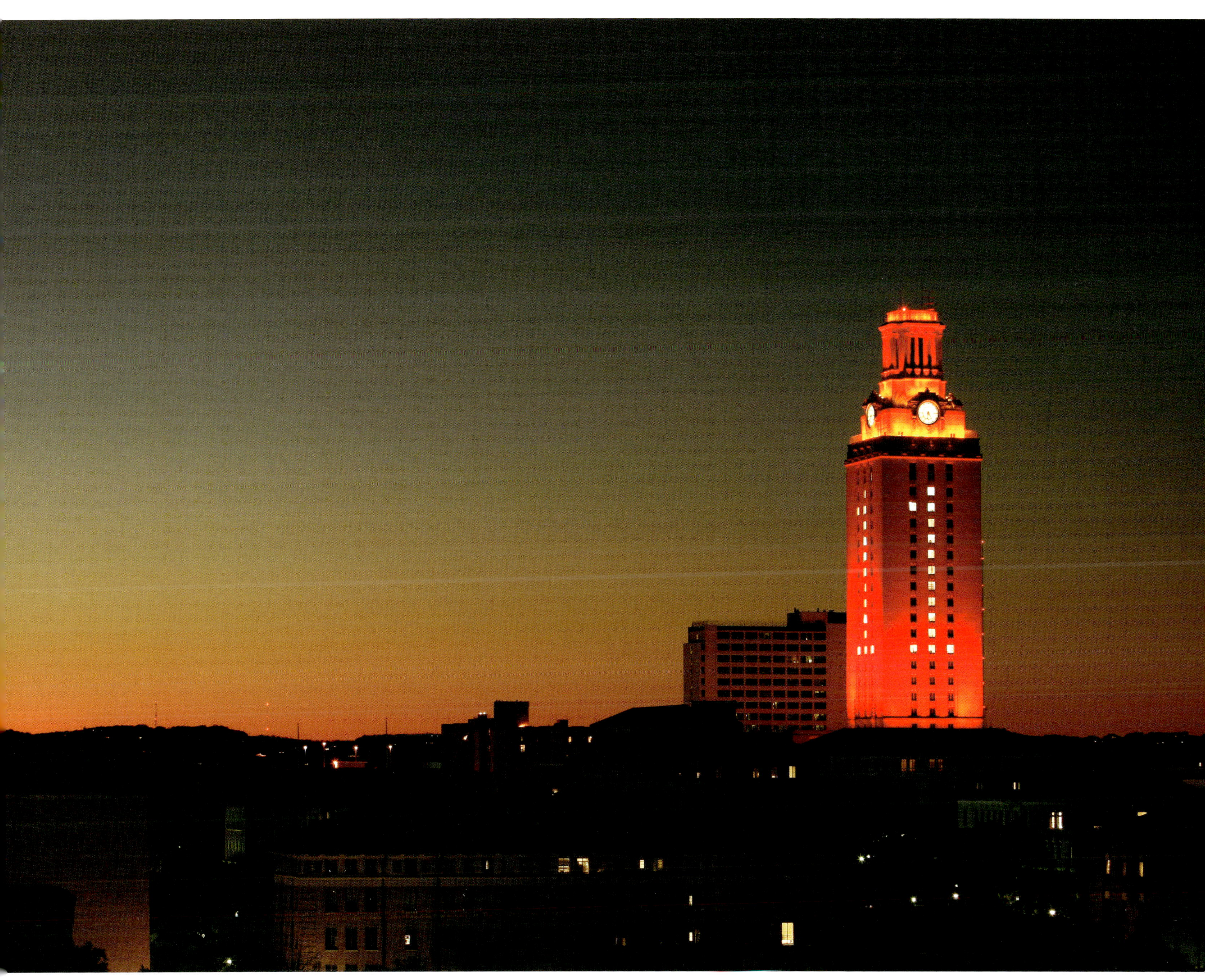

THE ASSOCIATION

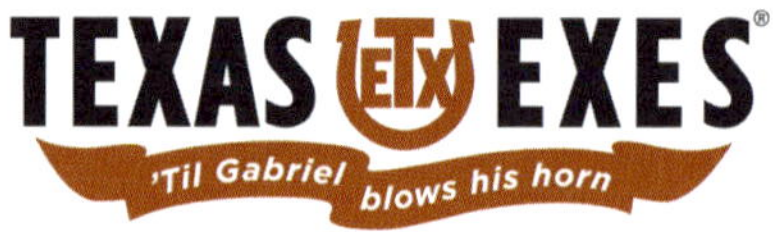

The Texas Exes is one of the strongest alumni associations in the country, supporting education through scholarships, teaching awards, public policy initiatives, and conferences. The Texas Exes connects more than 88,000 members to each other and to the past, present, and future of The University of Texas through career counseling, travel, reunions, continuing education, fellowship, the UT Heritage Society, and *The Alcalde* magazine.

The mission of the Texas Exes is to unite, inform, and involve alumni and friends for the purpose of promoting, protecting, and preserving The University of Texas.

Serving the University for more than 100 Years

On June 17, 1885, 34 new graduates of the two-year-old University of Texas organized the UT Alumni Association, later renamed The Ex-Students' Association. At first, the Association was an extension of the University, but the events of 1917 changed that, when Will C. Hogg led alumni to oppose Governor James Ferguson, who had vetoed the University's appropriation bill. Ferguson was impeached and removed from office. Two years later, in 1919, the Association separated itself from UT, which allowed it the freedom to act as an independent advocate for the University.

Keeping the "Public" in "Public University"

The Association worked with Texas A&M to pass legislation to use the Permanent University Fund to issue building bonds for both school. In 1982, the Association played a major role in passing a constitutional amendment to protect the PUF from further division after allotment of part of it to all schools in the UT and A&M systems. And in 1986, Texas Exes' fierce defense of the PUF against threats of additional raids is credited with saving the fund. The Association has now set up a full-time legislative advocacy program, UT Advocates for Higher Education.

Finding a Home on the Campus

The Association didn't acquire a home until 18 years after its founding, when the regents granted it the use of Room 43 in the Old Main Building. The offices wandered about the campus, and for a time were located in the Texas Union and later in the basement of Mary Gearing Hall. In the early 1960s, the regents offered a site for more permanent quarters on San Jacinto Boulevard between 21st and 22nd streets and donated $110,000 from the Lila B. Etter Fund to aid with construction. In 1965, the Association moved into the Etter Alumni Center. More than 1,000 Texas Exes helped to pay for the building. Between 1988 and 1990, the center underwent a renovation and addition that tripled its original size and made it into a showplace on the campus. Jack Harbin's name was added to the center in 2001 after his $1 million gift to improve the grounds. More than 9,000 tiles on the Texas Exes Plaza and Creekside Terrace were inscribed with names of donors to the $7.17 million expansion.

Fundraising from the Beginning

In 1892, the Association began its mission of fundraising by helping to raise money for a YMCA building adjacent to the campus and a year later gave its first recorded gift to the University: $53.59 for commencement ceremonies. Through the years, the Association has spearheaded many fund-raising campaigns, including those for Memorial Stadium, the Texas Memorial Museum, and the Longhorn Band, for a band hall and scholarships. The Association provided the main push behind the Union Project, which resulted in the construction of Gregory Gym, the Texas Union, Hogg Auditorium, and Anna Hiss Gym. In 1937, the Association helped to plan and establish the University Development Board.

As it looks to the future, the Association is pushing out in exciting new areas. It has built the first retirement community affiliated with The University of Texas, Longhorn Village, to keep alumni and friends even more involved in the life of the University, and at the other end of the spectrum, it is laying the groundwork for a massive expansion of its already robust scholarship program, an effort that will bring hundreds of America's top students to the Forty Acres. Through it all, the Association continues to build partnerships with entities across the campus and friends around the world to support the mission of The University of Texas in creative new ways. ✯

The Texas Exes • 2110 San Jacinto Boulevard, Austin, TX 78712 • 512-471-8839

TEXAS EXES BOARD OF DIRECTORS 2008-2009

PRESIDENT: Pam Willeford, BA '72
PRESIDENT-ELECT: Ron Kirk, JD '79
CHAIR: Darrell Windham, BBA '75, JD '78
SECRETARY: Melinda Perrin, BS '69
TREASURER: Mark Williams, BBA '81
CEO & EXECUTIVE DIRECTOR:
Jim Boon, BBA '69, MBA '72

Steve Ballantyne, BA '72, MBA '74
Mark Chassay, BBA '88, MEd '99
Alexandra Crook, UT Junior
Hector De Leon, BS '70, JD '73
Chuck Fraser, BA '80
N. Rudy Garza, MBA '91
Machree Gibson, BA '82, JD '91
Troy Glander, BBA '92
Steve Head, BA '72

Kevin Hegarty, BBA '77, MPA '79
Rick Kelly, BA '88
Aaron Kozmetsky, MBA '95
Elizabeth S. Massey, BS '61
Dennis McWilliams, BS '93
Alba Ortiz, PhD '76
Alisa Peppers, BA '90
Lynn Utter, BBA '84

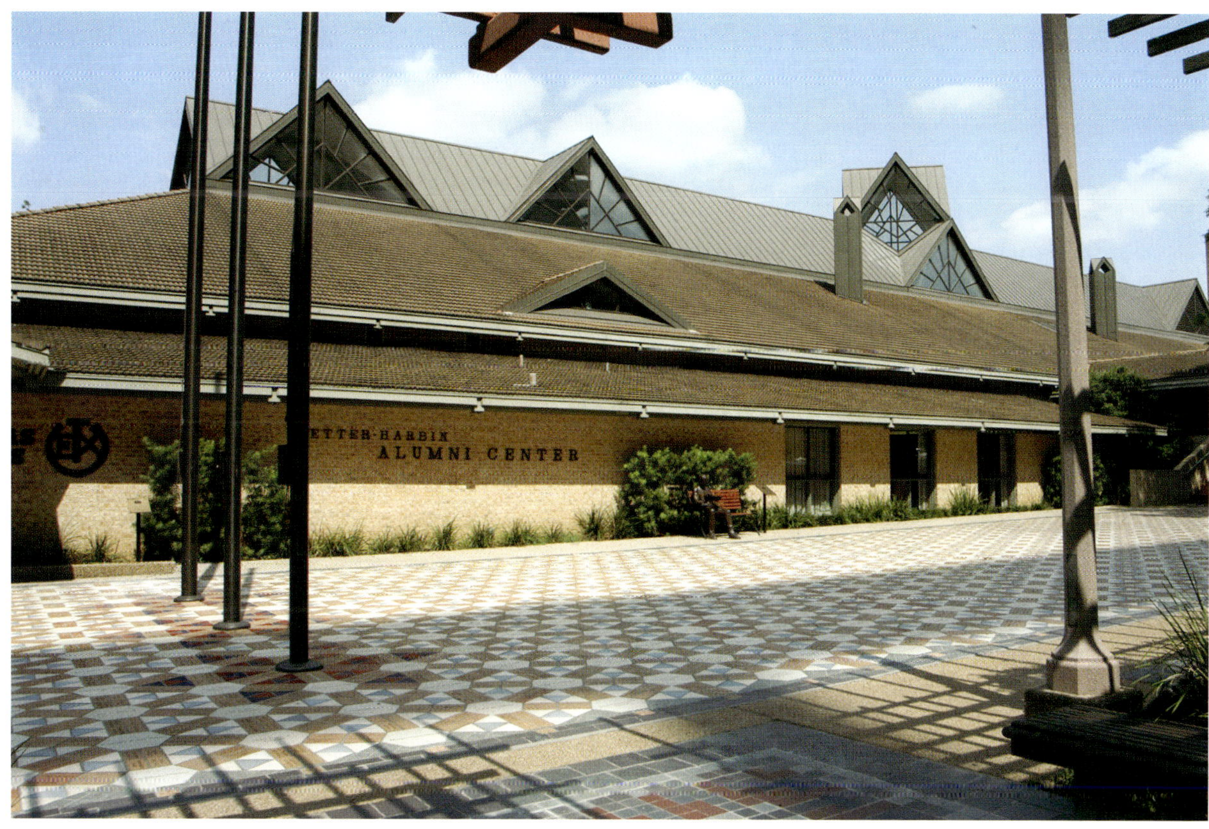

INDEX

INDEX

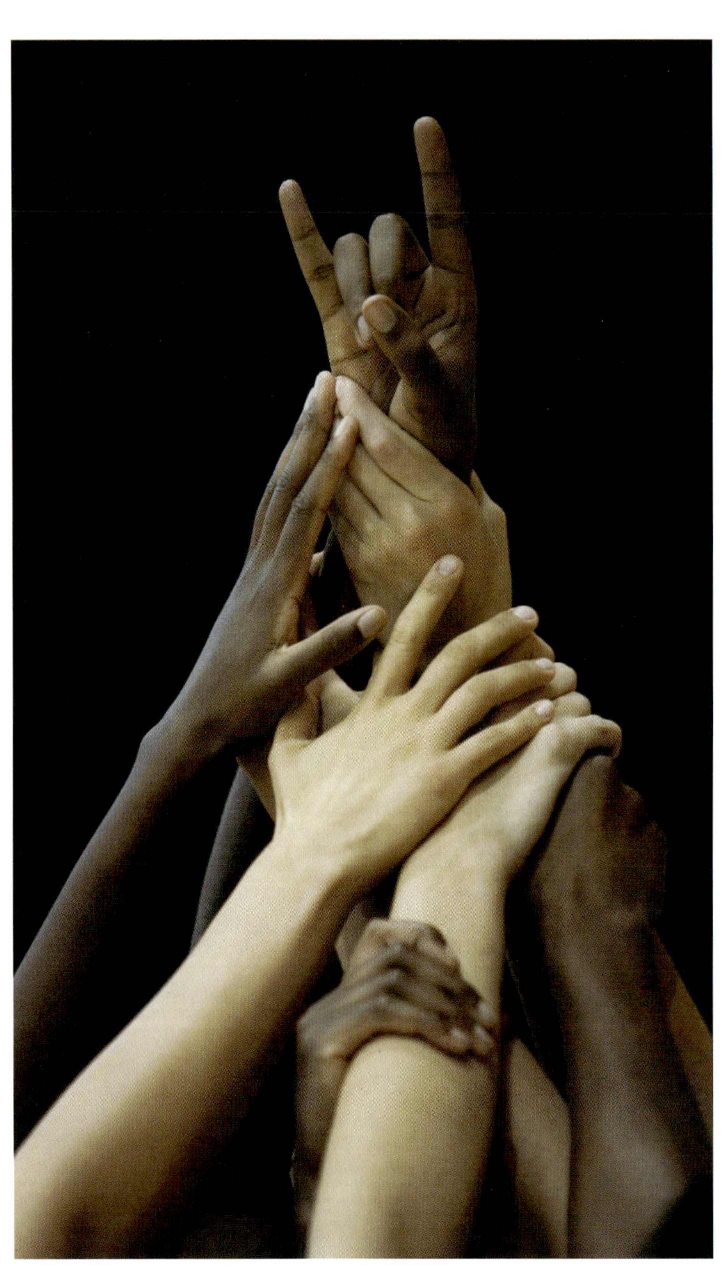